D0426619

THE BIRTH OF
THE CHURCH

THE BIRTH OF THE CHURCH

From Jesus to Constantine, A.D. 30–312

IVOR J. DAVIDSON

The Baker History of the Church, Vol. 1

John D. Woodbridge and David Wright,
Consulting Editors

Tim Dowley, Series Editor

BakerBooks
Grand Rapids, Michigan

© 2004 by Ivor J. Davidson

Published by Baker Books
a division of Baker Publishing Group
P.O. Box 6287, Grand Rapids, MI 49516-6287
www.bakerbooks.com

U.S. translation first published October 2004. This edition published by arrangement with
Monarch Books, Concorde House, Grenville Place, Mill Hill, London NW7 3SA.

Printed in the United States of America

Library of Congress Cataloging-in-Publication Data
Davidson, Ivor J.
    The birth of the church : from Jesus to Constantine, AD 30/312 / Ivor J. David-
son.
        p.   cm.—(The Baker history of the church ; v. 1)
    Includes bibliographical references and index.
    ISBN 0-8010-1270-8 (cloth)
    1. Church history—Primitive and early church, ca. 30–600., I. Title. II. Series.
BR165.D368 2004
270.1—dc22   2004011988

CONTENTS

Maps and Illustrations

PREFACE

Any number of guides exists for those who would learn about the early history of Christianity. This book was written in the conviction that there is nevertheless a need for a fresh narrative history of the early church that is accessible in style, comprehensive in scope, and—not least—up-to-date in scholarship.

It is of course a great deal easier to describe such aims than it is to realize them. Accessibility is always a matter of taste, and the quest for it involves authors and editors constructing illusory images of "average" readers who never quite match up to the actual individuals to whom they generally speak. Comprehensiveness is determined by the contingencies of word limits, time, energy, and knowledge. And the extent to which a work such as this can ever be "up-to-date" with all of the relevant literature is entirely relative: no scholar can be an expert in all of the component parts of such a vast and multidisciplinary field.

These have, nevertheless, been the ideals that I have tried to keep in mind as I have written. I hope the book will be of use to those who have some knowledge of early Christianity as well as to those who have none—it is designed, naturally, for students in universities, seminaries, and schools, but also for their teachers, and for all intelligent readers, Christian and otherwise, who wish to find out more about how the church began. While the content aspires to offer an appropriate level of substance and to incorporate the best of contemporary thinking in the field, I have sought to keep footnotes and references to a minimum in order to leave the text as unencumbered as possible by technical matters. I have tried to concentrate not only on issues of theology, politics, and ideas but also to look in some measure at the social, artistic, and cultural evolution of Christianity. I have also been conscious of the need to tell the church's story not merely as the doings of a few famous people but as a process in which all who professed faith in Jesus were involved. In every area of the work, the constraints of space have been very real, and judgments about what to include and what to leave out will always be contestable; but I trust that the overall picture is as wide-ranging in its detail as might reasonably be expected in a study of this length.

I have endeavored to produce an account that is balanced and fair to diverse interpretations of often-complex evidence. At the same time, no historian can or should shy away from offering opinions on contested issues. In many instances, the full reasons behind the judgments expressed here could not possibly be rehearsed in the space available, but interested readers can follow up the relevant themes by pursuing some of the further reading suggested at the end of the book. Bibliographies are notoriously ephemeral in their adequacy, but the list given here should provide a start at least. Internet-based sources in some of the areas in question are of mixed quality, and for that reason I have confined the suggestions to conventional printed media. There is undoubtedly a very large and growing body of useful material to be gleaned from the Web, but the wheat and the chaff are best sifted by those who have done some other reading first.

When I was first asked to write the book, I was advised that the aim was to furnish a new generation of readers with a work that might fulfill something of the function that earlier—and in some cases now classic—introductory texts on the period had provided for their predecessors. That is no small order, and I had then and have now no illusions about the challenges of fulfilling it. If the work should prove even a small part as useful as some of those that have gone before it, I shall of course be very pleased.

As always, an author must register his debts. I am very grateful to Baker Books for their enthusiastic sponsorship of the series, and in particular to my editor, Chad Allen, and his colleagues for their excellent work in overseeing its production. I appreciate the fine job done by Lois Stück in producing an American version of the text, and the skills of Kathleen Strattan who indexed the book. I am also grateful to staff at Monarch Books in London, especially Tony Collins, for their vital input. Dr. Tim Dowley has been an exemplary series editor, whose passionate commitment to the project has never wavered and whose encouragement, patience, and carefulness throughout the writing of this first volume have been greatly appreciated. I am grateful to an anonymous reader of the manuscript for his helpful suggestions. Not for the first time, I also owe much to Professor David Wright of the University of Edinburgh for his interest and generosity.

The University of Otago furnished me with research grants that assisted with the illustration of the book. I should like to record my appreciation to Jill Davidson, Bill Mooney, and in particular my research assistants Robyn Dold and Jacqui Davis for their hard work in that area. I am also grateful to those who agreed to allow reproduction of photographs from their personal collections: Professor Everett Ferguson deserves special thanks for lending me his image of the amphitheater in Lyons.

I dedicate the book to my parents: to my father, who has shown a lively interest in the project throughout its gestation, and who will, I hope, find some reasons for the reward of that enthusiasm now; and to the memory of my mother, who was called to a far better place several years before the work was begun, but who would undoubtedly have taken pride in perusing and discussing it had she been spared. I miss her, and her passion for the story of which this book tells a tiny part, more than any formal dedication can possibly record.

With her customary blend of extraordinary patience, good humor, and commitment, my wife Julie put up with me while I wrote the work, and gave up far too much of her own time in its interests. As ever, even a large "thank you" is a hopelessly inadequate return; but I offer it anyway, in the knowledge that the heart has further language of its own.

Ivor J. Davidson
Dunedin, New Zealand
April 2004

IN THE BEGINNING

The story of the Christian church has its genesis in the belief of a small group of Jews in first-century Palestine that a man who had been crucified had been raised from the dead. Jesus of Nazareth, the charismatic prophet, teacher, and healer whose ministry had caused a storm in Galilee and Judea, appeared to have died in defeat. He had called upon people to repent and had announced that the kingdom of God was at hand. He had shown special concern for the poor, the weak, and the outcasts of his society. He had taught that righteousness consisted not in outward conformity to moral conventions but in the attitude of the heart, and had summoned his hearers to a life of commitment to the truth and justice that God's Law in its essence demanded. But his teaching and his actions had brought him into collision with the religious and political authorities of his time, represented respectively by the priestly system of the temple in Jerusalem and the administrative and military power of Rome. He had met a fate commonly meted out to troublemakers in the Roman world: he had been put to death by crucifixion, sentenced by the Roman prefect of Judea, Pontius Pilate, around the year A.D. 30.

The First Followers of Jesus

This ought to have been the end of the matter. Jesus, it seemed, was just another failed reformer—courageous, no doubt, in his protest against religious and moral systems that he felt were wrong; commendable, certainly, in his principled concern for the needy and the marginalized and his practical efforts to address social injustices;

but in the end just another pious martyr to a cause. He had been an impressive teacher and miracle worker, and his brief ministry had made an impact on a wide variety of people, but he had died a common criminal's death, crying out to God in an apparent sense of being forsaken. His death left his band of followers without a leader and without any obvious sense of direction. Whatever Jesus had stood for, it appeared either that he had been mistaken or that his mission was a failure.

What changed all this was the conviction that, although Jesus had died a violent death and been laid in a tomb, he was dead no longer. Within a matter of days of his crucifixion, stories were circulating that his grave was empty and that he had been raised from the dead. Some of his closest friends were claiming they had actually seen him and heard him speaking to them. These experiences of the presence of Jesus resulted in the message that he was alive again, that his mission had not ended in defeat, and that he was commissioning his followers to go out and proclaim this fact.

The belief that Jesus was raised was not some pious idea that the events of his crucifixion had been reversed or that the dreadful reality of his suffering had somehow been canceled out. The Jesus who appeared was not a resuscitated corpse, amazingly brought to life again. Nor was he just a ghost or a phantom pictured in the minds of grieving—and perhaps guilt-ridden—disciples, looking back sentimentally on the individual they had known and failed in the hour of his greatest need. The appearances of the risen Jesus were not merely visions or shadowy encounters with the supernatural. At the heart of the first believers' faith was a conviction that Jesus was alive as a concrete, flesh-and-blood reality. For them, the Jesus who had been executed had been raised bodily to a new dimension of life.

Admittedly, Jesus's body now seemed to be capable of some amazing things, such as passing through locked doors and disappearing suddenly from sight. But however mysterious his resurrected form, there was an essential continuity between what he had been and what he now was. His physical body had not been abandoned to decomposition in a grave but had been transformed into a mode of existence that, although different in certain respects, was identifiable with his former self. His followers believed his appearances were confirmations that God had vindicated him and that his life and death, far from being in vain, were in fact the decisive means by which God was acting in history to effect not only the renewal of Israel but the redemption of the world.

Understanding Jesus

What was it that convinced the first followers of Jesus that he had been raised? In order to begin to answer this question, we need to understand something of the religious thought-world to which both Jesus and they belonged.

Jesus himself was first and foremost a Jew. He worshiped Yahweh, the one supreme God, the maker of all things and Lord of all, who had graciously elected Israel to be a special people and a source of blessing to all the nations of the earth. God had entered into a covenant with this chosen race, into a special relationship symbolized in the rite of circumcision and summarized in the Torah or Jewish Law, which laid down the moral boundaries within which Israel was to live. This bond was clear in God's dealings with Israel's kings and in the pledge that the descendants of David would reign forever. Israel had been unfaithful to her Lord, and God had judged his people for their sins, but the divine intention was still that Israel would be a channel of grace to the whole world. As the prophets had promised, one day a new covenant would prevail, and the obedience of God's people would consist not so much in outward conformity as in inner righteousness of heart. Jesus shared these religious assumptions and expectations. He participated faithfully in the rituals and duties of Jewish faith and was steeped in the Jewish Scriptures. Like other teachers, he offered his own interpretations of the Torah, but he insisted that he had come not to set aside the Law but to fulfill it.

Jesus regarded the temple in Jerusalem as the supreme site of God's holy presence on earth, the place where Israel's privileged relationship with God was most fully realized, and he was incensed at what he regarded as the lack of reverence for the temple reflected by a debased religious system. When he went around Galilee proclaiming that the kingdom of God was at hand, he was calling people not to abandon Judaism as such but to recognize that Israel's long exile from God's favor was coming to an end. At the same time, his understanding of how this was happening was deeply radical. Throughout his ministry, he spoke and acted as if God's purpose of salvation for Israel was being made manifest through his own presence, and he saw himself as commissioned by God to be not simply a reformer, boldly calling for spiritual renewal, but the *embodiment* of the means by which God would bring redemption to his people.

In his authoritative reinterpretation of the Law, and above all in his demonstration in the temple in Jerusalem (Matt. 21:12–13; Mark 11:15–18;

Luke 19:45–46; cf. John 2:13–22), Jesus displayed his belief that his role was not just to announce the kingdom of God but to personify its arrival. In Jesus's teaching, the word of God was now personally present; in his actions, he himself was the place of meeting with God. He was a prophet of Judaism, proclaiming judgment upon the corruptions that had befallen the great symbols and ideals of the Jewish faith and upon the misunderstandings that lay behind contemporary distortions of religious authority. But Jesus was a prophet like no other, for his conviction was that he was called by Israel's God to embody in himself the return of the presence of Yahweh with his people.

Jesus's position was distinct from that of all the other main groups within Palestinian Judaism in his time. The Pharisees, for example, stressed observance of the Torah as the way of maintaining Jewish identity amid the oppressive influences of Roman rule. The Gospels present the Pharisees as legalists and hypocrites, but their views commanded strong popular respect in Palestine. They emphasized both the study of the Law and the scribal traditions of interpreting it, and they were deeply concerned to maintain strict rules of ritual purity, tithing, and fasting. They were closely associated with the scribes, the guardians of religious lore who specialized in commenting upon and systematizing the moral obligations of the Law. The scribes elaborated a vast range of stipulations relating not only to religious rituals but also to everyday matters such as eating, drinking, and washing.

Jesus had certain things in common with the Pharisees. He shared their basic concern that the Law should not be a dead letter but a dynamic force in daily life. On issues such as the offering of gifts in the temple and Sabbath observance, Jesus was able to reason with the Pharisees on the basis of similar assumptions. More often, though, he sharply challenged their conceptions of the boundaries of moral purity and their definitions of the covenant community; he protested against their legal casuistry and called them hypocrites. Jesus, a product of Nazareth, an insignificant town from which no one expected anything good to arise (see John 1:46), drew most of his disciples from "the people of the land"—fishermen, farmers, and artisans from the villages of Galilee. He also associated with social untouchables, including tax collectors, who were believed to collaborate with the government, and prostitutes. His understanding of the limits of ceremonial cleanness and of the standards God required was much freer and more inclusive than most Pharisee sensibilities could accommodate.

Jesus was at much greater odds with the Sadducees, the privileged, priestly elite who ran the temple system in Jerusalem. Drawn mostly from the wealthy aristocracy, the Sadducees gave supreme religious authority to the Law of Moses and shunned the oral traditions prized by the scribes and the Pharisees. Unlike the Pharisees, they rejected belief in the resurrection, which most Jews believed would represent the ultimate reembodiment of the righteous dead at the end of the age, or, symbolically, the beginning of the new age in which Israel's exile would be over and God would renew the covenant with his people. The Sadducees lacked popular support, and they maintained their position by cooperating with the Romans and clinging tightly to their control of the temple. To them, Jesus's protest against the corruption of the priestly system represented a dangerous threat to the delicate balance of power that enabled them to style themselves the authoritative guardians of the survival of Jewish worship.

But Jesus was also different from other radicals. The Essenes, a diverse group of separatists, were also disillusioned with the operation of the temple system and sought to follow an alternative lifestyle in the expectation that God would bring deliverance from the harsh realities of a world dominated by the power of Rome (see pp. 39–41). They practiced asceticism of various kinds, particularly sexual abstinence, a strict piety, and a common ownership of goods. They appear to have had some connections with the community of sectarians based in the desert of Qumran on the Dead Sea. This group believed they were currently in the age of end-time fulfillment pointed to in the Scriptures, that they themselves represented God's faithful remnant of Law-keepers who were resisting the temptations to compromise with a corrupt world, and that God would shortly intervene to rectify their troubles and usher in a new era of blessing, peace, and holiness.

There were some similarities between the convictions of the sectarians in the desert of Qumran and the ideas held by John the Baptist, the man whom the Gospels depict as Jesus's forerunner, the radical prophet by whom he was baptized and whose message of repentance he continued. There were also shared general expectations between such separatists and Jesus about the imminent arrival of God's kingdom. But Jesus's teaching and example were in reality quite different from theirs, and his ideas generated some friction with other followers of John. Jesus showed a much more open attitude to those outside the Jewish community, adopted a far more cavalier approach to purity regulations, and did not advocate retreat from society. According to his vision, the kingdom had *already* arrived.

Nor was Jesus an enthusiast for political struggle in a conventional sense. Some groups of activists, the forerunners of those who would later be known collectively as the Zealots, urged resistance to secular authority, the nonpayment of taxes, and a preparedness to face death in the fight against the physical enemies of Israel. Although their religious affinities lay with the Pharisees, for them the political quietism accepted by conventional Pharisaism was too high a price to pay. The Messiah or Anointed One they expected was the triumphant Son of David: a nationalistic military figure who would spearhead a victory over the Romans who controlled their land and would bring about a restoration of the temple order to its former glory.

Jesus seemed to share some of this radicalism, for he condemned corruption, called upon his disciples to "take up the cross," and warned that there would be temporal cost in following his way. But he rejected the logic of political upheaval and distanced himself from the cause of armed rebellion, holding out the challenge of peace rather than turmoil. He envisaged himself as Messiah in a very different sense from that imagined by most reactionaries. He was the one who would act as the representative sufferer, paying the price of Israel's redemption by going to an inevitable death in consequence of his behavior. For Jesus, however, this messianic action was not about the liberation of Israel from Roman bondage but about the realization of the divine purpose that Israel would become the spiritual light of the whole world.

For these convictions, and the actions to which they led, Jesus had been crucified. To his Jewish enemies, especially the Sadducees, he seemed to be a dangerous messianic pretender, threatening to upset the vested interests of a religious system that was working to at least some people's satisfaction. To the Roman authorities, Jesus was a potential insurrectionist whose ideas were destabilizing an already volatile political environment.

Resurrection?

Yet now Jesus's followers were saying that he had been raised from the dead. Even for the majority of Palestinian Jews who, unlike the Sadducees, professed hope in the resurrection, the idea was bizarre. The first believers were not gullible or naive fools who somehow imagined that human beings rose from the dead as a regular occurrence. The notion that a person had been raised bodily from the tomb while history was still going on would have seemed almost as strange to first-century Jews as it does to most Western people today. The belief that Jesus was alive involved some major rethinking of the Jewish tradition. Instead of anticipating a general resurrection of the dead at the end of the present age, the followers of Jesus were proclaiming the resurrection of one person in particular in the middle of the age as the inauguration of God's kingdom. Instead of expecting the Messiah to be the one who would defeat the Romans, restore the temple, and inaugurate the era of God's justice for Israel, Jesus's followers were claiming that the Messiah had actually been *killed* by the Romans, had *not* restored the temple, and had *not* brought about the exodus from physical bondage or the renewal of the divine covenant.

Remarkably, these pious Jews were prepared to make the adjustments to their worldview that such beliefs involved. Jesus had led them to believe that he would undertake some dramatic action in order to establish God's kingdom. In the light of their conviction that he had been raised from the dead, they now saw what it was: his death was not the end but the commencement of the final phase of God's purposes. Jesus was not just another deluded liberator who discovered, too late, that he was mistaken and whose cross testified to the futility of his vision that Israel's spiritual exile was over. God had exalted Jesus to heaven, and the resurrection of Jesus was the prototype for the resurrection of all God's people. In raising Jesus, God had initiated the *last days,* in which the consequences of the triumph of Jesus over death and over all the forces that alienated from divine favor would extend to believers everywhere.

The period in which people had these compelling encounters with Jesus did not last very long. It was, however, deeply formative. Within a few weeks of his crucifixion, his resurrection was being boldly proclaimed in the city where he had been executed. While some of his followers no doubt remained in Galilee, the first community of believers congregated in Jerusalem. This was both natural and symbolic: natural, in that Jerusalem was the city where the events of Jesus's death and burial had taken place; symbolic, in that this city was regarded by the Jews as the center of God's purposes. The temple remained important for the first disciples in the immediate term, but they were increasingly persuaded that God's chosen dwelling place within Israel transcended this physical location. Now, God was to be found amid the community of those who believed in Jesus. Jesus's death and resurrection had revolutionized their understanding of how the living Lord was present in the world.

These believers were not "Christians" in any modern sense—they remained Jews. The name first used of them was probably "Nazarenes" (see Acts 24:5), indicating that they were disciples of Jesus "the Nazarene" (see Matt. 2:23). Their belief in Jesus did not amount to an attempt to establish a new religion but was instead a conviction that their ancestral faith had reached its climactic fulfillment in the liberating personal presence of God in this individual who had been crucified and raised from the dead. Jesus was God's Anointed One, the Messiah foretold by the prophets, the one through whom God was fulfilling the pledges mediated through Noah, Abraham, and Moses in the covenant of promise, symbolized in the rite of circumcision and summed up in the Law.

The primary task, as "the Nazarenes" saw it, was to bring their fellow Jews to acknowledge this reality. The Jesus movement—a small and inconspicuous sect within Judaism, with ostensibly dubious chances of long-term survival in its immediate context, far less farther afield—had begun.

1

THE WORLD OF JESUS'S FIRST FOLLOWERS

▼

The Roman Empire

The first followers of Jesus lived in a world in which there was only one real political, military, and economic superpower—Rome. The Roman Empire encompassed almost the entire Mediterranean region and spanned vast tracts of three of the world's continents. In the first century, Rome's territory extended from the shores of the English Channel in the north[1] to Egypt in the south, from the straits of Gibraltar in the west to Mesopotamia in the east. It covered all of Europe south and west of the Rhine and the Danube, much of North Africa, and a large swathe of Asia Minor, as well as Syria and Palestine. This empire constituted the whole of the civilized world; outside of it lay only barbarian or desert regions, subject, as far as Rome was concerned, to forces of lawlessness and savagery.

A system of rule over the whole of this territory by a single individual was created by the great-nephew of Julius Caesar, Octavian, who came to be known as Augustus (31 B.C.–A.D. 14).[2] Adapting structures and terminology inherited from the Roman Republic (established ca. 509 B.C.), Augustus had set up a regime in which ultimate political authority rested

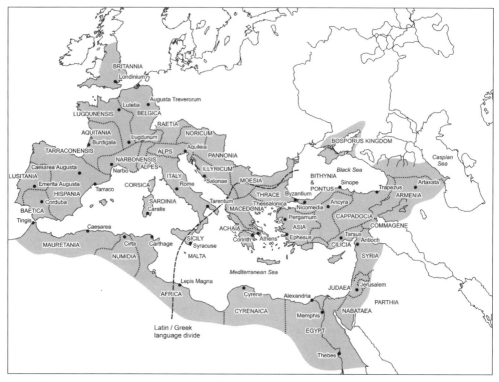

The Roman Empire around the middle of the first century A.D.

squarely in the emperor's hands. A formal configuration of traditional decision-making bodies such as the Roman Senate continued, and the running of the empire naturally required a bureaucratic apparatus, but the emperor himself held final control over the armies, the diplomatic channels, the fiscal system, and the public finances. In reality, the whole system was a huge military dictatorship, sustained by vast armed might and presided over by a figure who, although he eschewed the title of "king," had absolute power and whose commands amounted to law.

The great majority of the empire's inhabitants lived in the countryside, but, as in most societies, political power was concentrated in the cities. Rome itself had three-quarters of a million or more inhabitants, and it was in every sense the capital of the civilized world. It was *the* city like no other: the home of the gods, the heart of government, and the center of cultural sophistication. In the second quarter of the first century, the next most important place was Alexandria in Egypt, which had possibly

400,000 residents, followed by Ephesus with around 200,000, and Antioch with perhaps 150,000. Most other cities, such as Corinth, Sardis, and Carthage, had populations of little more than 100,000 to 120,000 at best, and many were much smaller. The most significant urban centers were melting pots of diverse cultural influences, made up of peoples of various ethnic backgrounds and many different beliefs.

In general, cities were left to run their own affairs with a fair degree of local autonomy, but they were also required to conform to Roman law and pay their dues to the Roman treasury. Their status was closely tied to the degree to which they possessed imperial privileges. It was also linked to where they were located in strategic terms. The so-called "senatorial" provinces were peaceful enough to be administered by the Senate in Rome via proconsuls or governors drawn from the ranks of former Roman magistrates. A majority of the provinces required an army presence, and much of Rome's military might was concentrated on the frontiers of the empire, where there were frequent problems from outside forces.

Roman military might was considerable. Across the empire as a whole, around 100,000 legionaries—highly trained forces, volunteers not conscripts, well-equipped, well-paid, and honored for their services—were kept in a position to fight at any one time. The legionaries were supported by as many as 150,000 auxiliary troops, drawn from confederates and subjects, who served as cavalry and light infantry. Colony cities, populated with retired soldiers, were dotted all over the empire as strategic outposts of loyal subjects dedicated to maintaining the Roman way of life in the provinces. The role of the armies in the imperial structure was vital; in the end, they alone could uphold the *pax Romana*, the Roman peace, upon which all cultural stability depended.

Forces of Unity

For all its vastness, the Roman Empire possessed various unifying forces. Among the most important of these were languages. In a world that embraced Africans, Asians, Europeans, Arabians, and Celts, it was possible to communicate from one side of the empire to the other with a knowledge of only two tongues: Latin and Greek. These were the two official languages of government, law, and commerce throughout the empire—Latin in the western part, Greek in the east, assuming a division roughly along a line running southward from the confluence of the Danube and the Sava rivers across Europe and into Africa. Regional vernaculars and dialects remained standard for most people in the countryside, but the educated members of urban society would learn at least Latin or Greek, and in many cases both, and a knowledge of either of the recognized tongues could carry a person a long way in geographical terms.[3]

In addition to language, there was law. Rome's legal system provided, in principle, a common system of rights and responsibilities throughout its dominions. Imperial legislation was a unifying force for all of Rome's subjects, providing a basis for the evolution of developed conceptions of natural justice. Legal structures were naturally allied to bureaucratic and economic organization. The empire saw an increasingly centralized system of control over regional administration, and various taxes had to be paid to Rome from all parts of the world, especially on agricultural produce, commercial activities, and property transactions. The operation of the legal and fiscal systems was heavily weighted in favor of the educated and the well-to-do, and tax collection in particular was pursued with a rigor that provoked popular resentment and sometimes revolt in the provinces. But however obnoxious its demands, the role of taxation as an integrating force in the imperial order was undeniable.

In terms of cultural influences, art, architecture, literature, and ideas naturally crossed boundaries. Both public and private buildings often reflected generic trends in their style and decoration, and intellectual culture in both Greek and Latin spread through the agencies of a flourishing book trade and the influences of itinerant teachers, rhetoricians, and philosophers. All of these movements were made possible by the empire's developed systems of communication. The Roman world was crisscrossed by a vast network of roads, the total length of which amounted to around a quarter of a million miles. There was considerable variety in the quality of the road system, but a large proportion of Roman roads were skillfully engineered and constructed, well-maintained, and durable. Their long, straight stretches cut a swathe through all kinds of terrain, using ingenious feats to overcome the difficulties posed by natural phenomena such as marshland or rock. Many of the basic routes chosen by the Romans are still in use today, and the remains of Roman bridges and aqueducts testify to the remarkably advanced character of Roman technical know-how.

Transportation along these roads was very slow by modern standards; progress was limited to the speed of the mules or donkeys employed to pull the various types of carts and carriages in use, and most people were obliged to go on foot. There were perils from roadside bandits, the discomforts of staying in dubious inns, and the costs of various tolls to pay. Nevertheless, for all the problems, travel and trade were more efficient in the Roman world than at any time prior to the nineteenth century.

Sea travel was much swifter than road transport and was a standard means of communication, despite widespread fears about safety. The major shipping lanes had been cleared of the worst threats from pirates in the first century B.C., and they were busy with a constant stream of commercial vessels. There were no special passenger ships, and travelers by sea had to book passage on merchant ships where facilities for passengers were often very basic. Schedules in the modern sense scarcely existed; in general, ships set sail whenever winds were favorable (see Acts 21:1–3). Routes tended to hug coasts wherever possible as vessels moved from port to port to deliver their cargoes. Larger grain ships, such as those plying the vital grain trade between Rome and Alexandria, had to venture onto the open sea, catching the summer winds from the northwest, which would take them from Italy to Egypt in around two weeks. They then had to labor back via a more circuitous route along the coast of Palestine and around Rhodes, Crete, Malta, and Sicily.

Generally there was much less sailing in winter, though ancient literature contains frequent criticism of merchants who were prepared to risk all in pursuit of extra profits off-season, and winter journeys inevitably did take place with fare-paying passengers and important shipments of military personnel. Even in summer the risks could be considerable, because the majority of ships, designed to maximize cargo space, were fairly unwieldy in any sort of rough weather and were furnished with rigging that was ill-equipped to sail in conditions other than a following wind. There were also some lingering dangers from piracy, in spite of the campaigns to reduce this problem.

All forms of travel facilitated the transmission of news, both in person and in writing. Letters were a favorite method of communication among the elite, both for business and the conveying of personal news. They were carried usually by private couriers, acquaintances, or anyone going in the right direction who might be trusted to pass them on. Designated officials had the right to use the Roman imperial post, which used the same dispatch carrier and a variety of means of conveyance to bear important information from person to person across the empire. Nevertheless, the writing and reading of letters or books was confined to a small portion of the population. It is likely that only 10 to 15 percent of the inhabitants of the Roman world were literate, and fewer could write than could read. For the great majority, news traveled by word of mouth, gossiped by merchants, officials, tradespeople, soldiers, and slaves, who carried ideas and stories of current events from place to place as they moved around on their business.

Social Structures

Amid all the outward signs of international unity, the Roman world was in reality a highly stratified and very mixed society. Significant social and cultural snobberies operated with regard to imperial geography, and there were many tensions between the rulers and the ruled. The diverse peoples of the empire could be variously viewed by the Romans as allies or subjects and could in turn regard their ultimate masters as either the guarantors of political stability or the repressors of personal freedom. Degrees of Romanization varied considerably, and there were widespread differences in the degree to which Roman cultural influences were accepted and the ease with which Roman authority operated.

In the social system as a whole, status was primarily determined by ownership of land and property. The elite were drawn from the Roman senatorial class, membership of which was determined by an onerous property qualification. From their ranks came the emperor's inner council of advisers and the most senior administrators of the empire. Some senators were able to trace their ancestry to the patricians who constituted the traditional nobility of Rome, but the numbers who could do so were declining, and senatorial status was increasingly available to those who won imperial favor, regardless of their family origins.

Below the senatorial order were the knights, or the equestrian class, a much larger group, whose property qualification was less than half that required of senators. Many equestrians, however, became very rich; direct engagement in business and trade was conventionally considered to be beneath the dignity of senators, and this left a lot of the most lucrative commercial opportunities open to knights. From this group many of the military, financial, and administrative posts of the empire were filled.

In local cities there were municipal aristocracies made up of councillors and other officials, who had to be rich enough to pay for public works and the running of civil society at a local level. Beneath all of these were the overwhelming majority of the empire's inhabitants: first its free persons, who were themselves made up of a variety of classes according to background, ethnicity, means, and opportunities; then the countless numbers of slaves (perhaps a fifth of the overall population) upon whom Rome's advanced agrarian form of economy critically depended.

There was a vast gulf between those at the top of the social pyramid and those at the bottom, though the position of individuals within the system would become more flexible in later centuries than it was in the first or second century. The ruling elite made up little more than 2 percent of the total population. They controlled the means of economic production, and they typically took a large slice of the economic surplus in order to sustain lives of considerable luxury. Their urban houses were frequently elaborate and well furnished, and they would usually own a country retreat as well. They enjoyed vastly better educational advantages than the majority and possessed a measure of control over the cultural opportunities available to others, not only because of their financial dominance but because they were able to monopolize the services of teachers and scribes. Alongside the privileges went obligations: the elite were obliged to pay significant taxes (though some of these were exacted in turn from their subordinates), finance public-works schemes and entertainments, and provide for the well-being of their extended households.

Compared with those at the opposite end of the spectrum, however, the ruling elite were highly privileged. For a large proportion of the slaves who did almost all the work in the households and large agricultural estates of the rich, there were very few rights other than the provisions of occasional legislation supposed to protect them from particular forms of abuse. In essence, slaves were chattels to be used by their owners as they saw fit. In practice, not all slaves were poor or weak, but their circumstances were closely affected by the status of their masters. Slaves of rich owners had the best chances of a reasonable life and of obtaining their freedom, and servants of powerful people, including the emperor himself, sometimes wielded a good deal of influence in the policies of their household. Those owned by less exalted people had a much worse lot.

Many slaves were able to earn or buy their freedom, and the liberated slave formed an important social type on the lowest rung of the ladder of the free. Many thousands of such individuals existed in first-century society. Some did very well and bettered themselves considerably; though barred from holding magistracies, their sons were capable of progressing as far as equestrian status. In practice, however, a majority lacked the opportunities to advance very far, and many continued to work for their former owners. Whether people were slave or free, there was no welfare provision if they were unable to work on account of illness, old age, or infirmity.

For the great majority, life in the towns and cities was cramped, squalid, and unhygienic. People lived in very overcrowded conditions, generally in small tenement apartments constructed around narrow streets with no sanitation or garbage-disposal systems other than the nearest window. Privacy was minimal, disease was rife, violent crime was common, and the destruction of poorly constructed buildings through fire or natural disasters such as earthquakes was a frequent occurrence. Food shortages were well-known among the general urban populace. The rich and those we might loosely think of as the upper-middle classes may have enjoyed some remarkable luxuries and benefited from the splendid aqueducts, baths, and heating systems for which Roman architecture and technology became famous. But for around 90 percent of the empire's residents, life was a dangerous, dirty, hand-to-mouth existence. The majority of the wealthy enjoyed a reasonable life span; for the poor, average life-expectancy was well under thirty years.

Imperial law may have been a unifying factor in geographical and cultural terms, but the full safeguards of Roman law were available only to Roman citizens, who had a right of appeal to Rome against the judicial decisions of local authorities and exemption from the most degrading forms of punishment, such as flogging (see Acts 16:37; 22:25–29). Citizenship was traditionally a highly valued prize, reserved for individuals and their families who were deemed to have served Rome well or demonstrated an appropriate degree of "Romanness." As a means of cementing provincial loyalties, the bestowal of citizenship was to be much used in the empire. In the first century, it was already being extended much more widely, especially under the emperor Claudius (41–54); nevertheless, it remained at this stage a status possessed by only a limited portion of the populace. In time it was necessary to develop new classifications of the legal privileges of citizenship, especially after the early third century, when it was extended to all free people of the empire.

Society at every level was underpinned by an intricate web of patron-subject relationships, the emperor himself being the supreme patron, through whose generosity—so the theory went—the people were provided with food and entertainment, such as circuses, games, and gladiatorial shows. In the cities, rich individuals would be waited upon early each morning by groups of hangers-on and suppliants to whom they would proffer various boons in exchange for loyal support and services rendered, especially in political causes. Society was highly competitive and driven by firm conceptions of honor and shame, which could be variously promoted or compromised by public behavior.

At the level of the prosperous household, the head was the man, and he was legally responsible for the protection of all his dependents: his wife, children, and slaves. Even his adult children ordinarily remained subject to his authority. His wife was considered to be the keeper of the hearth and the home, and while she enjoyed a good deal more freedom than women in some other ancient societies (she could, for example, initiate divorce, inherit property, or if widowed enjoy financial independence, wealth permitting), she nevertheless remained officially under her husband's guardianship. Lower-class women sometimes lived slightly more liberated lives in one sense, in so far as they were required to work at a variety of jobs outside the home; but very often their work was physically demanding and poorly paid. Women from the highest social ranks could exercise significant influence in certain areas of public life, but formal participation in political authority was restricted to men. Women could not vote, nor were they entitled to receive the free bread that was periodically distributed to the populace by politicians in order to buy favor or quell unrest.

Education was confined to those of means (though Jews of various economic backgrounds showed a stronger concern for the education of children than many other people, partly as a way of preserving their distinctive Jewish identity), and the opportunities were more extensive for boys than for girls. Almost all of the education received by girls took place in the home, and in general only the daughters of the most enlightened rich were given training in literature or language beyond a basic level. Girls were generally expected to marry at an early age (around twelve to thirteen) and bear children. Infanticide was widely practiced, especially as a way of reducing the number of daughters who would require a dowry.

Religion and Popular Belief

The Roman Empire was a world full of gods. Ancient city-states all had their patron deities, who were deemed to provide defense and ensure prosperity. Their cults were generally concentrated on particular images, maintained in a shrine or a temple, which would serve as a focus for special ceremonies once a year in a festival or in the event of special needs such as military peril or the threat of famine. Important civic occasions such as the installation of magistrates or the ratification of political and military treaties took place at temples; sporting activities and the world of the theater were also heavily pervaded by religious rituals. Priesthoods were filled by public servants appointed from the ranks of equestrians and freedmen. The rich might elect to build temples at their own expense, often in gratitude for some personal deliverance from evil, in fulfillment of a vow, or in response to a vision or other religious experience.

As the era of the empire unfolded, it became normal to hail the emperor himself as divine on his death, and he was honored with a temple at Rome and his own priesthood. In life, the emperor was seen as worthy of "heavenly honors," which was interpreted by a number of the first-century emperors—chiefly Caligula (37–41), Nero (54–68), and Domitian (81–96)—to mean that they should already be venerated among the gods. The cult of the emperor came to be promoted in the provinces especially as a means of ensuring political loyalty and stability in every imperial capital, and the emperor's virtues were associated with the personified powers of peace, concord, victory, and clemency.

Roman households honored the hearth (*Vesta*) and the guardian deities (*Penates*) who were believed to watch over and preserve the food supply. Houses typically contained a niche that served as a shrine to the *Lares*, the protective spirits (probably the deified spirits of dead ancestors) who looked after the household. The household shrine would have a little altar, and a small portion of the food at each meal would be placed before it, as well as regular offerings of flowers, incense, oil, or wine. Wealthier homes would also often possess small statues or paintings of the household gods. Images of gods and goddesses were to be found in gardens and in shop windows, and there were shrines and statues at crossroads and along the roadsides. Temples of all shapes and sizes were a standard element of public architecture, and votive offerings, ritual libations, and sacrifices of grain, bread, oil, and wine could be encountered at every turn. Animals and birds were sacrificed at major religious events and at important family or private occasions. The gods were distinguished from humans primarily by their possession of immortality. They varied in status and power but were believed to influence human affairs for both good and ill, and it was considered important to take the appropriate steps to ensure their favor.

Personal religion involved the widespread practice of divination and astrology, and at all levels of society there was a large amount of superstition, belief in magical practices and charms, and consultation of oracles and soothsayers (see Acts 19:19, 23–25). People would perform certain gestures as they passed wayside shrines, and it was vital in religious ritual in general that there was a careful implementation of prescribed procedures in the form of words, silences, and actions. The places of the dead as well as the living were part of the landscape of religious symbolism; tombs were often inscribed with imprecations against potential robbers, calling on the gods to punish anyone who dared to violate their sanctity.

In both private and civic religion, there was for the most part an unabashed syncretism. Travelers, traders, and military conquerors would often pay their respects to local divinities in other countries and regions and perhaps take their cults back home with them, especially in the form of plundered images or temple treasures. There were already acknowledged equivalents for most of the chief figures in the Roman and the Greek pantheons, who could be regarded as the deities of particular entities (such as earth, fire, wind, and sea), foodstuffs (such as corn, oil, or wine), activities (such as hunting, warfare, technology, music, and art), human relations (such as love, marriage, and death), conditions (such as childbirth and health), and so on. All over the empire there were also local divinities, whose associations with particular regions and settlements were buried in the mists of time. There were diverse Eastern mystery religions, such as the cults of the Egyptian mother-goddess, Isis; the Persian (male-only) religion of Mithras, which attracted considerable support from Roman army officers, particularly in the second and third centuries; and the cult of the Phrygian Cybele and her consort Attis, which had made its way into Roman religious life as early as the third century B.C.

Polytheism in antiquity was an extremely flexible phenomenon, and the religions of the Graeco-Roman world were well capable of absorbing new gods and goddesses in a spirit of openness and tolerance. To most people, the validity of a multiplicity of religious forms was simply self-evident, and atheism in a modern sense was almost unknown. When it came to encountering other religious traditions, the essential requirement for the Romans was simply that new cults should not conflict with the veneration of the emperor and that they should not pose any obvious threat to public morals. Inclusivity and principled pluralism were the order of the day, based on the dual assumption that the same deities could take many names and forms and that the expansion of empire naturally brought with it a widening of the boundaries of cultic expression. Many of the most acute thinkers and moralists were willing to acknowledge that there was perhaps in the end a single divinity behind all the diversity of human religious experience.

Philosophical Traditions

In addition to this religious openness, there were the influences of a range of philosophical traditions dating back to the worlds of classical and Hellenistic Greece,[4] which in varying ways posed their own particular questions for the practice of popular religion. The most significant was Platonism. Plato (428–347 B.C.) was deeply influenced by the great Athenian philosopher, Socrates (469–399 B.C.), whose ideas he conveyed and reinterpreted in his Academy in Athens and in his masterly literary dialogues, which continue to fascinate people today. Plato believed that the material world was transient and imperfect and that only a transcendent realm of "Ideas" or "Forms" was permanent and genuinely true. In physical objects, human beings knew only shadows of ultimate reality. Humans were composed, however, of two parts: a confining material body and an immortal soul, and the soul's origins were in the world of Ideas. The intellectual element of the soul saw the Ideas before it came to be imprisoned in the body, and this was how it came to recognize material things as copies of those Ideas: true knowledge was a matter of recollecting concepts learned in a prior spiritual existence.

All these Ideas or Forms were said to be encapsulated in one ultimate ideal, known as the principle of the Good. In Plato's thinking, the Good was not a personal God but a supreme Form. Nevertheless, Plato's theology pointed to a single transcendent principle as the source and goal of all things, and this was naturally taken by some to hint at a kind of monotheism, which might be loosely connected with the monotheism of certain religious traditions. In one of his dialogues, the *Timaeus*, Plato famously pictured the world as made by a Craftsman deity (in Greek, a *Demiourgos*) who copied the eternal Ideas in order to fashion the world. Plato and many of his heirs were sharply critical of the conceptions of divinity held by conventional polytheism. The myths of the poets, with their gods who engaged in passions and quasi-human behavior, were crude and unworthy distortions of the purity and stability of the world of the Forms.

After Plato's death, Platonism went through a series of phases, each with its own distinctive emphases and styles, and in time it would exercise a very strong influence over Christian thinking. Platonist philosophy from around the middle of the first century B.C. to the end of the second century A.D. tends to be described as "Middle Platonism," to differentiate it from earlier expressions of Platonist thinking and from the developments that ensued in the Platonist thought of the third century A.D. and beyond. Platonist thinkers in this middle period were quite eclectic, assimilating a number of ideas from other philosophical and religious traditions. In particular, they heightened the transcendence of the Good or "the One," arguing that the supreme Mind could not be known directly, but only indirectly; it was easier to say what it was *not* than what it *was*.

Next to Platonism there was Stoicism. Stoicism derived from the teaching of a Hellenistic philosopher named Zeno (ca. 336–264 B.C.). He came from Citium in Cyprus but settled in Athens around 313 B.C., where he taught in the *Stoa Poikile*, or the "Painted Porch," from which the school acquired its name. Zeno offered his disciples a philosophy of materialistic pantheism. God was the ordering principle or rationale of the universe, and the universe was akin to a giant, organically connected, living body, with this divine principle as its all-pervasive soul. God could be known by various names, such as *logos* (reason) or *pneuma* (breath, spirit), but divinity was no less material than any other physical object. Divine force held the universe together and would destroy it by fire. In fact, there was simply a constant cycle of cosmic conflagration in which the world was burned up and then remade time after time.

Stoic ethics argued that human beings ought to live "according to nature"; that is, as rational beings, they should exist in accordance with the reason that pervaded the world. Divine providence was utterly immanent in the physical order, and the task for human beings was to practice right judgment with regard to the business of practical living in order to realize the end that God determined. Right judgment, or moral wisdom, was expressed particularly in not allowing external realities to disturb one's mental and inward self-sufficiency. The Stoic sage was not moved by either physical suffering or physical pleasures but concentrated upon the display of virtue and the avoidance of vice.

Stoic philosophy after Zeno went through a variety of phases, beginning especially with Zeno's second successor, Chrysippus (ca. 280–207 B.C.), who was an impressive logician and systemati er. The "Middle Stoa" of Panaetius (ca. 185–109 B.C.) and Posidonius (ca. 135–50 B.C.) introduced a degree of eclecticism, concentrating on practical ethics and on prescriptions for doing the right thing in specific circumstances rather than on the idealized model of the perfect sage. It was this kind of Stoicism that passed into Roman thought in the first and second centuries.

Seneca (A.D. 1–65), who tutored the young Nero and acted as an adviser to him as emperor, blended aspects of Stoicism with Platonist ideas and argued for a mixture of practical good sense and moral asceticism (though he had few scruples about enjoying material affluence personally). His writings would in fact be taken by a number of Christian thinkers to approximate more closely to Christian ideals than those of any other classical philosopher, and in the fourth century an anonymous author constructed a fictitious correspondence between Seneca and the apostle Paul. Other Roman Stoics of widely differing backgrounds, ranging from the former slave Epictetus (A.D. 55–135) to the emperor Marcus Aurelius (who ruled A.D. 161–180), taught comparable forms of sober asceticism and suppression of desires for earthly possessions.

Other philosophical traditions existed besides Platonism and Stoicism. One was Epicureanism, begun by Epicurus (341–270 B.C.), who taught in Athens after about 307 B.C. One of the most controversial figures of ancient philosophy, Epicurus was a materialist. Following another Greek thinker of the fifth century B.C., Democritus, he believed that the world was made up of an infinite number of invisible atoms. Always in motion, these atoms often collided and intermittently combined to form material entities. The world should not be thought of as created but as eternal. There were gods, but these gods lived in the interstellar spaces outside the human sphere and paid no attention to earthly events; they were endlessly content within their own realm. There could be no place for prayer to them, nor should anyone be afraid of offending them or being punished by them. There was no such thing as divine providence in human affairs. The human soul, like the body, was also made up of atoms, and when the body died, the soul also disintegrated. There was therefore nothing to fear in death.

Epicurus and his followers believed the goal of life was "pleasure," but they did not mean wanton self-indulgence or unrestrained sensual gratification. Many of the opponents of Epicurean philosophy in antiquity assumed otherwise, and their misinterpretation is the source of our modern usage of *epicurean* as a term for the pleasure-loving. For committed Epicureans, however, "pleasure" meant an absence of pain in the body and trouble in the soul; it was the ideal of a trouble-free state in which the body was healthy and the mind was tranquil and undisturbed. The pleasures of the body were in fact regarded as the lowest kind of pleasures; what one ought to aspire to was an equilibrium of the soul, expressed in an absence of pain, discomfort, and fear. Epicurus was not an unabashed hedonist; he considered friendship with like-minded companions, not physical indulgence, the best form of human enjoyment.

Epicurean philosophy was immortalized for Romans in the magisterial poem of Lucretius (ca. 94–55 B.C.), *On the Nature of Things*.

Like his hero Epicurus, Lucretius saw it as his aim to disabuse his readers of the superstitious folly of fear of the gods. While there was no need to abolish forms of religious observance that might serve various social purposes, humans had no obligations to the gods and no need to be afraid of punishment for their actions. Unlike the Stoics, Epicurean devotees sought to distance themselves from public life and the world of political affairs and were often criticized for it. Epicureanism proved an attractive system for some, but it never caught on in the Roman world with the same measure of success that Stoicism achieved, for it seemed to place too much weight on the pursuit of individual fulfillment at the expense of service to society and the state.

Aristotle (384–322 B.C.) was a former pupil of Plato and tutor to the young Alexander the Great. He founded his own school in Athens, which met in a public building known as the Lyceum.[5] Aristotle had begun with similar assumptions to the later Plato but had gone in different directions, arguing that Forms existed only in concrete expressions and that knowledge might accordingly begin with sense-experience, though it had to proceed beyond this in order to abstract the universal from the particular. The soul animated the body and was its driving force, but the soul and the body were mutually dependent and were to be distinguished only in thought.

Ethical fulfillment, according to Aristotle, consisted of living a rational life, which involved the use of both intellectual or theoretical reason and practical or moral reason. Earthly things had potential perfection within them, and they moved toward the actualization of their complete reality—hence natural science, by which entities were closely scrutinized and investigated, was an entirely appropriate activity for the rational mind, and one that Aristotle and his pupils took with the utmost seriousness. The most perfect reality was thought, which was the prime mover of actions in that it was the object of their desire. At the head of a hierarchy of worldly substances was an eternal mind, the ultimate cause of all motion and change, but this mind was not a god of creation or providence as such.

Aristotle's overall legacy in science, logic, and philosophy—not least in later Christian thought—was enormous, and in the first century his works were the subject of scholarly interest in a number of quarters. In the period from the third century B.C. to the first century A.D., however, the traditions of Aristotelianism were not so influential, and Aristotle's ideas were not of strong popular significance in the earliest Christian age.

A much more obvious presence were the Cynics, whose origins lay in the fourth century B.C. The Cynics believed that virtue could be attained by moral self-effort and in particular by freeing oneself from dependence upon external things. Their alleged founder was Diogenes of Sinope (ca. 400–325 B.C.), who is said to have become known as "Diogenes the Dog"—in Greek, *kyon*, hence "Cynic"—for the shameless way he behaved in public.

Wandering Cynic teachers, or those who resembled them, were to be found widely in the first century. They deliberately adopted a countercultural style, dressing in rough clothes, engaging in provocative behavior in public, especially bold or insolent speech, and surviving by begging. Some of their devotion to asceticism and to detachment from material concerns resembled convictions held by the Stoics, but they were impatient of Stoic dogma, and insisted that the ideal of the wise individual was genuinely practicable for all. They were also very critical of conventional religion, although many were quite traditional in their belief in a god or gods. Not all Cynics were itinerants or radical attention-seekers; some lived milder, more settled forms of existence in the cities of the Roman world. Invariably, however, Cynics saw it as their role to challenge social conventions and to act as models of self-sufficiency through transcendence of the shallow needs and ambitions of the society around them.

Other more minor traditions also persisted in various forms. The Skeptics, who originally sprang from a particular phase in the history of Plato's Academy, argued that it was better to suspend judgment than to formulate dogmatic opinions about questions such as the existence of God, the meaning of life, and the nature of right behavior. In practice, they were often rather conservative on ethical matters, for they assumed that the best thing to do was to live according to the familiar patterns of society and to stay out of trouble. There were also movements such as Neopythagoreanism, which sought to revive some of the cherished ideas of the great Greek thinker of the sixth century B.C., Pythagoras. His philosophy, built upon the idea that number lies at the heart of the universe, advocated a system of mysticism, magical practices, ritual purifications of the soul, and self-denial.

Overall, however, by far the strongest philosophical influences were wielded by the twin streams of Platonism and Stoicism. Both of these systems had many variants, and they were not mutually exclusive; each came to nourish the other in a range of respects, as the middle phases of both traditions revealed. In very broad terms, those of a primarily Platonist bent were resistant to arguments that the material world or the realm of the senses is all that there is, and they looked for a principle of transcendent truth that went beyond what they saw as the simplistic images of conventional Graeco-Roman religion with its anthropomorphic gods and goddesses. Stoicism, for its part, essentially offered its devotees an integrated system of logic, physics, and ethics, in which they could hold to a belief in universal rationality without either devaluing the physical world or treating it as excessively important.

Taken together, all of these movements illustrate just how eclectic the religious and philosophical world of the first century was. Worship of many different divinities was commonplace in society, but alongside this lay frameworks of intellectual thought that variously challenged the logic of polytheistic faith. It was quite possible to go through the motions of civic piety and to participate in the imperial cult while also espousing the view that traditional mythology was not to be taken literally, or that the gods were not really to be feared, or that there was some kind of ultimate supreme being beyond all the expressions of classical religion. Sacrifice might be offered without believing that the deity in question really needed it; rituals could be performed without regarding them as literal means of placating divine spirits or satisfying absolutely necessary prescriptions for personal or societal prosperity. Opinions varied about the possibility and conditions of an afterlife and were very seldom concerned with punishment or reward for earthly behavior; where the gods were to be pleased, the aspiration to win their favor was overwhelmingly focused on the affairs of the present world.

A thinking person might read the stories of the poets as allegories of human behavior (of greater or lesser practical pertinence) while believing that the real concern of life was to engage in an appropriate kind of mental abstraction from the challenges of bodily existence and the shadowy deceptions of a fading material world. The imagery of many deities might be dismissed as superstition in the belief that there was ultimately only one overarching divine principle. Fundamentally, openness and tolerance were the norm, and most people could not understand why the practitioners of any religion should have felt the need to claim—as the Jews notoriously did—that their god was exclusive of all others. When the first stories about Jesus started to spread beyond the boundaries of Galilee and Judea, they were carried into a world that was not short of alternative belief systems, most of which were, in their various ways, capable of existing simultaneously with the practices and assumptions of theistic faith.

Judaism in the First Century

However influential the ideas of Athens, Rome, and Alexandria would in time prove for the unfolding of the story concerning Jesus's followers, the Jesus movement began not in the obvious heartlands of Graeco-Roman culture but in Palestine, and within Judaism, among a people of a faith that a majority of the empire's inhabitants found exceptionally strange, exacting, and difficult to comprehend.

First-century Judaism was itself a very eclectic entity. The designations "Jew" and "Jewish" originally referred to those whose identity was defined with reference to the territory of Judea and to its holy city of Jerusalem and its temple. They were thus, at heart, ethnic as much as religious terms. But in the first century far more Jews lived outside the motherland than within her borders. The population of Palestinian Judaism was probably not more than a million, but several million Jews were dispersed throughout the Graeco-Roman world, and together they may have constituted something like 7 or 8 percent of the total population of the Roman Empire. In order to understand the context within which belief in Jesus arose, we need to appreciate something of the sheer geographical expansiveness of the Jewish faith around the time of Jesus's death and resurrection.

There were very many differences between the expressions of Judaism found throughout the empire, but it is misleading to draw a simple distinction between Judaism in Palestine and Judaism elsewhere in the Roman world. It would be quite wrong to imagine, for example, that Palestinian Judaism had evolved entirely without Hellenistic influences. The rural Galilee to which Jesus belonged had remained fundamentally Jewish, and attempts to identify Jesus with Greek traditions such as that of the wandering philosopher-sage lack credibility. Jesus and his disciples spoke Aramaic, the popular version of Hebrew, while farther south in Judea, Hebrew laced with Aramaic was the norm for most people. Nevertheless, there was, at the same time, a very significant amount of Greek cultural influence in commercial, social, and public life throughout Palestine, the main centers of Lower Galilee, the Coastal Plain, Judea, Samaria, and parts of Transjordan.

The educated and mercantile classes of Jerusalem used Greek as a second language, and many individuals had Greek names. Jerusalem's public buildings included a gymnasium and a hippodrome, its architecture and pottery bore Greek influences, and its coins were minted with Greek inscriptions. Many Hellenized Jews from other parts of the Mediterranean settled in Jerusalem and met in synagogues where the

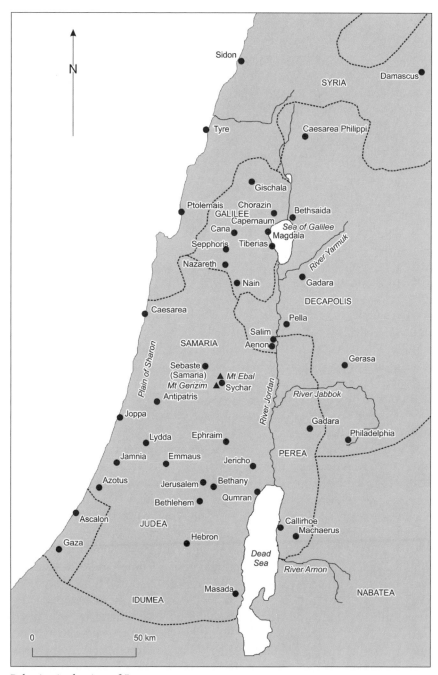

N

Sidon

SYRIA

Damascus

Tyre

Caesarea Philippi

Gischala

Ptolemais   Chorazin
GALILEE   Capernaum   Bethsaida
Cana   *Sea of Galilee*
Sepphoris   Magdala
             Tiberias
Nazareth

Nain   Gadara

River Yarmuk

Caesarea   DECAPOLIS

Pella

Salim
SAMARIA   Aenon   Gerasa

Sebaste ▲ Mt Ebal
(Samaria) ▲
Mt Gerizim ▲ Sychar   *River Jabbok*
Antipatris

Joppa   Gadara

Lydda   Ephraim   Philadelphia

Jamnia   Emmaus
                  Jericho   PEREA
Azotus
         Jerusalem Bethany
Bethlehem   Qumran

Ascalon   JUDEA   Callirhoe
                             Machaerus
Gaza   Hebron

                   *Dead
                    Sea*   *River Arnon*

Masada   NABATEA
IDUMEA

0   50 km

Plain of Sharon

River Jordan

Palestine in the time of Jesus

language used was Greek. Greek settlements existed in the so-called "ten cities" of the Decapolis, located mostly to the east of the Jordan, while in Lower Galilee itself, only four miles to the northwest of Jesus's village of Nazareth, lay the impressive and thoroughly Hellenized capital city of Sepphoris. Tiberias, built on the western bank of the Sea of Galilee between the years 17 and 20, was another strongly Gentile center in its early years, and there were other significantly Hellenized principalities dotted all around the region.

The main origins of Hellenistic culture in Palestine lay in the remarkable accomplishments of Alexander the Great, whose imperial conquests had carried the norms of Greek civilization all over the eastern Mediterranean world and far beyond. In Judea, Hellenism had been promoted in particular by those who came after Alexander, first the Ptolemies of Egypt and then especially the Seleucids of Syria. The Seleucid ruler Antiochus IV Epiphanes (175–163 B.C.), abetted by strong Hellenistic sympathizers in Jerusalem, pressed the agenda of Hellenization so hard that he provoked an armed revolt. The temple was desecrated and Jewish rituals were forbidden. The Jews of Judea rose in a series of armed challenges to Seleucid power and its idolatrous agendas. The Maccabean wars (168–142 B.C.) were initiated by a priest named Mattathias and spearheaded in inspirational fashion by his son Judas (who was given the name Maccabaeus—Greek *Makkabaios*, perhaps "hammerer") and then in turn by Judas's four brothers. These wars were a bloody and ultimately successful campaign to establish the freedom and dignity of the Jews to have their religious rites respected in their own land.

The Maccabeans and their successors had formed a number of alliances with Rome against the Seleucids, and the Romans had promised to respect the legitimacy of the Jewish people to follow their own customs. The earliest relations between Rome and the Jews were thus friendly. Judea was seen as just another buffer state on the borders of the empire, a virtually independent kingdom subject to Roman protection. Things changed in the mid-60s B.C., however, when the Roman general Pompey, who had been engaged in a campaign against Rome's eastern enemies, was confronted with rival claims for support from two feuding Jewish princes, Hyrcanus and Aristobulus. While awaiting Pompey's decision, Aristobulus in confusion launched rebellious activities against Pompey's authority and incurred his wrath. Pompey went to Jerusalem, where he was welcomed by the supporters of Hyrcanus but resisted by their opponents, who barricaded themselves in the temple. After a three-month siege and much loss of life, Pompey's forces were victorious. The sacred site was not looted, but there was outrage that a Gentile had penetrated the Holy of Holies.

From 63 B.C. onward the Jewish kingdom became a vassal state, officially subject to the authority of Rome. Absorbed into the Roman province of Syria, it was divided into two separated regions, Galilee in the north and Judea with part of Idumea and Perea in the south; between them lay Samaria. Hyrcanus was confirmed as high priest, and Antipater, an Idumean who was his principal political adviser, held the substance of civil power. Ultimate control, however, lay with the Romans, represented by the governor of Syria. After various revolts against Roman rule, spearheaded by Aristobulus and his sons, the governor extended his grip, and Hyrcanus was deprived of any authority other than his religious status. In 54 B.C., the temple was plundered in order to finance a major Roman military campaign against Parthia. The fate of the Jewish state was caught up in the various twists of Rome's civil war in the early 40s B.C., as Antipater switched allegiance with each change in Rome. The pragmatism paid dividends in the end, and Hyrcanus and Antipater secured guarantees and privileges when Julius Caesar emerged victorious over his rivals.

Under Antipater's son, Herod "the Great" (37–4 B.C.), Judea remained loyal to Rome. Herod was a nominal Jew, but his background and his sympathies lay with non-Jewish peoples. Designated "king of the Jews" by the Roman Senate in 40 B.C., he imposed himself on his kingdom three years later. Through firm measures and considerable expenditure of resources, he managed to bring a considerable degree of order to a resentful and highly troubled territory. He endeavored to put down banditry and ensure peace and stability. He actively promoted Greek culture and distributed significant benefactions to Hellenistic cities in Syria, Asia Minor, and Greece itself. Within Palestine, Herod rebuilt the city of Samaria and renamed it Sebaste (the Greek for *Augusta*) in honor of the emperor; he also rebuilt Caesarea, the great coastal city that later became the Romans' administrative capital. For all his patronage of Gentile causes and his sponsorship of pagan buildings, Herod appeared keen to conciliate Jewish sensibilities, and around 20 B.C. he also set about reconstructing the Jerusalem temple in magnificent style.

It is possible that Herod nursed a diplomatic dream of uniting Jews and Gentiles under Rome's final authority, which by this time had evolved into the principate of Augustus. Whatever his intentions, though, he was loathed by a large proportion of his Jewish subjects. Beneath the veneer of his success, his regime was marred by a great deal of violence and intimidation, and his own household was torn apart by intrigue and feuding. It was not only the Idumaean dynasty that most Jews hated but the collusion with foreign power that it symbolized. Whatever he had achieved, Herod had only exacerbated Jewish resentment of subjection to Roman rule.

On his death, Herod's kingdom was divided between his three sons, Archelaus, Philip, and Herod Antipas (the Herod referred to in the Gospels). Archelaus was to rule Judea, Samaria, and Idumea; Antipas was to be tetrarch of Galilee and Perea; and Philip was to be tetrarch of Iturea and Trachonitis, northeast of the Sea of Galilee. Philip and Antipas were able to retain their territories into the 30s, but after widespread revolts, protests, and cruel efforts to impose his authority, Archelaus's regime was judged a failure by the Romans, and he was removed from power in A.D. 6. His territory of Judea, Samaria, and Idumea became a Roman province, administered directly by a Roman governor.

Jews and Romans

In principle, the Romans allowed their Jewish subjects a good deal of religious freedom. The governor was based at Caesarea and only went up to Jerusalem on special occasions such as feast days. The Sanhedrin, the council of seventy-one members presided over at this time by the high priest, retained official authority over internal affairs and acted as the supreme court in matters of Jewish Law. The Romans showed considerable respect for Jewish sensibilities. A sacrifice in the temple "for Caesar and the Roman nation" was regarded as an acceptable expression of political loyalty; Jews were exempted from appearing before a magistrate on the Sabbath or on a holy day; and the copper coins that were minted in the country carried no image of the emperor or of pagan deities, in deference to Jewish opposition to graven images.

Nevertheless, the Romans maintained a large military presence in Jerusalem, and their taxation, whether gathered directly in the form of tribute to Rome or indirectly through the Herodian client-kings, was resented as a heavy burden. The upper classes, in fact, often did rather well socially and economically under Roman rule, and there were plenty of people who enjoyed positive relations with Roman officials, both at a general level and as their agents in local administration, tax collection, or the provisioning of Roman garrisons. For the great majority, however, upon whom the weight of taxation was especially heavy and the benefits of imperial control were slim, the Romans were resented as the occupying power, as idolaters and oppressors, and as the root cause of every national and social ill. There were many points of conflict both in Jerusalem itself and in the countryside, though rural resentment of collaborators within the holy city was particularly strong in areas such as Galilee. The differences in attitude between the few and the many highlighted and exacerbated existing social and regional divisions, and there were various periods when the Romans came down hard on seditious leaders and their followers.

Most Jews did not think of themselves as belonging to a particular party or representation of Judaism, akin to what we might think of as a religious denomination; they were simply *Jews*. Being Jewish was a lifestyle, and one that affected every part of existence. The overwhelming majority of the Jews of Palestine—like Jews everywhere—were united in their adherence to the one God, to his election of Israel as the covenant people, to the Torah, and to the temple in Jerusalem as the place where Israel possessed the privilege of God's special earthly presence. Those such as the Samaritans, who believed that Mt. Gerizim rather than Mt. Zion was the chosen dwelling place of God, were regarded as no better than uncircumcised Gentiles and outsiders to the covenant.[6] Because Judaism was an all-embracing commitment, it was not possible to separate religion and politics—least of all in a context in which political occupation was an ever-present reality. Being Jewish meant discerning and following the will of a God who was Lord of all and who therefore had a view about, and a purpose in, every area of life.

Yet there were many different perspectives on what it might mean to know God's will in a situation of bondage. For most people, the Romans were a menace to be grumbled about but a reality about which little could be done immediately. The best course was to cling to the essential hope that God would in time grant deliverance and the restoration of Israel's fortunes. For the Pharisees, as we have seen, this policy had to be followed in a particular way. Faithfulness consisted of loyalty to the Torah and tradition and the correct interpretation of the God-given symbols of Jewish identity. Divine rescue was to be achieved by the due maintenance of Jewishness. Degrees of strictness varied, and some Pharisees took a more critical line than others with regard to the Romans and the Herodians, but for the most part they were prepared to accept the political status quo and concentrate upon maintaining fidelity to their understanding of God's Law. For the Sadducees and other members of the aristocracy, by contrast, collaboration was in order; acquiescence in the right of the Romans to appoint the high priests was seen as the way to preserve a position of social importance and political influence.

The Qumran Community

A more radical approach was adopted by the Essenes and the Qumran community, based on the northwestern shore of the Dead Sea, with whom they appear to have been connected. They held that the positions adopted by groups such as the Pharisees and the Sadducees were not rigorous enough, indeed, that in vital ways they were badly mistaken. It was necessary to withdraw from temple worship not because—as the Samaritans thought—Jerusalem was not God's holy city but because the system in Jerusalem was corrupt.

God was indeed meant to be worshiped in his chosen place in Jerusalem, but the priesthood and sacrificial worship in the temple were compromised by the presence of idolatry and religious impurity. Only when God's kingdom came would the temple become what it should be and the divine presence be manifest in Jerusalem once again. This kingdom would arrive very shortly, but in the meantime, those at Qumran saw themselves as called to a life of separation and holiness in obedience to God's commands. They were the "children of light," an enclave of holiness amid a world made up of the "children of darkness," whose ranks included apostate (or all other) Jews as well as Gentiles.

The Qumran community adopted a monastic way of life, bound by a strict rule of discipline and entered in the fullest sense only after a period of probation. Ceremonial purity was taken extremely seriously, and initiates practiced ritual purifications, frugal communal meals, common ownership of goods, and the pursuit of holiness. They followed their own calendar of religious festivals, distinct from that of the authorities in Jerusalem and based upon a solar (364-day) as opposed to the usual lunar (354-day) sequence. The community revered a figure known as "the Teacher of Righteousness," who had taught his followers a special way of interpreting the Scriptures and had been persecuted by a "wicked priest." These characters are impossible to identify, although various suggestions continue to be made.

The distinction between the two constituencies of light and darkness was believed to symbolize a cosmic duel that was shortly to reach its climax in the triumph of God over the forces of evil and the vindication of God's chosen people. God's final victory would be foreshadowed by the coming of two Messiahs, a priestly "Messiah of Aaron" as well as a kingly "Messiah of Israel" from David's line. There would also be a third eschatological figure, the prophet predicted by Moses in Deuteronomy 18:15–18. These beliefs seem to reflect a range of messianic associations at Qumran as elsewhere among Jews; some expected a military deliverer from political bondage, others a religious savior-figure whose vindication of Israel would not be defined in violent conflict. Some among the Qumran believers were pacifists, but in the end a majority were prepared to bear arms; most would perish in the bloody Jewish revolt against Rome in the late 60s.

Our most valuable evidence concerning the Qumran believers comes from the famous Dead Sea Scrolls, and it is worth noting the significance of these remarkable discoveries for our awareness of Judaism around the time of Jesus. The first scrolls were discovered by accident by bedouin shepherds in 1947 in a cave at Wadi Qumran. Subsequent discoveries were made in a nearby cave in 1952 and in a series of further extensive excavations over the following years. In total eleven caves yielded an astonishing haul of ancient documents, extending to eleven scrolls written on leather and tens of thousands of fragments of papyrus and leather from around eight hundred original texts. One scroll is written on copper, the extreme oxidation of which has made it a particular challenge to decipher.

Scientific dating and analysis of these scrolls is a vast task, which (having proceeded extremely slowly for many years) continues to sustain a considerable industry of scholarly enterprise. The great majority of the scrolls were written in Hebrew, though a small proportion are in Aramaic and a few in Greek. They were almost certainly written or copied by the people who lived at Qumran. They contain almost all the books of the Jewish Scriptures, except for the book of Esther, possibly because that text had disputed status within Judaism. They also include a number of works in widespread use that were not finally included in the Hebrew Canon, such as the books of Enoch, Tobit, and the Wisdom of Jesus ben Sira (Ecclesiasticus). Copies of the Psalms, Deuteronomy, and Isaiah are particularly numerous. In addition, there are texts that appear to represent the lifestyle, rules, and beliefs of the movement to which those at Qumran belonged, including examples of their hymns and liturgies and works of scriptural commentary.

While the Qumran literature has not yielded any directly Christian material, its discovery has been of momentous significance for scholarship. In the first place, the scrolls of the Hebrew Scriptures are several hundred years (in some cases as much as a thousand years) older than any versions of these texts previously available to modern scholarship. These have proved an invaluable asset in the work of textual criticism and historical study of the Hebrew Bible. Second, the findings from Qumran have also been of considerable importance for our understanding of Jewish belief and practice in the first century. Claims have been made for fragments of Christian texts, notably of Mark 6:52–53, among the Greek material from one of the caves, but in each case there are alternative possibilities.

Even if there is no specifically Christian evidence with which to work, some interesting points of comparison can be made between the apparent beliefs and practices of the Qumran community and those of the first believers in Jesus. There are some parallels between Jesus's teaching, with its radical contrast between good and evil, life and death, and the Qumran belief in "two ways." The confident expectation that God's cause would finally triumph was obviously common to both traditions. The Dead Sea Scrolls certainly confirm that messianic expectations and hopes for the imminent arrival of God's powerful presence were widely shared in first-century Palestinian Judaism, and the Qumran conviction that the divine presence was not necessarily tied to a building was in certain respects similar to the conviction of Jesus's followers that God no longer needed to be worshiped in structures made by human hands. Jesus's place in the memory of the first Christians can appear faintly similar to the role of the Teacher of Righteousness, to whom the Qumran community believed God communicated special mysteries concerning the end times. In certain respects, the organization and discipline of the earliest community of Christians in Jerusalem also resembled Qumran practices, especially in matters such as the common ownership of property.

In the end, however, the similarities between Jesus's first followers and the Qumran believers should not be exaggerated, despite the sensational claims made in certain sectors of popular literature. For Jesus and his disciples, the last times had *already* arrived; they were not to be awaited in the coming of some future kingdom. The temple at Jerusalem was not just temporarily suspended in its significance, to be replaced by a new temple that God would build in an eschatological age shortly to dawn; it was seen as symbolically reconstituted by Jesus himself as the embodiment of God's presence to Israel. The moral obligations of God's people were not to withdraw from the world in pursuit of sectarian purity but to engage with society and to proclaim a message of divine love that extended, ultimately, to all people everywhere.

Diaspora Judaism

Meanwhile, what of all those Jews, by far the largest proportion of them, who lived outside Palestine? They were in part the children of the original captivities brought about by the Assyrians and the Babylonians several centuries earlier. Some Jews had never gone back to Jerusalem from exile in Babylon when offered the chance to do so by Cyrus of Persia on his conquest of Babylon in the 530s B.C. Large numbers of Jews remained throughout Mesopotamia and Babylonia. But "Diaspora" (dispersion) Judaism was also about much more than those Jews who had chosen to remain domiciled somewhere other than their ethnic homeland. For generations, many Jews had seized the opportunities opened up by the conquests of Alexander and his successors and had migrated for economic reasons as traders, farmers, and administrators, attracted by the rich prospects of life beyond the limited possibilities offered in Palestine. Others had been conscripted for military service, especially in the armies of the Ptolemies of Egypt, or taken into slavery as prisoners of war, not least in the aftermath of Pompey's conquest of Jerusalem, and had then gone on to earn their freedom and remain in the different environments to which they and their families had been brought.

As a result of all these historical movements, Jews were settled all over the eastern Mediterranean in Egypt, Cyrenaica, Syria, and the Greek cities of western Asia Minor. Egypt in the first century A.D. possessed as many as 750,000 Jews, and in two areas of its great capital, Alexandria, they formed a majority of the populace. There was also a strong Jewish presence in Italy, Sicily, Greece, and the Greek islands. Rome in particular had somewhere between 30,000 and 50,000 Jews and a dozen synagogues, and although most Jews were settled in predominantly humble surroundings on the right bank of the Tiber River, they were an established part of the Roman community. In the following centuries there would also be a significant Jewish presence as far west as Spain and as far south as Arabia.

Diaspora Jews lived in a wide variety of circumstances politically, socially, and economically, and over time they experienced many changes in their fortunes. So great was their diversity that it is precarious to generalize with regard to their defining characteristics or even over what it meant to be described as Jewish in these differing contexts. Some Jews were significantly assimilated into their surrounding cultures and participated extensively in the social and cultural life of their society. Others determinedly sought to maintain their distinctiveness, such as the group of ascetics known to us as the "Therapeutae," who seem to have lived on a sort of monastic commune near Lake Mareotis just outside Alexandria. Most were probably somewhere in between these two extremes. Jews represented almost every level on the social spectrum, from slaves and hired hands to prosperous traders, bankers, artisans, and civil magistrates. Although poverty was a reality for some, many others enjoyed considerable wealth and social status, and in many cities Jews were comfortably ensconced among the most affluent members of the population.

Throughout the Mediterranean Diaspora, Jews were subject to the powerful influences of Greek culture. Semitic languages may have remained standard for most Jews in Palestine, central and eastern Syria, and Babylonia, but for the great majority of Jews in the Graeco-Roman world, the Greek language was the common medium of communication in commerce, education, and everyday discourse. These Jews used a Greek version of the Hebrew sacred Scriptures, which was known as the Septuagint. Produced at Alexandria in the third century B.C., this version was traditionally said to have been completed by seventy (or seventy-two) scholars commissioned by King Ptolemy II Philadelphus—hence its designation "Septuagint" (Greek *septuaginta*, "seventy").[7] Various venerable legends had grown up around its production, including the belief that the books of Moses were translated by special divine enabling. It was said that the scholars had worked independently of one another yet miraculously came up with a common version. Others claimed that the whole project had been finished in the space of seventy-two days. The Septuagint was regarded as especially inspired by God, and in Alexandria the local Jewish community celebrated an annual festival in memory of its production.

The best-educated Jews were deeply familiar with Greek literature and thought. Most famous among these was the great Alexandrian scholar Philo (20 B.C.–A.D. 50), a descendant of a wealthy family, who wrote extensively on Scripture, philosophy, and apologetics and led a delegation to Rome to plead the case for Jewish religious rights before the emperor Caligula in 39 to 40. Philo was intimately acquainted with Greek philosophy, especially Platonism, and he confidently drew on Greek ideas and allegorical methods of interpreting texts in a bid to demonstrate that the Law of Moses contained the ultimate truth concerning the one God after whom the philosophers had sought. For learned Hellenistic Jews such as Philo, it was common to allege that Greek thinkers had in fact stolen their best ideas from the Jewish Scriptures.

Another educated Jewish writer was the historian Flavius Josephus (ca. A.D. 37–100), chronicler of the war between Rome and the Jews of Palestine in 66 to 73 and of the history of the Jewish people from their origins until his own day, and passionate apologist for his faith. Though born into the priestly aristocracy of Judea, he spent half his life as a figure of the Diaspora and wrote all of his surviving works in Rome. Josephus's background and instincts were a great deal narrower than Philo's, but his writings in Greek were intended for a Diaspora context.[8]

Whatever the differences in their lifestyles and contexts, most of the Jews of the Diaspora maintained a strong sense of their common bond to Judaism as an ethnic and religious tradition with its own values and customs. Some highly assimilated Jews did intermarry with Gentiles, but for the most part, such practices were frowned upon, in accordance with the traditional legal stipulations that Israel was to be kept pure. Children were instructed in the teaching of the faith, and in general a pattern of religious exclusivity was followed. Male circumcision was regarded as a vital token of identity. Almost every Jewish community had its synagogue or place of prayer, and attendance at regular Sabbath services was an essential element of a public religious life marked by reading and recitation of the Law, prayers, and participation in communal meals.

Dues were collected annually for the temple in Jerusalem, and pilgrimages to the holy city were frequent, especially for the major festivals of Passover, Pentecost, and the Feast of Tabernacles. The homeland occupied a powerful symbolic significance in the minds of most dispersed Jews, and many nursed hopes of returning some day to the special place that God had destined for them. Yet it was common also to feel a strong sense of attachment to present locations; rather than seeing the dispersion as a perpetuation of exile from the chosen land, the Jews of the Graeco-Roman world could equally see themselves as representatives of a worldwide expansion of their faith. The language of "captivity" was, for some, transposed into the imagery of "colonization."

In many ways, early imperial Rome showed remarkable indulgence to Jewish sensibilities. Often, of course, generosity was based upon political calculations and the attempt to play the Jews off against other constituencies. But in the early years of the first century, the Jews of the Diaspora were allowed to send in their donations for the upkeep of the temple, to show no particular respect to the traditional gods of Rome, and to collect corn handouts (where they were entitled to them) on the day after the Sabbath when necessary. They were also often allowed to evade military service. Under Augustus, the Jewish community in Rome flourished. Things changed significantly under Augustus's successor, Tiberius (A.D. 14–37), when in the year A.D. 19 the Roman Senate conscripted several thousand Jews for military duty and banished many others from Rome. There were further significant setbacks in subsequent decades, which would have important consequences for the Christian story, as we shall see. For a good deal of the time, however, the Jews of the first-century Diaspora were treated perfectly well by their political masters.

This is not to say that they were not widely resented. To many on-lookers, the Jews presented a lifestyle that was odd or obnoxious. They refused to engage in worship of the Roman emperor or to associate even indirectly with the practitioners of pagan cults. They would not eat meat that had been offered in sacrifice to pagan gods, and they regarded even common or garden pork as unclean. They circumcised their male children, a practice that seemed barbaric to most Gentiles. They observed one day each week as sacred and determinedly refused to work on that day, a habit that was often construed as laziness or stupidity, especially since the Jews themselves were frequently the losers in terms of income or their standing in legal processes.

But not all saw the Jews as quaint traditionalists or self-righteous separatists. Some were attracted by the moral dedication of Jewish worshipers, by Judaism's prizing of marriage and family life, its stress on sexual purity, and its emphasis on good works. Others found its intellectual ethos appealing: Judaism valued its sacred literature extremely highly, and its most sophisticated representatives could present good arguments in favor of a monotheism that attracted many in the Graeco-Roman world. Many Jews were also seen to care about charity as well as education. Diaspora synagogues often included not only libraries but hospices, and Jews were frequently assiduous in showing hospitality to strangers, visiting the sick, and giving alms to the needy.

Such practices commended the Jewish faith to Gentiles, and there were many converts to Judaism. Although there is little evidence from the time of Jesus and his immediate followers of any widespread pro-gram of organized proselytism, zeal for the truth of their religion and the rightness of its ways undoubtedly led some Jews to witness to oth-ers, and the testimony of Jewish lifestyles and values often had its own impact. When that impact reached beyond those of modest status and yielded converts at higher levels of society, it sometimes incurred hostil-ity from the Romans.

More common than wholesale converts to Judaism were people who were loosely attached sympathizers. They were usually referred to as "God-fearers," to distinguish them from committed proselytes. The term *God-fearer* is used in a variety of ways in first-century sources, and the details surrounding the status of such persons in this period are not al-together clear (see Acts 10:2; 17:4, 17; 18:7). Nevertheless, God-fearers appear usually to have been Gentile adherents who adopted Jewish religious practices without going through a process of formal conversion, which would have involved circumcision. They might attend synagogue services or give to Judaism financially, but they did not become Jews in the full sense.

In a world of religious syncretism, where various systems could be equally respected and some were scrupulous (or superstitious) enough to show deference to "unknown" gods (Acts 17:23), professions of admiration for the Jewish God and the way of life adopted by his worshipers were sometimes little more than religious insurance policies. Nevertheless, among the God-fearers there were undoubtedly individuals who were persuaded of the strengths of Jewish belief and were genuinely keen to exist somewhere within its scope.

The Launching of the Jesus Movement

It was in this world, with all its political, social, cultural, and religious diversity, that the movement arising from faith in Jesus was launched. The course of that movement in its first century cannot be understood in isolation from this context, for the message of Jesus variously engaged with, absorbed, and confronted aspects of all of the factors that made the first-century Graeco-Roman world the place that it was. The entity that we call "Christianity" emerged and developed in an environment that was at once Jewish, Greek, and Roman, and it still retains the hallmarks of this joint pedigree.

In time, this entity outgrew many of its original sources, and it certainly outlasted the political structures of the ancient Mediterranean world. But the challenges that the story of Jesus faced, the strategies that its advocates adopted, the mistakes they made, and the successes they attained can only be viewed correctly when seen against the backdrop of this first-century setting.

2

SPREADING THE NEWS

▼

The Nazarenes in Jerusalem

The group of Jesus's followers who gathered in Jerusalem around the year A.D. 30 were a fairly unimpressive bunch. They consisted of eleven of the twelve disciples whom Jesus had specially commissioned to speak and act on his behalf: Simon Peter, James, John, Andrew, Philip, Bartholomew, Matthew, Thomas, James son of Alphaeus, Simon "the Zealot," Judas Iscariot, and Jude, also known as Thaddaeus (Matt. 10:2–4; Mark 3:16–19; Luke 6:13–16). In addition were a number of women, including Mary, Jesus's mother, and Jesus's brothers, whose names are given in Mark 6:3 as James, Joseph, Judas, and Simon. In all, there were a few dozen individuals; Luke, the author of the Acts of the Apostles, numbers them at "about a hundred and twenty" (Acts 1:15).

At this stage, the term *apostle*, or messenger sent by Jesus, was used quite generally among the believers; only later on would it be restricted to a particular group of leaders, consisting chiefly of "the Twelve," who were deemed to have a special mandate from the risen Christ (see further p. 123). This narrower usage is on the whole assumed by Luke, who describes how a replacement was chosen for Judas Iscariot, the disciple

51

who had betrayed Jesus. Matthias, a figure who had been among the wider circle of Jesus's followers, was selected by lot to take Judas's place (Acts 1:15–26). Whether such deliberate reconstitution of a leadership of the Twelve was uppermost in the priorities of the believers from the start is unclear; in their minds, the future was none too certain. The narrative of Acts presents them as simply lingering in Jerusalem, praying together and taking comfort from one another's presence as they awaited a clearer sense of what to do next. They may have been convinced that Jesus was alive and that his body had mysteriously ascended into heaven, but they hardly seemed like the sort of people who were likely to spearhead a revolution on the basis of their belief.

The Feast of Pentecost, seven weeks after Jesus's death, represented a critical moment in these believers' confidence. Jerusalem was thronging with pilgrims from all over the Diaspora who had come to bring their offerings to the temple and give thanks for God's goodness in Israel's past and his continuing generosity in the present. Pentecost, or the Feast of Weeks (Lev. 23:15–21; Deut. 16:9–12), was the ancient festival of the firstfruits of wheat harvest, and it was the third most important of the great pilgrimage festivals of the Jewish year (after the Feast of Unleavened Bread or Passover, held in the spring, and the Feast of Tabernacles, celebrated in the autumn). It took place fifty days after Passover, hence the name "Pentecost," from the Greek for "fiftieth day."

Though smaller than the other two main festivals, Pentecost was typically attended by many thousands of Diaspora as well as Palestinian Jews, who came to remember that God had graciously given Israel the covenant and the exodus, and to affirm that he was to be acknowledged as owner of the land and giver of its bounty. According to Acts (2:1–13), a number of these pilgrims witnessed an amazing outpouring of spiritual power as the disciples of Jesus suddenly burst out in praise to God in languages other than their own. These visitors from many different backgrounds were able to hear those who were Galileans speaking in tongues they could understand. Bewildered, the crowd inquired what was going on; some thought the strange speech suggested that the speakers were drunk. According to Acts 2:4, the reason was plain: the disciples were "filled with the Holy Spirit," and their behavior was taking place under the control of divine power.

One of these disciples, the impetuous Peter—the fisherman and special friend of Jesus who had made the loudest protestations of loyalty to him and then gone on to deny that he knew him at all—is presented as declaring in unambiguous terms that Jesus has been raised from the dead: "God has made this Jesus, whom you crucified, both Lord and

Christ" (Acts 2:36). Everything that had happened to Jesus, including the terrible events of his crucifixion, had taken place in accordance with God's purpose; now he was alive, freed from "the agony of death" (Acts 2:24) and vindicated by God. The raising of Jesus, Peter declares, signifies the fulfillment of scriptural promises made in the Psalms and the Prophets. The last days spoken of by the prophet Joel (Joel 2:28–32) have dawned; "exalted to the right hand of God, he [Jesus] has received from the Father the promised Holy Spirit and has poured out what you now see and hear" (Acts 2:33; see Ps. 110:1). Peter's news was that the true Messiah, one of David's line yet greater than David, had come and the final times were now; repentance and the forsaking of sin had become urgent. This message of a crucified and risen Messiah seemed extremely offensive to Jewish ears, but a considerable number of converts were made (Acts 2:41 says "about three thousand"), and the community of believers in Jesus began to grow.

The account given by Luke was written at least a generation after the events it describes, and it paints a picture that reflects an apologetic concern to show the progress of the story of Jesus as purposed and enabled at every stage by the agency of God's Holy Spirit. Looking back on the experience of early Christian growth, Luke sees the success of the faith as something that only the Spirit of God could have brought about, and his characterization of the disciples as powerfully inspired by the Spirit from the start is part of that conviction. Luke's version of the early days of the Jerusalem community is influenced by particular theological emphases that reveal his own perspective and the situation of the readers for whom he writes. Nevertheless, for all the theological coloring, the Acts of the Apostles presents a picture that cannot be dismissed as implausible in historical terms, and its narrative offers us an important window on the earliest period of the faith.

The believers in Jesus were, to all intents and purposes, just another subgroup within Judaism. Those who believed that their Lord was risen continued to live as loyal Jews, worshiping at the temple and endeavoring to observe the Law. Jesus had predicted that the temple would be destroyed, but for the moment it still stood, and although his followers may well have regarded it as a doomed institution, as faithful Jews they could hardly have countenanced doing anything other than continuing with it while it lasted. Though it is clear that they also saw themselves as collectively constituting a new, eschatological temple, for them, unlike for the Qumran community, this was not because they had withdrawn from the Jerusalem temple but because they were convinced that through the risen Christ God's eschatological presence, or the presence of God in latter-day power, was now to be found among his believing people.

In most respects, the party of the Nazarenes behaved in ways that were not terribly threatening to their fellow Jews. Luke presents the believers as a pious and supportive network, meeting together regularly in the temple courts and in one another's homes, devoting themselves to fellowship and prayer, and sharing their possessions freely (Acts 2:42–47; 4:32–35). As far as at least some of the Pharisees were concerned, the Nazarenes could not be accused of seriously flouting convention or disregarding the Law, and although they adduced bizarre arguments that one who had been crucified was raised from the dead and was God's Anointed, they were certainly better than the Sadducees, who denied that there was any resurrection at all.

Other Pharisees certainly came to see things differently, and some would soon be arguing that the Nazarenes represented a dangerous challenge to the integrity of Judaism, but in the earliest stages, the followers of Jesus seemed to many to be harmless enough. They found no shortage of individuals to talk to in the temple courts, in their neighborhoods, and as they went about their daily business. They steadily attracted converts and interested inquirers, especially from among the ordinary people, who saw themselves as belonging to no particular party of Judaism but found something compelling about the story that Jesus was alive.

The Sadducees, who had colluded with the Roman authorities in the condemnation of Jesus, naturally looked with disfavor on his followers as dangerous enthusiasts and regarded their belief as based upon a false notion about resurrection. Attempts were made by the high priest and his associates to intimidate Jesus's followers into desisting from witnessing to their faith. But there were, in reality, no good grounds for legal suppression, however obnoxious the popular impact of the claims about Jesus. The Sadducee authorities could issue warnings to the apostles, but they had few options for successfully squashing their activities, least of all since there were other members of the priestly caste who were themselves drawn to the Nazarenes' teachings (Acts 6:7).

Hebrews and Hellenists

The first real challenges to the stability of the community actually came not from external enemies but from within, as the believers gathered converts not only among native-born Palestinians but also from people of other backgrounds. Tensions emerged between those whom Luke names the "Hebrews" and those he calls the "Hellenists" (see Acts 6:1–6). These two groups were probably made up primarily of Aramaic-speaking Jews from Palestine and Greek-speaking Jews of the Diaspora who had returned to Jerusalem, but the latter also included some Gentile converts to Judaism. The first group may well have known some Greek as well, but the latter probably knew no language other than Greek.

The distinction suggests that there were already distinct groups of believers, some worshiping in Aramaic and others in Greek. This in itself must have made the Greek-speakers conscious of their different-ness, but there is little reason to assume that they held a lesser view of the temple than their Aramaic-speaking counterparts or that the differ-ences represented a split between conservatives and liberals with regard to the Jewish Law. Neither constituency should be seen as monolithic. The details of the earliest dispute between them are not entirely certain, but it is clear that the Greek-speakers came to be critical of the way in which they were treated in the organization of the community. All were contributing to the common funds of the movement, but the Hellenists came to believe that the Hebrews were not affording a due share to the needy among the Greek-speakers, particularly their widows, who depended on alms for material support.

According to Acts 6:1–6, seven individuals, all of whom have Greek names, were appointed to oversee the distribution of food to the Hellenist widows. These seven—Stephen, Philip, Procorus, Nicanor, Timon, Parmenas, and Nicolas—were almost certainly Hellenistic Jews (one of them, Nicolas, was a proselyte from Antioch), and they formed a leadership for the Greek-speaking group. The most promi-nent among the seven (Acts 21:8) was Stephen, who is described as "a man full of faith and of the Holy Spirit" (Acts 6:5). Stephen came to be famous as more than a minister to the needy. He adopted a forceful style as a preacher of the new faith and went around propounding the message of Jesus with great energy and to significant effect. Soon he ran into problems with Jews from Greek-speaking synagogues in the city, and they provoked the authorities into investigating his teaching. Stephen was summoned before the Sanhedrin, where he was accused of blasphemy and, in particular, of expressing negative views concerning the Law and the temple (Acts 6:11–14).

In Luke's presentation of Stephen's speech of defense before the Sanhedrin (Acts 7:2–53), Stephen argues that from the time of Abraham onward God had repeatedly demonstrated that his presence was not to be confined to one specific physical place, and that from the time of

Moses onward the Israelites had persistently rebelled against God and rejected his messengers. The crucifixion of Jesus was but the climax to a long history of stubborn refusal to listen to God's word, spoken through his chosen servants. In harmony with Jesus's own emphasis, Stephen taught that the temple was a spiritual as opposed to a fixed physical entity, and he associated the lineage of Israel's salvation less with the temple than with Moses and the tabernacle (a movable tent as opposed to a settled house) as the symbols of divine presence for Israel. Stephen's blistering attack on his judges was hardly likely to win them over, and he was ritually stoned to death for his outrageous ideas. He was the first martyr for Jesus.

Dispersal from Jerusalem

The death of Stephen was the first stage in a more widespread persecution, which led to a dispersal of believers from Jerusalem. Probably the brunt of the troubles was borne by the Hellenists. In Acts 8:1, Luke says that "the apostles" (by which he usually means the Twelve) remained in Jerusalem. Wherever the believers went, however, they took their faith with them, and the story that Jesus was risen began to spread rapidly throughout Judea and into Samaria, beyond Palestine to the north, into Syria and Phoenicia, and as far as the island of Cyprus.

The mission in Samaria was spearheaded by Philip, another of the Hellenists, who subsequently took his gospel south toward Gaza before returning to Caesarea, the capital of Roman Judea, where he appears to have settled. As far as most Jews were concerned, the Samaritans were little better than Gentiles; the message of Jesus was thus being taken to a wider constituency than that of mainstream Judaism.

In Samaria, Philip was followed by two of the Twelve, Peter and John, who consolidated the work that Philip had done before they returned to Jerusalem. Philip, who became known as "Philip the evangelist" (Acts 21:8) to distinguish him from "Philip the apostle," one of the Twelve, is also pictured in Acts as instrumental in the conversion of an Ethiopian, the treasurer to Candace, the queen (mother) of the kingdom of Nubia, as he was returning home from a pilgrimage to Jerusalem (Acts 8:26–39). If this official shared his faith with others when he reached his home, the message would have spread far outside its original territory.

Throughout this period, Peter and John remained the most prominent leaders among the believers in Jerusalem. Originally known as Simon, Peter came from Bethsaida, a village on the northern shores of the Sea of Galilee, and he was following his father's trade as a fisherman when he was introduced to Jesus by his brother Andrew. He had been among the most trusted of Jesus's confidants and witness of some of his most compelling signs and wonders. He had passionately professed his belief in Jesus as "the Christ" (Mark 8:29) and boasted that his loyalty would be unshakable—yet he had denied his leader three times on the night of his arrest by the authorities.

Peter was nevertheless among the first to have an encounter with the risen Jesus, and he became the leading mouthpiece of the first community of Nazarenes in Jerusalem. In the early chapters of Acts, he is consistently depicted as the primary speaker, authority figure, and wonder-worker among the apostles. Next to Peter was John, son of Zebedee, and his brother James; together these three had formed an inner circle of Jesus's closest friends. John in particular is mentioned as Peter's chief associate in spreading the faith in Jerusalem and answering for it to the Jewish authorities (Acts 3–4).

Until the persecution that broke out with the martyrdom of Stephen, the faith of the Nazarenes had remained, for all the social and cultural diversity of its practitioners, an essentially Jewish affair. With the expansion into Samaria and northward into Syria and Phoenicia, it had begun to reach a potentially much wider constituency, comprising those who were either obviously Gentile or, in the case of the Samaritans, considered to be Gentile in all but name. The fundamental motivation, however, for a mission to the Gentiles came, ironically enough, from one who was by background an extremely conservative Jew—a man who would forever think of himself as a Jew—whose initial desire was to stamp out the sect of the Nazarenes altogether and whose activities, if they had succeeded, would have meant that there would have been no story of Christianity to tell. His name was Saul, though he is better known to us by his Roman family name of Paul.

Paul of Tarsus

Paul was a native of Tarsus, an important city near the southeastern corner of Asia Minor, the capital of the Roman province of Cilicia. The date of his birth is not known, but he was perhaps born around the same time as Jesus or in the very early years of the first century A.D. His parents were conservative Jews, but his father also possessed Roman citizenship, and Paul was born with the same privilege. His background was in the Greek culture of the Diaspora, but he was a "Hebrew of the

Image of the apostle Paul.
Illustration from G. Mitrevski.
Used by permission.

Hebrews" (Phil. 3:5; cf. 2 Cor. 11:22), which suggests that Aramaic as much as Greek may have been the language of his home. At some stage in his boyhood his family moved to Jerusalem, and there Paul received his education, under the tutelage of Gamaliel, one of the leading Pharisee teachers of his day.

By the second century, Pharisaism would develop two great schools of thought, which would come to be associated with the respective influences of two prominent teachers from around the time of Jesus, Hillel and Shammai. The followers of Hillel would be regarded as the lenient ones, whereas the Shammaites were strict. In the first century, such distinctions were by no means hard and fast, and we do not have solid grounds upon which to slot Paul into either of these later categories of opinion, despite various traditions and speculative attempts to identify him with one or the other. What we do know is that there were some fairly evident differences among Pharisees at this time with regard to Israel's political situation. More moderate Pharisees tended to argue for a policy of acceptance of the fact that Israel was subject to a Gentile yoke as long as the Jews were free to study and practice the Law without serious impediment. Others contended that this was not enough; fidelity to the Law meant being prepared to protest against the injustices and the indignities to which Israel was being subjected and, if necessary, to take up arms in that cause. For the latter group, mere acquiescence in the status quo was tantamount to a betrayal of the Law's demands that Israel must display her loyalty to her God.

Gamaliel was clearly a moderate. In Acts 5:33–39, he is described as cautioning discretion on the part of the Sanhedrin in handling the leaders of the Jesus movement. If their motives are merely of human origin, he claims, they will fail in any case; but if their work is intended by God, it would be dangerous and futile to oppose it: "You will only find yourselves fighting against God" (Acts 5:39). Gamaliel was a diplomat, who would not have approved of the stoning of Stephen. Paul had sat at Gamaliel's feet as a student and acquired under his guidance an intimate knowledge of the Jewish Scriptures in both Greek and Hebrew, but his inclinations were evidently a good deal more radical.

Whatever Paul learned from Gamaliel, one thing he did not learn was to take a tolerant line with those whose interpretation of their religion differed from his own. As far as Paul was concerned, the kingdom of God was coming soon, the prophecies of God's deliverance of Israel would shortly be fulfilled, and the task of God's faithful ones was to hasten the time of their realization. He had a burning zeal to see God honored and his people vindicated, and his conviction was that this would be brought about by a wholehearted commitment to the Law and a determination to deal summarily with those who were leading Israel astray from devotion to her Lord.

In Paul's eyes, the Nazarenes were prime targets for denunciation—and more than that, for forceful suppression. Their message of a crucified and resurrected Messiah was not only foolish, it was blasphemous. Although they appeared to care about the Law and the temple, the logic of their claims served, as he saw it, only to downgrade the importance of both. The followers of Jesus professed to obey the Law and revere the temple, but they did not show a sufficiently scrupulous concern for the Law, and they implied that the true temple was now, in effect, the people of God themselves. What was more, their ideas were spreading, not just in Jerusalem and Judea but much farther afield; many others were being encouraged to adopt similar attitudes. The Nazarenes needed to be stopped at all costs.

Paul was present at the stoning of Stephen and assented to Stephen's fate (Acts 7:58; 8:1), and it was he who took the primary role in the more general persecution that ensued upon Stephen's death. Paul was determined that the Nazarene community, and especially, it seems, its Hellenist members, must be crushed. Going from house to house and synagogue to synagogue, he personally organized the arrest of both men and women and ensured that significant numbers of believers in Jerusalem were condemned, flogged, and thrown into prison for their beliefs.

But Paul was not content with that. As the followers of Jesus fled beyond Jerusalem, Paul resolved to hunt them down wherever they were.

He obtained written authority to go north into Syria, to the synagogues in the capital, Damascus, and if he found believers in Jesus, he was to arrest them and bring them to Jerusalem for trial before the Sanhedrin. With the weight of the high priest's approval behind him, he had very strong grounds on which to act. The synagogue leaders were bound to respect his authority; the Romans too were committed to upholding the judgment of the high priest on matters of religious behavior, especially if there was any potential for unrest. If the new movement could be claimed to be hostile to the temple, it was also potentially a threat to the peace of the community.

Paul must have set off with not only an unshakable confidence that he was doing the right thing but a firm expectation that his mission to exterminate the Nazarenes was succeeding. On the way to Damascus, however, he had an experience that not only revolutionized his own life but had consequences that changed the course of human history. Somewhere close to his destination, he had an encounter with the risen and ascended Jesus. In the accounts in Acts of what happened (9:3–19; 22:6–16; 26:12–18), we are told that he saw a blinding light, and falling to the ground, he heard a voice saying to him in Aramaic, "Saul, Saul, why do you persecute me?"

The terms in which Paul himself described the experience in 1 Corinthians 15:3–7 do not imply that he simply had a mystical vision or some kind of hallucination. Paul never thought that he "saw" Jesus (1 Cor. 9:1) in quite the same way again, though he was ever afterwards intensely conscious of the presence of Jesus in his life. Those who were with him on the road to Damascus are said to have heard sounds and witnessed the blazing light, but they saw no one. Only Paul saw Jesus. He was convinced that he had encountered the reality of Jesus in a unique manner, as the one who had been crucified but was now physically raised to life and ascended into heaven.

Paul's experience was not just a moment of psychological breakthrough in which he at last found peace after struggling with a bad conscience. Nor was it a sudden realization that the Jewish Law somehow did not matter anymore and that it was possible for there now to be a people of God for whom the Law was of no significance. What Paul became convinced of was that Jesus was alive and that God had done for Jesus what Paul expected he would do for Israel. Paul had thought that God would vindicate Israel and bring about her deliverance; now he believed that God had vindicated Jesus and in him had acted definitively to transform the condition of Israel. Instead of Jesus being, as Paul had imagined, a failed Messiah who had deluded a group of Jews who were lax in their observance of the Law and lukewarm in their attitude to the temple, the resurrection showed that he was indeed whom his disciples said he was: the true Messiah, the one through whose actions the last times had already been ushered in.

The death and resurrection of Jesus, only a few short years ago, were, it seemed, the means by which God had acted in the midst of time to do that which Paul had expected would happen only at the end of time. The great reversal of present injustices and the arrival of the kingdom of God, in which peace and justice would reign, were not in the future; they were immediately present. The revelation of God's salvation was not some event in the future; it had already happened. The most startling consequence of this was that if the age to come had already begun, the message that the God of Israel was Lord of all was not just the property of Jews but urgently relevant for people everywhere. The gospel of Jesus was not only for Jews; it was for Gentiles too.

Not all of this became immediately clear to Paul on the Damascus road, but the process of conviction evidently did not take long. We are told that he was led into Damascus blind as a result of his encounter, that he remained blind for three days, and that during this time he did not eat or drink. A believer named Ananias was sent to him, and under his guidance Paul was restored to sight and baptized as a follower of Jesus (Acts 9:8–19; 22:10–16). Within a short time, the same Paul who had gone to Damascus to persecute and arrest the Nazarenes was found in the very synagogues to which he had intended to go, preaching that Jesus was indeed the Messiah. Paul the oppressor had become an apostle.

Jews and Gentiles

What did it actually mean, however, to say that the story of Jesus was of relevance to Gentiles as well as Jews? The narrative of Acts indicates that some potent tensions were emerging among the Nazarenes in Jerusalem over the practical implications of this question. We read in Acts 9:32–10:48 that Peter's itinerant ministry took him to western Palestine, to the Plain of Sharon and the towns of Lydda and Joppa near Caesarea. These were regions with significant Gentile populations, and there were already believers there prior to Peter's visit. At Caesarea, Peter baptized and stayed with Cornelius, a Roman centurion who is described as a pious God-fearer (see Acts 10:2, 22). This was an important encounter, for in Peter's eyes Cornelius, as a Gentile, albeit one with a

Sarcophagus of the Two Testaments from St. Paul's Basilica in Rome, showing scenes from the life of the apostle Peter. Illustration from FreeStockPhotos.com. Used by permission.

warm disposition toward the Jewish faith, was naturally to be regarded as unclean and not someone with whom to eat (though not all Jews were so strict). Though Peter's energies were still firmly concentrated on evangelizing his fellow Jews, he had been induced to take his message to a Gentile household and to share fellowship with those whom he would previously have regarded as beyond the pale.

On his return to Jerusalem, Peter was obliged to give account of his actions in eating with the uncircumcised (see Acts 11:2–3), a sign of how seriously the Jerusalem believers continued to take their commitment to the Law. Luke reports that Peter explained how he had been shown in a vision not to call anything impure that God has made clean, and this explanation satisfied his hearers, convincing them that God had indeed blessed a mission to the Gentiles (Acts 11:4–18). Luke's aim is not only to demonstrate that the expansion of the faith to Gentile hearers was divinely instigated but also to show that fellowship between Jewish and Gentile converts was authorized at an early date. In Luke's perspective, Peter's actions are controversial for the Jerusalem community not because he reaches out to Gentiles *per se* but because he dares to share a meal with them.

Some scholars have suggested that Luke invented the story of Peter and Cornelius in order to illustrate a concern in his own day that believers from Jewish and Gentile backgrounds should not be faulted for eating together. Certainly Luke may have had it in mind to answer those of his own time who were critical of such practices, and his placement of the Cornelius incident just prior to his description of the first major outreach to Gentiles may well be strategic rather than a straightforward reflection of the order of the events. Luke may be seeking to identify the Gentile mission with Peter's authority as well as with the actions of the Hellenists. But the fact that he goes out of his way to show that those who opposed close fellowship between Jewish and Gentile converts always were mistaken does not necessitate the conclusion that the Cornelius story is a fabrication. One thing is clear, and that is that although Peter evidently reassured the Jerusalem believers rather easily, there would still be very serious arguments about how to treat Gentile converts in the days to come. Peter himself would yet be accused of taking completely the opposite view regarding fellowship to that which he adopted in Acts 10.

Paul's Early Evangelistic Efforts

Paul, for his part, was in no doubt that Gentiles as well as Jews deserved to hear about the risen Jesus. After spending a short while in Damascus, he journeyed to Arabia. Scholars have long speculated as to why this was so, and it is impossible to be sure, but one of the most compelling suggestions is that he went there in order to seek out a place in which to begin the task of sharing the story of Jesus with non-Jews. If this was the case, his ideas soon got him into trouble. His actions in Arabia seem to have aroused the anger of King Aretas (IV) of Nabatea. There was a history of difficult relations between Jews and Nabateans, and Aretas would naturally have resented any Jew coming and proselytizing in his territory. After a while Paul returned to Damascus, but he was forced to flee from there, too, when Aretas's representative in the city was commissioned to apprehend him. Lowered from the city walls in a basket, he escaped (2 Cor. 11:32–33) and returned to Jerusalem. It was more than three years since he had first left on his mission to hunt down those who believed in Jesus (Gal. 1:17–18). Now he was one of them.

But was he really? Could he be trusted? In Jerusalem, Paul took steps to make contact with the followers of Jesus. It was not easy. There were plenty of memories of his vigorous persecution, and many believers were suspicious that if he was now making overtures to their community, it was only because he had decided on a change of tactics, to infiltrate their ranks and undermine them from within. Apparently thanks to Barnabas, a Levite (originally known as Joseph) from Cyprus whom he perhaps had known in earlier days, Paul was successfully introduced to some of the Nazarenes (Acts 9:27), but it is clear that suspicions persisted in many quarters. Among the leaders, he later tells us, he made contact only with Peter, with whom he stayed for fifteen days, and with James, the brother of Jesus (Gal. 1:18–19). His concern is to stress that he did not receive the specifics of his teaching or his commission to share the story of Jesus with others from the leaders of the community in Jerusalem. In his mind, the gospel he came to preach came directly by revelation from Jesus himself (Gal. 1:12).

It is unclear how long Paul stayed in Jerusalem, but after a time he went off to Syria, to his native city of Tarsus, and to the surrounding regions of Cilicia. He presumably set about spreading his message as he had in Arabia, but again the details of his activities are unknown. For as much as a decade, in fact, we remain in the dark about his movements, except to say that he seems to have spent most of this period in his home territory. We do not know what results were produced over the bulk of these years, but it appears that Paul's efforts in his native area met with significant opposition and suffering, including beatings and imprisonments (2 Cor. 11:23–29).

At some stage, Paul had a visionary experience, which he later described as being "caught up to the third heaven" (a Jewish expression for the immediate presence of God). As a result of it, he was left with a lasting affliction, a "thorn in [the] flesh," which was not taken from him despite his earnest prayers for its removal (2 Cor. 12:1–10). Much speculation has surrounded the question of what this affliction could have been. Suggestions have ranged from malaria to ophthalmia, from epilepsy to a speech defect. The reality is that Paul himself leaves the matter unspecified, and his point in narrating his experience is to underscore the assurance he received that God's grace was sufficient for him in his weakness, to the extent that he could claim to boast about his troubles for Christ's sake.

Further Troubles in Jerusalem

In Jerusalem, meanwhile, the early 40s had brought further problems for the Nazarenes. As a client-king under the Romans, Herod Agrippa I, the grandson of Herod the Great, had managed to acquire the territories of Judea and Samaria in addition to the regions over which he had initially been appointed. He now allied himself with the Sadducean high priesthood in Jerusalem and launched an assault on the leaders of the

Modern-day Jerusalem. Illustration from FreeStockPhotos.com. Used by permission.

Jesus movement. Peter was imprisoned, and James (son of Zebedee and brother of John) was executed, the first of the Twelve to suffer martyrdom. Peter managed to escape death, but he was obliged to flee Jerusalem, and from around this period he seems not to have been based in the city. Peter and John (and other apostles) continue to be mentioned in passages that refer to events that took place in Jerusalem up to about 50, but from the mid- to late 40s onward, most of the Twelve appear to have engaged increasingly in itinerant ministries rather than living and working only in Jerusalem and its environs.

Already at the time of Peter's imprisonment, James the brother of Jesus was emerging as the new leading figure in the Jerusalem community, and by the later 40s, he was clearly its main authority (he is mentioned before Peter and John in Galatians 2:9). It is conceivable that he stepped into a power vacuum generated by the dispersal of the other apostles under Agrippa's persecution, but it is clear that he had already been of prominence in Jerusalem as early as the late 30s, when Paul visited the city for the first time after his conversion. James proved a zealous and dedicated leader in a significant phase of the community's development, and during the time of his greatest influence, a period of relative calm seems to have ensued in Jerusalem for a number of years. Herod Agrippa I had died suddenly in 44, and James may have managed to be on rea- sonable terms with some of the Pharisees, which would have assisted with the public image of the followers of Jesus. James was himself a thoroughly Jewish figure, whose commitment to the message that his brother was the Messiah did not detract from his personal devotion to the Jewish Law and his careful observance of Jewish ritual.

Antioch: The First "Christians"

The gospel of Jesus spread not only through the work of leaders such as James in Jerusalem or prominent itinerant preachers such as the Twelve but also through the witness of other dispersed believers. As various waves of Nazarenes left Jerusalem, they carried the news with them far and wide, and many of their converts in turn became channels of the message to other constituencies, both Jewish and Gentile. It was through the testimony of unknown pioneers that the new faith came to be planted in a large number of the places where it would flourish most. One such place was Antioch in Syria.

Syrian Antioch was one of the great cities of the East. Founded on the Orontes River around 300 B.C. by Seleucus I, one of the generals of Alexander the Great, who named it after his father, Antiochus, it had been the seat of the Seleucid dynasty. After the Romans annexed Syria in 63 B.C., Antioch became their provincial capital. Though smaller in population than Ephesus, as far as the Romans were concerned, it was the

Some remains of ancient Antioch. Illustration from J. Oswalt. Used by permission.

third city of the empire, after Rome and Alexandria. It was a significant center of Diaspora Judaism, a meeting point for the sophisticated Greek culture of the coastal region with the customs of the nomadic tribes of the interior, and the interface for all major political, commercial, and military communication between Rome and the Persian frontier.

In the persecution that had followed the death of Stephen, converts from Cyprus and Cyrene had taken the gospel to Antioch and had begun to share it with Greeks (Acts 11:20). This had been a very bold move, but these evangelists had evidently been convinced that the story of Jesus was relevant not only for Jews but also for Gentiles. The results of their efforts had been very positive, and numbers of converts had been made. The first serious impact of which we know upon a Gentile audience had been mediated, not through some figure whose name would come to feature prominently in the churches' story, but by means of anonymous individuals.

When news of the developments at Antioch reached Jerusalem, there was evidently some concern. What were the implications of this significant extension of the boundaries of the covenant community to non-Jews? A few converts, perhaps, were one thing, but in this instance the numbers were much larger. For loyal, Torah-observing Jewish believers, the status of these new devotees of Jesus was a worrying puzzle. How should they be treated? What requirements should be placed upon them? In what ways should Jewish believers relate to them?

Barnabas, the disciple who had helped Paul in his difficult effort to introduce himself to the community in Jerusalem, was dispatched to Antioch to look into things. He was soon persuaded that what was taking place could only be occurring with God's blessing, and he gave his personal approval to the work and sought to encourage the new believers. At this point, he seems to have felt the need for a fellow worker, one who would share in his enthusiasm for the growth of the cause among the Gentiles. What about asking Paul? Many people still regarded him with suspicion, but he had by now demonstrated the seriousness of his commitment to Jesus and made clear his desire to reach out to non-Jewish constituencies. Whatever doubts lingered in others' minds, to Barnabas at least he was an obvious choice. Barnabas sought Paul out at Tarsus and invited him to accompany him to Antioch, and he agreed to go.

Paul and Barnabas remained in Antioch for a year or so. The Jesus movement prospered in the city, and a number of leaders emerged as "prophets and teachers" alongside Paul and Barnabas (Acts 13:1). Here, for the first time, believers in Jesus began to develop an identity distinct from that of Jews. To pagan onlookers, they were *Christianoi*, "people of Christ" (Acts 11:26). To a pagan, the term *Christ* was more of a name than a title; only a Jew or a proselyte would have associated it with the expectation of a particular figure, the Anointed One. So when pagans heard people describing Jesus as "the Christ," they came to think of them as "Christ's people." This is the first known use of the word *Christian* as a description of Jesus's followers, but it was not a name used by believers of themselves; it was a label applied by others. In fact, the name Christian never did become commonly used in the earliest churches (the New Testament records only two other instances of it, in Acts 26:28 and in 1 Peter 4:16), and it did not become a self-designation for Jesus's followers until late in the first century.

In response to a prophecy that famine would shortly afflict the region (something that we know did happen at least once in the late 40s), the Christians of Antioch collected a gift of money for their brothers and sisters in Judea, and Paul and Barnabas returned with it to Jerusalem. It is not easy to reconcile the sequence of events described in Acts, in which two visits to Jerusalem take place (Acts 11:29–30 and 15:1–4), and the description given in Galatians 2:1–10, which seems to imply a single visit. A variety of suggestions have been made by scholars, but perhaps the best suggestion is that Paul and Barnabas made one visit to Jerusalem around the year 48 and a subsequent one in the following year or in 50. On the first trip, Paul and Barnabas appear to have had a private meeting with the leaders of the Jerusalem community concerning the question of mission to the Gentiles. With them was Titus, a Gentile convert. An agreement was reached that Paul and Barnabas should continue to reach out to the Gentiles, but the Jerusalem leaders (or "pillars," Gal. 2:9), James, and after him Peter and John, should continue to concentrate their attentions on evangelizing Jews.

With regard to imposing the requirements of the Law on Gentiles, it was accepted that Titus did not need to be circumcised. Whether other issues were discussed we are not told. The only stipulation from the Jerusalem side was that Paul and Barnabas should continue to "remember the poor" (Gal. 2:10), which probably means that they were to take seriously the need to keep on sending money to the poor believers in Judea. The agreement was harmonious; some of the doubts that had existed about Paul's motives had, it seems, been slightly dispelled, at least among the leaders, and the respective parties finished their discussions in a spirit of fellowship. Paul and Barnabas returned to Antioch, taking with them from Jerusalem Barnabas's young cousin named John, also known by his Roman name of Mark.

Mission to the Gentiles

From Antioch, Paul and Barnabas were sent out together on further travels, and John Mark initially went along with them. Up until this point in Luke's account in Acts, Paul is called by his Jewish name, Saul, but from around this juncture onward he is consistently given his Roman name (Acts 13:9), perhaps signaling that his ministry henceforth was unambiguously aimed at Gentiles as well as Jews.

The expedition on which the friends set out has come to be thought of as Paul's first missionary journey, the first in a series of three great journeys described in the second half of Acts. Though Luke organizes his accounts of Paul's travels in this schematic fashion, Paul and his companions can hardly have been conscious that their adventures might ever fall into any neat pattern.[1] As far as they were concerned, they went out in accordance with a sense of calling to spread their gospel as opportunity permitted. In general, they remained in each place for as long as it took to ensure that a Christian community was firmly established, or until they were driven out by difficult circumstances. It is quite wrong to think of Paul and his associates rushing breathlessly from one place to another, leaving only half-taught converts in each location; their strategy was to seek to embed the gospel as thoroughly as possible before they moved on.

Nor should we imagine, of course, that the work of Paul and his fellow workers was in any sense the only, or even the main, missionary endeavor taking place. Luke's concentration on Paul is only one part of the story of growth; vital work was also going on in the labors of other preachers and teachers—not just the obvious figures such as Peter or John, but an incalculable number of unknown witnesses as well. Whether the focus was on Jews or Gentiles, there were any number of committed disciples sharing their faith with others, and the influence of the Jesus movement had already spread dramatically before Paul's travels began. In some of the places to which Paul and his companions would go, the message had gotten there before them, and, as was the case at Antioch, in many of the great cities and towns of the Mediterranean world the seed was first sown by believers whose names we do not know.

Leaving Antioch, Paul and his friends traveled first to Cyprus, Barnabas's native island. Cyprus was a place where there were some believers already; as we saw, the cause there had been advanced through the arrival of refugees from Jerusalem some years earlier, and natives of Cyprus had been among the pioneers of the gospel in Antioch itself. But there was obviously still no shortage of scope for expansion on the island. Adopting a pattern that would be characteristic of Paul's missionary endeavors almost everywhere, Paul and Barnabas made the main centers of population the base for their activities, presumably calculating that if the faith could be planted in the towns and cities, it would in turn spread into the surrounding countryside.[2] In Luke's presentation, they also concentrated on the Jewish synagogues, which strongly suggests that the Gentiles at whom they were primarily aiming their message were the God-fearers, those who were loosely attached to the Jewish faith but were not full proselytes.

From Cyprus they sailed to Pamphylia, and at this point John Mark left the party and returned to Jerusalem. We are not told why, but Paul at any rate seems to have felt that he deserted the work. When Barnabas later suggested that John Mark should accompany them on a return visit to the towns where they had evangelized, Paul dissented and went his separate way from Barnabas and his cousin (though reconciliation with Mark did come later on, 2 Timothy 4:11). From Perga in Pamphylia, the two missionaries moved to the southern part of the Roman province of Galatia, where they preached in Pisidian Antioch (so-called to distinguish it from the much more important Antioch in Syria, and because it lay close to the border with the region of Pisidia), Iconium, Lystra, and Derbe before retracing their steps back through these centers and down to the coast at Attalia. From there they sailed back to Seleucia, at the mouth of the Orontes, and finally arrived back at Syrian Antioch. It had been an ambitious circular tour of about a year's duration.

Paul and Barnabas experienced mixed success in spreading their message. In Cyprus, we hear no details of the results, except for the conversion of the proconsul in Paphos, Sergius Paulus (Acts 13:6–12);[3] it is impossible to tell how effective the mission was elsewhere on the island. Paul and Barnabas did not return there on their way back to Antioch, as they did to the other areas through which they passed. In the other regions, converts were won (the numbers at Derbe in particular are said to have been impressive, Acts 14:21), but in Luke's description there is also a strong depiction of hostility from the Jews, who orchestrated trouble for the apostles in various places. In Iconium the missionaries are forced to flee on account of "a plot afoot among the Gentiles and Jews" (Acts 14:5), and in Lystra, Paul is reported to have been stoned and left for dead (Acts 14:19).

Luke shapes his narrative in a way that points up an increasing "turn to the Gentiles" (Acts 13:46), who are in various regards presented as more reasonable and more amenable to the gospel than Jewish audiences. Whatever the background of the new believers, though, there is overall a positive tone to Luke's account. He describes how on the return leg of their journey Paul and Barnabas are able to consolidate a work that has been accomplished with some success and arrange the appointment of leaders in each of the centers they visited.

The growth of Gentile Christianity meant that the problems that had surfaced already concerning the relationship between Jewish believers and Gentile converts were not to go away. Many Jewish followers of Jesus continued to be deeply concerned that Gentiles were being admitted far too easily to the ranks of the covenant community. The heartland of a Gentile Christianity that took a liberal approach to the requirements of the Jewish Law was Antioch, and it was with the scene in Antioch in particular that some of the believers in Jerusalem and Judea were most alarmed. Even if a measure of agreement had previously been reached privately between Paul and the leaders of the Jerusalem community that Paul should concentrate on Gentile evangelism while figures such as James, Peter, and John continued to focus their activities on Jewish circles, there were others who felt strongly that Gentiles who professed faith as a result of Paul's preaching in Antioch should not be able to share meals with Jewish believers.

The objection was probably to the practice of "mixed" dining in general, but there was a particular religious implication in this instance: if Jews and Gentiles were not to eat together, Gentile believers ought not to be participating in the fellowship meals of the Christians at which the ritual of remembering Jesus—the "breaking of bread" (Acts 2:42)—was observed. A number of visitors arrived in Antioch from Jerusalem, apparently sent by James, and they began to challenge the laxity of the local system. Peter himself was present in Antioch at this time, and according to Paul he had previously been willing to eat with Gentiles, but when the people from Jerusalem came, he desisted from the practice, as did a number of other Jewish believers; even Barnabas was inclined to follow suit (Gal. 2:11–13).

In Paul's eyes, Peter's concession to the objections of the Jerusalem visitors was very dangerous. If it was not considered right to eat with Gentile believers, and if these converts were to be barred from the table of fellowship and remembrance, surely it would be only a small step from that to saying that Gentiles who professed faith were not believers at all. The next thing, logically, would be an insistence that Gentiles would have to be circumcised in order to be regarded as Christians. To separate from Gentiles on the grounds of ceremonial uncleanness was nothing short of "hypocrisy" (Gal. 2:13). Paul therefore confronted Peter publicly, accusing him of serious error.

We do not know how Peter responded, but some time afterward Paul discovered that some of his converts in Asia Minor had been infiltrated by those whose arguments went well beyond the issuing of condemnations concerning "mixed" fellowship. In Galatia, some had been "bewitched" (Gal. 3:1) into accepting that it was necessary to be circumcised and to adopt the requirements of the Law in order to be a Christian. The assumption was not that Gentiles could not become followers of Jesus but that in order to be recognized as such they would have to become Jews and observe the Law.

Crisis in Galatia

In response to this crisis, Paul wrote his impassioned letter to the Galatians, perhaps the earliest of the Epistles to survive under his name.[4] He was furious at what had happened, believing that his credentials as a leader had been called into question and that his message was being perverted. By insisting on circumcision as a sign of Christian belonging, his opponents had compromised the heart of the message that participation in the covenant people of God is a matter of grace. Paul agrees wholeheartedly that the Law is a good thing, but he insists that observance of the Law is not the means by which individuals demonstrate that they are part of the community of God's chosen ones. People are children of God solely by faith, and they prove that they have this status not by becoming subject to the rituals and requirements of the Law but by living as those who have been liberated by Christ.

At the heart of Paul's message is the cross and resurrection of Jesus: to be "crucified with Christ" and to have the risen Christ living within (Gal. 2:20) is to have one's standing defined not by Law but by grace. There is no longer a privileged differentiation in spiritual status between those who are Jews, observing the Law, and those who are not. In fact, even distinctions based on class and gender are overcome for those who believe in Jesus: "There is neither Jew nor Greek, slave nor free, male nor female, for you are all one in Christ Jesus" (Gal. 3:28). The death and resurrection of Jesus have done away with the significance of such lines of division in religious terms. The covenant community has been opened up to all who have faith, Gentiles as well as Jews, regardless of their background or status. All who share in Christ are justified by faith, as Abraham was; once people are "in," circumcision or the lack of it is irrelevant.

If initiation is simply by faith, Paul argues, then to be a follower of Jesus is to be set free from outward observance of the Law as a marker of elect status or moral separateness. It is possible to share in intimate fellowship with other believers regardless of their background or ancestry. Nevertheless, Paul goes out of his way to stress that such a position does not entail indifference to moral questions or undermine the importance of ethical behavior. Living as followers of Jesus means, for Gentiles as well as for Jews, "living by" (Gal. 5:16, 25) or being "led by" the Spirit of Jesus (Gal. 5:18), and this involves obedience to principles of self-control, not self-indulgence, and loving and caring for one another, not serving only one's own interests. Those who advocated any other approach misunderstood the truth; their message was "a different gospel—which is really no gospel at all" (Gal. 1:6–7).

The Council of Jerusalem

Paul could write these things to his newborn "children" (Gal. 4:19) in Galatia, but more than this was clearly necessary in order to address the issues more broadly. Similar demands for circumcision were being made in Antioch, and although Paul and Barnabas argued fiercely with those who sponsored such ideas, they and their supporters felt that further action was required. Paul, Barnabas, and a number of others from Antioch set off for Jerusalem, determined to raise the whole subject of the appropriate treatment of Gentile converts with the leaders of the Jerusalem community, among whom there were voices (especially from Pharisee backgrounds, see Acts 15:5) calling strongly for the necessity of Gentile circumcision. The conference of apostles and leaders that took place, described by Luke in Acts 15:6–29, has traditionally been known as "the council of Jerusalem."

Paul and Barnabas told of the remarkable spread of the gospel among the Gentiles and represented the view of the majority at Antioch that Gentile converts should not be compelled to "Judaize" (Gal. 2:14) by being bound to observe Jewish customs—above all, circumcision, but also the requirements of Jewish food laws, such as the principle that it was wrong to eat food that had been sacrificed to idols or meat with blood in it. The issue of Gentiles eating with Jews is not expressly mentioned in Luke's account, but we may assume that it was among the questions discussed in connection with the observance of such laws. Peter, who had recently been rebuked by Paul for his capitulation to pressures for separation, supported Paul, reverting, it seems, to the position of which he had earlier been persuaded in the context of the conversion of Cornelius. God had wonderfully shown that the Gentiles were accepted, and it was not right, he argued, to place unreasonable burdens on them in order to make them prove that they were indeed the recipients of divine grace.

A settlement was proposed by James, who perhaps became persuaded in the course of the debate that he should distance himself from those who were arguing that the Gentiles must be circumcised. His earlier actions in sending emissaries to Antioch who criticized Peter and others for their "mixed" dining suggest that his own instincts were very much to emphasize the importance of the Law and the moral distinctiveness of the believing people, but he did not think that this entailed the circumcision of Gentiles. James concluded that since the conversion of Gentiles was in accordance with the prophecy of God through Amos (Amos 9:11–12), it should not be made difficult for such converts to be recognized as belonging to the believing community. They should not be required to be circumcised, but the Jerusalem church should write to them, telling them to observe the stipulations of the Law about abstaining from food offered to idols, from sexual immorality, from eating the meat of strangled animals, and from blood.

This "apostolic decree" was based upon the prescriptions of Leviticus 17–18 for aliens living among Jews. What James advocated was a measure of compromise. The Law of Moses was still of profound importance, but those who came from Gentile backgrounds were not to be compelled to shoulder all of its obligations; they should adhere to its most vital principles concerning purity, but they were not to be subjected to circumcision. James's proposal was approved by the gathering, and it was agreed that the judgment should be sent in written form to the churches of Antioch, Syria, and Cilicia. The letter was to be carried not only by Paul and Barnabas, but by two representatives of the Jerusalem community, Judas and Silas (also known as Silvanus, possibly indicating that he was, like Paul, a Roman citizen), as guarantors of its endorsement in Jerusalem.

The Jerusalem council does not deserve to be seen as an instance of the believers in the founding city of the movement dictating terms to the communities in Syria and Asia. The occasion affords scant authority to subsequent church traditions seeking to use it as grounds for a regular system of handing down legislative stipulations from a central assembly to regional congregations. Nor was it a meeting of only people who were leaders in some official sense; it was apparently attended not only by the "apostles and elders" (Acts 15:6) but also by "the whole church" (Acts 15:22; see also 15:12). It was in many respects a unique situation—a gathering convened in order to discuss a pressing, practical issue generated by specific circumstances. In the wake of the remarkable growth and vitality of the Gentile mission far to the north, what was the relationship to be between Jewish and Gentile Christianity?

The vital importance of the meeting consisted in the fact that it represented an agreement on the part of (apparently) most or all of the original leaders of the Jesus movement that the practice of the faith was not to be confined to those who demonstrated complete commitment to the moral patterns of a Jewish lifestyle lived in accordance with the Law. Those from Gentile backgrounds who professed faith in Jesus were to be granted a greater degree of belonging in the Christian movement than the God-fearers had been afforded in Judaism; they were to be able to participate in close fellowship and be treated as bona fide members of the covenant people without being circumcised.

From Paul's point of view, the problems with Judaizers certainly did not disappear overnight, and for some years to come, he would find himself challenging the influences of the kind of people whom in his letter to the Galatians he had labeled "false brothers" (Gal. 2:4). Paul would also adopt a strategy of deferring to harder-line Jewish sensibilities in some instances, if he thought this policy would assist his work (Acts 16:3). Nevertheless, the agreement concluded in Jerusalem signaled the reality that the threshold for Gentile participation in the privileges of fellowship was to be lower than some of the movement's members wanted, and this represented in principle a triumph for the position of which Paul—for all his own enduring Jewishness—had been the primary champion.

Christianity continued to look like a very Jewish phenomenon to any outsider, but the council of Jerusalem represented one stage in a lengthy process of reappraisal on the part of the movement's Jewish core with regard to the status of the Law. Viewed from a later perspective, it was an important milestone on the complex journey toward an official parting of the ways between Judaism and Christianity.

3

PAUL: MISSIONARY, TEACHER, MARTYR

▼

The severance of the Jesus movement from Judaism was still, however, many years away. That particular development would not take place until well after Paul and his generation had passed from the scene. In the immediate term, all of the major emissaries of the new faith, Paul included, had plenty of energy still to expend in the service of their gospel.

Plans for Further Travels

Paul and Barnabas remained in Antioch for a number of months or perhaps as much as a year but then determined to set out on further travels. Paul was concerned to revisit the places through which the pair had passed on their previous journey in order to assess the progress of the believers in the towns of Syria and Cilicia.

In a disagreement as to who should accompany them, however, Paul and Barnabas parted company. Barnabas wanted to take John Mark once again; Paul refused, arguing that Mark had previously deserted them in Pamphylia. In the end, Barnabas and Mark sailed for Cyprus, while Paul elected to take Silas, one of the carriers of the decision of the Jerusalem council (Acts 15:36–40). Silas was a good choice of companion for Paul, for as a representative of the Jerusalem church, he could explain the assembly's decree to the communities to which they traveled and make it clear that Paul was not at odds with the leaders in Jerusalem.

A Second Phase of Outreach

Together, Paul and Silas set off on what has come to be regarded in the light of Acts as Paul's second great missionary journey. Again we must remember that Paul's movements were only organized into such a format with the benefit of hindsight, and in accordance with Luke's concentration on Paul's mission as constituting the main thrust of the faith's expansion. Not only was there a great deal happening over these years in addition to Paul's work, but even within the particular horizon of his focus on Paul, Luke's account presents a selective and carefully shaped version of events. In reality, Paul engaged in pastoral consolidation and settled ministry as well as in shorter phases of preaching as he traveled, and it is a mistake to think of his style as just a rapid progression from place to place on a mission of basic proclamation, as if he quickly sowed the seed of his message and then moved on. Sometimes Paul did stay in a place for only a short while, but at other times he settled down for lengthy periods, and a good deal of his work involved not just primary evangelism but sustained instruction and encouragement over months and years among existing communities of believers.

Paul and Silas journeyed through Asia Minor, stopping in centers such as Derbe, Lystra, and Iconium and making sure that the Christians in these towns were informed of what had happened in Jerusalem. At Lystra they were joined by another helper, a young man named Timothy. Timothy was the product of a mixed marriage, with a Greek father and a Jewish mother, and he had not been circumcised as a boy. Luke tells us that Paul chose to circumcise him so that his presence would not antagonize the Jews in his local area who knew of his background (Acts 16:3). This action seems very odd in the light of Paul's stance up to this point, especially his recent powerful rhetoric about the irrelevance of circumcision in the Epistle to the Galatians, addressed to the believers in these very regions. It seems to reflect a determination on Paul's part, however, that there should be no unnecessary obstacles to the progress of his mission. Timothy was circumcised not to *prove* that he was a true believer but as a voluntary gesture, designed not to satisfy demands for

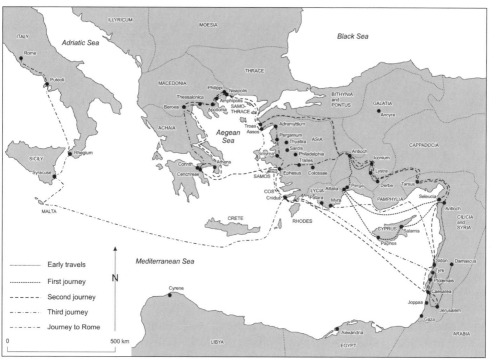

The travels of Paul

legal observance but to facilitate the reception of the faith. In any case, most Gentiles probably already regarded Timothy as a Jew, but only by receiving circumcision could he be considered as such by Jews.

The plan was probably that the mission would proceed from southern Galatia westward to the great city of Ephesus, the capital of the Roman province of Asia. However, Luke states that Paul and his companions were prevented by the Holy Spirit from venturing on this road at this point. One alternative was to head due northwards into Bithynia, but this was closed to them (Acts 16:6–7). Instead, the party turned in a northwesterly direction toward Troas, the Aegean port just to the south of the entrance to the Dardanelles. A few years later there would be a Christian community at Troas, which perhaps traced its origins to the arrival of Paul and his friends there on this occasion. In Troas, Luke tells us, Paul experienced a vision in which he felt himself called to strike out in a new direction—to cross over into Macedonia and thus to carry his message for the first time beyond the confines of the Eastern world and into Europe (Acts 16:9–10). Luke himself, a Gentile and a doctor, joined the group at this stage. Skilled physicians were in considerable demand in the first century, and like others of his kind, Luke may have made his living on an itinerant basis around the cities of the northern Aegean. He perhaps came to know Paul through ministering to him professionally.

From Troas, Paul, Silas, Timothy, and Luke sailed across to Neapolis, the seaport of the Macedonian city of Philippi, spending a night en route berthed on the rocky island of Samothrace. Philippi had been established in the 350s B.C. by Philip II of Macedon, the father of Alexander the Great, and it had become a Roman colony in 42 B.C. In 31 B.C., Philippi had officially become an Italian city, with the same rights and privileges as a place on Italian soil, and it had a strong Roman character.

There was evidently only a small Jewish community in Philippi, and there was no synagogue; instead, there was a place of prayer outside the city walls. There Paul and his companions met with a group of women, among them a merchant named Lydia, a native of the Asian city of Thyatira. Lydia believed and was baptized as a Christian along with the members of her household, and she invited the missionaries to stay with her. The time in Philippi was characterized by difficulties as well as some successes. Paul and Silas were beaten and imprisoned by the authorities as Jews stirring up trouble in the community, but while in custody they were instrumental in the conversion and baptism of their jailer and his household (Acts 16:12–40).

By the time Paul left Philippi, there was a nucleus of Christians. Luke appears to have stayed with them, while Paul, Silas, and Timothy moved on. After leaving Philippi, Paul and his friends moved in a southwesterly direction through Amphipolis and Apollonia to the city of Thessalonica, the largest city in the region and the seat of the Roman administration in Macedonia. There, as he often did, Paul made the local synagogue his base. His image of himself as a "minister of Christ Jesus to the Gentiles" (Rom. 15:16) did not stop him from using the synagogue as a natural starting point to reach Jews as well wherever possible. There his message might be articulated in a context in which people at least understood its informing ideas, even if many continued to disagree with the inferences he was drawing from them.

A number of converts were made among both Jews and God-fearers. There was also, however, some serious friction with other local Jews, and Paul and Silas were forced to flee to the town of Berea, a little farther south and off the main road from Macedonia to the Adriatic coast. The reception in Berea was warmer than in Thessalonica, but trouble again broke out, fomented by Paul's antagonists from Thessalonica (Acts 17:13).

Paul himself was smuggled away to the coast, leaving Silas and Timothy in the town for a period.

Paul was accompanied by a group of believers southward to Athens, in historical terms the principal cradle of European civilization. In this citadel of polytheism, surrounded by examples of the kind of pagan idolatry that were instinctively offensive to any Jew, he is pictured by Luke as reasoning with Jews, God-fearing Gentiles, and philosophers of Epicurean and Stoic persuasions (Acts 17:16–18). However, although there was some curiosity about his strange gospel of "Jesus and the resurrection," for many of the Athenians Paul was a "babbler" whose message sounded like a confused mishmash of other people's ideas (Acts 17:18).

There was perhaps concern in some quarters that Paul was introducing dangerous foreign notions into the city, and it is possible that he was called to account formally for his views before the court of the Areopagus, the conservative religious and moral council of the city. It was to this body that he is said to have delivered the famous address presented in Acts 17:22–31, which in Luke's version is a brief but sophisticated sermon on the reality of the one transcendent God to whom all people everywhere are accountable. There is no record that Paul was punished for preaching such ideas, and according to Acts 17:34, one of the members of the council, Dionysius, was persuaded by his arguments, as were a number of other people. Overall, however, the visible consequences of his efforts in Athens were few.

Since setting out from Antioch on this second wave of travels, Paul had experienced a number of setbacks and disappointments. Certainly some positive results had been achieved in Macedonia, but he had also encountered some serious opposition and had been forced to flee in a direction he had probably not intended to take, away from the northern region to which he had felt himself to be summoned and down into Greece. He was on his own; Silas and Timothy had rejoined him for a time in Athens, but he had thought it best to send Timothy back to Thessalonica, and Silas had perhaps been dispatched back to Philippi. Paul had been called to the Gentiles, yet the fruits of his labors in pagan Athens were sparse. There were few signs there, in one of the greatest historical centers of cultural sophistication, that the world was prepared for the gospel.

Not many, it seemed, were ready to abandon the patterns of their traditional religions or belief systems to accept Paul's outlandish claims that life and peace were to be found in following an obscure Jew who had been crucified some years ago in Jerusalem and was now supposed to be alive. A few had expressed some interest; more had laughed at what sounded like nonsense. In mid-first-century Athens, as in twenty-first-century urban societies, sophisticates did not listen for long to stories about people rising from the dead. Paul probably left Athens in a mood of some discouragement.

Corinth

From Athens, Paul traveled to Corinth. One of Greece's ancient cities, Corinth had been destroyed by the Romans in 146 B.C. and had lain in ruins for a century before being rebuilt as a Roman colony. In Paul's day, it was the capital of the Roman province of Achaia. Lying on the narrow isthmus between Central Greece and the Peloponnese, at the intersection of a number of crucial trade routes, Roman Corinth had soon recovered the commercial prosperity and cosmopolitanism of its predecessor. It had also become notorious for luxury and sexual indulgence, even in a world where urban sexual mores were very free everywhere. Ethnically, morally, and religiously, Corinth was a city in which pluralism reigned—a place with many possibilities but just as many challenges for the faith that Paul was seeking to spread.

Paul settled down in the city, and as in a number of other places, he found employment as a manual worker, reverting to his trade as a tentmaker (Acts 18:3; cf. 1 Cor. 4:12; 9:12; 1 Thess. 2:9). Tentmaking should have been a useful business to practice in Corinth because the city attracted many visitors, particularly for the great Isthmian Games held every two years, and there probably was a good market for tents to buy or rent. The work would have brought Paul alongside many people, both locals and visitors. Although tentmaking was a skilled trade and certainly not an activity of the lowest economic stratum, Paul, the educated teacher and thinker, was equally capable of inhabiting a social milieu well below what we might think of as comfortable. He showed no scruples about doing so if it would assist with his evangelizing. His letters reveal a man who willingly experienced varied material conditions, from abundance to poverty and security to hardship (2 Cor. 11:27; Phil. 4:11–13), in the interests of his gospel.

Paul worked alongside—or perhaps in the employment of—another Jewish tentmaker, a native of Pontus named Aquila, who with his wife Priscilla (or Prisca) had recently arrived from Rome. They were among a number of Jews whom the emperor Claudius had recently expelled from the capital, and it is probable that they were already converts to

Christianity. In our primary sources, Priscilla is usually mentioned before Aquila, which suggests that she had the more impressive personality of the two, and she may well have taken the leading role in their work of sharing and teaching the faith. The couple became loyal friends and fellow laborers of Paul, and they played an important role in the spreading of the faith in Corinth and elsewhere. Paul was also rejoined by Silas and Timothy from Macedonia. For a year and a half, he remained in Corinth, at first working at his trade and then, after the arrival of Silas and Timothy, supported by gifts from the Christians in Macedonia. He encountered some opposition from local Jews but also saw some notable successes, including the conversion of Crispus, the synagogue ruler, along with his entire household (Acts 18:8; cf. 1 Cor. 1:14).

With the help of Silas and Timothy, a significant community of believers was built up in Corinth, a community that embraced both Gentile converts and Jews. In time it came to include people of widely varying backgrounds, ranging from well-to-do officials such as a treasurer of the city (Rom. 16:23) to many who had been rescued from the margins of society—former thieves, prostitutes, and drunkards (1 Cor. 6:9–11). About halfway through his stay in Corinth, in the year 51, Paul was the victim of some concerted action from his Jewish opponents, who brought him into court on charges of propagating an illicit religion. The Roman proconsul, Lucius Junius Gallio (the brother of the famous philosopher Seneca), dismissed the accusation, deciding that he was faced with a simple matter of internal strife between different varieties of Jews—another instance of Christians looking no different from Jews to an educated pagan. Paul's frustrated accusers proceeded to vent their anger physically on the synagogue ruler, Sosthenes, but Gallio turned a blind eye (Acts 18:12–17).

Looking for Christ's Return

While living in Corinth, Paul corresponded with the believers he had left behind in Thessalonica. Timothy had brought encouraging reports of their faith and of their example to the other Christians in Macedonia and Achaia, but he had also informed Paul of some practical problems among them. Some of the Thessalonians, presumably Gentiles who had "turned to God from idols" (1 Thess. 1:9), were failing to observe the kind of standards of sexual morality that went with Christian profession. More commonly, many of them were so convinced that the final times were near that they were inclined to give up their daily work and simply wait for the present order to be wound up. There were also concerns that believers who had died in recent times would be deprived of some of the blessings that would follow at the *parousia*, or the imminent coming of the risen Lord in glory.

Paul's exhortation was that enthusiasm for the Lord's arrival must not distract from the business of responsible daily living. Paul himself clearly expected that Christ would return within his own lifetime, but he argues that since no one knows the day or the hour when this may happen, the Thessalonians have a duty to get on with whatever work they have to do and wait in patience and sobriety for God's chosen time. By doing this, their lives will be a witness to others concerning the truth of the gospel (1 Thess. 4:11–12; 5:1–11). At the *parousia*, those who had died as believers in Christ would rise first, and then, together with the Christians who were still alive, they would be united with the Lord (1 Thess. 4:13–18).

In another letter, 2 Thessalonians, it is said that the coming of Christ will not take place until certain terrible events have first occurred, namely "the rebellion" and the revelation of "the man of lawlessness" who is "doomed to destruction" (2 Thess. 2:3). There has been a good deal of debate about the authenticity of this letter, and some critics doubt that it is by Paul. If it is genuinely Pauline, as many scholars still contend, it may have been written prior to 1 Thessalonians, and 1 Thessalonians 4–5 is perhaps intended to deal with misunderstandings of its teaching. If 1 Thessalonians did come first, then 2 Thessalonians certainly followed very shortly after it. Either way, there was evidently some confusion in the Thessalonians' minds about the circumstances surrounding the second coming of their Lord. The language of 2 Thessalonians suggests that the *parousia* would be preceded by the outrage of a public desecration of God's holy temple, such as the sacrilege committed by Antiochus Epiphanes in 167 B.C.[1] Whatever this alludes to specifically, it seems clear that it refers to some act of dreadful blasphemy by a Roman emperor. In the end, a destruction of the Jerusalem temple by the Romans would not take place until the year 70, after Paul's death.

Ephesus

Paul left Corinth in about the spring of 52 and sailed with Priscilla and Aquila to Asia. He left his friends in Ephesus while he paid a brief visit to Judea to visit the believers in Jerusalem before returning to his base at Antioch. After a time, he set out again to the north. This journey has

A street in ancient Ephesus. Illustration from K. McGhee. Used by permission.

conventionally been described as Paul's third missionary journey, but in its first stages, he appears not to have engaged in primary evangelism as such but in a task of encouraging—or, in Luke's language, "strengthening" (Acts 18:23)—the existing disciples in Galatia and Phrygia.

In the latter part of 52, Paul finally arrived in Ephesus, one of the largest and most impressive cities of the Roman world. Situated near the mouth of the Caÿster River and at the end of a major Asian caravan route, Ephesus had been for centuries a great seaport as well as a commercial and cultural center.[2] Although predominantly Greek in flavor, it also contained large Jewish and Roman populations. Ephesus was especially famous for its magnificent temple to Artemis, or "Diana" as the Romans called her, the great Anatolian fertility goddess who had been worshiped for centuries in the area. The temple that existed in Paul's day was the fifth to stand on the site; four times as large as the Parthenon in Athens, it ranked as one of the seven wonders of the ancient world (only a single one of its columns survives today). Ephesus prided itself on being the temple warden of great Artemis, and it profited from a flourishing trade in religious tourism.

There was already a Christian presence in Ephesus when Paul arrived. Priscilla and Aquila were there, along with other believers. The community had been recently stimulated by the presence of an impressive Jewish convert named Apollos, a native of Alexandria, who was "a learned man, with a thorough knowledge of the Scriptures" (Acts 18:24). He may well have been a trained rhetorician and perhaps had studied philosophy. Apollos had become an enthusiastic follower of Jesus but had required some further clarification about the nature of the Christian path, particularly with regard to baptism. Priscilla and Aquila had helped him to understand the gospel more fully, and he had subsequently moved, with Paul's blessing, to Corinth, where he proved a powerful force in debating with his fellow Jews and attracted a strong following among the local Christians. There were also other disciples of Jesus in Ephesus who, like Apollos, were in need of further instruction and guidance. Between fulfilling this task and meeting the challenge of reaching out to a large pagan city, Paul had plenty of work to do.

As he had done in Corinth, Paul settled down for a protracted period, probably once again taking up his manual work in order to support himself. Luke pictures him meeting with opposition in the synagogue after a few months, and so he moved on to a base in a lecture hall of one Tyrannus, where he held daily discussions with the believers (Acts 19:8–10). In the two and a half years or so that Paul spent in Ephesus, the gospel made a powerful impact, both in the city itself and in the neighboring region. He spent most of his time in the city, attracting converts among both Jews and Gentiles and winning support among some notable as well as ordinary people. His helpers evidently spread the faith to other cities in Asia Minor, and it is likely that the Christian communities in Smyrna, Pergamum, Sardis, Philadelphia, Laodicea, Colossae, and Hierapolis were established during this period.

At the same time, there was also serious antagonism, danger, and possibly even imprisonment for Paul in Ephesus. In a city where the practice of magic was very strong, Paul's spiritual powers impressed, but they also led to resentment and imitation from other wonderworkers. Though many are said to have renounced sorcery under the influence of his gospel, others saw Paul's impact as a challenge to their own religious authority (Acts 19:11–20). In particular, Luke narrates how Paul became the victim of a public riot orchestrated by the artisans of Ephesus, who saw his religion as threatening their valuable trade in manufacturing miniature shrines of Artemis to sell to tourists. Paul escaped after the city clerk appealed for calm and invited Paul's opponents to press formal charges if appropriate rather than creating a breach of the peace (Acts 19:23–41).

Trouble in Corinth

In the aftermath of this disturbance, Paul was obliged to leave Ephesus. He traveled via Troas across to Macedonia and then went south into Achaia, arriving in Corinth, where he stayed for a number of weeks. His desire to visit Corinth was precipitated by a history of recent problems with the believers there as well as serious tensions in Paul's relationship with a number of them.

While still in Ephesus, Paul had received news that the Corinthian Christians had split into a number of factions. Some were professing loyalty to Paul, others to Apollos, while yet others boasted of attachment to Peter. There were rumors in some quarters that Paul's credentials as an apostle were suspect. In addition, there had been a sexual scandal among the believers in Corinth, and some Christians were taking others to court in business disputes. There were sharp debates about sexual ethics, about marriage, about whether or not it was right to eat food sacrificed to idols, about behavior at worship, and about the use of spiritual gifts. The factors underlying the problems were diverse. There were divisions between people from different social backgrounds, clashes of cultural attitudes between Jews and Gentiles, differing assessments of the importance of secular learning and rhetoric (areas in which Paul was held by some to be unimpressive compared with some of the skilled orators of the day), and simple personal jealousies.

In short, the community in Corinth was in a mess. Paul had written a letter to the believers that has not survived, which apparently instructed them to distance themselves from those who were practicing sexual immorality while professing to be followers of Jesus. This letter had solicited requests for further clarification, which Paul had offered in the pages of the Epistle that we call 1 Corinthians. There he set out in clear and forceful terms his views on the errors into which the Corinthians had fallen and urged them to return to the practical entailments of the gospel he had first preached to them.

Paul had paid a brief visit to Corinth from Ephesus to see if he could press home the message of 1 Corinthians and address matters more effectively in person. This visit, however, had turned out to be a disaster: Paul himself describes it as "painful" (2 Cor. 2:1). What happened, evidently, was that the opposition to Paul only intensified in his presence, and his authority was openly defied by one member of the community in particular. Unable to defend himself adequately in the circumstances, Paul had had little alternative but to leave the city. When he had arrived back in Ephesus, he had responded by sending a stinging letter of rebuke, which was conveyed to Corinth by the hand of Titus. This document, like Paul's first letter to Corinth, has not survived.[3]

After he left Ephesus, it seems as if Paul began to wonder if he had gone too far in some of his comments. At any rate, he was anxious to find out what the situation was in Corinth, and after doing some missionary work in Troas, he went over into Macedonia, hoping to find Titus there and hear how his letter had been received. When he managed to rendezvous with Titus, the news was reassuring: the Corinthians had taken Paul's rebuke to heart and were anxious to prove their loyalty to him by disciplining the individual who had most strongly opposed him on his last visit. From Macedonia, perhaps from Philippi, Paul had then written a further letter to Corinth, our 2 Corinthians, expressing his joy and thankfulness that a reconciliation had been achieved, though even yet pointedly defending his own status as an apostle and strongly rebuking those "false apostles" (2 Cor. 11:13) who won esteem from some for their clever speaking and bold performances but in reality were preaching a different Jesus from the one Paul proclaimed. This letter was again carried to Corinth by Titus.

The Epistle to the Romans

There are no reports of further difficulties when Paul finally arrived in Corinth for his third visit, where he probably spent the winter of late 56 to early 57. Presumably the animosities had been laid to rest, and his short time in the city must have been taken up with rebuilding relationships personally and endeavoring to underscore the essential points he had been seeking to make in his correspondence. While there he wrote perhaps his most remarkable letter, an Epistle to the believers in Rome.

Paul had never visited Rome, though he tells the recipients of his letter that he had long been keen to visit the city (Rom. 1:11–13). He had heard encouraging reports of the progress of the gospel there, though he was also aware of problems among the local believers. We do not know how the message of Jesus had first arrived in the metropolis. The Roman church was probably not founded, as later legend would claim, by the apostle Peter himself, though Peter almost certainly did go to

Rome and was martyred there for his faith in the 60s (see p. 96). There is good reason to suppose that Christianity in Rome first took root among the large population of Jews who lived in the capital. It had also spread considerably among Gentiles, however, perhaps initially among God-fearers, and it appears that tensions had arisen because of this fact. There may well have been differences of opinion about the standards for including Gentiles into the community, and these differences may have been forceful enough to contribute to the emperor Claudius's decision to expel Jews, including Jewish Christians, from Rome in 49. Though some of these Jews had by this time returned, Paul's letter is written to a church where there are still significantly strained relations between Gentile and Jewish members.

Paul's purpose in writing is to explain to these divided Roman believers the true implications of the gospel they have received. He could not address them as those who had been converted under his ministry, but he is keen to promote unity among them in preparation for a visit that he planned to make to the capital. His desire was to spend some time in Rome en route to further missionary work in the West, as far away as Spain (Rom. 15:23–24, 28). Paul wants them to understand what it means in practical terms for them to be followers of Jesus together, given that they have such different backgrounds and assumptions. If their community is to be a base for the further expansion of the faith toward the west, there are certain principles they will have to apply in their daily lives concerning the status of both Jews and Gentiles in the light of Christ.

At the beginning of the Epistle, Paul sets out the heart of his gospel, which is the announcement of the message that Jesus Christ is Lord (Rom. 1:4). This, Paul maintains, is precisely the good news promised beforehand in the Jewish Scriptures, and it has now been confirmed by the resurrection of Jesus from the dead. Jesus is the amazing declaration that the one true God of all the world has acted to deal decisively with all that is wrong in his creation, and that God is now about the business of restoring justice, peace, truth, and love to a realm that has been so dreadfully fractured by sin. The gospel is the proclamation that God is *righteous*—God is faithful to his covenant promises, and he has proved this by graciously dealing not only with the sin and humiliation of Jews, but with the sin and needs of Gentiles also. The message is "first for the Jew, then for the Gentile" (Rom. 1:16), but its astonishing announcement is that God has established a covenant community that goes far beyond the bounds of ethnic Israel to embrace all who will cast themselves on his mercy.

In the same way that Abraham, the archetypal recipient of God's promises, was "justified"—or reckoned to be in covenant relationship with God—not by his natural credentials but by his faith (Rom. 4:1–25), so those who have faith in Jesus today are similarly "justified"—or declared to belong to the covenant people of God—not by being part of physical Israel, demarcated by observance of the Law, but simply by believing in Jesus, "apart from [the] law" (Rom. 3:21, 28). By faith alone, Gentiles as well as Jews come to share with Abraham in God's covenant and to possess a right to be called full members of the people of God.

Where does all this leave ethnic Israel? Paul is writing in a context in which salvation is freely offered to the Gentiles but still rejected by most Jews, who do not have faith in Jesus. The people who have been privileged with countless evidences of God's favor have failed to recognize Jesus as Messiah, imagining that righteousness is defined by Law rather than by grace. In Rome, many Gentile believers seemed to assume that Jews were accordingly cut off forever and that God had abandoned his ancient promises to Israel. By no means, says Paul. On the contrary, Gentile Christians must recognize that it is *they* who have by grace become heirs to an inheritance that is, originally, Jewish. Paul glories in his own Jewishness and relies heavily on quotations from the Hebrew Scriptures in order to develop his argument. What has happened in the gospel of Jesus, he claims, is that God has acted to graft on new Gentile branches to the root of the ancient covenant people of Israel. The current rejection of the Jews is only a temporary state of affairs, purposed by God in his sovereignty in order to allow the gathering-in of the Gentiles. Paul's hope is that all Israel will in the end be saved (Rom. 9:1–11:36).

Later in his Epistle, Paul proceeds to explain the implications of his teaching for the way in which believers ought to live. Picking up themes that have been explored in earlier parts of the letter, he exhorts his readers to recognize that they are called not to conform to the pattern of the present world around them, which is passing and corrupt, but to be transformed inwardly in their attitudes, ambitions, and desires (Rom. 12:2). This way, they will live in love for one another, not seeking their own rights or pleasures but the good of others, tolerant of those among them who have differences of opinion about matters of ritual purity (Rom. 13:8–15:13). They will also be commendable members of their wider society, giving what is due to those in authority (Rom. 13:1–7), blessing even their enemies who persecute them (Rom. 12:14), and overcoming evil with good (Rom. 12:21).

On to Jerusalem

Paul's plan, as he tells the Christians in Rome, was to go and visit them and then head on farther to the west. First, however, he had another journey to undertake. The Christians in Macedonia and Achaia had collected a gift of money to send to the poor in Jerusalem. Paul, warned of a plot against him, traveled northward over land to Macedonia, while some of his friends sailed on ahead to Troas to wait for him. From Philippi, joined by members of the contributing churches, Luke once again among them, Paul sailed to Troas and then to Miletus, on the Asian coast south of Ephesus. From Ephesus, a number of the believers came down to visit him while his ship was in harbor, and Luke describes Paul's counsel to them and the tearful farewells that were said (Acts 20:17–38). Keen to hasten on to Jerusalem, the party continued on their way, sailing via the islands of Cos and Rhodes, putting in at Patara on the southwest Asian coast and then taking a course to the south of Cyprus before finally landing on the Syrian coast at Tyre. After further halts at Ptolemais and Caesarea to visit the local believers in these places, Paul and his friends at last arrived in Jerusalem.

Paul must have had no shortage of enemies in Jerusalem. He would have been seen as a traitor and a renegade by hundreds or thousands of Jews, including his fellow Pharisees and, inevitably, the Sadducean authorities. Furthermore, despite the agreements reached at the so-called council a few years before and some positive relationships in the period since then, Paul remained suspect to some of the local followers of Jesus, for whom his evidently liberal standards for the acceptance of Gentile converts remained a dangerous dilution of the essentials of spiritual identity. Greeted by James and the other leaders of the church, the visitors shared news of developments in their work among the Gentiles, and Paul presumably delivered the gift that he and his companions had brought for the poor. But it is clear that there were lingering concerns in a number of circles about Paul's position with regard to the Law and about the legitimacy of certain aspects of his actions during his extensive travels.

As a gesture to reassure these believers, Paul complied with a request from James to participate in a ritual purification process along with a group of local men. As Paul himself doubtless realized, however, this was hardly enough. When he appeared in the temple courts, his presence aroused a public riot, initiated by Asian Jews who happened to recognize him. Here was the man who had demeaned the teachings and traditions of the Law all over the world and who even showed contempt for the temple—for it was rumored that Paul had committed the capital offense of taking a Gentile into the inner sacred precincts. Paul was physically dragged into the outer courts of the temple and almost lynched. He was rescued only by the intervention of the Roman military commander and his troops stationed close by, who rushed to carry out their duty and restore public order.

Paul was taken into custody but escaped a flogging from his captors when he pointed out that he was a Roman citizen. The Roman authorities decided that since he was being accused of offenses against Jewish Law, the proper place for him to be tried was before the Sanhedrin. When the Sanhedrin could establish no proof that he was guilty of sacrilege, and serious arguments broke out between the Pharisees and the Sadducees concerning his talk of resurrection (Acts 23:1–10), Paul was kept in Roman custody. Soon he was removed to Caesarea, to the headquarters of the Roman procurator of Judea, Marcus Antonius Felix, where he remained for two years awaiting the resolution of his case. A deputation from the Sanhedrin pursued the case against him before Felix but without success. As a Roman citizen, Paul was well treated by his custodians and allowed a measure of freedom and regular visits from his friends. We are not told, however, that the believers in Jerusalem made any efforts to plead for his release. Maybe it suited some of them that he was out of Jerusalem, leaving them free to live on reasonable terms with their Jewish neighbors without the likelihood of trouble that Paul's presence among them would surely have reawakened.

We know little of how Paul passed his two years in Caesarea. It is likely that he engaged in further letter writing, and it is possible that one or more of the so-called "Captivity Epistles" that survive under his name—Philemon, Colossians, Philippians, and Ephesians—may have been produced at this time. In each case, however, other settings are also possible, and it may be more likely that these letters were written, as has traditionally been assumed, during Paul's subsequent stay in Rome.[4] He also engaged in some discussion with Felix and his young wife Drusilla, who was a Jewess (Acts 24:24–26).

At length, in A.D. 59, Felix was replaced by another governor, Porcius Festus. Finding Paul on his hands, Festus listened to a renewed presentation of the Sanhedrin's case, but Paul insisted on his innocence in terms of both Jewish and Roman law and exercised his right, as a Roman citizen, to appeal to the emperor for justice. He was thus conducted under guard to Rome, surviving a bad storm and shipwreck on the coast of Malta, which Luke describes in intriguing detail (Acts 27:1–44). He traveled not only in the company of other prisoners but with a few of his friends, among them Luke himself and a believer from Thessalonica named Aristarchus. After wintering on Malta, the company finally made it to Italy, arriving in Rome in the spring of 60.

Rome and Further Writing

Paul lived for two years in Rome under house arrest, in his own rented quarters (Acts 28:30). He would not have been allowed to practice his trade as a tentmaker and so would have been obliged to rely on others for support, but he was subject to only light custody (Acts 28:16) and was allowed free contact with the local Christians. The Romans would not have interfered with his freedom to observe his own religious devotions, and he was able to continue to share his faith with those who guarded him (Phil. 1:13). The remainder of his life is very much in the dark, since at this point the narrative of Acts ends. The wheels of Roman justice in this period ground very slowly, but it is likely that Paul was eventually acquitted, since at no stage in the judicial process had he been convicted of any crime against Roman law.

The most probable setting for the Epistles of Paul that make reference to the author being in captivity is in this period at Rome. His short letter to Philemon is addressed to a Christian of Colossae whose slave, Onesimus, had run away and somehow come to be with Paul. Paul sent Onesimus back to his master with the Epistle, in which he asks Philemon to show forgiveness to his servant because he is now a believer (Philem. 16). The Epistle to the Colossians, addressed to a community established not by Paul himself but by Epaphras, one of his associates from Ephesus, was probably sent with the letter to Philemon. Though some scholars doubt that the Epistle to the Colossians is by Paul, a number of its details and its likely connection with the letter to Philemon make such skepticism unnecessary. The letter exhorts the believers living in the Lycus valley to reflect on the exalted status of Jesus as their Lord and Savior and on what their calling to serve him must mean for their practical lives in the world. Unlike those who prized a worldly "philosophy" (Col. 2:8) based on rules and regulations, the Colossians are to appreciate that they have "died with Christ" (Col. 2:20) and "been raised with Christ" (Col. 3:1), and that their calling is to be, in effect, ordinary but different—not making a show of their spirituality, but living in humility, self-control, and love for one another.

The Epistle to the Philippians, written to the first community of believers Paul had planted in Europe and whom he obviously regarded with particular affection, alludes generally to some of the themes found in Galatians, 2 Corinthians, and Romans concerning the supremacy of the knowledge of Christ over every other way of defining human identity. Paul points out that naturally he has many reasons to be proud of his Jewish heritage, his Pharisaism, and his zeal for the Law, but now he has counted all these things as nothing in comparison with the knowledge of Christ (Phil. 3:4–10). Since membership in the covenant people of God comes solely through faith in Jesus, nothing matters more than commitment to Christ and wholehearted devotion to his service. To know Christ means to become gradually more like him in self-denial and obedience to the will of God (Phil. 2:5–11). If Jesus is indeed the Lord, the one whom God has exalted as the worthy sovereign over all things, then, as Paul himself can testify even as a prisoner, true joy is to be found in following him and making him known (Phil. 1:12–26; 4:4).

The Epistle to the Ephesians contains many close parallels with the Epistle to the Colossians, but in a number of other respects it differs from the rest of Paul's letters. Uniquely, there are no personal greetings and no references to the circumstances of the recipients. There are notable differences of language and theological nuance from Paul's usual style elsewhere. In reality, Ephesians is much more like a homily than a letter. Many scholars argue that the document is not by Paul himself but is the work of a disciple, who was seeking to put together a collection of Paul's teachings for general distribution. This might account for the similarities to the Epistle to the Colossians in particular and for other language that is akin to certain material in the Letter to the Romans. In other respects, however, it does seem plausible that the Epistle to the Ephesians was written during Paul's period of house arrest in Rome (Eph. 3:1; 4:1; 6:20; cf. Col. 4:18), and despite the unique characteristics in its language and content, it is not impossible that it is by Paul himself. It may well have been addressed not solely to those "in Ephesus" (the words of Ephesians 1:1 are not in some of the earliest manuscripts) but to Gentile believers more generally, though probably Gentile believers in Asia in particular, including the churches of the Lycus valley. Ephesians may well have been a circular, intended to reach a variety of Christian gatherings.

Whatever the circumstances of its composition, Ephesians offers a magnificent exposition of a range of themes that undoubtedly lie at the heart of Paul's theology, and in some cases, it expands upon their significance in ways that are not to be found earlier. Salvation is said to be entirely "in" Christ from first to last (Eph. 1:3–14). The story of grace is that God allows Gentiles, who by nature are estranged from the covenant, to be fellow members of God's family with Israel (Eph. 2:11–22). The church, in the Epistle to the Ephesians, is not simply a local entity, as it often is in Paul's writings, but the entire universal body of the risen Christ, and the establishment of this community of which Christ is the head is what God's purposes in history are ultimately all about (Eph. 1:17–23; 3:8–11). The unity of the body in spiritual and moral terms is therefore vital (Eph. 4:1–16), and believers must live in ways that show that they are "filled with the Spirit" of Christ (Eph. 5:18) and are, all in their distinctive ways yet all together, "children of light" (Eph. 5:8).

More Mission, and the End

Later evidence suggests that on his release by the Romans Paul went on to engage in further missionary activity. It is unclear whether this was in the eastern or the western end of the Mediterranean, or perhaps in both. The so-called "Pastoral Epistles," 1 and 2 Timothy and Titus, suggest that Paul spent at least a summer in Asia Minor and perhaps a summer and winter in Crete, Greece, and Macedonia. Timothy is pictured in charge of a community of believers in Ephesus (1 Tim. 1:3), and Titus is in Crete (Titus 1:5), where Paul himself has carried out a mission. Titus is also summoned to meet Paul in Greece (Titus 3:12) and goes on to Dalmatia (2 Tim. 4:10). First Timothy appears to have been written from Macedonia and the Epistle to Titus from Greece.

A majority of modern scholars believe that most if not all of the Pastoral Epistles as they stand are not by Paul, their claims to Pauline authorship and circumstances notwithstanding. The evidence for this is complex and beyond our current scope to assess in full, but it involves, among other things, issues of both style and content. Not only are the Pastoral Epistles written in a different idiom from Paul's, they also posit a much more ordered system of structures and offices among their respective Christian communities in Ephesus and Crete than we find anywhere else in Paul, and they lack some of the usual emphases of Paul's theology. For these and other reasons, most experts assume that these Epistles cannot be by Paul himself, and some historians argue that cities such as Ephesus possessed a variety of different church traditions, not all of which were sympathetic to the kinds of teaching presented in these pseudo-Pauline documents. Some commentators do, however, continue to defend the Pauline origin of one or more of the letters, while accepting that their material necessitates a setting toward the end of Paul's life. (Second Timothy, certainly, is presented as the vision of a man who believes that the time for his departure has come [2 Tim. 4:6].)

One conceivable middle way suggested by a number of scholars is to say that the letters were written not by Paul but by someone close to him and that they do contain significant fragments of authentically Pauline material. It is possible that they were composed not long after Paul's death by one of his co-workers, who wrote in his own hand but drew upon notes and instructions left by Paul himself. Names such as Luke have been discussed as possible candidates, but any precise identification is speculative. The theological contexts of the letters, and the kinds of relations that may have existed between allegedly Pauline and non-Pauline believers in Ephesus especially, are also susceptible to varying interpretations. Whatever is said on these matters, if the references to Paul's geographical movements are not to be dismissed as a complete fabrication, the letters do imply that Paul managed to fit in some further travels in the East, in accordance with his apparent expectation while in Rome (Philem. 22). At the same time, later first-century evidence says that Paul journeyed westward and carried his gospel as far as Spain, as he had definitely planned to do for some time (Rom. 15:23–24, 28). Possibly both happened; we cannot be sure.

What is subject to little doubt is that Paul at length found himself back in Rome around the years 64 to 65 and that he was arrested, probably in connection with an imperial effort to blame the Christians for a fire that had recently devastated Rome (see further pp. 191–93). This time he was subject to a much more stringent regime of custody: 2 Timothy describes its author as being in prison with death in sight (2 Tim. 1:8, 12, 16; 2:8–10; 4:6–8). At the end of a further protracted judicial process, Paul was sentenced to death and executed some time in the period 65–68. As a Roman citizen, he would have been spared the horror of crucifixion, being burned alive, or being thrown to wild beasts (fates that befell other believers), and legend confirms that this was so. Most likely he was beheaded.

Some later piety held that Paul and Peter were executed together, but this is unlikely. Peter almost certainly was martyred in Rome, but as an ordinary Galilean fisherman, not a Roman citizen like Paul, he would have had far fewer rights than Paul, and his fate was probably crucifixion. The two apostles may well have suffered in the same period of persecution, but they probably did not die on the same day. Both would be commemorated in increasingly elaborate style in Rome from the second century onward. Peter may have come to be regarded—dubiously—as the founding apostle of the church of Rome, but Paul's place in its early history was absolutely assured.

Evaluating Paul

To judge from the accounts of our dominant sources, the missionary endeavors of Paul were the central phenomenon in the spread of the early Christian faith. As we have noted already, this impression is regrettable, for a large number of other believers also engaged in zealous evangelism and consolidation in a wide variety of contexts, and without their efforts the message of Jesus would not have traveled and developed as it did in large areas of the Mediterranean world. It was through the proclamation of messengers other than Paul that churches were first established in Antioch, Rome, Ephesus, and many other places, and it was not Paul who first led such strategic witnesses as Apollos, Priscilla, and Aquila to confess faith in Jesus. In several instances, Paul built upon the achievements of earlier workers and made use of networks and opportunities that had been set up in previous phases of growth.

Even within Paul's own circle, the many men and women who served as his vital co-workers are too easily overlooked,[5] and in the contexts of the early faith as a whole, an incalculable number of other pioneers also deserve recognition. If Peter, James, John, and others of the first generation of leaders (to say nothing of all the anonymous disciples of that period) have occupied a limited place in our story, it is only because we know far less about their work overall than we do about Paul's, not because their labors were necessarily any less dedicated. Many other servants of Christ paid just as high a price for their faith as Paul did, and it would obviously be a huge mistake to suppose that Paul was somehow the only passionate preacher and teacher in the early Jesus movement or that he was the only one prepared to give his life for the cause.

Nevertheless, it was unquestionably to Paul more than any other figure that the Jesus movement that had begun in Galilee and Judea owed its remarkable expansion into the Gentile world, not only into Syria, Asia, and the eastern Mediterranean but across into Europe, through Macedonia, Greece, and Italy, and perhaps beyond. Paul remains a character of huge contrasts. The man who had tried to strangle the faith of the Nazarenes in its infancy had gone on to be its greatest champion and its indefatigable communicator. Paul lived and died thinking of himself as a Jew, and his ideas were fundamentally shaped by Jewish assumptions, yet to a vast number of his fellow Jews his views were outrageous, and even to many of his fellow Jewish Christians his attitudes were far too free. The one who considered himself a Hebrew of the Hebrews took his gospel to the Gentiles in ways that undoubtedly contributed to the subsequent severance of his version of Judaism from every other.

By the standards of some in the ancient world, Paul's oratory was quite feeble, yet his preaching was clearly highly effective and his letters, with all their torrential language and complex structures, were the work of a skilled and subtle communicator who knew very well how to move and inspire his addressees. In the oral culture of his day, his letters (usually written for the most part with the aid of a scribe) would have been typically read aloud, or orally "performed," and Paul could invest them with many kinds of rhetorical qualities that facilitated this process. He was a multilingual, multicultural person, yet his gifts for storytelling and persuasion were steeped in the Jewish Scriptures and nurtured by creative applications of standard Jewish techniques of exegesis. He was in theological terms a revolutionary, and his ethical teaching had the potential to affect social patterns in radical ways, yet he himself did not advocate political radicalism, nor did he directly challenge many of the existing conventions of his social world, including the existence of phenomena such as slavery.

Paul was by temperament a zealous man, prone to accepting no half-measures either in himself or in others. The truth was *his* gospel, about which he could be very possessive, and he did not take kindly to his authority being challenged. He was naturally impetuous, argumentative, prickly, sometimes boastful and defensive. Yet he was also capable of great warmth, tenderness, and loyalty to his friends and deep solicitude for his converts. It is little wonder that he evoked strong reactions, both positive and negative, wherever he went. Attempts to construct Paul's personality are in the end precarious, for all our access to him is via sources that have their own reasons for presenting him in particular ways. His own letters are aimed at persuading their recipients, and the author they reveal is a carefully crafted figure, whose stated emotions and aspirations are bound up with strategies designed to impress and convince his readers. In Luke's narrative in Acts, Paul is even more obviously depicted in a specific fashion in order to facilitate the telling of a larger story, the contours of which are determined by Luke's own situation and purposes as a writer.

What we can say is that Paul was without question a man driven by enormous passion. The Christ whom he met on the Damascus road was for him an all-compelling reality. Paul's belief that God had acted in Jesus to transform not only the situation of Israel but the condition of the whole world drove him to abandon the comforts of a settled life and the assurances of religious respectability to spend the rest of his days in taking the message of this Jesus to as large a constituency as he possibly could. Paul traveled many thousands of miles by land and sea, lived in all kinds of conditions, and suffered all manner of discomforts, indignities, and persecution (including passing several years of his life deprived of his freedom) for the sake of the gospel that Jesus was the Christ of God in whom God was making all things new. Within just a few years of Jesus's ignominious death on a Roman cross, Paul was spending all his energies in becoming all things to all people (1 Cor. 9:22), Jews and Gentiles, in order to persuade his world that this was so.

However important other leaders and teachers undoubtedly were, and however controversial some of his own ideas, it was Paul more than anyone who gave the Jesus movement its most formative ways of understanding its nature, purpose, and destiny. Does this mean that Paul should be thought of as the real founder of Christianity? It has often been suggested both in scholarly literature and in popular reevaluations of Christian origins that there is a significant gulf between Paul and the Jesus in whose name he claimed to speak, and that Paul in fact reinvented the message of Jesus by turning it into the religion that Christianity became. On this reasoning, it was Paul, not Jesus, who really designed the contours of the Christian faith, taking the ideas of Jesus in directions that were far removed from their original intention.

When subjected to close analysis, such arguments simply do not stand up. A careful assessment of both Jesus and Paul reveals that there is, at heart, a very high degree of congruence between them. Of course Paul lived in a much more eclectic, urbanized, and international world than Jesus, and naturally he adopted differing techniques to spread his message. His language, his intellectual framework, and his style were inevitably distinctive. He did not simply repeat directly Jesus's message of the kingdom, nor did he try to imitate the amazing actions that Jesus had performed. Such efforts would have seemed outrageous to Paul. He saw himself as the slave of Christ Jesus (Rom. 1:1), and his whole life's work from Damascus onward was devoted to working out and proclaiming the implications of his master's life, death, and resurrection.

Jesus had announced that the kingdom of God was present and had invited all who would come to celebrate its arrival. In giving his life, he had acted in the conviction that he was God's Anointed One and the means through which God would grant an enslaved people the deliverance they could never achieve for themselves. For Paul, the resurrection of Jesus from the dead was the proof that all this was true. *Election* was not just about ethnic Israel being chosen by God but about a whole world of sinners, graciously called "in" Christ to be the people of God. *Justification* was not about Jews alone living in covenant with God and demonstrating their special status by devotion to the Law; it was about

Gentiles also being declared righteous before God, with their sins forgiven and their standing vindicated in God's sight.

This inevitably meant that the works of the Law were relativized: Gentiles did not need to be circumcised or to obey all the detailed prescriptions of the Law on matters such as dietary regulations in order to show that they were believers. What they needed to do was to live in a way that demonstrated their moral commitment to the standards of truth, justice, holiness, and love that the Law had been designed to teach. The temple, too, though it remained an inevitable focal point for Jewish faith, was of only limited symbolic status; the presence of the risen Jesus with his followers through his Spirit meant that God was now to be met wherever these disciples of the Messiah gathered in his name.

Jesus had made all this possible. Paul had seen it as his task to go and tell the world that it was so—and in the end he had given his life in this conviction and hope.

4

BEING CHRISTIAN

▼

Estimating Numbers

The task of estimating the total number of believers at any stage in the history of the church is hazardous, but sociologists postulate that a growth rate of around 3.4 to 3.5 percent per year was likely in the first century of the Jesus movement. This may not seem very much, but when compounded it amounts to an expansion of as much as 40 percent per decade. One estimate has suggested that if we begin with the 120 or so converts gathered in Jerusalem in the year A.D. 30 (Acts 1:15), this would mean that there were perhaps 7,000 to 8,000 Christians in the world by the year 100. This was probably only about 0.01 percent of the total population of the Roman Empire. If a similar rate of increase is projected for each decade in the next two and a half centuries, there may have been by the year 350 almost 34 million Christians in the Roman world—and that, technically, may have represented a majority of the imperial population.[1]

Any such figures are speculative and highly contestable, and the effort to formulate them is subject to a number of criticisms. For example, those who make the foregoing calculation accept as plausible the claim of Acts 1:15 that there were in the first instance about 120 believers in Jerusalem, but disregard as implausible the claim of Acts 2:41 that "about three thousand" converts were added to their numbers on the day of Pentecost. Clearly if the second figure, or an estimate even partially toward it, was reckoned into the arithmetic, the projections for later periods would be much higher. It is also extremely likely that the growth rates for any movement will fluctuate from time to time rather than develop in a smooth and regular fashion. There is every probability that Christian expansion was more rapid in some periods than in others, and there is no reason necessarily to discount the possibility of certain large-scale influxes.

Calculations about development depend upon debatable assumptions about the nature of ancient society, about the social makeup of the churches, and about the kinds of people likely to have converted to Christianity. Some of these assumptions may be plausible, but it is always possible to cast doubt upon their validity in contexts in which the hard evidence is limited—as it often tends to be in ancient historical work. Given all of these variables, suggestions concerning annual growth rates in the early Christian period have ranged widely, from 2.5 percent or less to as much as 4 percent, depending on the differing presuppositions of those who have ventured a reckoning.

Sociological estimates provide us with some very rough guesswork as to the possible composition and growth of the primitive Christian movement and a broad context for our thinking about the earliest churches, but probably little more than that. What we can say with confidence, however, is that although the impact of the gospel in the first generation after Jesus's death and resurrection may have appeared, even to its most enthusiastic ambassadors, to be tiny, the long-term consequences of the story far exceeded anything that the first disciples of Jesus could have envisaged.

The Social Status of the Faith

Jesus himself and his first followers belonged to an essentially rural environment in Palestine, but within a decade of his death and resurrection, this culture had been largely left behind. Spreading out from Jerusalem, the gospel was planted primarily not in rural areas but in cities and towns. In a number of ways, this urban context was crucial to the expansion of the faith. In cities, people typically lived in very close proximity to one another; ideas traveled fast, and ways of living were closely observable. Given the very poor conditions in which the great majority of city-dwellers were housed, ill-health, disease, and death were constant realities, and every city contained large numbers of widows, orphans, and needy individuals. To many such people, the story of Jesus offered not only spiritual consolation and hope but also the present assistance of charity and the assurance of belonging within a family network.

It would be quite wrong to imagine, however, that the Jesus movement was essentially proletarian, made up primarily of the poor, the dispossessed, and the vulnerable. The charge that Christianity attracted only the weak, the vulgar, and the ignorant (or "women, children, slaves, and fools") was commonly made by pagan critics in the second century and beyond, and this interpretation has had plenty of supporters in modern times, not least among scholars influenced by Marxist approaches to sociology.[2] The evidence, however, is against it. Certainly the Nazarenes did not for the most part engage the attentions of the landed aristocrats, the senatorial class, or the rich equestrians of the Roman world. They, however, made up only a very small proportion of the ancient populace, and compared with them, more or less everyone was subject in some measure to the vagaries of economic circumstances. Very probably the Jesus movement did have some appeal for unskilled manual workers, hired menials, and laborers, and there were certainly constituencies of vulnerable believers for whom charitable collections and the distribution of aid were necessary (1 Cor. 16:1–4; 2 Cor. 8:1–9:15). The Pauline letters also give some instruction to slaves (Eph. 6:5–8; Col. 3:22–25; cf. 1 Cor. 7:20–24).[3] But the gospel appealed not only to the vulnerable; in fact, we have a greater degree of evidence of its effects upon those who represented what we might very loosely call the "middle" or "lower middle" classes[4] than we have of conversions at the lowest levels on the social scale.

It is thus mistaken to suppose that those at the edges of society made up the core of Christianity's followers. Although Paul states that "not many" of his converts in Corinth were "wise by human standards," or "influential," or "of noble birth" (1 Cor. 1:26), he also mentions in the same context other significant facts. Among the very few individuals he had baptized in the city were Crispus and Gaius (1 Cor. 1:14). Crispus, as the Jewish synagogue leader (Acts 18:8), was a man of some standing in his community, and Gaius was evidently of sufficient wealth to offer hospitality not only to Paul but to all the believers in Corinth (Rom. 16:23). Erastus, the city's director of public works, a wealthy individual capable of financing civic schemes out of his own resources, is also notably cited among the Corinthian Christians (Rom. 16:23).[5] It is in fact quite likely that some of the problems in the Corinthian church were attributable to tensions between individuals of different social strata, with different expectations about appropriate moral conduct. Even if they were not in a majority, the well-off or the successful in worldly terms were not entirely absent from the local body, and their attitudes may well have been a cause of resentment among more lowly members.

In Acts, we see the gospel achieving success or at least a sympathetic hearing from a number of figures broadly representative of a military, political, and economic elite,[6] such as the Ethiopian treasurer (Acts 8:26–39), the centurion Cornelius (10:1–48), Manaen, "who had been brought up with Herod the tetrarch" (13:1), Sergius Paulus, the proconsul of Cyprus (13:7), and certain Greek women and men of prominent standing in Berea (17:12). Asian officials are described as Paul's friends in Acts 19:31, and Paul is at home conversing with those in powerful positions, even if he does not persuade them of his message (24:24–26; 26:1–31). Although the proportion of socially prominent persons within the Jesus movement as a whole may have been small, it was not nonexistent.

The supposition that the poor and the uneducated are naturally more inclined to religious belief is in any case not borne out by the findings of more recent scholarship in the social sciences. Like every other movement that has emerged out of an existing religious culture, faith in Jesus must generally have taken root among those who were privileged enough in socioeconomic terms to be capable of giving serious consideration to the possibilities of immersing themselves in a new lifestyle. The privilege in question, of course, is relative: those who convert to a new faith need to be both in a position to understand the demands and opportunities it represents *and* at the same time sufficiently disaffected by their existing position within their inherited culture to be prepared to make a change. They will not be so lacking in physical security that they can give no thought to any religious message because they are preoccupied with the more pressing question of how they are going to stay alive, but they will also perceive that their present condition fails to satisfy their longings and needs. Had early Christianity been obviously a movement spearheaded by a restless proletariat or those with no sense of social belonging, it would almost certainly have been crushed by Rome at a very early date as a political threat. The fact that it was not suggests that it drew its converts from a wider cross-section of society.

Overall, the typical believer was in fact neither at the bottom nor at the top of the social pyramid but was likely to be an artisan, small trader, or skilled manual worker. Some such individuals were persons of reasonable wealth, as was probably the case with the tentmakers Priscilla and Aquila, who were able to move from city to city and act as patrons for both local believers and visiting evangelists (Rom. 16:3–4; 1 Cor. 16:19). Lydia, the first convert in Europe, was by background a merchant from Thyatira, dealing in luxury purple fabric, and she was of sufficient means to put up Paul, Silas, and their friends in her house in Philippi (Acts 16:13–15). The majority, however, were probably of more modest means—small-scale merchants, shopkeepers, and tradespeople with free status and adequate resources to manage some kind of reasonable life most of the time, barring disasters such as famines or the collapse of their local economies (the effects of which reached all but the very wealthiest)—but usually not people of significance or prestige within their society.

It may be that a greater degree of social mobility in cities such as the Roman colonies of Corinth and Philippi meant that in such places there were higher numbers of wealthy believers than elsewhere, and in the Hellenized cities of the East there were often significant numbers of prosperous Jews from whose ranks some converts were made. Figures such as the educated Jew of Alexandria, Apollos, were seemingly able to travel independently (Acts 18:24–28); Paul's friend Barnabas, a Levite, had owned property in his native Cyprus (Acts 4:36–37). Like other believers (Acts 4:34), Barnabas had sold his land and donated the profits to the apostles. On his missionary endeavors he engaged, like Paul, in manual work in order to support himself (1 Cor. 9:6). But notably Paul says that he and Barnabas were unusual in this regard; the other apostles were apparently able to rely on the generosity of others. Wherever the economic resources of early Christianity came from, the movement was not confined to the meager assets of those who lived at the margins.

Why Conversion?

The Jewish communities scattered throughout the empire provided the first messengers of the story of Jesus with a ready-made web of relationships and sites upon which to concentrate their evangelistic efforts. While the longer-term evidence may seem to suggest that only a minority of Jews overall turned to Christianity, there is good reason to believe that the preexisting networks of Judaism were vital to the expansion of the new faith and that Jewish conversions were in fact a critical part of the movement's growth.

Belief in Jesus was obviously entirely dependent on Jewish structures in Palestine, where those who professed faith in the Christian Messiah continued to represent a movement within Judaism until well into the second century. In the Diaspora, Hellenized Jews were used to hearing teachers who came from the "homeland" with messages of moral and spiritual counsel; there would have been some sympathy for accounts by Paul and other evangelists of a figure who had suffered unjustly at the hands of the Romans and the corrupt priestly regime in Jerusalem. In the cities of Asia Minor in particular, numbers of Jewish hearers must surely have listened with openness to the ideas of Paul, a fellow Hellenized Jew, as he expounded a new and potentially liberating understanding of their common faith. Even where the Jews remained unconvinced by or openly antagonistic toward the message of Jesus, as is regularly claimed in Acts, it was via contact with Jewish synagogues that many of the fruits of Gentile mission were reaped. The loosely defined category of God-fearers was made up of people already attracted to Judaism. The Christian gospel offered them a way of interpreting Judaism that offered a new kind of spiritual endorsement of its foundational concerns without requiring subscription to all the demands of Torah observance.

What about those Gentiles, progressively becoming the majority wherever the gospel traveled, whose natural habitat was in the diverse world of pagan polytheism? What kinds of inducements did they have to become followers of Jesus? Paul speaks of himself as becoming all things to all people (1 Cor. 9:22) in order to reach those whose thought-worlds and sensibilities were conditioned by differing assumptions. In Acts 17:16–31, his engagement with pagan thinkers in Athens typifies this strategy. Paul's approach, as Luke presents it, is not to depict Jesus as the Messiah of Jewish prophecy but to appeal to what he sees as the widespread religious instinct of people in Athens, evidenced by an inscription on an altar "TO AN UNKNOWN GOD" (Acts 17:23). The Athenians worshiped many deities, and they were concerned not to offend any by leaving them out for want of knowing their names. Paul's strategy is to say that the true God, who is the creator of all (and he quotes pagan poetry to show that his hearers might share the conviction that "we are God's offspring," Acts 17:28), transcends the temples and shrines constructed by human hands. The time has come, in the light of "the man he [God] has appointed" (Acts 17:31)—in Luke's account Paul does not actually mention Jesus by name—to repent of the folly of pagan idolatry in view of God's coming judgment, a judgment that has been guaranteed by the resurrection of this man from the dead.

A similar approach can be noticed in Acts 14:8–20, in the ministry of Paul and Barnabas in Lystra. There, the healing of a lame man by Paul excited a religious fervor among the people of the town, and they started to hail Paul and Barnabas as gods in human form; Barnabas was thought to be Zeus and Paul, Hermes, and a local priest of Zeus was prepared to offer sacrifices to them both.[7] Paul's response (which seems scarcely to have been very successful, for only with difficulty, we are told, did he prevent the crowd from sacrificing to them, Acts 14:18)[8] is to say that he and Barnabas are only human like the people of Lystra, and their desire is that their hearers should turn from paganism to the living God, the creator of the whole world. This God witnesses to his own reality by sending rain upon the crops and providing food and fulfillment for the inhabitants of Lystra. Again, the message is that the true God is there all along and that what the Christian gospel is summoning people to is the recognition that he alone is to be worshiped.

It is obviously not possible to extrapolate from such passages a complete analysis of the kinds of arguments that might have had weight with Gentile recipients of the Christian message—for one thing, in both of the instances mentioned, the proclamation did not enjoy great success. Nor should we reasonably suppose that, because the very condensed narrative of Acts omits to say that the preaching in each instance was focused directly upon Jesus or upon his death, it did not go on to speak of such matters in some form. Nevertheless, it is safe to assume that some people who were converted from pagan backgrounds must have been persuaded by some such arguments about the old gods being superseded by the story of the one divinity revealed in Jesus.

Many would have found compelling resonances in claims that, above all the medley of pluralistic religion, there stood the purposes and activity of a transcendent God. Such ideas were by no means unknown among intellectuals. In the Roman world, unified—supposedly—in political and even cultural terms, the message that all the people of this world were ultimately united as the children of a single deity may also have contained a certain plausibility for more pragmatic reasons. And an appeal to a coming hour of judgment, however it might have been understood by such respondents, might only have served to reinforce the sense of obligation that such monotheism implied in moral terms: if there was only one God, and human beings were accountable to him, it was indeed important to be on good terms with him.

The followers of Graeco-Roman religions would not have felt the same kinds of responsibilities spiritually as those from Jewish backgrounds. The idea of sin as moral guilt, concepts of estrangement and alienation from divine favor, and the prospect of judgment in a life beyond the present one would not have been automatically assimilable by pagan hearers. To some, Christianity probably looked almost as much like a moral philosophy as a religious faith, and it may well have been the Christian lifestyle as a comprehensive commitment to truth that appeared interesting in the first instance. Many in the ancient world would not instinctively have understood conversion as a process by which a guilt-ridden, broken individual found inner peace and joy through a crisis of repentance and dedication to God, but they would have known very well what was meant by a shift from one way of living to another in terms of intellectual commitments, social identity, and ethical behavior.

Whether the hearers of the gospel were Jewish or pagan, the story of Jesus was nevertheless, for a large proportion of its audiences, a peculiar, offensive business. Among Jews, the message of a crucified Messiah was scandalous, for it conflicted with every normal expectation of what God's Anointed One ought to mean. Equally, as Paul discovered not only in Athens (Acts 17:32) but all over the Hellenized Mediterranean world, talk of a person who had been vindicated by God by being physically raised to life was, to the Greek mind, sheer madness; it made no sense at all. Even the claim that there was one God who loved human beings and desired to live in close personal relationship with them would have struck a pagan hearer as bizarre; the members of the Graeco-Roman pantheon simply did not relate to the world in that way.

The proclamation of God's love and power expressed in the weakness and defeat of the cross of Jesus the Christ was at one and the same time "a stumbling block to Jews and foolishness to Gentiles" (1 Cor. 1:23). With such a challenging tale to tell, intellectual persuasion and rhetorical energy were only capable of achieving so much. It was no more possible than it was desirable to bully people into faith. They would come only if "called" by God (1 Cor. 1:24) and if their hearts were divinely opened to respond to the message (Acts 16:14), which, in all its apparent weakness, was yet, to faith, "the power of God for the salvation of everyone who believes" (Rom. 1:16).

In reality, for many in the first century—as in every subsequent period in Christianity's history—the first thing that would have elicited serious inquiry concerning the nature of the faith was personal contact with other believers. This must have been true regardless of the religious and cultural backgrounds of the seekers. To live and work alongside those who followed Jesus, to witness their behavior at close quarters, and to listen as they talked about the gospel amid their ordinary daily activities was to be confronted by the evidence of changed lives. In this sense, the drawing power of the Christian faith must often have consisted not so much in the public declarations of its most prominent representatives as in the quiet testimony of ordinary worshipers of Jesus witnessing to the credibility of their commitment by their integrity, constancy, and openness to others.

Doubtless for many adherents, awareness of inner need and a desire for repentance and reconciliation with God came later on, as a result of closer familiarity with the teachings of the Christian path. But in the earliest stages, Christianity may often have exerted a practical moral pull rather than a narrowly intellectual compulsion. In a world of many uncertainties and endless competing philosophies, the followers of Jesus had two great qualities to offer: first, they claimed to possess confident knowledge about the ultimate realities of human existence, and second, they appeared to live in the light of that confidence, even in the face of considerable difficulties and opposition, as those who were genuinely committed to their God and to his expectations for practical behavior. Others may have made similar claims, but the Christians must sometimes have seemed to make them best.

No doubt some of the conversions in the first century were in response to remarkable events of various kinds; according to the accounts in Acts, some people were drawn to the faith as a result of "wonders and miraculous signs" (Acts 2:43; cf. 4:30; 5:12; 8:6). These displays are said to have taken various forms, including the gift of communication in foreign languages (2:4–12), miraculous healings (3:1–10; 5:12–16; 8:7–8; 19:11–12), and exorcisms (19:13–16). In Luke's presentation, all of this is attributable to the outpouring of the Holy Spirit on the day of Pentecost and the Spirit's blessing of the endeavors of the first emissaries of the gospel. Luke sees the growth of the church as the Spirit's work; it is the evidence of the fulfillment of the promise of the risen Jesus that witness to him will extend far beyond the boundaries of Jerusalem, Judea, and Samaria, and reach "the ends of the earth" (Acts 1:8).

Conversions are depicted in Acts as sometimes occurring on a large scale, such as the profession of faith by around three thousand hearers of Peter's sermon in Jerusalem at Pentecost (Acts 2:41), but more often they are small-scale, the belief of individuals or small groups. In a number of instances, the conversion of an individual brought with it the conversion of that individual's entire household. This was so in the case of Lydia (Acts 16:15), and it was also true of the jailer in Philippi (Acts 16:31–34) and of Crispus, the synagogue ruler in Corinth (Acts 18:8). It is also implicit in the story of how the centurion Cornelius came to believe (Acts 10:1–48), as recalled by Peter in Acts 11:14. A similar reference occurs in connection with the initiation of the household of Stephanas in Corinth (1 Cor. 1:16), the members of which are described by Paul as "the first converts in Achaia" (1 Cor. 16:15). The practice probably meant that not only immediate family members but all who were part of the economic unit of the household were converts, including its slaves and perhaps even their families. The belief of the head of the household, whether male or female, entailed the belief of all the household's members. We do not know whether such a system happened on a large scale, but if it did, it must obviously have contributed substantially to the expansion of Christianity in statistical terms.

At the same time, conversion could also set up significant tensions within households, such as when a spouse became a believer but his or her partner did not, or when children professed faith against the wishes of parents, or when individuals elected to ignore the influence of their friends. Hostility and even ostracism could ensue within people's natural social units and among their peers. Converts were sometimes obliged to choose between the call of Christ and the approval of those with whom they lived and worked, and in a range of ways the demands of the gospel could radically destabilize their social world. If many were appreciative of the emphasis on a family ethos that evolved in Christian circles, it was not infrequently because the relationships within their conventional environment had become severely frayed as a result of their new commitment.

Participation in the Faith

Initiation into the Christian faith was seen as a radical change of orientation, loyalty, and lifestyle. Probably the earliest Christian confession was the simple but highly charged acknowledgment, "Jesus is Lord" (Rom. 10:9; 1 Cor. 12:3). To most readers of this book, such language is probably so familiar that its full significance in a first-century context is likely to be missed. In the earliest phase of the church's existence, the phrase was far more than simply a statement of assent to the importance of a name or a tradition. Jews believed that that name of God was too sacred to pronounce. The word *Lord* (Hebrew, *Adonai*) was customarily used for the tetragrammaton, the four Hebrew characters used in Scripture to represent God's holy name: YHWH (in English, "Yahweh," traditionally rendered with the capitalized form "Lord"). In the Greek version of the Hebrew Scriptures, the Septuagint, the term *Lord* with reference to God was rendered as *Kyrios*.

Jews refused to address the Roman emperor as "Lord," believing it blasphemous to ascribe to a human being a title reserved for divinity. Yet the Nazarenes were boldly saying it of Jesus. To call Jesus *Kyrios* was to say that Jesus was assimilated into the identity of this one true God, the Holy One of Israel and the Lord of all. For the person who came from a non-Jewish background, the confession equally represented an explicit break with actual or possible loyalty to every other deity. It was an acknowledgment that Jesus was to be recognized as the only worthy recipient of worship and service. Such a believer was renouncing life lived under the authority of any other master and stating that Jesus alone deserved to be honored and followed.

From the beginning, this transition from one life to another was symbolized by the rite of baptism with water. Baptism was practiced for the first converts at Pentecost, according to Acts 2:38–42, and it appears to have been widely observed thereafter, though Paul for one did not baptize as a matter of routine (1 Cor. 1:13–17). Those who received the message and professed their acceptance of it were publicly initiated into the new life by being baptized. The roots of the practice lay in the baptism of Jesus, which is attested to in all four canonical Gospels (Matt. 3:13–17; Mark 1:9–11; Luke 3:21–22; John 1:31–34), and Jesus himself had also periodically baptized people (John 3:22, 26; 4:1), probably in accordance with traditions of ritual washing that were well established in Judaism. The desert prophet John, by whom Jesus had been baptized, represented a contemporary Jewish movement in which baptism was adopted as a sign of penitence and inner purification, and some Jewish teachers believed in administering the ritual of *tebilah*, "the bath," to converts from paganism.

We know little of the details of the earliest Christian baptismal practice. It is not clear whether converts were invariably dipped or submerged in water, or whether the water was poured over them in one manner or another. We cannot be sure if there was a precise verbal formula that was used at most or all baptisms in the earliest period or what the formal requirements may have been of the candidate. Neither can we know if infants were ever among the candidates, or if there were any rules as to who should administer the baptismal process, or in what setting it was supposed to take place. It may well be that practices varied from context to context. In time, however, it is clear that baptism became regarded as something that the risen Jesus himself had commanded his followers to do. It was part of what it meant for them to "go and make disciples of all nations," and the process was to take place in, or more often *into*, the name of "the Father and of the Son and of the Holy Spirit" (Matt.

28:19). Prior to this, baptism was probably carried out simply "in/into the name of Jesus," or "into the name of the Lord Jesus."

Baptism was associated with a range of striking imagery, symbolic of the radical break the candidate was making with his or her former life. In Paul's theology, baptism signified the putting off of the old nature and the putting on of the new, or being "clothed . . . with Christ" (Gal. 3:27; cf. Col. 3:9–10). In being baptized—dipped or plunged into Christ—a person was signaling that he or she henceforth belonged to the Lord as his property. The ceremony stood for the unity of the believer with the death, burial, and resurrection of Jesus (Rom. 6:3–11; Col. 2:12–15). In other New Testament passages, baptism is associated with cleansing from or forgiveness of sins (Acts 2:38; cf. 1 Cor. 6:11; 1 Peter 3:21), with rebirth, or being born "from above" into the new life of the kingdom of God (John 3:3–21; Titus 3:5), with the reception of the Holy Spirit (2 Cor. 1:21–22; Eph. 1:13–14; 4:30), and with becoming part of a community that may be thought of as a body of which the risen Christ is the Head (1 Cor. 12:13). To be baptized was to become a new person, one who had renounced evil and identified with Jesus. The old life was buried and a new life begun in union with the risen Christ.

The Family of God

The community into which the baptized were ushered was distinctive. Its members were encouraged to think of themselves as an extended family and to call each other "brother" and "sister." They greeted each other with a "holy kiss" (Rom. 16:16; 1 Cor. 16:20; 2 Cor. 13:12; 1 Thess. 5:26; cf. 1 Peter 5:14). They professed a common mode of life in which, according to Luke's depiction of the Jerusalem believers at any rate, they would care for one another and share their possessions (Acts 2:44; 4:32). In Acts, the faith is described a number of times as "the Way" (Acts 9:2; 19:9, 23; 22:4; 24:14, 22; cf. 16:17; 18:25–26), a term that had some existing usage in Judaism, particularly among the Qumran community. It is clear that the believers saw themselves as having embarked on a path that had all-encompassing implications for their lives.

According to Paul, whatever differences there were among believers in respect of race, class, or sex, they were "all one in Christ Jesus" (Gal. 3:28). In terms of spiritual status, slaves were to be no different from free people, women from men, and, at least in Paul's vision, Gentile converts from Jewish ones. The slave was to be regarded as "a dear brother" (Philem. 16). The person with whom there was a disagreement about matters of ethical observance, such as what to eat and what to drink, was to be treated with sensitivity as a brother or sister "for whom Christ died" (Rom. 14:15).

The New Testament letters are of course full of indications that these ideals were frequently far from realized. Natural differences were hardly left behind entirely, and socioeconomic divisions were often simply replicated in new guises in the path of faith. The apostolic communities were beset with many practical problems, and divisions, social snobberies, selfishness, and moral failures were widespread, provoking often sharp rejoinders from leaders such as Paul. Nevertheless, the believers' loyalty to Jesus was what essentially unified them, regardless of other social, intellectual, or cultural distinctions, and it was to this basic fidelity that erring Christians were recalled. When things were awry, the assumption was that they had forgotten their primary obligation, which was to live not for themselves but for Christ, and they were reminded of their obligation to sacrifice their own interests and ambitions in devotion to his cause.

It is important to note that it was frequently in the expressing of very practical counsel that some of the most exalted theology was elaborated. Why should Christians practice humility and consideration of the rights of others? Supremely, because they should show the same attitude that Jesus himself displayed, who though divine in nature "made himself nothing," and took the form of a servant in the interests of others (Phil. 2:3–11). Why should Christians give to the poor? Above all, in reflection upon the grace of their Lord, who "though he was rich . . . he became poor," so that others "through his poverty might become rich" (2 Cor. 8:9). What does it mean to live appropriate lives as husbands and wives, parents and children, servants and masters? It means living as those who are "filled with the Spirit" of this risen Jesus (Eph. 5:18).

To belong to "the Way" was to be part of a new household of faith (Gal. 6:10), an expression of a new *ecclesia*, or "assembly," the term from which our English word *church* eventually was derived. From the time of Paul's letters, if not before, *assembly* became the most common term among Greek-speaking Christians to describe the community of believers as both a local entity, such as "the church [assembly] of the Thessalonians" (1 Thess. 1:1), and a body that included all followers of Jesus everywhere (1 Cor. 12:28). The word signaled both the intended continuity with Israel as the community of those who were called to belong to the Lord and also the differentiation of the Nazarenes from the Jewish synagogues, which were never known by this name.[9] The *ecclesia* was the constituency united by virtue of its common belief in the risen Jesus, the one in whom the God of Israel had acted for the salvation of the world; organically linked to Jesus, Christians were organically linked to one another. They confessed "one Lord, one faith, one baptism" (Eph. 4:5).

Believers were called by this Lord to be holy and distinctive, an alternative society in the midst of a corrupt world, and in spite of all their failures their hallmarks were to be fellowship (*koinonia*) and love (*agape*) for one another. Other related images for the people of God included designations such as "the saints" or "the holy ones" (a term reserved not simply for some elite believers but for all who had faith and were thus set apart for God); "the elect" or "the chosen ones," called by God; "the family," "the flock," and "the body of Christ." The psychology of belonging was reinforced in the language of intimacy and sharing. By the same token, the dreadfulness of sinning against Christ, offending against other believers, and causing division in the body was emphasized with images of violation and the prospect of exclusion from the privileges of participation.

Meeting Together

The believers met together regularly. In Jerusalem, the Nazarenes not only continued to congregate daily in the courts of the temple (Acts 2:46), but they appear to have continued at least a version of the Jewish pattern of prayer several times each day. Most Jewish Christians probably continued to pray in public at least twice and more commonly three times each day, in the morning and evening, and usually at noon or in the midafternoon as well (see Acts 3:1–5). Other private prayer times may well have been kept in addition. Although the pattern for Gentile converts was probably looser, Paul exhorts the Thessalonians to "pray continually" (1 Thess. 5:17). Fasting, another traditional Jewish discipline, continued to be observed, often in connection with dedicated seasons of fervent prayer and consecration (Acts 13:2–3; 14:23).

The rhythm of daily prayer was synonymous with an offering of daily praise to God. It was also associated with a spirit of watchfulness or vigilance (see Matt. 26:41; Mark 14:38; Luke 22:40). The early Christians believed that Jesus would return imminently to usher in the full realization of God's kingdom and that it was therefore of critical importance that they devote themselves to his cause so as to be found ready when he arrived (Eph. 6:18; Col. 4:2; see also Matt. 24:36–51; Mark 13:32–37;

Luke 12:35–40). Perhaps the earliest form of very short prayer regularly used by believers was the Aramaic formula *Marana-tha*, or "Our Lord, come!" (see 1 Cor. 16:22).

Within twenty years of Jesus's passion, it had become widespread practice to treat Sunday, "the first day of the week" (Acts 20:7; 1 Cor. 16:2), as the special day for worship, in commemoration of the day on which the Lord had been raised from the dead. The Jewish Sabbath was probably maintained alongside this by Jewish believers, at least for as long as the Jerusalem temple stood, though it is difficult to be sure. Gentile converts who adopted Paul's view of the Law probably saw no reason to observe any day as a Sabbath. Sunday had replaced the Jewish Sabbath for the overwhelming majority of Christians by the turn of the first and second centuries, though it would not be sanctioned in any formal sense as a day of rest until the fourth century; prior to that, it remained for most a regular working day. Sunday came to be designated "the Lord's Day" (Rev. 1:10), and in later Christian reflection this was taken to mean that it was a day not so much for remembering Jesus but for encountering him and enjoying fresh communion with him in his risen power. Sunday was not just about looking back but about meeting with Jesus in the present; it was also about looking forward to a future day of the Lord when Jesus would be definitively acknowledged as Lord of all.

The first generations of Christians had no special buildings in which to worship. In Acts 2:46, the believers in Jerusalem are said to have shared fellowship together "in their homes." The New Testament letters often include references to the church in the house of an individual or individuals (Rom. 16:5; 1 Cor. 16:19; Col. 4:15; Philem. 2), and certain households clearly provided a nucleus for the community in various places, as was apparently the case with the house of Stephanas (1 Cor. 16:15; cf. 1:16). Multiple house-churches came to exist in several of the larger cities to which Paul went; Corinth may have had six or more of these, and Rome had even more. As we have seen, the conversion and baptism of a head of a household could bring with it the conversion and baptism of all the house's members (Acts 11:14; 16:15, 34; 18:8). Those who were able to serve as patrons of house-churches were typically people of greater social standing and means, whose homes were large enough to accommodate numbers of their fellow believers. They offered hospitality both to visiting evangelists, such as Paul and his companions, and to the local believers. In Romans 16:23, Gaius is described as one whose generosity benefits both Paul and "the whole church here."

Such household leaders were not always male. Besides the case of Lydia mentioned in Acts 16:15, Paul refers to a number of other women who were either leaders of household groups or in some other way significant servants of the church, women such as Chloe (1 Cor. 1:11), Priscilla/Prisca (1 Cor. 16:19), and Nympha (Col. 4:15). In Acts 12:12, the house of Mary, the mother of John Mark, is a place where believers gather to pray in Jerusalem. Phoebe, who was a valued servant of the church at the Corinthian port of Cenchrea (Rom. 16:1–2), seems to have carried Paul's Epistle to the Romans to its destined audience. Mary (Rom. 16:6) and Junia (Rom. 16:7)[10] were other dedicated workers in Rome, and the latter had suffered imprisonment for the faith. Women such as Euodia and Syntyche (Phil. 4:2–3) are described as co-workers with Paul, and others such as Tryphena and Tryphosa, or his "dear friend" Persis are said to have been hard workers "in the Lord" (Rom. 16:12). A substantial proportion of the believers to whom Paul sends personal greetings at the end of his Epistle to the Romans are female; in addition to the names already mentioned, there are the mother of Rufus (Rom. 16:13), Julia (Rom. 16:15), and the sister of Nereus (Rom. 16:15). "Sister" Apphia is one of the main addressees of Paul's Epistle to Philemon (Philem. 2).

We do not know exactly what roles were played by many of these women. It is clear that not all were heads of house-churches or patrons in the same sense, nor were they all travelers or bearers of apostolic letters. Nevertheless, some undoubtedly were leaders and teachers, either on their own or as part of a husband-and-wife team,[11] and a number provided vital accommodation, funds, and support for Christian activities. Others perhaps engaged in different kinds of ministry, such as charitable work or other practical activity. Yet others may have labored in work of another variety, such as the task of prayer, which was seen as a demanding labor of great strategic importance (e.g., Rom. 15:30; 2 Cor. 1:10–11; Col. 4:2–4, 12). Whatever they did, there can be no doubt that women took an active part in the life of the early house-churches, and the roles in which at least some of them engaged were considered to be comparable in significance to those played by men. Whether as householders or as other workers, they labored side by side (Phil. 4:3) with their male counterparts in the Christian movement.

The system of house-churches persisted for generations. We have archaeological evidence from the third century that some houses had been adapted architecturally to facilitate worship, and this marked the first step toward the evolution of dedicated church edifices. But the ordinary domestic setting remained the primary context for both Jewish and

Gentile assembly for a very long time, and there were house-churches in use in many places well into the fourth century. Other buildings were deployed in particular situations, including school halls such as that of Tyrannus at Ephesus, in which Paul led daily discussions for a period of two years (Acts 19:9), and evangelism in particular went on in many different environments, ranging from synagogues or other less formal places of Jewish religious assembly (Acts 16:13) to open-air settings such as the great marketplace in Athens (Acts 17:17). Predominantly, however, it was in private houses that Christians were obliged to gather, comforting themselves with the knowledge that the temple of God was a spiritual rather than a physical reality (1 Cor. 3:16; 2 Cor. 6:16) and that God did not dwell in buildings framed by human hands (Acts 7:48–50; 17:24).

In its own way, the ethos of house-churches naturally facilitated the characterization of the Christian community as a family network and fostered the emergence of Christian moral codes that projected the household as the context in which discipleship was given true practical expression. In reality, this did not mean that Christian social structures were entirely egalitarian. Indeed, as time went on, the grafting of Christian values onto the patterns of family life served increasingly to reproduce conventional social divisions within the household of faith, as certain individuals were regarded as more appropriate to lead than others on the grounds of means, gender, status, or capacity to manage. Nevertheless, the domestic setting of the early churches was an important aspect of their moral as well as organizational character and almost certainly contributed to the spread of the faith.

Sunday Worship

When the believers met in Sunday worship, they naturally prayed together, sharing in the experience of thanksgiving, praise, and petition to God, whom they approached in the name of Jesus. In conformity with Jewish practice, there was almost certainly reading from the Jewish Scriptures, with some comment upon them (as Jesus did in the synagogue in Nazareth in Luke 4:14–30). Much of the time such exposition can hardly have been preaching in a formal sense, but there was clearly regular interpretation and application of biblical texts and a sustained concern to ground ideas and practices in Scriptures that were believed to declare God's word. Engagement with this word cannot routinely have followed the patterns of the stylized apostolic sermons presented in Acts, which are in any case evangelistic rather than educational in nature.

Nevertheless, there was undoubtedly a strong emphasis on listening to the messages of sacred texts, recognizing in Jesus the fulfillment of their promises, and instructing one another in the moral implications of this fulfillment for contemporary life. Teaching of this kind was seen as a significant element in worship, and from early on, Christian literature contained many exhortations on the importance of being instructed in the truths of the Scriptures.

There was also singing of "psalms, hymns and spiritual songs" (Eph. 5:19–20; Col. 3:16). The Jewish Psalter was the primary songbook, and believers found clear images of their Lord, his sufferings, and his exaltation in the Psalms (e.g., Pss. 2; 16:9–11; 22; 55:12–14; 110; 118:22–23). Psalms were read aloud as well as sung, as they were in Jewish worship, and singing in general would almost always have been undertaken without any kind of instrumental accompaniment. Indeed, in later Christian writers there would be a great deal of polemic against musical instruments, which were strongly associated with worldly entertainment.[12]

Psalms and *hymns* were often interchangeable terms in the first century—the "hymn" said to have been sung by Jesus and his disciples at their last supper together (Matt. 26:30; Mark 14:26) was probably part of the Hallel or praise sequence recorded in Psalms 113–18. But this was not always so, and both descriptions were used for other material besides the conventional Jewish Psalter. We cannot be sure what these other hymns or spiritual songs of the first believers may have been, how extensively they may have been used alongside scriptural psalms, or whether there were differences between the kinds of songs considered appropriate in different settings. Nevertheless, it is highly likely that from an early date Christians began to produce their own compositions for praise. In the earliest phases, such songs perhaps typically paraphrased the language of the Jewish Scriptures, which was understood by the worshipers to refer to Jesus. But it was not long before there were hymns specifically identifying the Christians' Lord as the object of worship.

Many scholars believe that the New Testament contains material that may be derived from early Christian hymns. Passages such as Ephesians 5:14; Philippians 2:6–11; Colossians 1:15–20; 1 Timothy 3:16; 2 Timothy 2:11–13; and perhaps Hebrews 1:3 are cited as examples. But it is difficult to establish if the verses in question are genuinely quotations from hymns or simply instances of rhetorical or quasi-poetic prose. Whatever the status of such texts, there is little reason to doubt that songs to Jesus and celebration of his saving work and living presence through singing hymns were a significant part of the early believers' experience. In contexts besides Sunday worship, the singing of traditional Psalms or other songs also proved a comfort in difficulties (Acts 16:25), a way of expressing Christian joy (James 5:13), and a natural medium for showing gratitude of heart to God (Eph. 5:19–20; Col. 3:16). In the writing of at least one of the Gospels, too, hymn forms were an important stylistic element (Luke 1:46–55, 68–79; 2:29–32), whose content would later become part of Christian liturgy.

In addition to prayer, reading, exposition, and singing, there were various other dimensions to worship, as we can see from Paul's First Epistle to the Corinthians, which offers the earliest extensive evidence on what might be deemed Christian liturgy. One evidently standard activity was prophecy, which involved not so much the prediction of future events (though sometimes this did occur, e.g., Acts 11:27–30) as the sharing of inspired messages for the edification or encouragement of the assembled company (1 Cor. 14:1–5, 29–40). Prophecies, like hymns, readings, or the articulating of other forms of instruction or revelation, could be contributed by worshipers in a spontaneous fashion (1 Cor. 14:26), though it was required that their content be weighed carefully and discussed in an orderly fashion.

Another practice was speaking in tongues (*glossolalia*). This was apparently different from the gift that came to the first believers at Pentecost and so impressed the diverse crowd of pilgrims present in Jerusalem. According to Luke in Acts 2:4–13, the gift on that occasion was the ability to speak in other languages (consider also the gift that accompanied conversion in Acts 10:46). In a worship context, however, speaking in tongues, although recognized as an important sign of the Holy Spirit's power, required interpretation (1 Cor. 14:1–25). Whatever it amounted to in psychological and social terms, it is clear that it was not regarded as an ultimate sign of spirituality. Paul pictures it as not the greatest of spiritual gifts and as something that is useless unless employed to the edification of the whole body (1 Cor. 13:8; 14:9–12).

The details relating to some of these activities are not altogether clear, and it is not certain to what extent we can generalize on the basis of the evidence from Corinth in particular. Nevertheless, it is plain that in Corinth at least the believers engaged in a fairly informal, spontaneous style of worship, exercising a good deal of freedom in their practice of these gifts of the Holy Spirit. In fact, their behavior ends up, in Paul's eyes, as too much of a free-for-all, and he scolds them for their subjectivism and abuse of freedom. Paul considers it vital that the Spirit's gifts not be treated as private resources, to be used only as individual means of self-expression. Instead, they should be used as ways of building up the entire community and promoting the unity of the whole church. Paul insists that all things must be done "in a fitting and orderly way" (1 Cor. 14:36–40). Mutual edification had to take priority over personal whims, and one Christian's exercise of liberty is not to be at the expense of another's. Revelations and a "word of instruction" (1 Cor. 14:26) are to be shared for the good of all. Even the task of taking disciplinary measures against those who sinned is the responsibility not just of a few but the obligation of the whole assembled community (1 Cor. 5:1–5).

Paul also counsels the Corinthians to adopt a system that he had advocated elsewhere, with the Galatian churches, in which they should set aside a sum of money weekly, according to ability, for distribution to other needy Christians (1 Cor. 16:1–3; cf. Acts 24:17; Rom. 15:25–28; 2 Cor. 8:1–21; Gal. 2:10). Christian charity, and the consecration of funds to the needs of the church not only locally but farther afield, was regarded as an important practical necessity and a sign of spiritual devotion. There are no indications that particular rules applied as to what was considered an appropriate donation; giving was to be voluntary and in accordance with means, not undertaken "reluctantly or under compulsion" (2 Cor. 9:7). It was a vital way of reinforcing the principle of fellowship between believers and, above all, an expression of gratitude to God for the "indescribable gift" of Christ himself (2 Cor. 9:6–15).

Giving Thanks

The central focus of Christian worship, though, was the breaking of bread ceremony in which the believers participated (Acts 2:42, 46; 20:7), which later came to be known more commonly as the "thanksgiving" or "Eucharist" (Greek, *eucharistia*, "thanksgiving"). Even more than was the case with baptism, the eucharistic meal had a background in existing Jewish tradition and in the example and teaching of Jesus himself. Jesus had shown considerable freedom in sharing meals with tax collectors and sinners, and his inclusive approach to social types regarded by many Jews as undesirables symbolized the breadth of his vision of the kingdom of God. In the Gospels' presentations of his Last Supper with his disciples prior to his trial and crucifixion, Jesus gave thanks for the gifts of bread and wine and instructed his followers to take them as symbols of his body that would be broken and his blood that would be shed for their sake (Matt. 26:17–30; Mark 14:12–26; Luke 22:7–23).

Many years prior to the writing of these accounts, however, Paul recounts to the Corinthians the teaching he had passed on to them about engaging in a meal of thanksgiving in obedience to a command given by the Lord Jesus, "on the night he was betrayed" (1 Cor. 11:23–34). Regular participation in this meal was a hallmark of the earliest communities. We cannot be entirely sure how often it was celebrated; the pattern of life followed by the early apostolic church in Jerusalem described in Acts 2:42–47 (cf. 5:42) may imply that these believers at least broke bread daily, but it may well be that practices varied from church to church. It is likely that celebration each Sunday was the general norm (see Acts 20:7).

For most of the first century the thanksgiving was part of a larger communal meal, probably held in the evening, and the whole occasion was known as "the Lord's Supper" (1 Cor. 11:20). The pattern enunciated by Paul in 1 Corinthians 11 became the basic sequence for the rite. Food was taken, blessed, broken, and shared. "After supper," or after the remainder of the meal proper had been consumed, a cup was similarly blessed and distributed (1 Cor. 11:25; cf. Luke 22:20). The order in which the bread and the cup were taken varied. Sometimes the cup came first, and sometimes a number of cups were passed around. A single bread-cup sequence was, however, probably the commonest pattern. The basic elements in the ritual meals were typically bread and wine, but there is evidence that some believers came to use a variety of other items as well, including cheese, fruit, vegetables, fish, milk, honey, and water, in symbolism of their rejection of the dietary habits and ritual practices of pagan society. Ascetic bread-and-water Eucharists became common in some circles, though often among those whose beliefs were controversial (see p. 314).

The eating and drinking were seen as a sacred commemoration of Jesus, especially a commemoration of his sufferings and death, and a way of communing with the risen Lord. The bread was his "body," the cup contained his "blood"; those who partook were "eating the flesh" of Jesus and "drinking his blood" (John 6:53–56) and rendering thanks to God for the fact that Jesus's body and blood had been surrendered for their sake—"given" and "poured out" in his death. This "participation" in his body and blood symbolized both the union of the believers with their Lord and their unity with one another as a single body (1 Cor. 10:16–17). Ultimately, the process was about more than just remembering or offering gratitude for the sacrifice of Jesus or being one in fellowship with the risen Savior and all who worshiped him; it was also about "proclaim[ing] the Lord's death until he comes" (1 Cor.

11:26). To partake of this supper was to anticipate a feast that would yet be eaten, an eschatological banquet in which Jesus and his followers would share when he returned in glory.

The house-church system provided an obvious context for the association of eucharistic activity with the practice of eating together more generally. The food and drink were perhaps provided by the participants on a contributory basis. The style, in other words, was informal, and the ethos of the occasion was about sharing and corporate charity. The sacredness of the thanksgiving dimension was nevertheless taken very seriously. The apostle Paul taught that certain forms of ethical behavior were incompatible with participation in the supper. Those who partook at idol feasts, for instance, were disqualified from the communion, since it was impossible to sit at "the table of demons" as well as at "the Lord's table" (1 Cor. 10:18–22). Paul also issued stern warnings about inappropriate behavior at the meal itself, such as drunkenness or selfish eating and drinking to the neglect of others (1 Cor. 11:20–22). This kind of "unworthy" conduct (1 Cor. 11:27) meant that the occasion was not genuinely "the Lord's Supper" (1 Cor. 11:20), and such abuse was an extremely serious matter; those culpable of it were guilty of "sinning against the body and blood of the Lord" (1 Cor. 11:27) and were said to eat and drink judgment on themselves (1 Cor. 11:29). Participants needed to examine themselves and not fail to recognize the Lord's body (1 Cor. 11:29). They had to be conscious of the organic interdependence of all believers and thus to be sensitive to the needs of their brothers and sisters.

Abuses of the common meal apparently became a problem in other places besides Corinth (see 2 Peter 2:13; Jude 12), and by the end of the first century the sacred action of remembrance and proclamation had begun to be distinguished from the context of eating and drinking together generally. The latter, the *agape* meal (love feast or charity meal) tended to be held in the evening; the Eucharist as such was observed more often in the morning. By the middle of the second century, the *agape* meal had for many Christians become an occasional rather than a regular meeting, and the Eucharist was isolated as the essential ritual. There are some hints that the vital liturgical activities surrounding the Eucharist were Scripture-reading, exhortation, and prayer, but not singing, which may imply that the practice of singing had traditionally been part of the informality of the *agape* meal in particular. Singing continued to be highly valued all the same, and it certainly remained important in worship long after the communal meal had disappeared from regular liturgical practice.

Leadership

When it came to leading and instructing in matters of the faith, continuity with Jesus was deemed to be transmitted in the first instance via the authority of those whom the risen Lord had personally commissioned. The title of "apostle" applied to those who had lived with Jesus during his earthly ministry, encountered him after his resurrection (1 Cor. 9:1; 15:3–11), and been specially sent by him to preach and teach. Initially, however, as we saw in chapter 2 (p. 51), the term was used quite loosely to describe a variety of ambassadors of the gospel. For Paul, it applied not only to the Twelve (1 Cor. 15:5) but to a variety of other witnesses of the risen Jesus (1 Cor. 15:7), including James the brother of Jesus (Gal. 1:19), and to disciples both male and female, such as Andronicus and Junia (Rom. 16:7). Even those who were enemies of Paul's message in Corinth were identified as "false apostles," masquerading as genuine apostles of Christ (2 Cor. 11:13–15). Paul was insistent that he was himself a genuine apostle (1 Cor. 9:1–6) with authority comparable to that of the Twelve. Though Paul had not been an acquaintance of Jesus in his former days, he saw himself as endowed with authentic apostolic authority by virtue of his dramatic encounter with the risen Christ (1 Cor. 15:8).

Luke and other later writers primarily used the term *apostles* to refer to the Twelve, though Luke also refers to Paul and Barnabas as "apostles" in Acts 14:4, 14. The criteria of apostolic status were subject to dispute and evolution, and there were clearly some significant tensions over the question of who was to be regarded as a true apostle. Eventually, the label came to be restricted to a particular group, made up chiefly of the Twelve and Paul; Jesus's brother James was sometimes included, but not always. In the earliest churches, things remained a good deal more fluid. Nevertheless, the tendency to recognize a small constituency as specially commissioned leaders was undoubtedly already present. Many had been witnesses of the resurrection of Jesus, and many more were zealous emissaries of the faith, but none of these individuals was believed to have been charged in quite such a special sense with the task of overseeing the shaping of the faith.

After the apostles (1 Cor. 12:28) came *prophets* such as Agabus (Acts 11:28), who exercised a ministry of offering inspired messages and prayers in the Spirit. Then came *teachers*, probably a general term for those deemed suitable to instruct converts and communicate the faith, as distinct from people who spoke with direct inspiration or originality. Acts 13:1 lists the prophets and teachers of the church at Antioch as

Barnabas, Simeon called Niger, Lucius of Cyrene, Manaen, and Saul (who is not here described as an apostle). Women as well as men could prophesy, as we can see from the example of the four daughters of Philip the evangelist in Caesarea (Acts 21:8–9) and from Paul's instructions to the Corinthians concerning propriety for male and female behavior in worship (1 Cor. 11:3–16, especially 4–5).[13] There is equally no unequivocal indication from the earliest Christian literature that teaching or preaching in the house-church settings were necessarily seen as roles restricted to men.

In addition to those who undertook such tasks as teaching, preaching, prophesying, and leading worship, there were also "workers of miracles, also those with gifts of healing, those able to help others, those with gifts of administration, and those speaking in different kinds of tongues" (1 Cor. 12:28). All of these responsibilities or gifts were considered to be important ministries distributed to particular members of the body by the Holy Spirit in his wisdom, and none was to be treated lightly or regarded as only a marginal contribution to the life and witness of the community. In Ephesians 4:11–13, the nomenclature is slightly different again, but the basic gradation of primary roles is consistent: the risen Christ "gave some to be apostles, some to be prophets, some to be evangelists, and some to be pastors and teachers. . . ." All ministry was to be seen as a form of service, not as a means of enjoying precedence or a step toward personal advantage.

A more widespread term for leaders, though not one found in indisputably Pauline usage, was *presbyteroi*, "presbyters" or more commonly "elders." The designation was used already in Jewish synagogues for the older men who formed the governing body. The Jerusalem church in Acts was administered by a council of such elders, alongside its apostolic leaders, Peter, James, and John (Acts 11:30; 15:1–35; 21:18), and such elders were appointed also in Gentile churches (Acts 14:23; 20:17). The word *presbyteroi* is used interchangeably with another term, *episkopoi*, "overseers," or traditionally "bishops" (Acts 20:17, 28; Titus 1:5, 7). The duty of such overseers was not to inspect the churches in terms of subjecting them to a process of intrusive scrutiny but to "keep watch over" them (Acts 20:28), like shepherds watching over their flock, to protect their spiritual sheep from the dangers of false teaching and ungodly influences. Related language was used in secular Greek society in various political and social connections.

Others were *diakonoi*, "deacons," who are mentioned alongside the "overseers" in the case of the Philippian church (Phil. 1:1). Their duties in the earliest period are not very clear, but their name suggests that they were expected to minister or serve, probably in practical ways. The seven individuals appointed in the early days of the Jerusalem church, in the context of the dispute between the Hebrews and the Hellenists, to look after the daily administration of charity are not called "deacons" in Acts (6:1–6), but it is likely that Luke's account is intended to account for the origin of such an office, and from the second century onward it became common to identify "the Seven" (Acts 21:8) as deacons. By this time, the status of deacons had become much more formalized in terms of qualifications and responsibilities (see 1 Tim. 3:8–13), and a number of churches (especially the church of Rome, but also others in the Greek East) came to appoint seven deacons in accordance with Acts 6:1–6. To begin with, however, *diakonia* simply meant practical service of one kind or another performed for the church. Like a number of other terms, it was used of ministry carried out by women as well as men: Phoebe is described by Paul as one who performed such a role in the church in Cenchrea (Rom. 16:1).[14]

It is impossible to know how much diversity existed between forms of worship and organization in different places in the first generation. It is entirely likely that styles of order and expressions of ministry did vary according to circumstance, degrees of Jewish or Gentile influence in the makeup of particular congregations, cultural milieu, and economic and social factors such as the prosperity, education, and personalities of local believers. What does seem to be the case is that worship in the earliest period was characterized at least in many instances, if not generally, by a looseness of structure and a concentration on forms of ministry that were "charismatic," that is to say, attributed directly to the gifting of the Holy Spirit. Gifts could be exercised on a regular basis, or, as was evidently the case with the gift of tongues, experienced only at certain times as the Spirit chose.

The distinction between full-time and part-time ministry was initially unknown, and as we have seen, Paul and at least some of his companions worked with their hands at various stages. With the exception of the status afforded to those who came to be regarded as "the apostles" in the narrower sense of that term, there were also few signs of a firm differentiation between those who exercised official ministries and those who served the church in less formal ways. Hard-and-fast distinctions cannot be drawn between local leaders and itinerants. Nor have we any evidence that only certain persons could baptize, lead worship, celebrate the Eucharist, or read out apostolic letters to assembled believers. There is little to indicate that any of these roles was necessarily restricted to leaders in a technical sense or to men rather than women or to those who had experienced any special training.

All the same, the practice of setting some people apart for specific tasks was evident from earliest times, typically accompanied by prayer (and sometimes fasting) and the laying-on of hands, in accordance with long-standing Jewish ritual (Acts 13:3). The sequence of apostles, then those whom the apostles in turn instructed, whether designated as "elders," "deacons," or something else, also established a certain implicit order of spiritual and practical authority. As the reaction of Paul to the excessive libertarianism of the Corinthians indicates, there were impulses toward order and cohesion from an early date. Ministry was for all, but gifts were not to be exercised in a selfish fashion or in a way that did not contribute to the edification of the community as a whole. The enjoyment of individual spiritual and moral freedom was not to be regarded as an excuse for ignoring the voice of authority. Paul sees himself as speaking with special power and as one able to rebuke, correct, and discipline, both in writing and in person, even though the responsibility for ensuring the moral integrity of the Christian family rested upon all its members together.

Moves toward Formalization

The beginnings of a more formal organization of ministry roles and of the stipulation of some of their requirements can be seen in the so-called Pastoral Epistles: 1 and 2 Timothy and Titus. As we saw in the previous chapter, the authorship of these letters is disputed, and a large number of biblical scholars argue that they are not by Paul but are "deutero-Pauline"—that is, produced by a later author or authors seeking to claim Paul's authority. Estimates for such a later dating vary widely, but one of the primary arguments for a later context is the degree of formality that the Epistles seem to suggest with regard to ministry structures and matters such as the respective roles of men and women in the churches.

Can the Paul of 1 Corinthians, who seems to envisage a rather informal and inclusive style of worship, have gone on to say some of the things said in these documents? For example, can the Paul who spoke so warmly of the ministry of women in the Epistles to the Romans and the Philippians have gone on to insist that no woman should "teach or have authority over a man" but must instead "be silent" (1 Tim. 2:12)? Quite strong arguments can in fact be mounted that the differences between the Pastorals and Paul are not necessarily as stark as may at first appear and that these letters, for all their changed contexts, may represent a fairly logical elaboration of some of the teaching about ministry and authority that is already implicit in the definitely Pauline corpus. If the letters are not Pauline, they can still plausibly be located close to Paul, and quite possibly within a very few years of his death.

Whatever their precise origin, the Pastoral Epistles show that at least some of the churches established by the apostles or other itinerant missionaries had come to be led by local individuals whose authority was deemed to derive from apostolic commission. Timothy is functioning as a leader at Ephesus, and Titus is in Crete. The young Timothy is gifted for his calling "through a prophetic message," given "when the body of elders laid their hands on [him]" (1 Tim. 4:14; cf. 1:18). It is clear that not all were content to acknowledge such authority, and there were plainly theological and ethical tensions with other professing Christians in both Asia Minor and Crete. The instructions to both Timothy and Titus contain a range of warnings about the evils of false teachers and speak of the importance of giving the believers solid instruction in order to inoculate them against falsehood, both doctrinal and moral. There is a strong sense that, although the *parousia* is not yet, believers are living "in later times" (1 Tim. 4:1) or "in the last days" (2 Tim. 3:1) and that moral decay and theological apostasy will only grow worse. The vital importance of sound doctrine is emphasized several times (1 Tim. 1:10–11; 2 Tim. 1:13–14; 4:3–4; Titus 1:9, 13–14; 2:1).

Clear directives are given in the Pastoral Epistles concerning the qualifications for serving as either an overseer or a deacon. Both positions need to be filled by people who have proved themselves to be of good character, self-controlled, sober, and capable of managing their private lives (their marriages and their households) circumspectly. These Epistles call for individuals who know the truths of their faith and who, in the case of the overseers at least, are capable of teaching others. Overseers are "entrusted with God's work" (Titus 1:7), and anyone who aspires to this task desires a noble thing (1 Tim. 3:1).

The Roles of Women

While the roles of leaders are unquestionably more formalized, the fundamental advice concerning those who ought to fill them is perhaps not as different from the teaching we find in earlier material as it may appear. Even such a problematic passage as 1 Timothy 2:11–15, which severely limits the place of women in this context compared with their position in earlier Christian settings, may possibly be interpreted as a localized prohibition for a particular situation rather than as a blanket ban on women undertaking teaching or leadership roles in all churches from this point onward.

Scholars continue to argue over the appropriate exegesis of 1 Timothy 2:11–15, but it is possible to present a reasonable case that the prohibitions in question applied to a specific situation in which certain women were abusing a legitimate kind of authority in the churches in Ephesus and behaving in a way that was detrimental to the well-being and harmony of their communities. It was conceivably this particular problem, not an issue that applied to all Christian circles, that was being addressed, just as it was probably a particular abuse that had also been confronted years earlier in the case of certain women in Corinth (1 Cor. 14:33–35). Similar problems were apparently also being encountered in Ephesus in the behavior of some men, who were equally acting wrongly by displaying anger or quarreling; they too had to learn to deport themselves properly (1 Tim. 2:8).

Many questions remain for further discussion, but whatever view is taken of 1 Timothy 2:11–15, there is evidence elsewhere in the Pastoral Epistles that women are viewed as continuing to undertake a variety of Christian ministries in this same context, including, most probably, a diaconal role (1 Tim. 3:11). Priscilla and Aquila, the couple who had been Paul's friends and associates in earlier years, are sent greetings in 2 Timothy 4:19, implying that there was certainly at least one woman in Ephesus who had been a notable teacher in the past and who in all probability continued to teach in one way or another.

Overall, it is true that the Pastoral Epistles do stress the need for women to display modesty and to show respect for men, and some of the counsel on social propriety is certainly similar in tone to the kinds of advice that might have been given by other teachers in antiquity, who saw no reason to proffer anything other than frankly patriarchal stipulations on female submission. There may well have been some debates about the overall place of women within the context of the Pastoral letters; nonetheless, there is nothing in these Epistles to suggest unambiguously that women were necessarily intended to desist from all ministry and leadership activity in the churches at large.

In other Christian literature of the later first century, especially the Gospels, women feature prominently, and they occupy a range of positive roles that in various ways challenged conventional assumptions, especially in a Jewish context. The Gospels present Jesus as interacting closely with women, defending them against their critics, caring for them and healing them, highlighting their faith and activities as examples, and showing particular concern for women of special vulnerability or "untouchable" status, such as impoverished widows, prostitutes, and ethnic outsiders. He was followed and ministered to by different types of women, ranging from those who had been converted from a previously sinful life, such as Mary Magdalene, to women of means, who were able to provide for him and his disciples out of their own resources. Women are portrayed as among his most loyal devotees, who remained faithful to him right to the end, even after his male disciples had forsaken him and fled. According to the Gospels, it was women who observed his burial and visited his tomb, and it was women who first carried the news of his resurrection—much to the incredulity of some of his male followers.

Both the nature and the details of all of these characterizations are subject to a good deal of scholarly debate. Though much of Jesus's treatment of women and his teaching concerning them in the Gospels is undoubtedly quite radical, not all of it is, and the case for a wholesale subversion of patriarchy can sometimes be overstated. The logical outcome of his example was a powerful reformation rather than an unqualified rejection of patriarchal assumptions. Furthermore, some scholars think that the fact that women are given prominence in the Gospels may be because their place within the Jesus movement had indeed become controversial by the time the Gospels were written—both in society at large, where it raised issues of credibility in the minds of men, and within the Christian community itself, where some men, maybe especially from Jewish backgrounds, had come to resent the degree of freedom exercised by some women. It is possible that the Gospel writers were deliberately recalling their readers to realities that had existed in Jesus's own time and—to some extent at least—in the earliest days of the new faith.

Christian arguments limiting the rights and opportunities of women to lead would certainly be presented over subsequent generations, and many of these would be based one-sidedly upon selected aspects of the Pastoral Epistles' teaching, taken in isolation from the overall testimony of early Christian behavior. The consequences of such reasoning would be both tragic and far-reaching for the Christian churches and undoubtedly carried much Christian moralizing some distance from the ministry of Jesus himself and from some of the practices of his earliest followers. Although it is easy to see how excessively negative assessments of the place of women could have been legitimized by appeals to the language of the Pastoral letters, there is no good reason why the apparent implications of a few verses in these documents should ever have overridden the stronger witness of the apostolic churches as a whole that women and men initially acted as co-workers in the gospel of Christ.

Wherever the Pastoral Epistles originated, whatever particular issues and challenges they sought to address, and whatever degrees of continuity deserve to be identified between their teaching and the principles assumed by believers in earlier times, they do testify to a scene that had undoubtedly changed in a number of respects from the earlier days of the Jesus movement. The expected *parousia* of the Lord had not occurred; the content of the faith both conceptually and morally was deemed to be under significant challenge; and a more settled pattern of ministry and leadership was being promoted as necessary to ensure the stability and good order of the communities that had been planted in the heyday of apostolic expansion.

The changes toward a more formal, and in various ways more conservative, style of Christian practice may seem quite striking, but they probably should not surprise us very much when we consider the circumstances in which they took place. It is time to consider these circumstances a little more closely.

5

ISRAEL OLD AND NEW

▼

Jerusalem: The 60s and Beyond

In A.D. 62, James the brother of Jesus and leader of the Jerusalem community was executed. This was a great blow, for James was a deeply dedicated figure whose obvious piety and prudent leadership had commended the new faith to many over more than two decades. His most striking testimony had been that commitment to Jesus in no wise required severance from Jewish roots. The consistent Jewishness of James's theology is evident in the Epistle of James that exists in our New Testament. This letter may or may not have been written by James himself,[1] but either way it presents a very Jewish picture of the ethical implications of belief and the practice of wisdom. A circular Epistle addressed to the twelve tribes of the Diaspora from James, "a servant of God and of the Lord Jesus Christ" (James 1:1), it is sharply critical of any view of the Christian life that downplays the importance of good works as the evidence of faith. The Law is described as "the royal law" (James 2:8) and the "law that gives freedom" (James 1:25; 2:12), and there is no indication that it is no longer of relevance.

Despite the fears of many later Christians that James somehow compromises the message of free grace, [2] there is no necessary tension between the logic of this letter on the moral obedience of faith and the position of Paul on justification. It is likely that James's reasoning is directed not against the authority of Paul but against extreme interpretations of Paul's teaching in Jewish-Christian circles, especially his teaching that in Christ believers are no longer "under law" (Rom. 6:14–15; 1 Cor. 9:20; Gal. 5:18). Paul himself was insistent that this did not mean Christians were free to live as they liked, since to be "under grace" spelled freedom from sin and slavery to righteousness (Rom. 6:1–23), and he vigorously repudiated allegations that he was indifferent to ethical endeavor (see Rom. 3:8). Nonetheless, there were those who imagined that if the Law was incidental then believers could disregard moral effort and the practice of holiness.[3] Such conclusions were very far from Paul's own thinking, but those who drew them could obviously appeal to aspects of Paul's language. James was anxious to refute such distortions from his own perspective.

As had been evident at the Jerusalem council, James stood for an unambiguously Jewish version of the gospel, which continued to cherish the Law as the marker of covenant identity.[4] His stance had probably won significant numbers of Jewish converts in Jerusalem and Judea, and as far as the high priest and his party were concerned, James—like his brother before him, whose servant he professed himself to be—represented a danger to their power. For his refusal to disown Jesus as the Messiah, James was put to death. His enemies had seized the opportunity of an interval between the departure of one Roman governor and the arrival of another to secure his condemnation. It was a shameful piece of behavior, and many Jews were shocked at what had happened.

If, however, the removal of James was intended by the Sanhedrin to calm the situation in Palestine, it failed dismally. James was succeeded by Symeon son of Clopas, one of Jesus's cousins, and the Nazarenes continued to practice and spread their faith in Jerusalem and Judea. In Galilee, Jesus's other brothers had been active as traveling missionaries for several years (1 Cor. 9:5), and their itinerant work went on, fanning out over the countryside around Jesus's hometown of Nazareth and another village in the hills to the north of Sepphoris called Kochaba.[5] If the realities of Nazarene expansion continued, so too did the political problems. The Jewish historian Josephus describes how abuses of power, heavy taxation, and increased corruption and ineptitude on the part of Roman governors had produced mounting resentment among the Jews of Palestine from the mid-40s onward. In the 60s this mood worsened still further, and a variety of would-be revolutionaries and messianic deliverers emerged, championing the cause of freedom. Moderates were also provoked by the political climate, but many people remained unenthusiastic about changing the situation by force, and there were fierce disputes between different factions over how to respond. There was a broadening base of sympathy for resistance to Rome among Jews of both upper and lower classes, each of whom stood to gain different prizes if political change were to ensue.

By the year 66 the radicals, now increasingly referred to as the Zealots, had gained the upper hand in Jerusalem, and in the wake of further outrages by the Roman procurator of Judea, Gessius Florus (64–66), armed revolt broke out. In the first instance the uprising went the Jews' way: the Roman forces in Jerusalem were decisively beaten, and the Romans lost control of the eastern Negev, Galilee, and parts of Transjordan. However, the successive Roman commanders, Vespasian and his son Titus, were able to mobilize much larger forces, and by the year 70, most of the territory controlled by the Jews had been retaken. In the spring and summer of 70, Jerusalem was besieged and sacked, and the temple itself was destroyed. Pockets of resolute Jewish resistance remained—those holed up in the fortress of Masada, on the western shore of the Dead Sea, held out against the Romans for a further three years or so, and some (though not all, despite the traditional account) of the defenders ultimately chose suicide rather than surrender. But, in psychological terms at least, the revolt was effectively over when Jerusalem fell.

The destruction of the temple was a disaster for Judaism, in symbolic terms at any rate. The destruction of the temple robbed the Jews of the holy place where God was believed to be present, and it ended the sacrificial system. No longer was there a center of priestly power, a Sanhedrin in the traditional form, or an elite who could combine the maintenance of their religious authority through cultivating an alliance with the political might of the Romans.[6] At the same time, for all the brutality of their military methods in crushing the resistance (and even by ancient standards the violence was gruesome), the Romans did not go on to take serious punitive measures against the Jews in terms of their religious rights. The war was seen essentially as a local, not an ethnic, revolt.

Judea remained an imperial province, but in legal terms it lost its "allied" status and became the emperor's private property. It was to be run by senatorial governors, assisted by equestrian procurators. The tax traditionally paid to the temple was now to be handed over to Rome for the maintenance of pagan ritual in the imperial capital. Nevertheless,

Judaism remained a tolerated religion, and aside from the diversion of their temple dues, no serious measures were taken against most of the Jews of the Diaspora, who had in general taken no part in the uprising.[7] As the Pharisees urged, the catastrophe that had befallen Jerusalem represented God's judgment on Israel for her moral backsliding, but there were widespread hopes that with a due period of repentance and reformation the temple would yet be restored to its rightful place at the heart of the faith.

Judaism without the Temple

The most significant result of the fall of Jerusalem consisted in the impetus it gave to Jews of all varieties to think about their identity as Jews. A new center of Jewish learning and teaching slowly began to emerge, based not in Jerusalem but farther to the west, at Jamnia (Yavneh), south of Joppa. The leading spirit in this movement was Rabbi Johanan ben Zacchai. Legend has it that this pioneering leader was smuggled out of Jerusalem in a coffin during the siege of the city and eventually was given permission by the Roman authorities to establish an academy for the interpretation of the Law.

The group that formed at Jamnia was at first small and of only limited influence, but in time its teachings and decisions came to exercise an important role in Judaism. The rabbis of Jamnia promoted the evolution of a form of orthodoxy on such issues as the boundaries of Scripture and the due interpretation of the Law. They discussed the status of certain biblical books such as Ecclesiastes and Song of Songs, which occupied a disputed place in the collection of Hebrew Scriptures accepted at this time. They saw themselves as constituting a sort of ad hoc, spiritual Sanhedrin, making judgments about the parameters of their faith.

The logical extension of the rabbis' position was that certain forms of Judaism came to be regarded more bluntly as unacceptable or as transgressing the boundaries of an appropriate Jewish faith. The full flowering of rabbinic Judaism into the rich and multicolored traditions that it came to represent in later centuries lay in the future, and few if any Palestinian Jews of the late first century would have thought of the early work of Jamnia as anything other than a temporary expedient pending the rebuilding of the temple. Nevertheless, the beginnings of rabbinic reflection on the contours of a "normative" form of Judaism were part of the decisive consequences of the events of 70, and in their own way they furthered the divergence of Judaism and Christianity.

The Nazarenes had distanced themselves from the violence of the revolt years, and at least a proportion of their number had apparently fled Jerusalem in 66 and taken refuge in the Transjordan, chiefly at Pella in the Decapolis. Others had traveled farther afield, to Asia Minor and elsewhere. Wherever they had gone they had taken their faith with them, thus furthering the expansion of the message about Jesus. The witness of the relatives of Jesus in Galilee had also continued. Some form of Nazarene presence may have been maintained in Jerusalem during the war, though it is difficult to be sure. A number of refugees never returned, but in the aftermath of the conflict a nucleus of believers did regroup, led as before by Symeon son of Clopas.

For the followers of Jesus in Jerusalem and Galilee, as much as for other Jews, the desolation of the temple provoked big questions. The sacred symbolism and rituals of temple worship had been deeply formative for their thinking about the nature of Jesus and his achievement, and in a variety of ways the traditions of the temple had also shaped the liturgical celebration of his status. At the same time, from the earliest Gentile missions onward, debates had gone on about what it meant to accept a Jewish Messiah if it was also possible to do without certain key aspects of Jewish practice. With the destruction of the temple, it became necessary to address at a new level the question of what was entailed by the reality of the risen Jesus in the midst of his people.

If God's presence was no longer genuinely made manifest through a physical building, then was not the destruction of the temple simply a confirmation that the temple was irrelevant? Jesus himself had prophesied that the temple would fall, and this had now happened. Why, then, should those who worshiped Jesus entertain any hope that the temple would be restored or consider it necessary that this happen? Had God shown his definitive judgment not only of Israel but also of former ways of thinking about the relationship between belief in Jesus and the traditional symbols of Jewish piety?

Jewish-Christian Reflection

A fair proportion of Christian literature from the late 60s onward shows that the place of the Jesus movement within Judaism was already a matter of serious reflection for many Christian believers. In the so-called Epistle to the Hebrews, which in style is actually much more like a homily than a letter (except for its closing verses), the readers are directed to appreciate that faith in Jesus is superior to Judaism; rather, he is the fulfillment of all that for which Jewish faith at its truest had longed.

Scholars debate the question of to whom this Epistle was written. It is equally possible that the recipients were Jewish believers or Gentiles who, like those to whom Paul wrote in Galatia, were tempted to "Judaize." The writer to the Hebrews certainly presupposes a knowledge of the Jewish Scriptures and the Jewish religious system, and those whom he addresses are warned against lapsing from their faith in Jesus. Probably they were Jews already, though they may well have been living in a Gentile environment, perhaps in Rome. Although regarded from an early date by some Christians as Pauline, the document is not Pauline in style, and its author remains unknown, despite many guesses at his identity over the centuries.[8]

The date of Hebrews may be before or after the fall of the temple; there is no unambiguous reference to the temple's destruction. The implications of Jesus for Jewish faith are, however, crystal clear. The writer argues that while the Jewish Law and worship should not be seen as untrue, properly understood they are only an imperfect shadow of the reality and substance that have come in Christ (Heb. 10:1). Jesus, a truly human representative of human beings yet sinless and divine in status, is the perfect high priest, who in offering himself as a definitive sacrifice has abolished forever the need for repeated animal sacrifices (Heb. 7:23–28; 9:11–10:18; 13:11–12) and become the mediator of a new covenant, which has superseded the temporary covenant of the old dispensation (Heb. 8:1–13). The symbolism of Judaism is transposed to a new key; there can no longer be any need for the earthly realities of the Jewish religious system, for their spiritual fulfillment has come in the person and achievement of the one who suffered for sins, was accepted by God, and ascended to heaven to appear on his people's behalf.

The letter of Jude was written by "Jude . . . a brother of James" (Jude 1), who is probably to be identified as the Jude mentioned in the Gospels as one of Jesus's brothers (Matt. 13:55; Mark 6:3).[9] Like the Epistle of James, it breathes a thoroughly Jewish air, drawing upon the Jewish Scriptures and upon other Jewish writings such as 1 Enoch. There is no reference to the Law or to the destruction of the temple, but the letter warns its Christian recipients (who were presumably, though not necessarily exclusively, Jewish by background) about certain false teachers who have infiltrated their ranks and are leading them astray with erroneous notions and immoral behavior. The allusions are not easy to unpack, but the letter is reflective of a late-first-century Jewish eschatological mindset. It also suggests a time in which Jewish apocalyptic ideas were being rethought in the development of a new, Christian version of orthodoxy, which appealed not only to the Jewish sacred writings but also to the teaching of the apostles (Jude 17) and "the faith that was once for all entrusted to the saints" (Jude 3) as the benchmark of truth.

In 1 Peter, the anticipated readers are located in the churches of Pontus, Galatia, Cappadocia, Asia, and Bithynia (1 Peter 1:1), and they are encouraged to persevere amid difficult circumstances, when persecution and hardship are a reality. Although they are characterized in thoroughly Jewish terms, it is probable that the readers are mainly Gentile by background. The author's key strategy for exhorting them in their time of trial is to press upon them the assurance that they possess full membership in the household of God, despite their origins in "darkness" rather than light (1 Peter 2:9–10). As those who have come to faith in Jesus and been baptized, they have received "new birth into a living hope" (1 Peter 1:3; cf. 1:23; 2:2–3), and they are heirs to all the glorious promises made to Israel.

The dating and authorship of the letter are disputed,[10] but what is quite clear is that the status and identity of Israel are claimed directly for the believers to whom the argument is addressed. As a product of Jewish Christianity, the letter reflects a kind of reconciliation of the earlier Petrine conception of the faith with the views championed by Paul. There is no emphasis on the keeping of the Law and little apparent interest in the earlier disputes about the terms upon which Jewish and Gentile believers might share fellowship together. There may not be the kind of extended appropriation of Jewish symbols that we find in the Epistle to the Hebrews, but in the light of Jesus, the symbolic order of Judaism is certainly assumed to apply to Gentiles as much as to Jews. Whether reflective of Peter's personal views or not, the letter shows that the tradition of Jewish faith in Jesus associated with Peter's name had come to endorse an authentically Jewish identity for those who did not live as Jews.

Though it expresses awareness of a previous letter written in Peter's name (2 Peter 3:1), 2 Peter is probably not by the same author as 1 Peter, and it is likely that it also originated in the church in Rome. Writing perhaps toward the end of the first century, its author draws significantly on the Epistle of Jude (Jude 4–18) and presents a polemical argument against false teachers in very similar terms (2 Peter 2:1–3:3). As in Jude, the intruders are seen as doomed to destruction, according to scriptural prophecies. Although there is nothing particularly Jewish about the dispute with the practitioners of error, the fact that the clearly Jewish polemic of Jude is employed so deliberately implies that the writer of

2 Peter considers true Christian belief to have taken over the inheritance of the Jewish faith.

Remembering Jesus

One of the most crucial developments to emerge from the late 60s onward as far as Christian identity was concerned was the writing down of traditions relating to the history of Jesus. The transmission of the gospel had taken place from the start in an oral culture, with low rates of literacy, where narratives were essentially "performed" by storytellers who would bring the character of their subject to life by improvising their accounts in different ways according to circumstance. The expansion of the Christian faith from its original Aramaic-speaking environment into predominantly Greek-language contexts, and the differing emphases of the missionary strategies deployed by Christian messengers, had lent various unique features to the traditions about Jesus. As a result, there was inevitably a range of stories told about Jesus's life and teachings amid the communities of believers scattered around the Mediterranean.

Many storytellers focused particularly on the details of Jesus's suffering and death; others were fond of quoting his sayings or telling of his amazing feats as a healer. There were certainly many common elements among the different traditions, but the overall impact of Jesus's ministry and achievements found expression in a diversity of forms. The believers' faith was a living thing, and their recollections of their Lord were naturally subject to differing emphases and fresh development as they told his story anew.

More than a generation had now passed since Jesus's resurrection, and his second coming, which had been so keenly awaited, had still not occurred. Outbreaks of persecution or harassment may have reminded Christians of the vulnerability of oral traditions and fueled a concern in some quarters to put more things down in writing in order to clarify those aspects of the Jesus tradition that really mattered and preserve them for the future. At least one continuous version of the story of Jesus's passion was already in circulation, having perhaps first emerged in the midst of the troubles under Herod Agrippa in the early 40s, when believers might naturally have linked their own peril with the fate of their Lord a dozen or so years earlier. One or two small collections of some of Jesus's sayings had probably also begun to evolve, distinct from the passion tradition and perhaps grounded in earlier memories of his Galilean ministry. From the late 60s or very early 70s onward, a number of authors began to write down more extensive versions of what Jesus had said and done, which combined aspects of both the passion narrative and the accounts of Jesus's teaching and healing. These versions represented only a limited selection from the traditions in existence, but their production reflected a strategic stage in the history of the Jesus movement.

The Gospels were written both to corroborate existing faith in Jesus and to persuade others to believe in him. Unlike modern biographies, they do not aspire to describe the whole of their subject's life in chronological sequence, nor do they try to analyze his psychology or probe the reasons why he acted and spoke as he did. This was not the style in which biographies were usually written in the Graeco-Roman world. The Gospels follow many of the conventions of ancient biography by presenting a carefully selected series of small snapshots of their subject, concentrating particularly on his own words and deeds as directly expressive of his character. Also, like a number of Graeco-Roman biographies and in keeping with existing traditions of narrating the story of Jesus's sufferings in particular, they devote a disproportionate amount of attention to the final stages of their hero's life. It was common to see the last days and death of the subject as reflecting his greatest achievement and revealing his true importance.

The Gospel portraits are built up out of short stories chosen, edited, and organized in a particular fashion in order to construct a specific impression of their central figure and his relationship to others. The authors employ a variety of techniques in order to achieve their results, from historical investigation and sifting of sources to literary and rhetorical devices designed to highlight features such as irony or patterns of symbolism and context. Many of their emphases naturally reflect the circumstances in which they wrote, as they sought to use strategies of language and social registers that were appropriate to some of their anticipated recipients. The theological as well as literary creativity of the writers testifies to their respective preoccupations with differing aspects of Jesus's character and their interest in relating these to the various circumstances of their intended readers.

At the same time, there is little evidence that these texts were designed only for particular communities. Despite what many scholars have assumed, there are good grounds for believing that the Gospels were intended to be circulated widely among churches in different locations and potentially to be relevant to all kinds of believers, not just to those in a few specific congregations. The names of the canonical Gospel writers are not given in the original documents but were ascribed to their texts in the second century. Although their styles varied, these authors saw themselves as the heralds of a common message that was ultimately valid for people everywhere.[11]

Almost certainly the first of the canonical Gospels to be written was the Gospel according to Mark. Written in unpolished style in ordinary *koine* or "vulgar" Greek, Mark's Gospel reveals an author who thought not in Greek but in Aramaic. Its narrative style is brisk and vivid, and its subject is a figure who speaks and acts with boldness and authority. Mark's Jesus shows a disregard for the kinds of ritual laws that many Jewish peasants found it difficult to observe—concerning ceremonial purity, dietary practice, and Sabbath observance—and he comes into inevitable conflict with the religious elite of his world. The status of Jesus is made clear in the opening verse of the Gospel: he is the Messiah and the Son of God (Mark 1:1). Although this identity is confirmed at his baptism, implicit in his miracles, and understood by the demons he confronts, it is repeatedly missed by every other character in the first half of the story.

The Jesus of Mark's Gospel maintains a curious element of secrecy about his own status, instructing those to whom his identity is revealed not to divulge their knowledge, and preferring to style himself with the somewhat enigmatic phrase "Son of Man," which variously hints at his identification with the lowly condition of humanity and at his perceived special status as a representative of divine agency. In the second half of the Gospel, from Mark 8:27 onward, the confession of Peter that Jesus is the Messiah leads into an extended account of Jesus's passion, climaxing in his death and resurrection. His sufferings are seen as inevitable, both as the fulfillment of Hebrew prophecy and as the offering of a perfect sacrifice that inaugurates the new covenant.

The Gospels by Matthew and Luke were probably written in conscious dependence on Mark's account, but they both contain quite distinctive emphases of their own, reflective of their authors' use of other material and their particular contexts and intentions.[12] Matthew's Gospel, written in better Greek than Mark's, presents a thoroughly Jewish Jesus but a different kind of figure from the outspoken village artisan depicted by Mark. Jesus's human genealogy is traced back to Abraham, as is Jesus's descent from the royal line of David (Matt. 1:1–17). He is seen in a variety of ways as a new Moses, a new teacher of Israel, and it is repeatedly emphasized that his ministry does not abolish but fulfills the Law and the Prophets (e.g., Matt. 5:17–20). His teaching, structured in five major blocks of material in Matthew 5–25, stresses the moral righteousness of the kingdom of heaven, and the sharpness of Jesus's demands for inner as opposed to outward conformity to God's standards brings him into increasing conflict with Israel's leaders, especially the scribes and the Pharisees, against whom there is some fierce polemic.

In Matthew's perspective, Jesus's death represents the ultimate rejection of his messianic identity by the power-blocs of contemporary Judaism, but his resurrection is the divine vindication of his claims. Jesus had prophesied that the temple would be destroyed (Matt. 23:38; 24: 1–2; cf. 26:61; 27:40), and this had now been fulfilled. Matthew's portrait depicts a Jesus who is the fulfillment of Jewish ideals, but the author's assumptions are firmly at odds with other competing conceptions of where Judaism should go in the aftermath of the temple's destruction, especially the views of the Pharisees and the rabbis. For Matthew, the temple was over; God was now present in transforming kingdom power in the risen Jesus, who promised to be with his people to the end of the age (Matt. 28:20).

The Gospel according to Luke is even more obviously in the style of an ancient classical work than is either Mark's or Matthew's version, and the author is careful to point out his concern to write "an orderly account" based upon faithful investigation of traditions (Luke 1:1–4). Luke's narrative is written with confidence and a fair degree of literary polish.[13] It proceeds quite slowly, with detailed descriptions of the context of Jesus's birth and his presentation as a child in the temple. Jesus is anointed with the Spirit of God to be a healer and teacher, a man of both prayer and action, who shows great compassion and care for the needy and the vulnerable. He challenges the social and religious conventions of his society, associating with undesirables, valuing women among his followers, censuring the rich for their selfishness, and blessing the poor as spiritually favored. The record of Jesus's ministry in Galilee concludes with his determination to go to Jerusalem (Luke 9:51), the holy city, which Luke sees as central to God's purposes.

Luke presents Jesus as a great Jewish prophet who must go to Jerusalem to suffer for his teaching and be rejected by his people (Luke 13:33). He is also Christ the king, who enters in triumph into David's royal city, yet he rides not on a charger but on a lowly colt: he is a *different kind* of king (Luke 19:28–44). The one who has affronted the sensibilities of his world dies a submissive victim, but his resurrection proves that his death was divinely ordained as a sacrifice, and his personal appearances to his disciples prior to his bodily ascension into heaven have confirmed that he is indeed the living Lord, who has promised to be with his people in power until the end of the age. As Jesus showed repeatedly in his ministry, his good news is not just for Jews but for the whole world. Luke's account of the spread of the faith to the Gentiles in the Acts of the Apostles takes up the further dimensions of what this means and forms a companion volume to his Gospel (Acts 1:1–2).

The three accounts ascribed to Mark, Matthew, and Luke thus all have their own distinguishing features. The study of the sources upon which they draw and of the particular techniques of editing and crafting deployed by the writers is a matter for specialists and occupies many biblical scholars over their entire lifetime. The individuality of the three versions is not to be downplayed, for each of them presents one particular image of Jesus's significance, aimed at inspiring and persuading in differing ways. In their varying styles, all three are highlighting vital aspects of Jesus's character, and their differing emphases remain as crucial for Christians today as they were in the first century. Whatever the distinctiveness of each of them, however, they can legitimately be described as "synoptic." That is to say, they present complementary perspectives on an essentially shared narrative, and their individual characteristics do not mean that they were intended only for isolated groups of believers with disparate experiences.

When we turn from the Synoptic Gospels to the Gospel according to John, written some years later, we seem to enter a strikingly different world. John's Gospel shares the same underlying story of a Jesus whose ministry brings him into conflict with the authorities, leading to betrayal, crucifixion, and resurrection, and some of the episodes and sayings ascribed to Jesus are similar to those in the Synoptics. John has a different chronology and geography, however. There are no parables or exorcisms, and Jesus talks directly and extensively about himself and his relationship to God rather than uttering concise sayings about the kingdom of God. Jesus is conscious of his identity as one sent by God, and the narrative of his mission is structured around a series of signs or miracles confirming this status and an account of his passion in which he first expounds his unique relationship to God to his disciples and then confirms it, in the face of betrayal, injustice, and unbelief, by going to his death and being raised again on the third day.

For all the differences between John and the Synoptics, the writer of John's Gospel was well aware of other versions of the Jesus story, and a good case can be made that he expected his readers to know Mark's portrait of Jesus in particular. This hints at how a document such as Mark's Gospel may have circulated among Christians in different circumstances within a few years of its production. John may be thought of as providing a kind of theological commentary upon an existing Gospel tradition, and thus as opening up a complementary set of perspectives on the significance of Jesus without simply repeating, as Matthew and Luke broadly do, the narrative sequences of Mark. To the reader (or hearer) of John, unlike many of the characters in his drama, who remain blind and in the dark, it is clear from the start who Jesus is: he is the eternally preexistent Son of God, the divine "Word" by whom everything has been made (John 1:1), who has "become flesh" and dwelt in the world (John 1:14) in order to make it possible for those who believe in him to know "the true light" (John 1:9) and to have "eternal life" (John 3:16) by virtue of his sacrifice on their behalf. This gift of salvation is the gift of life from above (John 3:3, 7) or life lived in the presence and power of God. Although only brought to final completion at "the last day" (John 6:39–40), it is also entered into directly in this present life, through faith (John 5:24).

Such a message, in John's account, provokes serious hostility from the Jews of Jesus's time, both in his ministry and in his passion. John's narrative can look bitter about Jewish rejection of Jesus, even though its central figure is himself strongly Jewish and the author is well aware of the state of Palestinian Judaism a generation earlier. All the same, in working out his synthesis of Jesus's significance, John paints a masterly theological interpretation of a Savior whose achievement is transformative for both Jews and Gentiles precisely because he is the unique Son of God made flesh.

The Partings of the Ways?

In their own ways, then, the Gospels, like the later New Testament Epistles, reveal just how preoccupied many Jewish Christian believers continued to be with the question of their relations with "old" Israel. As is true of all of the earliest Christian literature, in fact, such documents show that followers of Jesus were distinguished not so much by what they *denied* in Jewish tradition as by what they *asserted* about the fulfillment of that tradition's hopes in the person of Jesus and the implications that this fulfillment carried for Jews and Gentiles alike. The essential Jewishness of the Jesus movement continued to be widely emphasized, but the disciples of Jesus were increasingly bold in articulating their claims that Jewish expectations of the kingdom of God had been realized in the crucified and resurrected Messiah.

With the temple gone, the Jesus movement in Palestine probably enjoyed a period of growth. The relatives of Jesus continued to be energetic in itinerant evangelism in Galilee, and other converts were made in Judea. The leadership of a number of the communities of disciples both in Galilee and in Jerusalem came to display an almost dynastic character over subsequent generations, as those connected to Jesus by blood seem to have been recognized as especially suitable leaders by their fellow believers. The household of Jesus's brother Jude, particularly his two grandsons, would play very significant roles in later years. In time, the work of Jesus's wider family may well have affected not only Palestine but farther afield, perhaps as far as Mesopotamia, where the Jewish Diaspora had close links with its religious homeland.

The relatives of Jesus boldly claimed that their kinsman, who had been crucified in ignominy, an apparent failure, was the fulfillment of all their Jewish hopes. Such assertions were, of course, astonishing—but in their support, it could also be argued with some force that the very thing Jesus had plainly prophesied, the destruction of the temple, had indeed come true and that those who followed him were now the true servants of God, worshiping in spirit and waiting patiently for the final vindication that was guaranteed to come when their risen Lord arrived in his ultimate splendor, to be acknowledged by all. The growing preparedness of these believers to contend that the temple no longer mattered may well have appealed to many of their fellow Jews who were looking for a way to understand their religious plight in the aftermath of the war.

At the same time, as we have seen, the rabbinical traditions that were beginning to gain momentum elsewhere in Palestinian Judaism were showing greater signs of wanting to define the *true* Jewish faith over against deviant versions of it, and the consequence was more and more open hostility to the worshipers of Jesus. Quite possibly the rabbis saw the Nazarenes as their primary rivals in their quest to dominate the Judaism of Palestine, and it was not least for that reason that their antipathy toward the Christians' ways of being Jewish became increasingly fierce. The Nazarenes not only held unacceptable views about Jesus, they also showed no signs of wanting the temple to be rebuilt, and their differentness from much of the Judaism around them was looking more and more obvious.

In the last quarter of the first century, one of the prayers used in the liturgy of Jewish synagogues formally denounced "apostates" and appealed for their exclusion from the divine "Book of Life." At some stage, among those who came to be cursed as *minim*, "heretics," were *Notzrim*, "Nazarenes." Some such curses had probably existed for some time as tests of Jewish loyalty (see Acts 26:11; 1 Cor. 12:3; 16:22), their purpose being to strengthen the unity and purity of the *true* Jewish community by excluding false believers from the fellowship of the synagogue. The date of this particular *Birkat ha-minim*, or "benediction concerning the heretics,"[14] and the point at which the Nazarenes came to be mentioned specifically within it, are not at all clear, and all of the details surrounding the denunciation have been subject to a great deal of scholarly dispute. Nevertheless, the curse against Christians was almost certainly in use in some places before the end of the first century. Although it was targeted at holders of a range of different positions, its specific extension to the followers of Jesus[15] as transgressors of the bounds of normative Judaism was inevitably of some significance for Jewish-Christian relations. It is conceivable that John's Gospel was written in a context in which such attitudes were already prevalent, for John's readers are expected to understand what he means when his narrative alludes to people being put out of the synagogues for confessing Jesus as the Christ (John 9:22; 12:42; 16:2). There is certainly evidence that Christians were the objects of Jewish curses and active hostility by the middle of the second century.

From the Christian side, also, the rhetoric became more heated. A potent argument concerning faith in Jesus can be found in the *Epistle of Barnabas*, an Egyptian document from the turn of the first and second centuries, written in the name of the Barnabas who was Paul's companion. The work presents a strong polemic against the enduring significance of Judaism as such. Jesus is said to have fulfilled all God's covenant promises, and "the Jews" have repeatedly misunderstood the teachings of their own faith by interpreting the injunctions of the Law literally rather than spiritually. Christians alone have a right to claim the Hebrew heritage as their own: the sacrifices, the promises, the covenants—all looked on to Christ. All of these aspects of the Jewish Scriptures nevertheless require allegorical interpretation.[16] Even the temple never should have been taken literally as the physical place of God's presence: the *real* temple is the community of believers among whom God dwells.

Although the work advocates a spiritual interpretation of the Law, the author of the *Epistle of Barnabas* also urges moral endeavor, in case his readers should imagine that faith in Christ is a license to sin. The document closes with an adaptation of a Jewish catechism known as the "Two Ways," a copy of which was known to the Qumran community (see p. 44). It consists of a fundamentally Jewish series of ethical injunctions about right and wrong behavior (the way of righteousness and life versus the way of wickedness and death). The treatise thus evinces a curious mixture of anti-Jewish language and an ongoing desire to appropriate certain Jewish ethical ideals.

Of particular concern to *Barnabas* was the possibility that believers in Jesus might sympathize with the Jewish dream that the temple would be rebuilt. This remained the serious hope of most Jews, and the same curse pronounced against the heretics contained a prayer that "the insolent kingdom," namely Rome, soon would be "uprooted." When Simon ben Kosiba emerged as the leader of a guerilla rebellion in Palestine in 132, many Jews hailed him as a messianic figure and called him Bar Kochva, "son of the star" (see Num. 24:17), following the example shown by the leading rabbi, Akiba, who seemed convinced that Simon was God's anointed one. As in the earlier Jewish war, events initially favored the rebels, and Bar Kochva was able to wrest control from the Romans and establish his own regime in Judea. There appeared to be a serious prospect that the temple would indeed be rebuilt, in accordance with the key intentions of Bar Kochva.

As in the 60s, Jewish Christians were again reluctant to get involved in armed resistance, and they naturally refused to acknowledge Bar Kochva's messianic status. They were also wholly unwilling to participate in a plan to reconstruct the temple. Their opposition to the restoration project threw into sharp relief the differences between them and most Jews around them, and they were severely punished as traitors to the Jewish faith and driven out of Jerusalem.

Bar Kochva's revolt was put down by Rome after three years, at the cost of heavy losses on both sides, and his plan to reconstruct the temple remained unfulfilled. Jerusalem was rebuilt as a Hellenistic Roman colony and was renamed Aelia Capitolina, after the family name of the emperor Hadrian, Publius Aelius Hadrianus, and the god Jupiter, whose temple stood on the Capitoline in Rome; a shrine to Jupiter was dedicated on the site of the former temple. The city was to be an entirely Gentile place into which, officially, no Jew was permitted to enter. The Roman territory of Judea was renamed Syria Palaestina—it was now formally (for the first time, in fact) "Palestine," named after the Philistines, not the Jews. Hadrian ordered fierce reprisals against the inhabitants of Judea, destroying hundreds of settlements and slaughtering very large numbers of people—the worst atrocities ever committed against the Jews in the Roman world. In the emergency situation, the rabbis were even obliged to concede that Jews were temporarily exonerated when they were forced to break the Law, except in cases of idolatry or fornication. Rabbi Akiba was martyred. The practice of Jewish spiritual life was placed under severe strain, and there began a further shift of Jewish intellectual activity farther to the north and to the east, with new schools emerging especially in Babylonia.

The nonparticipation of the Christians in Bar Kochva's revolt and the persecution of the followers of Jesus as apostates probably sealed the fate of the Christians' cause as far as Palestinian Judaism was concerned. The consequences of the war were painful for both sides. Jews had to suffer the desecration of their holy city, the proscription of their sacred rituals, and the death of their hopes for the temple, and Christians had to endure harassment, dispersion, and the knowledge that shrines to Jupiter and Venus were erected on the reputed sites of Jesus's crucifixion and burial. Some Christians were doubtless killed by Roman forces because in the eyes of the agents of Hadrian there would have been little difference between Christian and non-Christian Jews.

Hadrian's policies did not survive the end of his regime in 138, but the long-term implications of the Bar Kochva uprising saw the hardening of the distinctions between Jews and Christians, both of whom increasingly concentrated on the business of defining their respective faiths in an environment in which the apocalyptic expectations of the first and early second centuries were ever more muted. For Jews, deliverance from Rome showed no signs of happening in the foreseeable future, and the temple was not going to be rebuilt any time soon. For Christians, Jesus's return in triumph to usher in the final appearance of God's kingdom had still not taken place, and the faith was increasingly differentiated from its original context. Jews might look to rabbinic scholarship to provide theological guidance in such times; what were Christians to do?

Christian Self-Definition: Views of Judaism

The shape of Christian self-definition in the early second century was determined not only by events in Palestine but by the growth of the faith elsewhere. By the end of the first century, Christianity had reached at least forty or fifty of the Roman Empire's cities. Most were in Asia Minor, but other centers that the gospel had reached ranged from Rome in the west to Syria in the east, from Macedonia in the north to Libya in the south.[17] In all of these places, at least a significant number—and in many cases a majority—of Christian converts were of Gentile background, whether they had come from a pagan religious context or from the periphery of Judaism.

Jewish converts undoubtedly continued to be made, and probably in larger numbers than some historians have been prepared to acknowledge, but they were generally converts from the Hellenized Judaism of the Diaspora, which was, in all its diversity, a somewhat different entity from the Judaism of Palestine, whatever their common convictions. Although there were significant Jewish revolts against Rome in various regions in the period 115 to 117, particularly in Egypt, Cyrenaica, and Cyprus, these were fueled as much by socioeconomic factors as by messianic hopes. The Jews of the Diaspora took almost no part in the wars in Palestine in 66 to 73 or 132 to 135, and they were minimally affected by their political consequences, though the fall of the temple was obviously a serious blow in psychological terms. Many of the Diaspora Jews who became Christians came out of a more flexible faith than their coreligionists in Palestine and were less firmly wedded to the maintenance of Jewish traditions, particularly in the company of Gentile brothers and sisters. With all the diversity that undoubtedly existed among the Christian churches, Christianity overall was becoming a less Jewish movement.

This certainly did not mean that the Jewish inheritance ceased to be of crucial importance to the self-understanding of Christians. On the whole, Christians continued to embrace the Jewish Scriptures with enthusiasm and to argue that their faith was the fulfillment of the prophecies of Hebrew tradition. Arguments from prophecy continued to be at least as important in the second century and beyond as they had been in the apostolic period and in the writing of the Gospels; Jewish Scripture was avidly searched for proof-texts concerning Jesus's status, sufferings, and significance.[18] However, other aspects of Christian reasoning, such as the in-house debates that a generation earlier had concentrated on the relevance of circumcision and the status of the Law in the light of Christ, now took a different turn, and there was a greater readiness to paint Jews as persistent dwellers in error, stubbornly refusing to recognize the plain truth concerning the Messiah whose identity was foreshadowed in their own holy texts.

What we see from documents such as the *Epistle of Barnabas* is a growing willingness to repudiate not only the mistakes but even the continuing place of Judaism as such. The literature of the first century had, in all its variety, argued for the fulfillment of Jewish expectations in Jesus while remaining fundamentally Jewish in its orientation; now it was increasingly being argued that Jewish faith had quite simply been superseded in its conventional forms. If the Scriptures had been fulfilled and God had indeed acted decisively in Jesus, what possible reason could there be for remaining Jewish at all, other than willful spiritual blindness? Or—more ominously still—was it the case that God had rejected the Jews and that they were to be cut off from the inheritance to which they aspired? The early second-century self-defining of Christianity took place in part amid a strengthening vilification of Judaism that would have appalled earlier leaders of the Jesus movement. Within a few years, the seeds would be sown that would develop into the shocking traditions of Christian anti-Semitism, in which the Jews would be blamed directly for the crucifixion of the Messiah and regarded as apostates upon whom God's judgment had justly fallen.

Yet alongside all of this there remained in parts of the East significant groups of believers in Jesus who continued to prize their Jewishness highly. They were resistant to arguments that this aspect of their faith was to be seen as a spiritual heritage only, rather than as an enduring badge of moral identity. These proudly Jewish Christians traced their roots to the Jerusalem church, where their forebears were undoubtedly among those who had been most antagonistic to Paul's views on the acceptance of the Gentiles. However, they had come to be located farther to the east and the north, in Transjordan and in Syria (where they existed as late as the seventh century; they also came to be found in Egypt). Some derived from the migration of Jerusalem believers to Pella and elsewhere in the context of the first Jewish war; others probably came from the ranks of Judean Nazarenes who were displaced from their native area during subsequent periods of persecution, especially Hadrian's exclusion of Jews from Aelia Capitolina.

Much of what we know about these Jewish Christians comes from their opponents, fellow believers who regarded their ideas as mistaken or heretical, and so it is not easy to build up a clear picture of their identity. They were certainly quite diverse in nature, and the labels that we have for them tend to oversimplify the complexities of their distinctive characteristics. According to conventional ways of classifying these Jewish Christians, the best-known grouping are those called the "Ebionites," whose name, apparently a self-designation, means in Hebrew "the poor" (*ebionim*), a label also used at Qumran. According to their critics, the Ebionites adhered strictly to the demands of the Jewish Law, including circumcision, and rejected the authority of Paul. They avoided contact with Gentiles and practiced various forms of self-denial, including abstention from eating meat. They are also said to have believed that Jesus was a great prophet but not the divinely preexistent Son of God. Jesus was the natural son of Mary and Joseph (reference to his virginal conception was absent from the Ebionite gospel), and the divine Spirit descended upon him at his baptism and left him just before he died. Not surprisingly, it was for such views of Jesus that the Ebionites incurred most censure, and they were condemned as heretics by a number of later Christian writers.

Other Jewish believers were regarded less critically. The name "Nazarenes," which had traditionally been used as the most common designation for all followers of Jesus, came to be applied in particular to a group of Jewish Christians who resembled the Ebionites in their view of the Law but held a much higher view of Jesus, regarding the Messiah as divine, not just human, in origin. These Nazarenes also differed from the Ebionites in accepting the validity of Paul's message and the Gentile mission. All that marked them out as belligerently Jewish was, in the end, their strict attachment to the Law. Others may have belonged somewhere in between the Ebionites and the Nazarenes, cherishing the Law and acknowledging mission to the Gentiles but refusing to accept the teaching of Paul. Some who professed strong loyalty to the legacy of James the brother of Jesus (certain scholars go so far as to label them "Jacobites") may have existed in approximately such a category.

Such broad characterizations of Jewish Christianity are questionable, however, for we cannot be sure where the boundary lines lay between one group and another, nor can we confidently posit the historical sequences within which the various strands developed. Certainly there were some shared influences and preoccupations between them, and the literary evidence points to some common assumptions about the story of Jesus, if not about his status. The *Gospel of the Nazarenes* was an Aramaic version of the story of Jesus, bearing some resemblance to the Gospel according to Matthew, which is said to have been of particular importance to the Ebionites. The *Gospel of the Ebionites* was evidently a Greek composite or harmony of our three Synoptic Gospels, although it is only known to us from fourth-century quotations by a Christian leader who regarded the Ebionites as heretics, Epiphanius, bishop of Salamis in Cyprus (ca. 315–403). Another Greek gospel, known as the *Gospel according to the Hebrews*, was in use among Jewish Christians in Egypt in the fourth century. It is possible that all three of these documents represented variants on a single Jewish version of the gospel favored by the second-century groups. The Ebionites took a lower view of Jesus's person than did the Nazarenes and others, but all of these Jewish believers preserved some traditions about what Jesus said and did that were partly independent of those that were included among the Gospels accepted as canonical, not least the most obviously Jewish one among them, the Gospel according to Matthew.

In various ways, many of these people saw themselves, quite reasonably, as preserving some of the core traditions of the faith as it had begun in Jerusalem. In imaginative accounts such as those found in the *Ascents of James*, Jewish Christians eulogized the first leaders of the Jerusalem community and aimed thinly veiled criticism at the Pauline perspective on the observance of the Law. In a work entitled *The Preaching of Peter*, which probably reflects Ebionite influences, the evangelistic activity of Peter is opposed by a figure depicted as the sorcerer Simon Magus of Acts 8:9–25 but clearly intended to be seen as an alter ego for Paul. The Nazarenes may have been prepared to recognize Paul, but for some Jewish Christians, Paul's attitude to the Law remained seriously questionable long after his death. The tensions that had existed since the 40s and 50s had not gone away, even in the light of significant Gentile conversions and amid the altered world of Judaism after the destruction of the temple.

In the second-century context, however, the prospects for believers who maintained such a faithful adherence to the Law of Moses were looking less and less bright. Both Jews and Christians were increasingly determined to define themselves as mutually distinct and to circumscribe their respective positions according to certain criteria of acceptable and unacceptable teaching. In the process, resolutely Jewish Christians, who saw the traditions of the Jewish faith not just as a symbolic legacy to be appropriated but as a perpetual obligation in practical terms, found themselves squeezed between the two and regarded more and more as deviants by the emerging consensus positions within both Judaism and Christianity. As one later Christian writer, Jerome, would put it, such individuals wanted to be both Jews and Christians, and in the end, they were able to be neither.[19] The reasons for their exclusion on the Christian side lay in the cluster of factors that went into the pinning down of an official, normative version of the faith in the communities of the second century.

6

A CATHOLIC CHURCH?

▼

The thickening of the boundary line between Christianity and Judaism was part of a process toward the formal identification of a certain fund of beliefs, values, and practices as the common inheritance of Christian people everywhere. On the face of it the obstacles to such a process were not inconsiderable, for as the debates over the relevance of Jewish symbols testified, there were obvious differences of opinion and practice among those who followed Jesus. Some had received the gospel in more Jewish garb than others; some had been reached by missionaries concerned to locate Jesus firmly within a biblical matrix; others had been won over by appeals to wider intellectual and moral categories. Quite apart from differences of conscience over the practical entailments of their faith, Christians in distinct cultural situations inevitably had their own particular ways of doing things in accordance with local customs and various ways of thinking and traditions brought with them from their former lives.

Early Christian Diversity

Tracing the processes by which traditions had evolved in all of these different contexts is a virtually impossible task. Apart from our evidence regarding Paul, Peter, John, and James the Lord's brother, and some glimpses of the vitally important work undertaken by other relatives of Jesus in Palestine and perhaps beyond, we know relatively little about the ways in which the apostles and their associates spread their message to their diverse constituencies, or even about the places they eventually reached. Peter and Paul are both securely connected in their latter days with Rome, and John went at some stage to Asia Minor, where he came to be associated with Ephesus and its surrounding area. For the most part, however, we cannot be sure where the apostles and their co-workers finally traveled.

The apocryphal *Acts* of the apostles, produced in the late second and third centuries, claim that various remarkable missionary feats were accomplished by others among the Twelve. Thomas is said to have taken the gospel to Persia and to India, where he was eventually martyred for his faith.[1] Andrew is reported to have engaged in evangelism in northern Asia Minor and Greece, especially in some of the territories evangelized by Paul, including Philippi and Corinth, and to have been martyred in Patras.

It is impossible to gauge the reliability of these claims. To this day, the Syrian Christians of Malabar consider Thomas to be the founder of the church in southwestern India, but the tradition is only possible rather than certain. Later legends connect Andrew not only with Greece but with southern Russia, and his relics are said to have been widely dispersed, allegedly traveling as far as Scotland, where he eventually became the nation's patron saint. The apostle James was also said to have preached in Spain. Many of these traditions are, however, simply pious fictions, designed to embellish the spiritual sanctity of particular localities.

What we can say is that the apostolic period witnessed the spread of Christianity in places as diverse as Syria and Italy and in cities as far apart culturally as Jerusalem and Rome. Diaspora Jews from Egypt, Libya, and Arabia had witnessed the outpouring of the Holy Spirit on the day of Pentecost, according to Acts 2:9–11, and Philip was instrumental in the conversion of an official from Ethiopia on the upper Nile (Acts 8:26–39). Assuming that the message had been spread in turn by these and other converts, varying types of African influences were also part of the Christian blend by the end of the first generation.[2] The churches that the apostles or their followers founded reflected a wide variety of circumstances and range of ways of thinking and operating.

It is regrettable that most of our historical sources focus primarily on the growth of the churches in the Graeco-Roman world and do not pay much attention to the many expressions of Christianity that also evolved in other regions. By the later second century, churches were flourishing not only around the territories of the Mediterranean but also much farther to the east, in Edessa (modern Urfa in southeastern Turkey) and in Persia (modern Iraq and Iran). These places inherited very different cultures from the Hellenized cities of Asia Minor or Europe.

In Edessa, the capital of the kingdom of Osrhoene, the primary language was not Greek but Syriac, an Eastern version of Aramaic. Legend has it that the church in Edessa was founded by Addai, who was said to have been one of the seventy (or seventy-two) disciples of Jesus mentioned in Luke 10:1.[3] He was also said to have been sent by the apostle Thomas to heal the Edessene King Abgar V (4 B.C.–A.D. 7, and A.D. 13–50) and preach the gospel to his people, in fulfillment of a promise made in a letter to Abgar by Jesus himself. Such stories were constructed in later centuries, partly in order to claim a venerable legacy for the orthodox faith in a region where there were many rival versions. In reality, we do not know when the church in Edessa began. What we do know is that from the second century onward, Edessa had begun to evolve its own distinctive traditions of liturgy, scriptural exegesis, and theology, and its energetic missionaries had begun to travel all over the East and as far to the north as Armenia and Georgia.

Another important center was Nisibis, an ancient city of great strategic significance farther still to the east, at the interface of the Roman and Persian cultures. Such Syro-Mesopotamian Christianity was a great deal more Eastern in flavor than that of any of the churches on the Mediterranean seaboard, and its rich traditions of literature and spirituality have too often been overlooked in the writing of histories that see the story of the church as essentially a European affair. In the West, too, Roman North Africa was not Italy, and Central Gaul (France) was not southern Spain. The diversity represented by all of these evolving communities was considerable.

But Also Unity

Nevertheless, there is plenty of evidence that there was already within the apostolic churches a strong impetus toward a broad form of unity.

This unity was fostered by the degree of communication that existed between believers in different locations. We should not think of the first generations of Christians as existing only in localized communities, isolated from one another. For all the scattered nature of the churches, a very large number of believers in apostolic times lived no more than a week or so's travel from one of the main hubs of the Christian movement: Jerusalem, Antioch, Rome, Ephesus, Corinth, or Philippi. Communities received regular visits from itinerant teachers and leaders, from believers traveling in connection with work or leisure, or from those who had been uprooted because of political circumstances. Travelers inevitably brought news, letters, and other communications (such as Gospels) with them (as well as practical items such as gifts of money), and there were widespread exchanges of ideas and experiences.

New Testament literature contains plenty of exhortations about the responsibilities of extending due Christian hospitality to visitors (e.g., Rom. 12:13; 1 Tim. 5:10; Titus 1:8; Heb. 13:2; 1 Peter 4:9),[4] and it was expected that servants of the gospel would receive lodgings and support from those in a position to offer them (e.g., Rom. 15:23–24; 16:1–2; 1 Cor. 16:6–7, 11; Philem. 22). Similar principles are to be found widely in second-century and later texts.

Believers in one place might receive investigatory or disciplinary visits from leaders in another, as was the case at Antioch in Galatians 2:11–13 or with Paul's "painful visit" to Corinth referred to in 2 Corinthians 2:1. They might also request clarification of doctrinal matters or solicit prayer from their brothers and sisters elsewhere. So far from being entirely enclosed in their own contexts, a large proportion of the Christians of the first century may well have formed a much more integrated and cohesive social network than we imagine and kept in quite close touch with each other's developments, ideas, and practices.

This unity was focused upon the essentials of belief in Jesus as the one who had died for sins and been raised to life, which was expressed in the shared practices of baptism, thanksgiving, and fellowship. The disputes between Paul and his fellow Jews were regarded, at least by Paul (and doubtless no less so by his questioners), as being about the heart of a clear and unambiguous gospel (Gal. 1:6–9). As we have seen, Paul did not hesitate to say sharp things against those whose doctrinal or ethical tendencies he regarded as violating the logic of that message, whether they were in Galatia, Corinth, or Colossae. By the later New Testament period, we find numerous warnings against false teaching and false teachers, who had departed from the bounds of what had been handed down. Those who would instruct faithfully must resist such influences and inoculate others against them (e.g., Acts 20:28–31; 1 Tim. 1:3–7, 18–20; 4:1–5; 6:3–5; 2 Tim. 1:13–14; 2:14–19; 4:1–5; Titus 1:9–16; 2:1; 3:9–11; 2 Peter 2:1–22; 1 John 2:18–27; 4:1–6; 2 John 7–11; 3 John 9–10; Jude 3–22).

Orthodoxy and Heresy

What did it mean in this context to designate someone a "false teacher" or, in the language that would become more familiar, a "heretic"? The term *heresy* comes from the Greek *hairesis,* meaning originally a "choice," and so a "party," "sect," or "school" as a "chosen" position or lifestyle. The word appears in Acts to describe the parties of the Pharisees (Acts 15:5; 26:5) and the Sadducees (Acts 5:17), and it is also used of the Nazarenes or Christians themselves (Acts 24:5, 14; 28:22). Formally, it is a neutral term in these contexts, but a pejorative tone is not too far away (see especially Acts 24:14), and the description could also refer to a schism or faction within a group of Christians (1 Cor. 11:19; Gal. 5:20). By the later New Testament period the word was clearly associated with a deviant position, or the adoption of a view or way of life that differed from what the person using the word considered to be acceptable. In the Pastoral Epistles, one who has adopted such a stance, a *haeretikos,* is to be warned twice about the error of his ways, and if he does not heed these warnings, he is to be shunned as "warped and sinful; . . . self-condemned" (Titus 3:10–11). In 2 Peter, the false teachers are those who will "secretly introduce destructive heresies . . . bringing destruction on themselves" (2 Peter 2:1).

On the basis of such evidence, it would seem logical to assume that the first heretics in this negative sense were people who dissented from an existing position of orthodoxy and that they were clearly perceived to be departing from an established expression of belief. In the twentieth century, this picture was seriously challenged. In the 1930s, the German historian Walter Bauer argued that, at its origins, Christianity was in fact widely variegated and embraced many different styles of belief.[5] For Bauer, and the many interpreters who have been influenced by his analysis, it is *heresy* that comes first rather than *orthodoxy. Orthodoxy,* as we think of it, was the imposition of a narrower spectrum of belief upon what was hitherto a richly diverse range of perspectives, in order to solidify or protect one dominant position.

The triumph of orthodoxy, Bauer suggests, was as much as anything a triumph of power—the victory of some people in leadership positions over others who proved less able to command support for their views. The denunciation of "heresy" involved the deliberate exaggeration of the opinions held by the losers in this political struggle. According to Bauer, it was in the end the church of Rome, from an early date the most powerful among the major Christian communities, that sought to eradicate the diversity of earlier values, lifestyles, and ideas in the interests of a homogeneity reflective of its own control over other churches.[6]

Bauer's thesis is subject to a number of weaknesses. For one thing, it fails to consider the wide diversity of opinion with which the church of Rome itself was affected in the first two centuries and beyond, and the degree to which political cohesion in the Roman Christian communities actually evolved quite slowly. For another, it does not pay sufficient attention to the potency of Jewish Christianity and to the early significance of the Jerusalem church in particular in the delineating of a line of "authorized" belief and practice. In addition, it exaggerates the extent to which any believers were in a position to repress their peers during the period in question, given that Christianity in its entirety remained a technically illegal movement.

Above all, however, Bauer's theory overlooks the degree to which there clearly was from the beginning a certain set of convictions about Jesus that bound a majority of believers together, and it underestimates the intrinsic impetus that existed within these convictions to work out the logical parameters within which the gospel and its advocates could be said to exist. The process of discerning truth and falsehood that evolved in the late first and second centuries was implicitly grounded in the attempts by the first followers of Jesus to think through the consequences of their newfound faith with regard to personal salvation and practical living.

Nevertheless, there is an important lesson to be learned from the argument that early belief was in fact quite elaborately stratified and that the classifying of *orthodoxy* and *heresy* was complex both theologically and sociologically. Christians who hold to the importance of tradition in some sense and believe that the emergence of the churches' thinking was a process in which God as well as human beings were involved cannot accept the idea that the success of orthodoxy was *simply* the political triumph of the weak over the strong or a regrettable flattening out of divergent opinions in an otherwise delightfully plural world. All the same, it is important to remember that dissent and radicalism in one form or another lie at the heart of Christianity's origins. The pressures that in the end led to the Christian break with Judaism were themselves generated by those who challenged inherited assumptions in the light of their experience of Jesus. If the earliest years of the faith were anything to go by, ideas could not necessarily be rejected merely on the grounds that only a minority held to them, for the theology of Paul himself had begun as a minority position, and the final acceptance of his views was assured only by the success of his missionary activities.

Heresy in any context is never about attack entirely from the outside but about pressure from within and the contention from some internal quarter that existing patterns, while partly right, are inadequate or wrong as they stand. Dissent can sometimes foster renewal and reorientation, and at other times it ventures off on paths that prove to be unhelpful or dangerous. The decisions as to which internal challenges are, in the end, positive and which are negative are always bound up with political and social factors and the contingencies of circumstances and personalities. It was no less so in the early church. To recognize that fact is not to dismiss the role of providence in the overall shaping of the gospel's story.

Early Definitions of the Faith

The apostles themselves had set out some very clear guidelines as to the fundamental matters of the faith. Writing to the Corinthians, Paul summarized the gospel as follows:

> For what I received I passed on to you as of first importance [or "in the first place"]: that Christ died for our sins according to the Scriptures, that he was buried, that he was raised on the third day according to the Scriptures, and that he appeared to Peter, and then to the Twelve. After that, he appeared to more than five hundred of the brothers at the same time. . . . Then he appeared to James, then to all the apostles, and last of all he appeared to me also.
>
> 1 Corinthians 15:3–8

A number of things are immediately striking about this passage. First, Paul highlights certain elements of his message as primary, either in time or (more likely) in significance; there are particular aspects to the gospel that matter above all. Second, he emphasizes that he has transmitted a message that he himself inherited; his gospel is not something he personally invented but a narrative he has "passed on," a deposit entrusted to him that he in turn has entrusted to others. Third, at several points the message is stressed to be biblical: "Christ died for our sins" and "was raised on the third day *according to the Scriptures*" (emphasis added);

the account of Jesus's saving significance and his vindication by God is grounded in the sacred texts of the Jewish faith.

Paul's synopsis of the gospel's essentials is brief and to the point, and its stress on continuity and scriptural authority is clearly intended to highlight features that Paul regarded as vital. Paul does not see the theology of the gospel as something to be determined by the ingenuity of the individual reflecting imaginatively on his or her personal experience; it is about historic events that God has recorded in Scripture, confirmed in Christ, and passed on in a living tradition of shared faith. The strategy that Paul follows in these verses reflects a tendency replicated quite widely in the New Testament. In a number of other places we find certain vital elements of the faith described in a few succinct clauses, as in Romans 1:1–4. In beginning his Epistle to the Romans, Paul describes himself as one "set apart for the gospel of God":

the gospel . . . regarding his Son, who as to his human nature was a descendant of David, and who through the Spirit of holiness was declared with power to be the Son of God, by his resurrection from the dead: Jesus Christ our Lord.

In Romans 4:24–25, the scriptural account of Abraham's justification by faith (Gen. 15:6) was written also "for us who believe in him who raised Jesus our Lord from the dead. He was delivered over to death for our sins and was raised to life for our justification." Similar passages can be found in later writings as well:

Beyond all question, the mystery of godliness is great: He appeared in a body, was vindicated by the Spirit, was seen by angels, was preached among the nations, was believed on in the world, was taken up in glory.

1 Timothy 3:16

For Christ died for sins once for all, the righteous for the unrighteous, to bring you to God. He was put to death in the body but made alive by the Spirit, through whom also he went and preached to the spirits in prison . . . by the resurrection of Jesus Christ, who has gone into heaven and is at God's right hand—with angels, authorities, and powers in submission to him.

1 Peter 3:18–19, 21–22

In sketching the essential constituents of their foundational narrative, the early Christians were continuing a practice that lay at the heart of Judaism. If it is right, as some scholars have suggested, to see the elementary confessional claims of the early Christians as, in effect, very primitive "creeds," such expressions did not originate as tests of orthodoxy so much as summaries of belief—brief descriptions of who God is and what God has done. This, for the early followers of Jesus, was entirely traditional. Jews daily confessed their faith in the absolute uniqueness of their God in the words of Deuteronomy 6:4–9, known as the *Shema* (from the opening imperative verb, *hear*):

> Hear, O Israel: The LORD our God, the LORD is one. Love the LORD your God with all your heart and with all your soul and with all your strength. These commandments that I give you today are to be upon your hearts. Impress them on your children. Talk about them when you sit at home and when you walk along the road, when you lie down and when you get up. Tie them as symbols on your hands and bind them on your foreheads. Write them on the doorframes of your houses and on your gates.

Such affirmations became part of more elaborate liturgical recitations of a defining story concerning the salvation God had wrought for Israel, such as the one recorded in Deuteronomy 26:5–9:

> Then you shall declare before the LORD your God: "My father was a wandering Aramean, and he went down to Egypt with a few people and lived there and became a great nation, powerful and numerous. But the Egyptians mistreated us and made us suffer, putting us to hard labor. Then we cried out to the LORD, the God of our fathers, and the LORD heard our voice and saw our misery, toil and oppression. So the LORD brought us out of Egypt with a mighty hand and an outstretched arm, with great terror and with miraculous signs and wonders. He brought us to this place and gave us this land, a land flowing with milk and honey."

The articulation of such a narrative was—and remains to this day—a basic part of Jewish worship. The Christians of the first century were carrying on this convention by describing what, to their minds, the same God had done in Jesus.

When individuals were baptized into the name of the Lord Jesus and professed their allegiance to Christ, they were pledging their commitment to a new, foundational story, and the context for rehearsing the essential outlines of that story was in the first instance the process of Christian initiation. As people became Christians, they were reminded of the heart of the gospel to which they were committing themselves. In a world where a large proportion of converts were illiterate, the memorizing and oral recitation of the main points of the gospel was an essential way of learning and professing its rudiments. As the believers met together for worship and communion with their Lord and with one another, there too they recollected the basic truths regarding Jesus and the salvation God had wrought through him. Some of the earliest kinds of teaching to be deemed false were those that related to the status of Jesus; if people held wrong views about who he was and what had been accomplished in him, how then could they be part of this community that defined itself by naming him as Savior and Lord?

As the churches grew and the possibilities for confusion or misrepresentation of Jesus became ever greater, particularly through the assimilation of mistaken ideas and superstitions carried over by converts from paganism, it was quite natural that the details of the narrative or the length of the basic story told became more expansive as the apostolic faith was defined in contrast to other versions of the truth. The embryonic statements of faith in passages such as 1 Timothy 3:16 and 1 Peter 3:18–22 probably originated in circumstances in which false doctrine was an issue and where there was an increasing concern to specify what should and should not be said about Jesus. The same motivation that led to the writing down of the gospel traditions about Jesus also encouraged the expansion of the confessional details of the summaries used to describe the boundaries of truth.

We glimpse an example of the kinds of issues at stake when we read the Epistles of John, which are dated late in the first century. These documents are not all "Epistles" in an obvious sense: It is clear that 2 and 3 John are indeed brief letters, one addressed (probably) to a church, the other to an individual Christian named Gaius. But 1 John is better regarded as a tract or a homily, perhaps delivered to the same believers who are addressed in 2 John.[7] The context for all three is almost certainly Asia Minor, in or near Ephesus. Both 1 and 2 John contain strong criticism of certain people in this milieu who held that Jesus was not truly a flesh-and-blood human being but (apparently) a kind of purely spiritual being (1 John 4:1–3; 2 John 7). In countering such claims, the opening section of 1 John strongly emphasizes the physicality of Jesus as the Word made flesh, the one "we have looked at and our hands have touched" (1 John 1:1). The bodily reality of Jesus is seen as essential to his role as Savior, and the person who does not recognize this fact is described in 2 John as "the deceiver and the antichrist" (2 John 7). Comparable stress on the bodily nature of Jesus is to be found in John's Gospel, which asserts at the beginning that the Word "became flesh" (John 1:14), notes the reality of Jesus's susceptibility to physical needs (John 4:7; 19:28), and points out that when his side was pierced it yielded real "blood and water" (John 19:34).

The tendency to deny the reality of Jesus's physical humanity was not confined to the context in which the Johannine letters originated. Some kind of apparently similar (although not necessarily identical) problem seems to have affected other believers in Asia Minor in the early second century, and in this instance it evoked a response that directly appealed to a quasi-credal summary of the gospel's key truths. Ignatius, bishop of Antioch (see pp. 181–82, 203), speaks of the Savior as one who is "truly of the family of David with respect to his human descent . . . , truly born of a virgin, baptized by John in order to fulfil all righteousness, truly nailed in the flesh for us under Pontius Pilate and Herod the tetrarch."[8] In another letter he writes, "Turn a deaf ear whenever anyone speaks to you apart from Jesus Christ, who was of the family of David, who was the son of Mary, who was truly born, ate, and drank, was truly persecuted under Pontius Pilate, was truly crucified and died in the sight of beings heavenly, earthly, and under the earth, who also was truly raised from the dead when his Father raised him up."[9]

There can be no doubt about what Ignatius is endeavoring to achieve in these passages. He is pressing home what he regards as the essential truth of the gospel that Jesus lived an absolutely normal flesh-and-blood existence, and that his human nature was not, as some claimed, a mere phantom. He is arguing against the kind of people whose views would later come to be known, generically, as "Docetism," from the Greek verb *dokein*, "to seem"—to them, the Savior only *seemed* to be human.[10] Such wrong views of Jesus were fatal to the Christian story of salvation. If Jesus was not authentically human, he was not genuinely related to those he came to save, and his crucifixion was a sham rather than a real event.

Gnosticism

In a Gentile world in which popular religion was characterized by all kinds of ideas and superstitions about what the gods could and could not do and what the physical structures of the world did and did not represent, there were many reasons why people might assume notions about Jesus and salvation that were at odds with the convictions of his first followers. Nowhere were the influences of religious and philosophical syncretism in early Christian thinking demonstrated more obviously than in the loose assortment of movements conventionally known as "Gnosticism."

As an umbrella term for a variety of influences pertinent to the history of the churches in the early second century and beyond, the name *Gnosticism* is a relatively modern designation. It derives from the regular Greek word for knowledge, *gnosis*, and refers to the fact that those who were deemed Gnostics *(gnostikoi)* claimed to possess a special type of knowledge that was superior to the knowledge of others. The knowledge in question was a matter of salvation: those who had it were said to be saved; those without it were not. Gnostic views varied considerably, and in many respects the generic name *Gnosticism* to describe all of them is of only limited value; complex debates surround the scholarly classification of individual types of Gnostic teaching and their historical roots. We must also remember that not all of those who came to be regarded as Gnostics would have thought of themselves in accordance with the criteria of Gnosticism with which their critics (or their modern scholarly analysts) have tended to work.

Until modern times, almost all of what was known about the Gnostics came from evidence provided by their opponents, of whom there were many. But the late eighteenth, nineteenth, and twentieth centuries saw the discovery and publication of a number of original Gnostic texts, mostly in Coptic, a late version of the Egyptian language, and these have greatly added to our understanding of Gnostic teachings. The most significant finds were made in 1945 to 1946 when a priceless collection of twelve papyrus codices and fragments of a thirteenth were discovered at Nag Hammadi in Upper Egypt, where they had been deposited between the third and the fifth centuries. These documents, forty-eight in all, were mostly translated from Greek into Coptic.

Coptic is also the language of other important modern finds uncovered prior to the Nag Hammadi texts. One is the manuscript of the *Pistis Sophia* ("Faith-Wisdom"), which purports to record instruction given by Jesus to some of his disciples over a twelve-year period after his resurrection. Another is the so-called Berlin codex, discovered in 1896 (though not published until 1955), which contains, among other things, part of a gospel of Mary Magdalene. The Nag Hammadi material, however, belongs to an earlier phase of Gnosticism, and most of it was previously unknown. It includes the so-called *Gospel of Thomas*, claiming to be written by the apostle Thomas (not a historical narrative, but a collection of 114 sayings attributed to Jesus); the *Gospel of Philip*, a series of reflections on the quest for spiritual salvation; the *Gospel of Truth*, a synthesis of familiar and unfamiliar thinking on the mission of Jesus as dealing with the problem of human ignorance; and various other documents purporting to describe dialogues between the risen Jesus and his disciples.[11]

Gnostic ideas flourished in various parts of the eastern Mediterranean, particularly around Alexandria in Egypt and in Asia Minor, and they spread to Rome and other areas of the West, including Gaul, owing to the influence of a number of charismatic teachers, among them Basilides (fl. 125–50), Valentinus (fl. 130–65), and Heracleon (fl. 145–80), a pupil of Valentinus and the earliest known commentator on John's Gospel. These figures saw themselves as presenting true Gentile Christianity by relating the redemption achieved by Christ to the disclosure of a special saving knowledge. While Jewish influences are by no means absent from Gnostic traditions, the Gnostics' thinking also reveals affinities with pre-Christian religious and philosophical ideas from the Greek East and from Persia.

Some scholars have tried to argue that Gnostic beliefs not only predated early Christianity but influenced it, so that the theologies of divine redemption that we find in Paul and in John were allegedly shaped by Gnostic assumptions. This is certainly too simplistic. It is true that there were notions around in the first century that had superficial resemblances to Gnosticism. In Corinth, for example, Paul found himself contending against those who prided themselves on already possessing a superior wisdom or perfection (1 Cor. 1:10–4:21) that allowed them to treat the physical world as inferior—something to be either despised or, conversely, indulged in with abandon because of its intrinsic worthlessness.

Writing to the believers at Colossae, Paul challenges people who held that it was necessary to engage in the worship of heavenly beings such as angels (intermediaries between the spiritual and the physical) and that a strict asceticism was also essential (Col. 2:6–23). Against such distortions of the gospel, Paul insists that "all the treasures of wisdom and knowledge" are already to be found in Christ (Col. 2:3). Paul's perspective is that believers are set free from human regulations and from unspiritual preoccupation with special achievements in moral or intellectual terms. In Christ alone is true completeness to be found, and this completeness was already a present reality (Col. 2:9–10). In 1 Timothy, there is a scathing reference to those who peddled "opposing ideas of what is falsely called knowledge [*gnosis*]" (1 Tim. 6:20); their views are to be shunned as the hostile teachings of apostates. For all the perceived seriousness of such errors, though, there is no evidence that most of the first century witnessed the kind of developed views that we find among the major Gnostic thinkers of subsequent generations.

The Gnostic teaching of the second century and beyond was drawn from so many different sources that it is precarious to try to describe it in broad terms. There are, however, a number of common features that can serve to characterize the beliefs of the Gnostics as a general tradition of thought, albeit a very loose and factional one. Pervading all forms of Gnostic thinking was a strong dualism of the spiritual and the material, the good and the evil. The Gnostics believed in a doctrine of the fall, but for them this was a fall of the divine, spiritual element into the material realm. The material world was evil. It was the work not of the supreme, transcendent, good God but of a lesser being, a crafts-man or "demiurge" (after the deity of Plato's *Timaeus*), who was often identified with the God of Israel. The physical world was held captive by malevolent powers who lived in the planets.

As a result of the fall, particles or sparks of goodness had become imprisoned in the earthly bodies of certain "spiritual" individuals, who were destined for salvation. God's plan of salvation consisted in the sending of various redeemer figures (above all, in a Christian context, Jesus the Christ), to enlighten these privileged persons as to their heav-enly origins and their special destiny and to communicate to them the special *knowledge* that would enable them to take the appropriate measures finally to escape the corruption of the material world and be reunited with God. Without this redemption, the divine element remained forgetful of its heavenly home; it needed to be awakened in order to appreciate its true status.

The process of spiritual ascent was deemed to take a variety of forms. Most Gnostics believed that the material was escaped by some kind of asceticism, and they taught an abstinence from sexual activity and marriage as a way to subdue bodily appetites and concentrate the soul upon higher realities. Dietary frugality was also typically enjoined. Some, however, took the opposite approach and argued for physical indulgence and promiscuity, either as a way of demonstrating the ultimate irrel-evance of the body or as a putative means to a higher, spiritual union. For all of them, death represented (in strongly Platonist terms) the release of the soul from the prison of the body. Thereafter, the soul of the elect had to undertake a hazardous journey through the planetary regions, infested with hostile demons, in order to return to God. It was vital that the correct passwords and rituals were learned that would enable the soul to proceed safely past the obstacles that these spiritual forces represented.

The Gnostics proposed an unashamedly elitist system, with a special class of believers superior to all others. Their ideas made considerable inroads among educated Christians in the second century. The Gnostics were generally well aware of the Jewish Scriptures and sought to derive some of their basic doctrines from expositions of Genesis and the history of Israel. Such exegesis, however, was not intended to revere the God of the Hebrews but to portray him as either foolish or evil. Thus, for some Gnostics, the serpent in Genesis 3 was to be venerated, not reviled; in tempting Eve, the serpent was in fact imparting knowledge to which the maligned creator deity did not wish humans to have access. Those who regarded the serpent this way were known as "Ophites," from the Greek word for "snake," *ophis*. Others read the story of Israel's bondage and exile as a plot against the elect; the lesser deity, the God of Israel, was ignorantly or wickedly persecuting a secret remnant and disrupting their efforts to achieve knowledge.

The most influential forms of Gnosticism as far as Christianity was concerned were those of Valentinus and Basilides. Both were connected with Egypt, but Valentinus spent a significant part of his life in Rome, whereas Basilides (who may have been Syrian by birth) remained based in Alexandria. Both were deeply interested in the Christian Scriptures and sought to ground core aspects of their doctrine in exegesis of texts such as Matthew's Gospel and certain of Paul's Epistles. In the teaching of Valentinus, whose ideas were especially seminal,[12] Jesus was the Redeemer sent by the true God to enlighten the spiritual. Crucially, however, Jesus could not be seen as truly a flesh-and-blood human being, for if the material world was debased, there could be no purposeful incarnation of the good God within it. Jesus may have *looked* human to people without discernment, but in reality he was pure spirit. Highly elaborate schemes were proposed to explain how such a one was able to live an ostensibly human, temporal life.

Other forms of Gnosticism spoke of additional savior-figures besides Jesus, such as Seth, the third son of Adam, who was also said to have been a heavenly being (in some versions he appears to have been equated with the one who comes in Jesus), or the sorcerer Simon Magus (Acts 8:9–25), who pioneered an influential cult of his own under a Christian name in Samaria and perhaps in Rome in the first century. Simon also came to be regarded by many of the Gnostics' opponents as the original source of the Gnostics' errors, and he was accused of various outlandish crimes. In reality, the relationship between Simon and the second-century "Simonian" Gnostics is not very clear. In certain Greek texts (primarily pagan in background but also influenced by Judaism), the so-called "Hermetic" corpus, the principal bringer of salvation is said to have been the Greek god Hermes (the equivalent of the Egyptian Thoth, the father of all knowledge), and Jesus occupies a very minor role.

In Valentinian Gnosticism, those who were not elected to possess spiritual knowledge and full salvation were not entirely written off. Between them and the definitely hopeless "carnal" constituency—those who were mere earthly beings with no sense of anything beyond the physical sphere—lay a group of people of the *psyche*, "psychic" or "soulish" individuals (after 1 Cor. 15:44–46; cf. also, loosely, 1 Thess. 5:23). This middle group did not have knowledge, but they possessed faith and would therefore enjoy a certain limited form of salvation in a life to come. There was thus a clear hierarchy of humanity: the Gnostics at the top, ordinary/psychic believers in the middle, and the majority, the carnal heathen, at the bottom. The membership of all of these groups was believed to be predetermined by God from eternity.

The influence of Gnosticism was immense and raised enormous issues for the churches. If the ideas of the Gnostics were to be regarded as unacceptable or dangerous, on what grounds could this be established? It could only be done, it seemed, by recourse to the story of what was basic. But how precisely was that story to be defined? After all, many of those who spoke of "knowledge" and prized a higher path of spirituality also sought to ground their claims in the language of the Jewish Scriptures and in some of the familiar aspects of Jesus's teaching. Yet at the same time, they were denigrating the material world, which God had declared to be "very good" (Gen. 1:31), saying that the Son of God was a kind of docetic Savior who had not genuinely become incarnate, and setting up spiritual hierarchies among believers that were plainly at odds with the concepts of unity and fellowship advocated by leaders such as Paul. How were these notions to be tackled?

The Rule of Faith

The solution that emerged in the second century was that there was a certain line of teaching that was in harmony with the apostles' position, and the vital narrative of the faith was to be located with reference to that line. In the later second century, Irenaeus, bishop of Lyons in Gaul (ca. 140–200), appealed directly to tradition to summarize what he believed to be the true gospel. He spoke of the "rule of truth," "the tradition," "the preaching," or "the faith." Others, like Tertullian, a prominent teacher in the church in North Africa (ca. 160–225), would refer to a similar notion as "the rule of faith" (*regula fidei*, loosely evoking Paul's reference to a "rule" in Galatians 6:16) or the "Canon of truth."

The essence of all these ideas was that there was a particular fund of beliefs and values that had been faithfully transmitted by the apostles' preaching and writing and passed on in turn by those whose teaching was demonstrably in the same mold. All believers who were true to this consensus were part of the "catholic" (Greek, *katholikos*, "general" or "universal") Christian community, the fellowship of the body of Christ that transcended social, geographical, and temporal boundaries. Those who deviated from the consensus were not.[13]

While the specific pressures that elicited such arguments varied, Gnosticism was among the commonest targets of the polemic. In the mind of Irenaeus and others, what the rule firmly implied was that over against the vast diversity of Gnostic ideas stood the essential consistency of a mainstream Christian tradition, and over against the secrecy prized by Gnostic teachers stood the public, open practice of this Christian consensus—clear, unambiguous, and widely prevalent in the behavior of true believers everywhere. In one passage, Irenaeus puts it like this:

> Although the church is dispersed throughout the whole world, to the very ends of the earth, it has received from the apostles and their disciples this faith: in one God, the Father Almighty, who made the heaven and the earth and the seas and everything in them; and in one Christ Jesus, the Son of God, who was made flesh for our salvation; and in the Holy Spirit, who proclaimed through the prophets the times and the advents, and the birth from a virgin, and the passion, and the resurrection from the dead, and the bodily ascension into heaven of the beloved Son, Christ Jesus, our Lord, and his future appearing from heaven in the glory of the Father to sum up all things and to raise up anew all flesh of the whole human race.[14]

Irenaeus's emphases are plain. There is belief in one God, the Father, the Creator of all things, physical as much as spiritual; in one Jesus Christ, his Son, the Savior, who is genuinely incarnate; and in one Holy Spirit, the inspirer of the Hebrew prophets. Jesus is fully human as well as fully divine; the Son of God was genuinely "made flesh," and after his death and resurrection, he ascended "bodily" into heaven. His saving work is part of a divine plan that embraces the whole of reality. No wedge can be driven between God the Creator and God the Redeemer nor between the purposes of God in the old dispensation and the strategy of God in the new. Jesus is the fulfillment of the prophecies of the Jewish Scriptures; his ultimate saving purpose is to sum up all God's dealings with humanity (Eph. 1:10). Irenaeus goes on to say that the church has received this preaching and this faith, and it believes them as one, though it is widely scattered and multilingual. The rule that the apostles have bequeathed derives originally from the Lord himself, who sent them to preach, and all who adhere to this tradition, however diverse they may be, are his true disciples.

The rule was seen as a summary form of the gospel preached at the origins of the Jesus movement, and it served as a criterion by which to gauge the "Christianness" of an idea or practice that was alleged to be traditional. For Irenaeus, this standard was not a norm higher than or supplementary to the written form of this gospel in the apostolic literary legacy, but it was a kind of précis or set of catchphrases that epitomized the essentials of the biblical story. Others would speak of the rule in similar terms, including Hippolytus (ca. 170–236), Origen (ca. 185–254), and especially Tertullian. Tertullian extended the rationale of the rule somewhat so that it was taken to represent virtually a source of revelation in itself. The heretics could argue about the interpretation of biblical texts, but Tertullian believed they could not deny that the rule of faith represented a consensus way of interpreting them—and because this way was so widely shared and of such venerable lineage, it must be treated as divinely approved and thus, in effect, as offering divinely given insight in itself.

For all of these thinkers, though, the rule of faith was not a fixed creed with a verbal form that did not vary; it was a broad narrative pattern and a means by which to determine the soundness of beliefs and practices. On these terms, Gnosticism was plainly heretical, for while it maintained aspects of conventional thinking, it was also in clear tension with a number of the vital elements of the apostolic gospel. For all its obscurities, Gnosticism had served as a catalyst for creative thinking about the ways in which the heart of the faith was to be specified in the context of the second century and beyond.

Marcion

Another issue implicit in the debates with Gnosticism was the question of what it meant to appeal to certain texts as embodying particular religious authority. What was the relationship between the Scriptures of Judaism and the literary efforts of Christian writers, and on what grounds might some Christian writings be deemed preferable to others? These questions, too, were thought through in the midst of controversy.

Around the year 140, a man named Marcion arrived in the church of Rome. What we know of him comes largely from his numerous opponents, but we can be confident that he was a wealthy ship owner from Sinope in Pontus and that his views got him into serious trouble in Rome, for he was excommunicated by the church there around 144. Thereafter, he formed an alternative community of his own, whose ideas spread significantly around the Mediterranean world, reaching Egypt, Arabia, Syria, and Armenia, and in some areas enduring for several centuries. He died some time in the later 150s. Marcion was not a Gnostic, in the sense that he does not seem to have espoused the same kind of speculative beliefs about the origins of the world or about hierarchies of spiritual beings, but he did hold a number of views that were vaguely Gnostic in ethos, and it was alleged that he had been taught at Rome by a Gnostic teacher, Cerdo.

Marcion's views are set out in a work entitled *Antitheses*, in which he lists what he believed to be the contradictions between the Jewish Scriptures and Christian teaching. He posits a rigid distinction between the creator God of the Hebrew tradition and the savior God of Jesus. The former is essentially a vengeful and vindictive being; the latter is loving, gracious, and good. The Hebrew God, Marcion argues, is inferior to the God and Father of Jesus: he is responsible for a world that contains nasty creatures as well as pleasant ones; he demands sacrifices, orders the massacre of people groups, and is not consistent with himself, changing his mind over a number of things. The God revealed in Jesus, by contrast, is pure goodness and love, and he sent Jesus out of his compassion for a creation harassed and oppressed by its creator.

The creator God, according to Marcion, was deceived by Jesus and agreed to exchange the souls of all who were condemned by his Law in return for the life of Jesus. But Jesus could not be held in death and was raised to life. From this, the message of free forgiveness arose, which persuaded both Jews and Gentiles of the reality of grace. However, the creator God duped the apostles of this message into imagining that Jesus was in fact sent by him rather than by the loving God, and thus they confused the gospel of Jesus with the principles of the lesser God. The true gospel is not to be found everywhere in the Christian writings but only in selected texts, and above all in those by Marcion's real hero—Paul. Yet even Paul's letters, he felt, need to be purged of "Judaizing" elements, or aspects that relate to the creator God's purposes.

Marcion's teaching made a significant impact on many. It is easy to see how his message might have appealed to those who had sympathies with some form of Platonist philosophy, who tended to look on the material world as inherently inferior, or, more generally, to people who felt the moral demands of the Jewish Law were odd, or who found it hard to reconcile some of the Hebrew pictures of God's character and actions with the concept of a God of love and mercy. It was not that the Marcionite ethic itself was at all easy; Marcion's followers were called to renounce marriage, practice sexual abstinence, follow a spartan diet, and be prepared to die for their faith. Still, such stipulations exercised a certain pull for people who were perhaps disillusioned with the world and inclined to suppose that the realm of the spirit was necessarily better than the pleasures or challenges of the material order. Marcionite traditions were especially potent in Asia Minor and Syria. Beyond the frontiers of the Roman world, in the equivalent of modern Iraq and Iran, they were still very strong as late as the sixth century.

Christian Scripture

Marcion's real importance, however, lay not so much in the converts he attracted or the churches that his followers established but in the issues he raised about the status of sacred texts. It was he who compiled the first extant list of "approved" Christian Scriptures. It consisted of an abbreviated version of the Gospel according to Luke and ten letters of Paul, in the following sequence: Galatians, 1 and 2 Corinthians, Romans (minus some sections), 1 and 2 Thessalonians, Ephesians (called "Laodiceans" by Marcion), Colossians, Philippians, and Philemon. The Pastoral Epistles were not included.

Marcion's followers produced a number of prologues to some of the Pauline Epistles that purported to explain how the message of Paul had been corrupted by those who had sought to obscure his hostility to the Jewish God. Alleged evidences of such corruptions were deleted from Paul's writings. From Luke's Gospel, Marcion excised in particular the narrative of the birth and childhood of Jesus, in accordance with his apparent conviction that Jesus was separate from the physical processes of creation, and he pictured Jesus as appearing on earth as a fully grown man, arriving in the synagogue of Capernaum (Luke 4: 31). He also stripped away the stories of the resurrection as unworthy of Jesus's proper status as a spiritual being.

Around the time of Jesus, Palestinian Judaism had a working collection of sacred texts. These consisted, first and foremost, of the five books of "the Law" or Torah, followed by "the Prophets," which included the historical books, and finally, a group of miscellaneous texts known as "the Writings." There were debates as to which of the non-Torah material should be regarded as appropriate for reading in the synagogue and for private study, and, as the debates of the rabbis of Jamnia indicated, many were unconvinced about the status of works such as Esther and Song of Songs. Nevertheless, for the most part it was assumed that the threefold division of the Law, the Prophets, and the Writings constituted a body of authoritative books, of which the Law was the undisputed chief part. This was the Scripture from which Jesus had quoted, and which, according to John 10:35, he had said could not be broken.

Outside Palestine, and thus for the overwhelming majority of Jews, the Scriptures existed in the Greek of the Septuagint. The Septuagintal version embraced a somewhat larger range of books than the Palestinian collection, and the threefold division of the Law, the Prophets, and the Writings was abandoned. The Torah was regarded just as highly as it was in Palestine, but the non-Torah material included not only the Prophets and the Writings, as widely assumed in Palestine, but also additional books and parts of books, such as the Wisdom of Solomon, Ecclesiasticus, Judith, Tobit, Baruch, and 1 and 2 Maccabees (literature that Protestants would come to deem "apocryphal"). This Alexandrian collection served as "the Bible" for the great majority of early Christians, and it was from it that the apostles typically quoted in their writings. Sometimes its language lent important nuances to Christian interpretations of Jewish Scripture, as can be seen in passages such as Matthew 1:23, where the prophecy of Isaiah 7:14 about Immanuel's birth is quoted as foretelling birth specifically from a "virgin" (the word used in the Septuagint) rather than from a "young woman of marriageable age" (the sense of the term originally used in the Hebrew).

By the later first century, it can be assumed that most Christian communities outside Palestine had a working assemblage of the books of our Old Testament as well as the additional material (accorded equal status) in the Septuagint. For them, as for the majority of Jews outside Palestine, this would have been a generally accepted list of holy books. (Christians would later call it a "Canon," from the Greek *kanon*, originally a "rod" or a "measuring stick," and thus a touchstone of rightness or purity.) But what about specifically *Christian* texts? In the last quarter of the first century, the Christians not only possessed the Septuagint; they also had various numbers of occasional letters from apostles and other leaders and the first written versions of the stories about Jesus. Some communities of believers had doubtless acquired more of these texts than others, but most would have had some. Apostolic letters and the primary Gospels were widely copied, circulated, and discussed from one community to another. What was the status of these books to be alongside the Jewish Scriptures?

Paul's letters refer frequently to the Jewish sacred texts as *he graphe/ hai graphai*, "the writing(s)" or "the Scripture(s)," and it is clear that he believed they were marked by a divinely given authority. The importance of such material is expressed most famously in 2 Timothy 3:16, which, if not written by Paul, reflects a perspective that Paul would have endorsed: "All Scripture [*graphe*] is God-breathed and is useful for teaching, rebuking, correcting and training in righteousness." By the time of 2 Peter, the writings of Paul himself are described as being on a par with these same *graphai* or Scriptures. Evidently some kind of collection of Paul's letters was by then in circulation. Its contents are unclear, but the texts it included are said to contain "some things that are hard to understand, which ignorant and unstable people distort, as they do *the other Scriptures* [*graphai*], to their own destruction" (2 Peter 3:16, emphasis added). Paul's teaching is here implicitly equated with the authoritative Scriptures of the Jewish faith. By the time of *2 Clement*, a sermon perhaps dating from some time in the second quarter of the second century,[15] a saying of Jesus, "I have not come to call the righteous, but sinners" (Matt. 9:13; Mark 2:17; Luke 5:32), is quoted as *graphe*,[16] suggesting that a number of the gospel traditions were also already being regarded as classical or inspired in some sense akin to the Jewish Scriptures.

The challenges posed by false teaching intensified the conviction that certain Christian writings were to be regarded as especially authoritative. Ignatius, for example, expects his readers to be familiar with a body of Pauline texts that includes 1 Corinthians, Ephesians, Romans, Galatians, Philippians, Colossians, and 1 Thessalonians; of the Gospels, he at least knows Matthew and very probably Luke and John as well. While Ignatius does not formally cite these works, he alludes to them copiously, and he clearly regards their teaching as foundational in combating heresies. The same pattern can be seen in other second-century teachers. In the work of Justin Martyr (ca. 100–165), we learn that the Gospels were read alongside the Jewish Scriptures when Christians met to celebrate the Eucharist, and it is probably the case that Pauline and other apostolic letters had been read and discussed in similar worship settings since earliest times. This practical merging of the personal authority of the apostles with the authority of the Jewish Scriptures must have contributed heavily to the formal elevation of Christian writings to the same level of authority as the sacred *graphai*.

When Marcion rejected certain texts such as the Gospels according to Matthew, Mark, and John as unworthy to be included in his collection, he was therefore proposing an alternative to some fairly widely observed conventions. On the positive side, however, he was obliging Christians to think about why they regarded some texts as Scripture and not others. If Marcion was wrong, *on what points* was he wrong? On what grounds were some writings to be afforded normative status while others received some other ranking? As we might well expect, essentially the same kinds of criteria started to operate in this area as in the delineation of orthodoxy in other contexts. The extent to which texts could be claimed to reflect apostolic authority or mirror apostolic teaching was in the end to be decisive. This naturally meant that *new* writing was inherently less likely to be regarded as scriptural, for new writing, by definition, was not part of an established tradition of works used profitably by believers over a period of years. It also meant that texts that were already widely read and valued could not lightly be dismissed, for to dismiss them was to fly in the face of consensus Christian practice.

For teachers such as Irenaeus, the pattern of existing usage by most Christians was of axiomatic status. "It is not possible," Irenaeus writes, "that the gospels can be either more or fewer in number than they are, since there are four directions of the world in which we are, and four principal winds. . . . The four living creatures [Rev. 4:9] symbolize the four gospels . . . , and there were four principal covenants made with humanity, through Noah, Abraham, Moses, and Christ."[17]

Some time around 160, just a few years after Marcion's death, Justin Martyr's disciple Tatian produced a harmony of the Gospels of Matthew, Mark, and Luke with the Gospel of John. It was known as the *Diatessaron*, the harmony of "the four," or "the fourfold chord," and was widely used in Syriac-speaking churches until the fifth century as their standard version of the Gospels' story.

The Gnostics claimed that their "gospels" were of value, but most believers followed the tradition of four Gospels only.[18] The Gnostic gospels are useful for building up a picture of some of the different ideas that went under the name of "Christian" in the second century, and they demonstrate the ways in which certain teachers sought to connect their claims with established traditions regarding Jesus's words and actions. All the same, despite the sensational claims made about these gospels in some quarters of modern scholarship, they actually add little to our understanding of the course of early Christianity that is not fairly evident from other sources. For a very large proportion of believers in the mid- to late second century, the Gnostic gospels were nowhere near equivalent in authority to the fourfold tradition, and many of the texts uncovered at Nag Hammadi were already regarded as heretical by this time. The fact that no Gnostic gospel survives in anything other than fragments testifies to the reality that these documents never did possess the same popularity or acceptance.

In the late second century, we find the beginnings of attempts to compile lists of canonical texts over against the series produced by

Marcion. The earliest of these is the so-called "Muratorian" list. This document was probably first written at Rome, in Greek, around the year 190. It was discovered in the Ambrosian Library in Milan in 1740 by the Italian scholar Lodovico Antonio Muratori, after whom it has acquired its modern name. It is in fragmentary form, in a poor-quality Latin translation some eighty-five lines long, dating from the eighth century. It lists the Christian Scriptures as: the four Gospels, the Acts of the Apostles, thirteen letters of Paul (including the Pastorals), Jude, 1 and 2 John, the Wisdom of Solomon, the Revelation of John, and the *Apocalypse of Peter*, an early second-century work, though it is said that not all are willing that the last of these be read in church. The *Shepherd* of Hermas, a widely read book of revelations allegedly granted to a former slave in Rome in the form of visions, mandates, and similitudes, is said to have been produced very recently: it "ought indeed to be read, but it cannot be given out publicly to the people in church either among the prophets, whose number is complete, or among the apostles, for it is after [their] time."[19]

What the fragment thus seems to suggest is, broadly, a threefold classification of texts. First, there are definitely canonical works, which ought to be read in the churches. Second, there are works that are probably canonical but about which there is some dispute as to whether they should be read in church. And third, there are books that deserve to be read, but not as part of the church's worship. Over against all of these, the fragment refers to texts that are rejected because of their associations with false teachers, including the Gnostics Valentinus and Basilides.

Implicit in this categorization are a number of details that point to the criteria of canonicity, as these were assumed by the late second century. The most obvious among them was, as we might expect, apostolic authorship. Did a particular text claim to be the work of one of the apostles of Jesus? This was one of the critical tests applied to letters in particular: if Epistles claimed to be Pauline, then their claims were to be treated seriously. With regard to the Gospels, all four of the canonical documents were technically anonymous, but they were nonetheless associated with apostolic authority. In the case of Luke, the author was one of Paul's circle, and something of Paul's authority rubbed off on him. In Mark's case, a tradition as old as Papias, a Phrygian bishop of the early second century, maintained that he had written his Gospel in accordance with the recollections of Peter. Matthew and John were validated on more direct grounds as having been composed by the apostles in question, and John's Gospel was regarded as compatible with the accounts of the Synoptics.

With some documents, though, it was clear that evidence of apostolic authorship was insufficient of itself as a basis for establishing canonicity. Other tests were called for. As we have seen, the Muratorian fragment points to antiquity as one such criterion. The *Shepherd* of Hermas, however valuable, is said to have been produced too recently to be included among the apostles or the prophets. Furthermore, not all works that purported to be apostolic were genuine. The Marcionites, for example, had letters written under Paul's name to other churches, but these were not authentic, since (implicitly) they did not contain sound doctrine. Thus, the question of whether the substance of a text was consistent with a genuine and shared interpretation of apostolic wisdom became a vital supplementary concern. The fragment also mentions the issue of whether a document was to be read in public or in private; books acquired a certain status by being used widely in the context of shared worship. If they were not read in public, this did not necessarily indicate that they were dangerous or to be rejected, but it did lower their chances of being included as canonical.

When one or another of these criteria was pressed to the exclusion of the others, debates inevitably ensued. If purely apostolic authority were at issue, then the Epistle to the Hebrews, for example, was an uncertain candidate for inclusion in the Canon, for it was not clear who its author was—the Muratorian fragment omits any reference to it. If orthodoxy alone were the key, then should relatively recent documents—such as those that offered imaginative but doctrinally mainstream accounts of what the apostles had done—be included after all, as long as their content was sound? If some texts were regarded as of lesser value and not to be read in the churches, was there any point in associating them at all with canonical lists? Such questions continued to preoccupy Christian minds in the third and fourth centuries and beyond. Doubts persisted about the cases of Hebrews, Jude, 2 Peter, 2 and 3 John, and Revelation in particular. Discussion concerning the apocryphal literature of the Septuagintal Bible endured much longer, to the extent that to this day somewhat different positions are formally held about the status of these latter texts among Roman Catholics, Protestants, and Orthodox believers.

Nevertheless, by the late second and early third centuries there was a remarkable measure of consensus about a very large proportion of the Christian Canon, and from around the time of Tertullian onward it became standard in the West to refer to the "New Testament" as a collection of Christian sacred texts over against the books of the "old covenant" (2 Cor. 3:14) or "Old Testament" of the Hebrew tradition.

The earliest exact list of the twenty-seven books of our New Testament is found in a letter by the Alexandrian churchman Athanasius in 367, and by the end of the fourth century, the great majority of Christians had come to regard the New Testament collection we have inherited as canonical. Differences remained between the churches of the Greek East and the Latin West about the order in which particular books ought to be placed, but by the early fifth century, the Christian Canon was regarded by almost all believers as effectively closed. Its boundaries were little discussed again until the Reformation.

At one level, it might be said that Christians created their Canon, for the decisions as to which books were *in* and which were *out* were obviously made by Christian leaders over a period of time and in response to particular internal and external challenges. At another level, however, these believers would have claimed that they were simply recognizing an authority that had already come to be appreciated by a large number of Christians in widely differing situations. Rather than imposing legitimacy on a particular set of texts, they were, as they saw it, acknowledging and conserving the inspired authority that was already inherent in these works according to their origin, content, and proven usefulness over time.

Other Literature

Alongside the texts that would become most familiar as Scripture, there was plenty of other interesting spiritual literature around in the second and third centuries. There were, for example, "protogospels," or narratives that sought to narrate aspects of Jesus's life that received little attention in the accounts of the Synoptics, especially his birth and childhood. These works were not intended to rival or challenge the conventional gospel stories but to supplement them, partly to provide edifying reading for Christians and partly in response to Jewish polemic against Christian beliefs. One seminal work of this type was the *Protevangelium of James*, which claims to have been produced by James the brother of Jesus, describing the background of Mary as prelude to the birth of Jesus. Another was the *Infancy Gospel of Thomas*, which narrates a series of miracles allegedly performed by Jesus during his childhood, between the ages of five and twelve.

Other imaginative literature related not to Jesus but to the apostles. It was designed to serve as popular fiction, aimed at encouraging believers and attracting others to the faith by telling impressive stories of the amazing things that the apostles had accomplished. There were *Acts* written of the feats of apostles including John, Andrew, Peter, Paul, and Thomas. These accounts were indebted to the canonical Acts of the Apostles in a number of ways, but they tended to paint the miracles of their heroes in much more sensational colors, and to reflect a much sharper vision of asceticism, especially sexual abstinence, as an exemplary Christian virtue.

Church Ministry and Order

As we saw in chapter 4, the first century witnessed a gradual movement toward a more limited structure of church leadership, from the rather informal style that characterized the earliest communities to the prescriptions concerning elders and deacons that we encounter in the Pastoral Epistles. The literature from the end of the first and beginning of the second centuries testifies to a continuing fluidity in the ways in which church leaders were designated but also to a concern to validate a certain system of authority. The evolution of this system was also of major significance in the development of a tradition of orthodoxy.

The document traditionally known as *1 Clement* was apparently written by Clement, one of the leaders in the church of Rome, to the Christians in Corinth some time in the early 90s. The carefully constructed argument of *1 Clement* is that unity is vital in the church. At Corinth, it seems, there had been a dispute in which the elders of the church had been removed from office by younger people and replaced by other leaders. Writing in the name of the church at Rome, Clement produces biblical examples to argue that there needs to be mutual submission and charity within the body of Christ, and he contends that the risen Jesus established the principle of a divinely ordained ministry of presbyters or overseers (which remain equivalent terms) in his commission to the apostles.

There is thus, for Clement, a clear doctrine of apostolic succession: Jesus anointed the apostles, then they in turn appointed the first overseers and set out the rules within which they were to operate. The presbyters of Corinth, even if they were not directly appointed by the apostles, should be deemed to stand in authentic continuity with the apostles if they teach and preach according to apostolic principles. Those who had challenged the legitimacy of such leaders in the Corinthian community were guilty of resisting a tradition that stretched back to Jesus himself.

We have another fascinating glimpse of one form of early Christian order from roughly the same period as *1 Clement* in the compendium known as the *Didache*, or *Teaching of the Twelve Apostles*. This work was much revered in the early church, though it disappeared at some point and was unknown to modern scholarship until the 1870s. It dates to the late first or early second century, and its likeliest location is in the church in Syria. Its context is very clearly Jewish Christianity, though, as with much of the literature of this period, there is also an explicit concern to differentiate Christian and Jewish behavior. Its milieu is rather similar to that of the Gospel according to Matthew, written some years earlier, and there are several allusions to Matthew in the work. The text of the *Didache* is made up of a variety of different documents, and the version we have has evidently gone through some considerable editing and alterations. For all its unevenness, though, it represents a handbook of a church order that is of great significance to our understanding of how at least some Christians were worshiping and behaving (or being exhorted to behave) at this period.

After opening with a contrast between the "Two Ways," the fundamentally Jewish series of ethical injunctions about right and wrong behavior that we also found in similar form in the *Epistle of Barnabas* (p. 145), the work concentrates on church order, liturgy, and discipline. There are detailed prescriptions for the correct administration of baptism and the Eucharist as well as instructions on the importance of fasting. The candidate for baptism must be instructed in the "Two Ways" and must demonstrate an appropriate moral character. He or she preferably ought to be baptized in cold, running water,[20] but it is not so much the mode of baptism that matters as its meaning. Both the candidate and the person administering the baptism should fast before the ceremony. The Eucharist, to which only the baptized may be admitted, follows a sequence in which the cup is taken before the bread (see Luke 22:17–18; 1 Cor. 10:16–17). Fasting is deliberately to be observed on different days from the Jewish fast days of Monday and Thursday so as to heed Jesus's injunction that Christians when they fast must not be like "the hypocrites" (Matt. 6:16); believers should fast on Wednesdays and Fridays instead.

Leaders are described in the *Didache* as "apostles," "prophets," and "teachers," as in 1 Corinthians 12:28, but the final part of the section on leadership also mentions "overseers" and "deacons."[21] It would appear that, in this Syrian context at least, the overseers and deacons were starting to be appointed alongside, and probably as potential successors to, the apostles, prophets, and teachers, and the *Didache* is insistent that they should be regarded with the same honor that had been afforded to their predecessors. As in the Pastoral Epistles, there is concern about false prophets and teachers, and it is regarded as very important that the overseers and deacons be people of proven character—truthful, hardworking, charitable, hospitable, and not lovers of money. The believers are to appoint such leaders for themselves and give them the esteem they deserve as they direct the affairs of the church in the way that the apostles and the prophets did before them.

The earliest evidence for the appearance of a single, authoritative *episkopos* ("overseer") as a bishop in something akin to what would become the standard sense of that term is to be found in the letters of Ignatius of Antioch. Ignatius seems to have served as the sole bishop of Syrian Antioch, the city from which Paul had launched his missionary activities among the Gentiles. He wrote a number of epistles to churches in western Asia Minor and to the church in Rome while on the way to Rome to be executed for his faith. The date, context, and authenticity of these letters are all disputed, but there are reasonable grounds for locating them around the second decade of the second century, and although Ignatius may not have been martyred quite as early as 107, the traditional date of his death, he may well have been writing only a few years later, possibly in 110. As he traveled to Rome, probably in the company of other condemned prisoners, he was allowed to receive visits from believers from the churches in Ephesus, Magnesia, and Tralles, and he wrote back to them and forward to the church in the city of his destination. While in Troas, he also wrote other letters, including ones to the Christians in Philadelphia and Smyrna.

All of Ignatius's letters to Asian churches are addressed to named bishops, which suggests that in these communities at least, as at Antioch, there was already a system in which one overseer had come to assume overall responsibility. Ignatius envisages each community as governed by a single *episkopos* with the assistance of a group of presbyters and deacons. In the case of his letter to the church of Rome, this is not so, which implies that the Roman church continued to be led, as it had been in Clement's time, by a collegial board of elders.[22] In the Asian churches, however, the presence of a single, overall episcopal figure is, in Ignatius's perspective, of considerable importance for the nature of the church and for its liturgical actions. Baptism and Eucharist are assumed not to be valid unless performed with the bishop's authorization. The bishop is not the guarantor of the efficacy of the rites as such, but his role is to safeguard the unity of the flock in whose midst they are practiced. There is little emphasis on the bishop as a successor of the apostles, but he is pictured as a divinely commissioned minister, representing Christ to the people and the people to Christ.

One of the Asian bishops to whom Ignatius wrote was Polycarp of Smyrna. Polycarp, who had reputedly been a disciple of the apostle John at Ephesus, was the recipient of a separate personal letter from Ignatius, in addition to Ignatius's letter to the Christian community at Smyrna. The personal letter is not entirely private, for it offers instructions addressed to believers in the plural regarding submission to church leaders. Polycarp was responsible for sending on copies of Ignatius's other letters to the church at Philippi (a city through which Ignatius had probably passed but to whose church he did not, for some reason, write), and he thus served as a conduit for Ignatius's teaching. In a letter of his own to the Philippian believers,[23] Polycarp pressed the obligations he himself considered to be incumbent upon elders, deacons, and family members. He did not, however, specify anything directly about the role of a monarchical bishop; those in authority are still addressed collectively as "presbyters." For Polycarp, certain individuals might function as bishops in a leading sense, but a body of elders was still seen as a basic pattern.

Polycarp was martyred for his faith around 155 or 156, but his influence endured considerably longer, not least for the courage with which he went to his death (see pp. 203–5). His views were formative for Irenaeus, the future bishop of Lyons, who was a native of Smyrna and, in his turn, one of the most important theologians of the early church (see pp. 225–28). Irenaeus would see every church as led by one bishop, whose authority derived ultimately from the Lord himself and reflected the great tradition mediated by his apostles. The rule of faith was preserved in the great centers of Christian tradition, where the leaders could trace their teaching and their status back to apostolic foundations.

The assumptions of Ignatius and those under his influence, concerning church structures and the authority of leaders as guarantors of unity and judges of false teaching, begged a crucial question. What was the relationship between ordered ministry and a belief in more immediate and spontaneous forms of divine guidance and inspiration in leadership, teaching, and worship? The Corinthian church of Paul's time had shown a marked preference for the latter, and while it had earned his rebuke for its preoccupation with sensational and possibly selfish expressions of spiritual energy, it seems clear that a measure of informality and openness was standard not only in Corinth but more widely in the house-church communities of the earliest period. With the evolution of a more structured approach to church government, how free were individual believers to exercise their own gifts and ministries?

A strengthening resolve to exclude certain expressions of the faith as wrong brought a corresponding emphasis on the need to assess claims to ministries such as prophecy in particular in the light of inherited teaching. First John had already enjoined a testing of the spirits (1 John 4:1–6), effectively building on earlier judgments on the authenticity of prophecy (1 Cor. 12:3) and warnings against those who peddled false messages. This was not, however, to be seen as a disparaging of prophecy itself. The *Didache*, for its part, contains advice about the discernment of true and false prophecy and stern admonition about the rise from within the community itself of those who will propound error, but it also assumes that prophets occupy a very important place in the life of the congregation. Similar assumptions are also to be found in the *Shepherd* of Hermas. In the early second century, the kind of freedom of ministry represented by prophecy was assumed to coexist with the need for settled forms of leadership.

The New Prophecy

Such accommodations were nevertheless to be tested significantly in the succeeding generations. The greatest example of the tensions that could arise between different conceptions of Christian practice is to be found in the movement that has come to be called Montanism, which first arose in Asia Minor in the late 160s and 170s. Montanism cannot be appropriately characterized as a clash between a power-hungry hierarchy and ordinary believers set on freedom of expression, but it highlighted the practical problems that could ensue when some Christians saw the leadership of the church as functioning in one way and others in another.

Montanus was a Phrygian prophet who was joined by two prophetesses, Priscilla (or Prisca, as Tertullian called her) and Maximilla. Together, they claimed to be prophesying under the direct inspiration of the Paraclete, the designation used of the Holy Spirit in John 14–16. Their teaching, which became known as "the New Prophecy," was ecstatic; that is to say, they spoke not as prophets had traditionally done, declaring the word of God in the third person ("Thus says the Lord . . ."), but in the first person, presenting themselves as the Spirit's actual mouthpiece. Their prophetic manifestations were probably accompanied by speaking in other tongues, noise, and open displays of fervor. Part of their message was that the end was near and that Christ was about to return. In view of this, they enjoined a wide-ranging asceticism for the last days, including the suspension of marital relations in favor of chastity and the adoption of a simple diet and frequent fasting. Priscilla and Maximilla abandoned their husbands and became the leading members of an inner circle around Montanus. Not all believers were called upon to prophesy, but it was insisted that "the Three" must be recognized as those specially chosen to deliver the Paraclete's message.

The New Prophecy began in a rural backwater, but it spread rapidly throughout Asia Minor and soon became an urban as well as a rural phenomenon, extending not just through Phrygia but also into Galatia, Lydia, Cappadocia, and beyond. Study of inscriptions (epigraphy) has revealed evidence of the sect's presence over a very significant area. Montanism traveled well beyond the Greek East, to Rome, Gaul, and North Africa. Its teaching was vigorously opposed by many Christians, who saw the Montanists' style of ecstatic prophesying as bizarre, spurious, and conceivably demonic.

Not the least of the movement's dangers, in the minds of some church leaders, was its promotion of a prominent role for women as mediators of the Spirit's power. While women had engaged in teaching and prophesying in many circles from earliest times, the New Prophecy seemed to give at least some women a status that challenged conventional cultural assumptions about the overall primacy of male leadership, not to say the established structures of family life in which the man was head. The prophetesses Priscilla and Maximilla were very much equals with Montanus, and other women also came to exercise leadership roles. The most prominent among these was a third-century prophetess named Quintilla, who established a variety of Montanism (the so-called "Quintillian" branch) especially preoccupied with the imminent end of the world. In time, Maximilla's status seems to have waned somewhat, largely because she had issued prophecies that had not been fulfilled, and no immediate successor to her appeared. Her memory was eventually eclipsed by that of Montanus and Priscilla.

As the movement spread and established its own forms of organization, it offered potential empowerment to a wider constituency than more traditional expressions of the faith sometimes seemed to do. The Montanists may have been the first to pay their leaders to lead, and this may have not only attracted a wider social spectrum but also diverted donations away from mainstream churches. Collections of Montanist sayings and prophetic oracles circulated, and these were revered as holy texts by supporters of the movement. In Asia, the New Prophecy split many churches, and the

Montanists became the first believers we know of to be excommunicated by a synod of bishops.

Montanists were accused of many errors, including the denigration of marriage, the propounding of false teaching about the coming of the end times, and (especially later on) the holding of wrong ideas about God's nature as triune. They were said to have held that the heavenly Jerusalem would descend in Phrygia, where Montanus seems to have established an idealized religious community called "Jerusalem," based in the villages of Pepouza and Tymion (the modern identities of both sites are extremely difficult to verify). Their followers were also allegedly taught to relish the prospect of martyrdom for their cause in anticipation of the coming of God's kingdom. Archaeology has revealed some support for the impression that the Montanists were "faithful unto death"; inscriptions from probable Montanist tombs suggest that their subjects suffered openly as Christians and faced death bravely as those who were spiritual rather than wedded to this world.

There can be little doubt that the New Prophecy's fervor and the rigor of its discipline intensified over the years in the face of opposition and persecution. It is likely that several of the charges against Montanism were exaggerated, especially as time went on. As far as we can tell, the movement shared many basic beliefs with catholic Christianity, and it was distinctive more for the degree of its spiritual zeal than for the doctrinal assumptions that underpinned it. North African Montanism attracted its most famous convert in Tertullian, who became a devotee of the movement in the later years of his life, from around 207 or 208. He was impressed by its focus on the Spirit's power, and he in turn taught that the Paraclete enjoined a more stringent discipline on believers in a variety of areas: those who committed grave sins after baptism were not to be forgiven; those who remarried after the loss of a spouse were guilty of a grievous error; and no true believer ought to flee from persecution but should embrace death as the gateway to spiritual glory. Tertullian berated the non-Montanist Christians of his time for their sensuality and lack of spiritual commitment: they were "psychics," people of nature, as opposed to the "pneumatics," the people of the Spirit. He and his supporters in Carthage were increasingly marginalized within the church because of their fanaticism, but they were never formally excommunicated.

The enthusiasm of Tertullian testifies to the broad doctrinal orthodoxy of Montanism. It is most improbable that Tertullian would have elected to associate with a movement that he believed to hold aberrant views on such fundamental issues as the nature of God. Many other

Christians clearly saw things similarly and did not consider the core teaching of the Montanists to be at odds with inherited assumptions. In Rome, for example, the New Prophecy seems to have enjoyed a brief period of favor before its opponents won the day, and even then it did not disappear entirely. In North Africa in particular, Montanism lasted in some measure until the fifth century. In its heartland in Phrygia, it endured even longer.

Some scholars suggest that Montanism is best seen as a renewal movement, challenging believers to recover a more authentic style of Christian experience, one that did not confine the exercising of spiritual gifts to those who held official roles, or to men rather than women, or to formal ways of teaching within the church's liturgy. Some of these interpretations go farther than our information on the history of the movement allows. It is evident, for example, that the New Prophecy was not anticlerical or lay-centered in a modern sense, and its ways of worshiping were not entirely informal. As their apparent system of paying their leaders indicates, the Montanists certainly did believe that some were leaders in a special sense, and Tertullian, for one, was no protestor against the need for ordained ministers. While they may well have offered women a greater place than some male sensibilities could accept, they may not have had a recognized class of female clergy in a formal sense. In many instances, it seems, the Montanists were controversial as much for their views on fasting, self-denial, and the imminent end of the world as they were for their ideas about ministry.

Nonetheless, although we should not overstate the superficial similarity of the sect to later charismatic movements, it is clear that the Montanists were felt to pose a challenge to the emergence of catholic structures of authority, and it is not difficult to see why their brand of spirituality would have been regarded by some as divisive and offensive. Perhaps they were seeking to preserve a tradition of revelation that was in danger of being eclipsed. But in an age marked by increasing efforts to consolidate and demonstrate the power of episcopal leadership, the New Prophecy represented a threat to the assumptions of many that the bishops knew automatically how (and by whom) the believing communities should be directed. An individual bishop expounding an established and shared tradition of beliefs, values, and practices could control his church within some fairly manageable parameters; it was much harder to keep a hold upon the possibilities when new prophecies and new revelations were allegedly being granted on a regular basis. The crisis that Montanism provoked testifies to the challenges that attended the implementation of a generic system of leadership bound by common conceptions of tradition and order.

In Retrospect

Viewed in retrospect, the Gnostics, the Marcionites, and the Montanists make for peculiar bedfellows. They were driven by very different motives and interests, and the degree to which each of them represented a departure from apostolic thinking varied considerably. The Montanists in particular were far more conventional doctrinally than any of the others, and despite the common accusation of their opponents that they were linked to the Gnostics, they consciously sought to counter Gnostic views about the humanity of Christ and the spiritual privileging of an elite.

The Gnostics, for their part, raised issues of unique complexity and subtlety about the nature of the Christian life and the reality of God's saving presence in Jesus, while the contentions of the Marcionites, though they were less influential overall, precipitated significant further reflection upon the relationship of Christianity to Judaism and upon the status of authoritative texts. The diversity of all three constituencies makes it perilous to conceive of them as identifiable sectarian groups, for all of them thought of themselves as authentically Christian, and as far as they were concerned, they existed entirely within, if not at the heart of, the true believing tradition. In the end, however, they all stood for ideas or practices that were objectionable to a stronger consensus of those with authority.

In their various fashions, all of these currents provided the stimulus to the churches to think through what it was that essentially bound true believers together, and in an important sense they energized the Christian communities in a formative period. The story of the second and early third centuries is in part an account of the ways in which the faith of the apostolic age came to be seen as something that was both fundamental and finished; it was both the basis for a right understanding of the church's present configuration and a standard to which believers had to keep appealing. Its traditions were to be regarded as a broadly unified system of beliefs and practices; its texts were more and more to be seen as a fixed corpus of special material. And although patterns of organization and ministry still varied widely, in a range of contexts its authority was coming to be recognized as mediated through a fairly narrow lineage of official leaders, conceived, by some at least, according to a threefold pattern of ministry, with monarchical bishops at the head, assisted by presbyters, in turn assisted by deacons.

A great deal of diversity of structure and organization remained, and dissent from every one of the arguments about authority and order was widespread. It would be quite wrong to imagine that there was any kind of easy convergence either in doctrine or in forms of leadership. The delineation of a catholic faith took place amid the white heat of controversy and the tensions of complex political struggles, and the battles went on, frequently in vicious forms, for a very long time. In some cases, especially that of Gnosticism, they never did disappear, and essentially Gnostic ideas of one sort or another have continued to plague Christian thinking in almost every age.[24] Nevertheless, without the specific challenges posed in this early period by those we loosely call Gnostics, Marcionites, and Montanists, the tradition that we regard as mainstream would not have come to reflect the shape that it did.

Yet the church was also molded just as much by external as by internal forces. It is to these, in the form of pagan challenges, both physical and intellectual, that we now turn our attention.

7

EXTERNAL PRESSURES:
SUFFERING FOR
AND DEFENDING THE FAITH

▼

The Early Period

Christianity's relations with Roman imperial authority had gotten off to a very unpromising start: Jesus had been sentenced to death by a Roman prefect. Nevertheless, according to the Gospels, Pontius Pilate had condemned Jesus in order to satisfy Jewish demands, not because he had considered him guilty of any crime against Roman law. The first believers in Jesus were regarded by the Romans as just another Jewish sect, and for the most part, they probably seemed harmless enough in political terms. In principle, the Romans were not interested in interfering in what they saw as a dispute between rival groups of Jews over finer points of their religious tradition (see Acts 23:26–30).

The followers of Jesus, for their part, had no wish to jeopardize their potential to spread the gospel among the Gentiles. Leaders such as Paul exhorted their converts to be decent, law-abiding people, who paid their taxes, showed respect for those in authority, and prayed for the emperor (Rom. 13:1–7). Although Paul was insistent that Jesus's lordship took precedence over every other allegiance (1 Cor. 8:5–6; cf. Phil. 2:9–11), he was quite prepared to claim his rights as a Roman citizen when it came to legal process (Acts 22:22–29) and to appeal to Caesar against the judgment of Jewish authorities, protesting his innocence under Roman as well as Jewish Law (Acts 25:1–21). In Palestine, the Nazarenes distanced themselves from the cause of nationalistic opposition to Roman rule, believing that their Lord had taught that God's kingdom was not brought in by violent means and that his followers should render to Caesar his rightful dues (Matt. 22:15–22; Mark 12:13–17; Luke 20:20–26). For as long as Jesus's followers could be treated as a peaceful constituency within mainstream Judaism, they were both tolerated and protected by Roman law.

The most serious opposition to the initial spread of the message of Jesus came not from the Romans but from other Jews. As we have seen, documents such as the Acts of the Apostles make much of the fact that the Jews were to blame for a variety of disturbances and attacks upon early Christian evangelism (Acts 6:8–8:3), especially the forceful persecution ordered by Herod Agrippa between 41 and 44 (Acts 12:1–24), in which James the brother of John was executed. Far from seeing the Romans as invariably hostile, the narrative of Acts presents them as sometimes opposing rather than abetting would-be hostility to the Way (Acts 18:12–17). Among the Romans of whom we read in Acts, there are intelligent seekers who become converts, such as the centurion Cornelius (Acts 10:1–48) and the proconsul of Cyprus, Sergius Paulus (Acts 13:6–12). There are officials who treat Paul with judicial fairness, such as Claudius Lysias (Acts 21:27–23:35), others who are capable of being impressed by him, such as Felix (Acts 24:24–26) or Porcius Festus (Acts 24:27–25:27), and one, Publius, the chief magistrate of Malta, who offers hospitality and sustenance to Paul and his companions after their shipwreck en route to Rome (Acts 27:7–10). None of these individuals is said to have regarded Christian profession as an offense punishable in Roman law. Our text of Acts ends with reference to Paul, at Rome, being allowed to live in his own rented house and spread his gospel without opposition (Acts 28:30–31). In other sources, too, it is from within Judaism itself rather than from Roman antagonism that calamity arises for the worshipers of Jesus.

Some Christians were caught up in the emperor Claudius's expulsion of Jews from Rome in 49. It was this expulsion that took Priscilla and Aquila to Corinth, where they would meet Paul (Acts 18:2). It appears from the narrative of Acts that they were already Christians before their arrival in Corinth. The Roman writer Suetonius says that Claudius expelled the Jews from Rome "because they were constantly creating disturbances at the instigation of Chrestus."[1] The "Chrestus" he mentions may have been a Jewish troublemaker of whom we otherwise know nothing. Alternatively, Suetonius may have misunderstood the spelling of "Christus" (possibly because the word could be pronounced "Chrestus"), and he may be saying that riots occurred at Rome when the message of Christ was spread among the city's Jews. Either way, it looks as if there was no singling out of Christians for particularly hostile treatment, even if it was the name of their Savior that provoked the disputes. Jesus's followers were removed from the capital as part of a wider constituency of Jews whom the authorities regarded as undesirables. Similar measures against the Jews of Rome had been taken before; this time, some Christians simply happened to be among the victims.

Persecution in Rome

The first significant action taken by the Roman authorities against the Christians as a specific target came under the emperor Nero in 64. Nero has gone down in history as a notorious tyrant, but in fact the first five years of his reign, from 54 to 59, were largely peaceful and prosperous. It was during this period that Paul had urged respect for civil authorities (Rom. 13:1–7), and it was to Nero that Paul had appealed from the tribunal of Festus (Acts 25:11). It was only when the young emperor had begun to take political control more directly into his own hands rather than relying on his advisers that things had taken a different turn. Nero had ordered the murders of both his mother and his wife, and he had scandalized upper-class Roman sensibilities by his performances as a musician and a charioteer, but criticism of his extravagance and mounting despotism was brutally repressed. Even so, when Christians at length became victims of his regime, the persecution was precipitated not by an important point of principle but by an accident.

On 19 July 64, a massive fire broke out in Rome. It lasted for six days and seven nights and gutted perhaps three whole sections of the city, leaving thousands homeless. According to the account by the Roman historian Tacitus, the emperor was under suspicion for having started the conflagration himself. The speculation was that Nero had ordered a district of the city to be cleared in order to make room for a rebuilding project, and the fire had gotten out of control owing to an unexpected

Roman coin (A.D. 67) showing the emperor Nero. Illustration from Otago Museum, Dunedin, New Zealand. Used by permission.

strong wind. Tacitus states that Nero turned away the odium directed against him by blaming the fire on "a class hated for their crimes, called Christians by the populace." Tacitus goes on to say that on the information of a few, "an immense multitude" were arrested and put to death with extreme forms of torture, convicted "not so much of arson as of hatred of the human race."[2]

Tacitus's account, written around fifty years after the event, is designed very much to portray his own contempt for Nero, and he emphasizes the brutality inflicted on the Christians in order to underscore the emperor's wanton cruelty. He does not deny the legitimacy of punishing those found guilty of wrongdoing, but he says that the sufferings imposed on the victims aroused some sympathy for them, since it seemed as if they were being put to death not so much for the public good but in order to satisfy the cruelty of one man. "Mockery of every sort was added to their deaths. Covered with the skins of beasts, they were torn by dogs and perished, or were nailed to crosses, or doomed to the flames."[3] Nero's persecution was probably the general context for the martyrdom of the apostles Peter and Paul; this is certainly where their deaths are placed by later writers.

The language of Tacitus's account is of interest. The reproach of the Christians for "hatred of the human race" was typical of the kind of slur that Romans elsewhere directed against the Jews for their withdrawal from pagan society. Tacitus saw the Christians as a Jewish sect, but, as the agitation of other Jews against them showed, they had apparently gone off at a tangent from regular Judaism and become even more peculiar. Their belief was a "deadly superstition" that conjured up, in the educated Roman mind, images of the weird, emotional cults of the East as opposed to the stable and venerable public religion of Roman tradition. As offshoots of Judaism, the Christians were already followers of an outlandish system; they had added a further absurd twist by contending that a dead man, crucified as a common criminal in a notoriously odd part of the empire, was alive (see Acts 25:19). In Tacitus's terms, the Christians were loathed for their "crimes."[4]

Such descriptions can be paralleled in other Roman authors. They probably say more about how Christians were seen by aristocratic

Romans in the first quarter of the second century than they do about the image of Roman Christians in the 60s, and they relate to some particular misconceptions about Christian practices to which we shall shortly come. It is important, however, to appreciate the circumstances within which the Neronian persecution took place. The Christians were plainly capable of being distinguished from Jews, and no doubt Jews in Rome were keen to distance themselves from them when it became clear that trouble was in the air.[5] Whatever the numbers of Christian believers martyred, the assault upon them was confined to the city of Rome and did not become a more widespread attack on Christians elsewhere in the empire. It was essentially an ad hoc phenomenon—one emperor's effort to extricate himself, at appalling cost to others, from an awkward situation and to divert hostility toward a convenient class of scapegoats.

Nevertheless, although the events in Rome provided no formal precedent for the systematic persecution of Christians (and the extent of Nero's cruelty may have been officially condemned after his death), in psychological terms they did establish a chilling precedent to which Roman authorities might look in the future. Victims in a misjudged town-planning exercise or not, in reality people had, for the first time, been put to death by the Romans simply for being Christians. Judaism was a recognized cult (*religio licita*), but the actions taken against the Christians made it clear that *their* faith was now regarded as a prohibited movement, not licensed by Roman law—a *religio illicita*. Individuals could in principle be arrested and tried simply on suspicion of being believers and then charged with associated crimes. This would remain the official position until 312.

Further Opposition

In texts such as 1 Peter and the Epistle to the Hebrews, the believers being addressed are familiar with some kind of harassment from secular authorities. First Peter is written to those who are "strangers in the world, scattered throughout Pontus, Galatia, Cappadocia, Asia and Bithynia" (1 Peter 1:1). They have had to "suffer grief in all kinds of trials" (1:6), and are going through a "painful trial" (4:12). They know what it is to be called to account and slandered (3:15–17). They are exhorted, nevertheless, to show respect for the authorities and to live circumspect and honorable lives among their pagan accusers (2:12). If they suffer, it must be as Christians, not as wrongdoers, trusting that this is God's will and committing themselves to God's faithfulness (4:15–19); indeed, they are to count themselves blessed if they are "insulted because of the name of Christ," for they are participants in Christ's own sufferings (4:13–14). The language of 1 Peter does not necessarily suggest the presence of official persecution, and the emphasis on believers as temporary sojourners in the world is governed by theological interests, but the recipients were clearly experiencing at least some difficulties in professing their faith.

In Hebrews, some or most of the addressees (cf. p. 136) were probably Jewish converts who were considering reverting to their former faith, no doubt on the grounds that they had lived perfectly peacefully as Jews whereas now they were experiencing hostility and oppression (Heb. 6:4–12; 10:19–12:13). The writer points out that they have not—as yet—been called upon to shed their blood (12:4), and if anything their current condition seems to be more stable than it was in the first period of their Christian allegiance. They are reminded of the particular challenges that they faced "in those earlier days"—public ridicule, persecution, and (in at least some cases) imprisonment and the confiscation of their property (10:32–34). Nevertheless, hardship and difficulties are still a present reality (12:1–13), and some are yet in prison or are being ill-treated (13:3). The readers are to remember the example of their former leaders (13:7) and to submit to those now occupying their position (13:17), taking heart where the pressures are somewhat lighter and persevering in the face of continuing hostilities.

The Imperial Cult

One of the focal points for trouble between Christians and Rome was the imperial cult. For much of the first century, the cult of the emperor was observed in a formal manner throughout the empire but without excessive stipulations on Rome's subjects. Jews were exempted from the worship of Roman deities, and a fairly simple ritual observance was regarded as acceptable evidence of their loyalty. In Jerusalem, a twice-daily sacrifice for Caesar and the Roman nation was offered in the temple until 66, when its discontinuance was one of the final triggers for the Jewish revolt against Rome. The emperor Caligula (37–41), whose reign was marked by repeated tensions with the Jews, attempted in 40 to have his statue set up in the temple but was thwarted by his legate, Petronius, governor of Syria, who successfully stalled on the order, knowing that it would incite an uprising. (Paul possibly alludes to this crisis in 2 Thessalonians 2:3–4.) Even in the aftermath of the crushing of the Jewish revolt of 66–73 and the destruction of the temple, the cult of the emperor was treated lightly by both Vespasian (69–79) and Titus (79–81).

Things worsened, however, under Domitian (81–96). Domitian styled himself "Lord and God" (*Dominus et Deus*), and he insisted that the oath to the emperor's *genius* or "creative life-principle" become compulsory. This posed a significant problem for Jews, and presumably no less so for Christians. The third-century Roman historian Dio Cassius reports that a number of aristocratic Romans were arrested and put on trial for "atheism, for which many others also were condemned who had drifted into Jewish ways."[6] Among these was the emperor's own cousin, Titus Flavius Clemens, the consul of 95, and his wife, Domitian's niece, Flavia Domitilla. Clemens was put to death, and his wife was banished to the island of Pandetaria, off the coast of Campania.

It is possible that the charge on which they were condemned, a mixture of atheism and Judaism in Dio's words, implied that they were Christians; *atheism* would certainly become a standard term in the second century for the Christians' rejection of the pagan gods. If the couple were Christian, they represent an interesting illustration of the extent to which the gospel had made inroads into the household of Caesar. This was already the case in Paul's time (Phil. 4:22), and it would continue to be so in the second and third centuries, when there were regularly believers among the slaves and freedmen of the imperial palace, and even some members of the emperor's family had contacts with Christian leaders.[7] It is equally possible, however, that the main reasons for the emperor's action in this instance were political rather than religious, and in general there is insufficient evidence to conclude positively that Domitian pursued a policy of political oppression against upper-class Roman Christians, despite his grandiose cultic pretensions.

Nonetheless, it is likely that the persecutions of Christians in Asia alluded to in the book of Revelation have their context at this time. John the seer writes from the island of Patmos, off the coast of Asia Minor, to a group of churches in seven major cities on the mainland—Ephesus, Smyrna, Pergamum, Thyatira, Sardis, Philadelphia, and Laodicea. A Jewish Christian prophet, John describes himself to these believers as "your brother and companion in the suffering and kingdom and patient endurance that are ours in Jesus" (Rev. 1:9).[8] The communities in these places, all of them important centers of the imperial cult, have already known various trials and hardships (2:3, 9), including, at Pergamum, the martyrdom of one Antipas (2:13), and it is predicted that worse is yet to befall them (2:10; 3:10). While some of the opposition involves Jewish enemies of various kinds, including "those who say that they are Jews and are not" (2:9; cf. 3:9), the overriding threat is clearly from pagan forces, whose power is symbolized in a variety of ways, most notably as that of Babylon, the city responsible for the most significant oppression of God's chosen people before the coming of Jesus. Babylon serves as a cipher for Rome.[9]

In the series of visions that make up the main body of Revelation, Rome is depicted in a range of powerfully negative images. She is a woman "dressed in purple and scarlet," the "mother of prostitutes," "sitting on a scarlet beast . . . covered with blasphemous names"; she holds a golden cup "filled with abominable things and the filth of her adulteries," and she is "drunk with the blood of the saints, the blood of those who bore testimony to Jesus" (Rev. 17:3–6). The imperial cult is likened to the worship of a proud and blasphemous beast (13:1–10), and the number of the beast, 666 (13:18), is perhaps a cryptogram for "Nero Caesar," hinting that Domitian was regarded as *Nero redivivus*.

Revelation deserves to be read, on one level at least, not so much as a coded prediction of events at the end of world history as a political message to suffering Christians in the later first century, exhorting them not to quiet submission or passive acceptance of their lot but to bold resistance to the idolatries and corruptions of Roman authority. This resistance is called for not just because Rome oppresses believers but because the whole system of Roman power is intrinsically evil. In dissociating themselves from the perverted political, economic, and moral structures of the empire around them, Christians are highly likely to suffer persecution. Nevertheless, their action is to be motivated by the awareness of two realities: that those who compromise with such a world will incur God's fierce judgment (Rev. 14:9–12), and that those who remain steadfast, even though they suffer, will be avenged in the end at the coming of their divine deliverer, the conquering "Lamb" himself (6:9–17).

Like other writers of apocalyptic literature, John sees it as his purpose to reassure his readers that God is sovereign over their circumstances and that the power of God that is already evident in heaven will yet reward those who are faithful and wipe out all the forces of evil ranged against God's will on earth. Confrontation of political powers may well mean suffering and death, but such witness is a vital part of the divine strategy to usher in an alternative future, in the coming of a kingdom that is universal, righteous, and unending.[10]

Popular Resentment

Christians in general needed such inspiration about the transcendence of their God and the sovereignty of his purposes. Though they were not routinely subjected to physical oppression, they were despised and hated at a popular level for many reasons. Their rejection of the usual gods and cults was an offense to traditional values. When they refused to make offerings to the emperor or to conventional deities, they were often seen as jeopardizing political stability or dangerously risking divine wrath on their communities. Roman society was thought to depend upon the maintenance of the *pax deorum*, the peace of the gods, by the observance of the contractual obligations of civic religion. The Christians appeared to throw this into doubt by their religious exclusivism and their determination to avoid idolatry.[11]

The refusal of Christians to participate in the imperial cult meant that they frequently disqualified themselves from military service, which required an oath of allegiance to a divine emperor and regular presence at polytheistic rites. It was accepted that Jews might be exempt in this way, but as large numbers of Christians came from non-Jewish backgrounds, there was a significant increase in those adopting such a stance. In at least a number of cases, the believers also posed a significant practical threat to local economies. It is clear that as early as the ministry of Paul, the success of Christian evangelism undermined important commercial interests. In Philippi, the opposition to Paul and Silas described by Luke was initiated by the owners of a fortune-telling slave-girl, whose conversion meant that she was no longer able to make money for her masters (Acts 16:16–21). At Ephesus, still more famously, Paul was accused of threatening the livelihood of the metal-workers and other traders who did "no little business" in connection with the great cult of Artemis (19:23–41).[12]

Christians were also seen as generally antisocial; they kept close to their own circles and sought to distance themselves from the recreational activities, associations, and festivals that went on in society around them, a large proportion of which were associated with traditional religious values. Christians could not belong to trade guilds or social clubs, for membership entailed participating in religious rites in honor of patron deities, and they were equally supposed to stay away from civic processions, feasts, and even traveling markets set up in the precincts of pagan temples. Their separatist tendencies must often have been resented by neighbors, relatives, and acquaintances as expressions of self-righteousness, and their apparent concentration on their own spiritual preoccupations must often have seemed like an obnoxious resistance to the patterns and practices of normal social life.

Even where believers engaged in demonstrative acts of charity such as almsgiving, their behavior was subject to misinterpretation and distortion. One of the most important forms of early Christian witness was the care and generosity that believers extended to the needy, such as widows, orphans, the sick, the destitute, the imprisoned, and the elderly. These expressions of good works were always capable of being abused, and especially so in a society in which there were as many vulnerable dependants as there were in the average Graeco-Roman city. From an early date there were problems with false mendicants and those who feigned need in order to line their own pockets. The Christians could accordingly also be ridiculed by their critics as gullible fools, taken in by people with obviously dubious credentials. There were also allegations that church leaders benefited personally from funds raised for the poor.

A second-century pagan satirist, Lucian of Samosata, tells the story of a charlatan philosopher named Peregrinus Proteus who at one stage in his life had converted to Christianity, advanced to a leading role in a church, and been imprisoned for his beliefs. During his time in prison, Peregrinus had duped his followers into showing him such devotion that by the time he was released, he had made his fortune and was able to go off on his next adventure. Peregrinus (who became a Cynic and eventually burned himself to death) is painted in better colors elsewhere, and Lucian's point is not about the evils of Christianity as such but about the general absurdity of human life. Nevertheless, in taking the Christians as such a striking example of human folly, his portrait illustrates the contempt in which believers were often held even when they sought to do good.

The Christians through Roman Eyes: Pliny and Trajan

The everyday pressures suffered by some Christians in the later first and early second centuries were probably quite significant. Even so, we do not have evidence of sustained or widespread political persecution in these years, however graphic the images of hostility and hardship in some of the later New Testament literature. Under Domitian's successors, the transitional ruler Nerva (96–98) and the astute expansionist emperor Trajan (98–117), life for Christians was on the whole relatively stable vis-à-vis the state, even if popular antipathy continued. It is from

Trajan's time that we have one of the most famous pieces of evidence about the relationship between the Christians and the Romans in the early second century.

Around 112, the Roman official Gaius Plinius Caecilius Secundus, known to us as Pliny the younger,[13] governor of the Black Sea province of Bithynia, wrote to his emperor asking for guidance in the matter of how to deal with people within his jurisdiction who were accused of being Christians. Pliny had been charged with looking into the administration and finances of his territory, in which there were reports of widespread corruption and abuses, and with quelling political disorder and settling outstanding legal cases. He had slowly toured the cities of Bithynia, starting at Prusa in the west, and had reached the northern coastal area of the province. In one of the cities of this region, he had been presented with a number of complaints about Christians living in the vicinity. It appears that the petitions had been generated by local merchants, perhaps butchers and those engaged in the slaughter and sale of sacrificial meat, whose sales were suffering because of the presence of—presumably—a fairly large number of Christians who would not participate in pagan ceremonies. The temples too, it seems, were fast being deserted in both urban and rural areas, and local interests were being affected.

Pliny knew that Christianity was illegal and therefore punishable as a criminal offense, but he reported to Trajan that he had not been present at the examination of Christians before, and he was not sure as to the kinds of factors that should enter into his decisions. Should allowances be made, for example, for the age of a professing Christian, or should young people and adults be treated alike? Should pardon be extended to those who renounced their beliefs, or ought this to make no difference? Pliny in fact expresses uncertainty as to whether it is the mere name of "Christian" that is punishable, or the "crimes" associated with the name. Pending further clarification, he had in the meantime not hesitated to order the execution of those who persisted in their confession after being warned three times about the seriousness of the charge, on the grounds that they deserved to be punished in any case for their "obstinacy and unbending perversity"—or resistance to a governor's threats.[14]

Pliny goes on to say that he has released those who denied that they were Christians if they were first prepared to recite a prayer to the Roman gods, offer incense and pour out a libation before a statue of the emperor, and curse Christ. This was clearly an improvised test to determine whether someone was a Christian and to ascertain imperial loyalty; Pliny acknowledges that genuine Christians refused to comply with it. Pliny was particularly troubled, though, by another category of individuals—those who acknowledged that they had been believers at an earlier stage in their lives, perhaps as many as twenty years previously, but who were now willing to repudiate Christianity and perform the appropriate religious acts. He had been presented with an anonymous pamphlet denouncing a large number of people as Christians, but many of them insisted that their attachment to Christ was firmly in their past. If people were to be punished just for being Christian, then those who confessed that they had been believers three, five, or twenty years ago but were so no longer deserved to be pardoned. If, however, the offense lay specifically in the "crimes," then inquiries would have to be made and trials take place no matter how long ago the "crimes" had been committed.

Pliny does not specify what these alleged "crimes" were. Perhaps the Christians were thought culpable of regular offenses such as theft, fraud, and adultery. It is much more likely, though, that Pliny suspected them of evils of a more sensational variety, such as the secret nocturnal orgies that Romans associated with proscribed Eastern rituals like the cult of the Bacchanalia. We know from evidence dating to later in the second century that Christians had by then come to be widely suspected of enormities such as cannibalism and incest. They ate the "flesh" and drank the "blood" of their Lord; they called each other "brother" and "sister," greeted one another with kisses; and, in some quarters at least, they were alleged to have engaged in gatherings called "love feasts." There were also accusations of magical practices. The Christians prayed "in the name of Jesus." They met during the hours of darkness. They chanted strange hymns and spoke in strange tongues that sounded like gibberish. They made ritual gestures, such as the sign of the cross. They spoke of spiritual powers and sometimes practiced exorcisms.[15]

Some of the rumors of immoral and illicit activity were no doubt based on confused ideas about the nature of Christian ritual, as Christian spokesmen would regularly insist, though they cannot always be put down to complete ignorance, since life in ancient society, especially in the urban locations where most Christians were concentrated, afforded little room for privacy or the keeping of strict secrets about religious or cultic practices. What mattered was not the truth or falsehood of the claims in real terms, however, as much as the fact that they enabled people to perceive the Christians as cultural nonconformists whose behavior violated the accepted conventions of their society. The followers of Christ could be labeled in stereotypical ways as dangerous deviants.

While we cannot be sure that perceptions of this kind were necessarily widely prevalent in Pliny's time, the tone of his language suggests that he had indeed entertained some dark suspicions about what the Christians were doing. After having interrogated former believers, though, he concedes that the rites of the Christians have turned out to be innocuous:

> They declared that the total sum of their guilt or error amounted to no more than this: they had met together regularly before dawn on a fixed day to chant verses alternately among themselves in honour of Christ, as though to a god, and also to bind themselves by oath, not for any criminal purpose, but to abstain from theft, robbery, and adultery, to commit no breach of trust and not to deny a deposit when called upon to restore it. After this ceremony it had been their custom to disperse and reassemble later to take food of an ordinary, harmless kind.[16]

Pliny's description is valuable for a number of reasons, not least for the testimony he offers to Christian practice in this period. The believers' meetings were not sinister nocturnal feasts of the flesh, and the food they ate was a regular meal. Their early-morning gathering was probably on a Sunday; their hymns were sung in worship of Christ (which suggests that they sang not just psalms, but hymns specifically naming Christ); and they swore allegiance, whether in the rite of baptism or more generally, to an honorable code of ethics. They met later in the day, not to consume a murdered child or engage in some other ghastly ritual, but to eat together as associates. Pliny records that they had also agreed to suspend their common meal when he had published an imperial order banning clubs or associations (which were frowned upon as potential sources of political factionalism in the community). This was all that Pliny could ascertain about the Christians, despite having tortured two professing believers, "female slaves who were styled as deaconesses" (who were presumably taken to be easy targets). He determined that Christianity was just a "squalid superstition."[17]

Trajan's response to Pliny assured him that he had adopted essentially the right course. "Nothing can be laid down as a general ruling involving something like a set form of procedure," Trajan says.[18] The Christians were not to be sought out in any kind of systematic fashion, and unsigned documents of mass denunciation could be ignored. If individuals were accused and convicted according to the proper processes of law, then they were to be punished—Christianity remained illegal. But those who denied being Christians and proved this by worshiping the Roman gods should be pardoned, regardless of suspicions about their past conduct. The imperial position was clear: Christians were members of an illicit sect, but they were not to be persecuted by the state in an organized way. If someone wished to allege that a person was a Christian, let him. But in Roman law, malicious prosecutions on capital charges were firmly discouraged by the rule that an accuser would find himself the victim of the punishment if his case were found to be slanderous. Those who repudiated former adherence to Christianity and backed this up by participation in the rituals of pagan religion were to be treated with tolerance and absolved of wrongdoing. As far as Trajan was concerned, the Christians, for all their obnoxious hostility to traditional religious observance, posed no serious threat to society, and the punishment of their faith, while appropriate, ought to be kept within reasonable bounds.

Trajan's judgment was reaffirmed by his successor, Hadrian, around 125 in a letter to Caius Minucius Fundanus, the proconsul of Asia. As we saw in chapter 5, Christians as well as Jews were caught up in Hadrian's suppression of the Jewish revolt in Palestine and his transformation of Jerusalem into a pagan city. But in the case of Asia, Hadrian ruled that Christians had to be proved to be doing something "contrary to the laws" in order to merit punishment; anyone seeking a writ of prosecution against a Christian merely for the sake of libeling him should be punishable with heavier penalties, "according to the heinousness of the crime."[19] This remained the official position in the empire as a whole until the middle of the third century, and Christian spokesmen were ready to quote Hadrian's ruling in support of an argument that Christians ought to be exempt from legal harassment.

This was, however, wishful thinking, for proven participation in the faith still remained a capital offense. All the while, under Trajan, Hadrian, and beyond, individual Christians in various regions were put to death for their beliefs, though there were no large-scale assaults such as would occur later. The very absence of a firm legal principle that could apply in all circumstances allowed provincial authorities a good deal of discretionary power according to political circumstance, and it was easy to exercise this against the Christians when local exigencies were pressing.

Esteemed Martyrs: Ignatius and Polycarp

Nevertheless, the most famous instances of Christian martyrdom in the first half of the second century actually became famous, in part, because they represented fairly infrequent cases. Among the most celebrated was the martyrdom of Ignatius, bishop of Antioch, perhaps around 110. Ignatius was arrested and condemned to death in the East and taken to Rome under military guard, probably in the company of other prisoners who had been similarly sentenced. Others are also said to have taken the road to Rome before them, "for the glory of God." The letters that Ignatius wrote on his final journey became justly famous for several reasons, not the least of which was Ignatius's stated determination to die as a martyr. He wrote ahead to the Christians in Rome, imploring them not to try to intercede on his behalf:

> May I have the pleasure of the wild beasts that have been prepared for me; and I pray that they prove to be prompt with me. I will even coax them to devour me properly, not as they have done with some, whom they were too timid to touch. And if when I am willing and ready they are not, I will force them. Bear with me—I know what is best for me. Now at last I am beginning to be a disciple. May nothing visible or invisible envy me, so that I may reach Jesus Christ. Fire and cross and battles with wild beasts, mutilation, mangling, wrenching of bones, the hacking of limbs, the crushing of my whole body, cruel tortures of the devil—let these come upon me, only let me reach Jesus Christ![20]

As we saw in the previous chapter, one of Ignatius's key theological emphases was his opposition to docetic views of Jesus; it was essential, he argued, that Christ's suffering and death were real, physical processes. In resolutely going to his own death, Ignatius saw himself as following in the footsteps of his Lord, and he was determined to show his commitment to Christ by paying the ultimate price himself. He was given to the wild beasts in the Roman amphitheater.

Under the emperor Antoninus Pius (138–161), Ignatius's friend Polycarp, bishop of Smyrna, was executed (along with a small group of other victims) around 155 or 156, at the age of eighty-six. The account of his suffering, the *Martyrdom of Polycarp*, is the oldest surviving record of a Christian execution, and although it has been subject to significant revisions, it is at heart an authentic document. Originally written as a letter from the church of Smyrna to the church of Philomelium in Phrygia, it became much more widely known at an early date. It contains a remarkable description of Polycarp's trial, narrating his defiant refusal to swear by the *genius* of Caesar or to repudiate the Christ whom he had followed over the course of his long life, despite the authorities' appeals to him to consider what his resistance would mean even at his advanced age: "Eighty-six years

The Colosseum, Rome. Dedicated in A.D. 80, this vast amphitheater was used
for a variety of games, shows, and spectacles, including gladiatorial fights.
Illustration from author.

have I served him, and he has done me no wrong; how then can I
blaspheme my King who saved me?"[21] Polycarp makes it clear that
whereas pagans consider Christians to be atheists for rejecting their
gods, to him it is the pagans who are really the atheists, for it is they
who deny the one true God.

Polycarp was regarded as an especially venerable martyr, not only because of his age but because he represented a final link with those who
had known Jesus in the flesh: in his youth, he was said to have been a
disciple of John the apostle. In reality, the fact that he had been able to
live his Christian life unmolested for so long points to the relative stability
of his political environment, but the drama of his final end is none the
less poignant for that. Polycarp's suffering and death are depicted in the
Martyrdom of Polycarp in heroic style, as patterned after the passion of
Christ, and the narrative is invested with miraculous elements, such as the
detail that when his body was pierced, out of it came a dove, accompanied
by enough blood to quench the fire that had been lit to consume him.

The *Martyrdom of Polycarp* set the tone for what became a large genre
of martyr literature from the mid-second century onward. Sufferers were
portrayed in elaborate hagiographical fashion as the ultimate witnesses

to the faith (the Greek word *martys* means "witness") and as those whose inspirational fortitude bestowed an aura of special sanctity upon the communities from which they came. Such literature represents an interesting fusion of cultural inheritances. It evokes very frequently the traditional veneration of Jewish martyrs as a persecuted minority who were prepared to face death rather than commit acts of idolatry. The chief heroes of that legacy were the Maccabees, who became exemplars for the characterization of a great many Christian confessors. There were also parallels with Graeco-Roman idealizations of courage amid suffering, especially in political portraiture influenced by Stoic philosophy. In addition, there were similarities with the style of Greek biographies, which typically wove together fictional and historical aspects in their material in order to bolster the status of their subjects. Amid such features, however, there also ran an increasingly strong polemic by Christians against both Judaism and paganism. Judaism was regularly depicted as responsible for the death of Jesus and complicit in the cruelty meted out to his faithful followers (as in the case of Polycarp); paganism was naturally seen as corrupt, sadistic, and blasphemous.

From the late second or early third century, it became increasingly common to observe the anniversary of martyrs' deaths with ceremonies of remembrance, typically held at their tombs (which in turn frequently became the sites for later shrines or church buildings). The martyr's death was said to be his or her "birthday," or day of entrance to heavenly life. Alleged relics of martyrs became the prized possession of churches or (often wealthy) individuals, and various special powers came to be attributed to them. Initially such veneration was largely a private affair, shared in by a few local devotees, but it was soon taken over by clergy, who often used public celebrations to great effect in their communities, especially in the fourth century and beyond. Martyrs came to be seen as special saints, with particular intercessory powers, and their fame often spread well beyond their local region. To pagan critics, the degree of public theater that came to characterize the self-sacrifice of the Christians and the commemoration of their courage underlined the absurdity of Christian beliefs and pointed rather worryingly to their capacity to make significant impressions on naive people.

The Mid- to Late Second Century

Other martyrs of the middle of the second century included Telesphorus, bishop of Rome, who gave his life for his faith around 137, and then, much more famously, Justin, a Christian teacher in Rome, whose witness earned him the designation "Justin Martyr." Justin was put to death during the reign of Marcus Aurelius (161–180), which proved a difficult time for believers. The anonymous Christian author of the document known as the *Letter to Diognetus*, an apologetic tract written to an unidentified inquirer into the faith, possibly around this period, speaks of believers, who "live in the world but are not of the world," being harassed, condemned, and persecuted by all.[22] Justin himself protested against the injustice that saw Roman Christians summarily executed in the 150s for no crime other than confession of the name of Christ. In this context, it was not only church leaders who paid the price but the faithful of all kinds.

Marcus Aurelius's period as emperor was marked by a number of serious political, military, and economic challenges for Rome. There were invasions on the empire's northern frontiers and a variety of natural disasters, including plague, floods, and famine. When circumstances were difficult at an imperial level, it was normal to look for local scapegoats. More than ever, the Christians were a convenient target of blame for all sorts of problems, and they took over from the Jews the unenviable position of being hated as the primary enemies of social and political order. It is even possible that the legal process by which an informer could denounce someone for being a Christian was relaxed somewhat in these years in order to encourage the extermination of Christians from society. Very often, though, the primary initiative for persecution came from the general populace rather than from the authorities. If anything, magistrates seem to have tried to get Christians to conform outwardly in order to forestall unrest and to save them from death, and there is evidence that the determination of some believers to lose their lives rather than compromise was a source of genuine puzzlement and sadness to their political masters.

Marcus Aurelius was an educated Stoic, whose personal *Meditations* became an influential expression of later Stoic thought; they represent the aphorisms of a sober and reflective man grappling with the responsibilities of his imperial role in difficult times. Marcus could scarcely comprehend the Christians' readiness for martyrdom. His Stoic creed allowed for suicide, but only if it was a rational decision; as far as he could see, the Christians obstinately and recklessly threw their lives away when they were offered a reasonable way of escape. His personal tutor, the scholarly rhetorician Marcus Cornelius Fronto, may have encouraged him in reaching such conclusions because Fronto believed the Christians constituted a depraved and superstitious band of dangerous malcontents, whose actions only fomented civil instability and whose ostensible courage amounted to sheer perversity.

Justin (ca. 100–165) was a native of Samaritan Palestine, from Flavia Neapolis (the modern Nablus), but of Greek parentage. As a young man he had searched for truth in a variety of philosophical schools, and he had eventually become convinced that Christianity represented ultimate enlightenment and the highest path of morality. Part of the inspiration for his conversion, according to his own account, was the bravery shown by Christians in the face of death. After a period in Ephesus, Justin moved to Rome, where he established a school devoted to the teaching and defense of the gospel of Christ as the perfect philosophy. His writings represent the most substantial body of literature surviving from the group of second-century authors whom we call the apologists, and they are of great significance for our picture of Christian intellectual activity in this period.

We shall come to these works in more detail shortly, but for now it is sufficient to note that Justin's bold efforts to persuade his world that Christian philosophy was the way of the future ultimately failed. Brought before the prefect of Rome as a result of what began as a private dispute with a rival Cynic teacher, Crescens, he acknowledged that he was a teacher of Christianity. The elderly prefect, Junius Rusticus, endeavored to dissuade him from incurring the death sentence that this confession entailed and urged him to prove his loyalty to the Roman state in the usual manner by offering incense to the gods. On refusing, Justin, along with a number of other Christians, was condemned to be scourged and beheaded.

A more brutal fate still befell a group of Christians in Gaul in 177. According to a letter sent from the churches in Lyons and Vienne to the churches in Asia and Phrygia, there had been a violent mob uprising against the Christian community in Lyons. After some ugly public harassment, a number of believers had been arrested and tried for the crime of being Christians. Some of them apostatized, denying that they had ever been followers of Christ; others were condemned by "evidence" extorted from their slaves that they were guilty of crimes such as cannibalism and incest, just as was suspected.

When the local governor discovered that one of the confessors was a Roman citizen, he wrote to Marcus Aurelius for advice. The emperor's response was that Roman citizens who admitted to being Christians should be beheaded (as opposed to being crucified, burned alive, or thrown to the beasts, and thus a concession to their status); all others who confessed should be put to death by torture, though clemency should be extended to any who recanted. The latter provision seems to have benefited few, as a number of individuals who had first denied their faith then withdrew their renunciations. They were kept in prison under appalling conditions of torture and deprivation, where some of them died; the rest were substituted for gladiators in the amphitheater in Lyons, as the highlight of the games at the annual feast of the "Three Gauls" on 1 August.

Among those who perished was the first bishop of Lyons, Pothinus, who was over ninety years of age and physically infirm, and a fourteen-year-old boy named Ponticus. The most heroic victim was a slave-girl named Blandina, who is said by the later church historian Eusebius of Caesarea[23] to have steadfastly refused to renounce Christ or state that evil practices were perpetrated among the believers. Her courage is reported to have been so outstanding that she did not go to her own death until she had first inspired her fellow sufferers, encouraging them "as a noble mother" to advance resolutely toward their fate before she followed on behind.[24] In all, forty-eight Christians were martyred in the amphitheater of Lyons.

Amphitheater at Lyons, scene of Christian executions in A.D. 177. Illustration from E. Ferguson. Used by permission.

The incident in the Rhone valley was not so much an act of political oppression as an expression of mob justice at which the authorities connived. It is conceivable that the roots of the tragedy lay in local hostilities to the Christians, not just as Christians but also as foreigners, for the believers may well have been in many cases immigrants from Asia Minor (Pothinus, for one, was almost certainly Asian). It is also quite likely that the local nobility saw their victims not only as legitimate targets for persecution but also as a convenient way of avoiding the expense of providing gladiators for the annual games. Dreadful as the deaths of the Christians were, there is no reason to believe that the local believers had been harried over a protracted period; the governor had, after all, allowed Pothinus to reach old age unharmed in his role of bishop. The effort to halt the judicial proceedings pending guidance from the emperor in the case of a Roman citizen also bespeaks a desire on the governor's part to follow official procedure, even if no serious steps were taken to prevent the ill-treatment of other defendants. Overall, it would seem that the events of 177 were more to do with political expediency than organized efforts to liquidate Christians. All the same, this local pogrom could hardly have taken place had not the emperor been hostile to Christianity.

A smaller-scale repression took place in North Africa on 17 July 180 at a town called Scillium, near Carthage, where a group of twelve Christians, both men and women, were put to death. The local governor again appears to have offered them every chance to recant, and they were not tortured. The governor's instincts were humane, and all he seems to have sought was evidence of basic conformity with the law, but his offer of a period for further reflection was rejected; finally his patience was exhausted, and the believers were executed for their resolute refusal to swear by the *genius* of Caesar. The account of the Scillitan martyrs is the first surviving document from Christian North Africa, and it shows the zeal with which from early times the believers in that region viewed their commitment to Christ. These ordinary Christians are pictured as giving thanks for their death sentence, convinced that martyrdom guaranteed direct entrance to paradise. Such enthusiasm for the martyr's crown would be a typical feature of North African spirituality from the later second century onward.

The story of the Christians' lot in the Roman Empire is a complex one. Sometimes emperors who are traditionally regarded as positive rulers presided at a time when Christians found life difficult, as was the case with Marcus Aurelius, while otherwise "bad" emperors granted Christians a fair degree of freedom. The latter was the case with Marcus

Aurelius's son, Commodus, who reigned from 180 to 192. Commodus was an unsuccessful emperor in many respects and was in the end assassinated, but during his tenure the churches enjoyed a period of relative calm. A number of believers were released from servitude in the mines of Sardinia, where they had been sent by Marcus Aurelius. It is possible that some of the relief for Christians was secured by the agencies of Marcia, Commodus's concubine, who had been converted or was at the least strongly sympathetic toward Christianity.

Under the first emperor of the "Severan" dynasty, Septimius Severus (193–211), an imperial edict (202) banned conversion to either Judaism or Christianity. Bans had been placed on Jewish proselytizing before, but this was the first time such a stipulation had been made against the Christian faith. The law precipitated a number of outbreaks of persecution in Alexandria, Carthage, Corinth, and Rome. In the first of these, Clement, the leader of the Christian school in Alexandria (see pp. 251–56), was forced to flee the city, and a number of believers were martyred, among them the father of a zealous young student of the Bible named Origen, soon to become one of the great figures of early Christian scholarship (see pp. 256–69). According to Eusebius, Origen himself was thwarted in his desire to suffer along with his father, when his mother hid his clothes.[25]

Perpetua and Felicitas

At Carthage, the Christian martyrs included two young women, Perpetua and Felicitas, who were at that time catechumens (that is, undergoing "catechesis," or a course of instruction in the Christian faith in preparation for baptism; see pp. 272–78). Perpetua and Felicitas did not suffer alone; at least three men, Revocatus, Saturninus, and Secundulus, are said to have been arrested along with them. Perpetua was a well-born married woman[26] with a young child, and Felicitas was perhaps a pregnant slave-girl (though there is some doubt about her servile status). They and their companions were exposed to the beasts in the amphitheater before having their throats cut by a gladiator. In a valuable work known as *The Passion of Perpetua and Felicitas*, we have a record of Perpetua's account of her arrest and trial, including a narrative allegedly written by the subject herself (though perhaps penned by another author). The text as a whole is a composite of various layers and may reflect a Montanist source; Perpetua is celebrated for her visions, and one of the contributors to the text may have seen her as a Montanist convert, even if she was not this in fact.

Part of ancient Carthage. Illustration from M. North. Used by permission.

However terrible the suffering of Christians such as these, we should not overstate the degree to which believers in general were actively pursued in this period. From the record of Perpetua's and Felicitas's suffering, it is clear that there were no mass arrests in Carthage, nor did the victims' fellow Christians flee; instead, they openly visited them in prison. As elsewhere, it appears that the Roman authorities would have been content to release their prisoners on proof of a sacrifice on behalf of the emperor. The victims in each case were catechumens, not clergy, which seems to reflect the pattern of Septimius Severus's repressions; the emperor's concern may have been to try to inhibit conversion by acting against those in preparation for baptism or the newly baptized.

After the initial, sporadic troubles in 202 to 203, most of Septimius's reign proved fairly tolerant as far as Christian believers were concerned. Such repressions that did occur were often rooted in personal disputes or popular grudges at a local level or were carried out by officials keen to sound a warning note of their judicial authority over their communities. As ever, Christians continued to be easy objects of blame for problems ranging from barbarian invasions to natural disasters. As Tertullian famously objected: "If the Tiber rises to the city walls, if the Nile does not rise to the fields, if the heavens do not move or if the earth does, if

there is famine or plague, the cry is at once: 'The Christians to the lion!'
Really? All of them to one lion?"[27]

The images that continue to lurk in the minds of some modern
Christians—that the believers of the first and second centuries were
routinely subjected to persecution and physical danger by the Roman
authorities—cannot be substantiated in the hard evidence of history.
There were some particularly ghastly instances of cruelty and violence,
and there was undoubtedly a great deal of criticism, gossip, innuendo,
and resentment that from time to time flared up into personal denunciations and mob brutality. Nevertheless, with a few exceptions, during
this period there was no concerted effort on the part of Rome to crush
Christianity. For all the official disdain for their beliefs and the illicit
status of their faith, Christians in large part were able to live, assemble,
and worship without serious hindrance.

There were some short, sharp persecutions in the early third century
to which we shall come in a subsequent chapter, but serious, systematic
oppression did not occur until later on, in the campaigns of the emperors Decius (249–251) and Valerian (253–260), and then especially in the
Great Persecution, which began under Diocletian in 303 and lasted until
312. In these later imperial policies, Christianity was indeed seen as a
serious threat to the stability of the Roman Empire generally, and the
hostility that had hitherto been confined to popular emotions, philosophical critique, or local harassment found much more dangerous and
sustained expression in official political strategies. The reprisals on the
churches then were severe indeed, particularly in the early years of the
fourth century.

Intellectual Opposition and the Beginnings of Christian Apologetics

All the same, everyday tensions and intermittent political troubles were
only one aspect of the pressure placed upon Christians. Challenges also
came from intellectual quarters. The significance of these was greater
than we might instinctively suppose, for the thinkers and scholars who
opposed Christianity were not simply conducting academic discussions
among a small elite; they were also offering implicit intellectual validation
for the kinds of resentment directed at Christians at a popular level. The
industry of a pagan intelligentsia arrayed against the ideas and practices
of Christianity testifies to the seriousness with which the spread of the
gospel was viewed by many educated Graeco-Roman minds.[28]

The apparent exclusiveness of Christian convictions was seen as not just eccentric but illogical and dangerous, and even if their beliefs were not always to be met with political measures, they increasingly deserved to be addressed with cultural and intellectual ones. In order to appreciate what was entailed in this process, we need to look at the work of the protagonists on both sides—both the defenders and the critics of Christianity. Amid the ferment of the respective arguments deployed by friends and foes, the second and early third centuries produced some of the most seminal thinking in the history of Christian theology and bequeathed ideas and frameworks that profoundly shaped doctrinal discussion ever after.

Intellectual opposition took various forms. Christians already faced polemic from Jews; in the second century they also began to encounter serious critique from Greek and Roman philosophers and literary figures. While Christian leaders were evolving principles such as the rule of faith (see pp. 168–70) and catholicity to define the essentials of their faith against unacceptable ideas from within, they were at the same time dealing with ideological attacks from the outside, in the form of rhetorical debates and written polemics framed by gifted opponents in Rome, Athens, and Alexandria. They responded to these external challenges with a number of strategies, ranging from direct rebuttal of caricatures and false allegations to the use of arguments deliberately designed to build bridges toward those who saw the world differently from themselves. Apologetics was a mixture of self-definition, defense, and outreach—a simultaneous demarcation of Christianity over against competing worldviews, an appeal for due understanding of its beliefs and practices, and an effort to persuade its critics that the faith really was true.

The first Christian apologist of whom we know was a man named Quadratus, who lived during the reign of Hadrian and was perhaps bishop of Athens. Around the late 120s, he wrote a defense of Christianity to Hadrian. From a surviving fragment of the work, and from Eusebius's report of its author's contribution,[29] we learn that Quadratus appealed to the healing miracles of Jesus as evidence of his divine power and claimed that some of those whom Jesus had raised from the dead had even survived to his own day. A few years later, an Athenian writer named Aristides presented an apology to the emperor Antoninus Pius (ca. 140). This document is lost in its original Greek form, though it survives in an expanded Syriac translation, and parts of the Greek version made their way into a later Greek legend. Aristides argued that the existence of an eternal, perfect creator God was proved by the order of the world, but only Christians rightly knew and honored this God. Pagans, barbarians, and Jews all failed to recognize and respond appropriately to what was disclosed of God's character in creation.

Justin Martyr

The most significant of the apologists, though, was Justin Martyr (ca. 100–165). Justin wrote two Apologies, the first of which is by far the more substantial. His *First Apology* was addressed to Antoninus Pius around 151. A few years later, the work was reissued along with a supplementary text less than a quarter of its length, and this latter work became known as the *Second Apology*. At some point in the later 150s, Justin also published a longer treatise entitled *Dialogue with Trypho the Jew*, which purports to be the record of a conversation he had held with Trypho, an educated Hellenistic Jew, around 135. In addition to these books, we have some fragments of other texts by Justin, including one on the resurrection of the flesh and another refuting Gnostic heresies, but his main contribution lies in the three works for which he is famous, all of which were preserved by a single manuscript (itself sadly destroyed during the Second World War).

The *First Apology* sought to respond directly to pagan criticisms of Christianity. Justin dismissed crude ideas that Christians were guilty of cannibalism and incest and argued that in fact their morality was exemplary, for they practiced obedience to God, sexual restraint, and community of goods, and they cared for one another. They prayed for their enemies, and when necessary they were prepared to face death bravely. Their worship practices were not secret rites involving magic or immorality. Baptized after a process of careful preparation and a solemn declaration of commitment, believers became part of a community characterized by a new life. Their gatherings for Sunday worship focused on a Eucharist taken as the flesh and blood of Jesus, who was the Savior of the world; they also involved prayers, readings from the apostles and prophets, and the taking of a collection for those in need—the poor, widows, and orphans. Justin's descriptions of Christian behavior offer very valuable information on liturgical and structural organization in his time (see pp. 280–81). He speaks, for example, of the worship service as led by a "president," who gives thanks at the communion feast and then gives bread and "wine mixed with water" to deacons to distribute to the people. Some of the Eucharist is set aside for people who are absent. Prayer is conducted with the congregation standing. Baptism is specifically into the triune name of God.

The weightiest aspect of Justin's argument in both versions of his *Apology* is his case that Christian theology is the true "philosophy." Although he utterly rejects pagan mythology as absurd superstition, Justin labors to point up the connections between the best insights of Greek philosophy and the beliefs of the Christians. The transcendent, mysterious God spoken of by Platonist thinkers is the God of biblical revelation. This God was made known throughout history by his divine Word or *Logos*, in a manner reminiscent of the Stoic idea that the *Logos* is immanent in all reality. Not only is it the case that all people have a sense of God's existence; the light that they have is implanted by the *Logos*, for, as the Stoics saw, seeds of the *Logos* are present throughout the world. For Justin, the *Logos* was present in the patriarchs, prophets, and philosophers, and it was this *Logos* that had become incarnate definitively in Jesus Christ (John 1:1–18).

Those who saw aspects of the truth in the past, such as Abraham and Socrates, did so as enlightened by the same Word, and so they were implicitly Christian. Teachers who opposed the falsehoods of pagan religion in every age found themselves condemned as "godless"; Socrates was put to death for the same alleged crime of which Christians are regularly accused because he, like them, dared to criticize the corruptions of traditional piety. However great the insights in truth and morality attained by people like Socrates and Plato, though, they are now relativized, for Christ represents the fullness of everything that these thinkers were seeking.

Justin weaves together a variety of themes to make his points. Hellenistic Jewish apologists such as Philo had long contended that Plato's wisdom was derived from the Pentateuch. To this argument Justin adds a further synthesis: the language of "Father" and "Son" that Christians use to describe the relationship of God and Jesus is akin to philosophical arguments that the immanent *Logos* is both derived from and yet distinct from the transcendent One. The Platonists saw that the supreme God interacted with material creation via the mediation of the *Logos*; the Stoics believed that the *Logos* could be thought of as both "essential" and "expressed" (like the difference between an idea in the mind and the utterance of it in speech), and that once expressed it was both derived from and yet "other than" its source. Such Platonist and Stoic ideas represented a measure of apprehension of the Christian claim that God is both transcendent and immanent. The Son derives his being from the Father, as light from light, and is other than the Father, yet the oneness of God is not violated. By drawing on an assortment of philosophical concepts,

Justin seeks to make his case that Christianity is entirely reasonable and that it is the perfect expression of that to which the best of pagan wisdom has always aspired.

Justin's *Dialogue with Trypho the Jew* reveals something of the character of Christian-Jewish exchanges in this period. As a wearer of the philosopher's cloak, the recognized dress of the teacher of philosophy, Justin argues that the true philosophy of the Christian faith has its roots in the Jewish Scriptures. These Scriptures themselves, however, speak of Christ, and in him they are completely fulfilled, so that the true "owners" of their teaching are Christians. Jesus is the climax of the prophets' messages: the one who perfectly keeps the Law and so sets it aside ever after as a way of salvation. He is the realization of everything to which the most potent symbolic events of the Scriptures were pointing. The survival of Noah and his entourage in the ark at the flood; the exodus from Egypt and the crossing of the Red Sea; Joshua's conquest of the Promised Land—all were "types" or foreshadowings of what God would do in Christ to redeem sinners from judgment.

Justin draws on a rich tradition of Jewish interpretation to argue that Christ is the fulfillment of messianic texts and that his achievement represents the consummation of God's purposes of salvation. Some of the scriptural arguments are decidedly forced, and a measure of confusion sometimes affects the debate with Trypho in that Justin at times assumes a form of the Septuagintal text that his interlocutor does not recognize. He rejects Trypho's suggestion that he ought to become a Jewish proselyte and criticizes Jews who acknowledge Jesus as the Messiah but do not regard him as divine. The treatise provides further evidence that there continued to be at this time many Jewish believers who professed to follow Jesus but did not accept the full implications of a mainstream Christian position. Justin indicates that some of these people were concerned to persuade Gentile converts to adopt Jewish rites, which he believed showed they were not true Christians. (Gentiles who gave in to their stipulations were equally alienated from salvation.) But he believed that Jewish followers of Jesus who did not make such demands on Gentiles were genuinely Christian. Justin is nevertheless insistent that the Jesus who was crucified must be recognized by Jews as the very God who appeared to Moses in the burning bush and spoke through the prophets.

Justin wrote in an age when contacts between Jews and Christians, while still close, were increasingly strained. He testifies to the reality of Christians being cursed in Jewish synagogues (see pp. 144–45) and to the existence of propaganda and vigorous attempts at proselytism on both sides. In this milieu, the respective positions adopted by Justin and Trypho in their stylized literary exchange are a good deal more tolerant than those that might have been found among a number of their contemporaries in both camps. Here the dialogue is courteous and respectful on both sides. Justin himself seeks to show an inclusive attitude toward genuine Jewish believers in Jesus, aware that not all of his fellow Christians would agree with such a stance. Trypho, for his part, comes across as an entirely reasonable conversation partner, who is completely faithful to his position without being narrow-minded or unduly hostile to other intellectual perspectives. In the end, however, he is not persuaded by Justin's arguments.

Justin's writings offer fascinating insights into the nature of Christian attempts to respond to criticism from both pagan and Jewish sources. In the one case, he calculates that Christianity is best defended by the argument that the wisdom for which the world has sought is to be found definitively in Christ. In the other, he seeks to contend that Judaism in its conventional form is no longer an appropriate expression of the truth of its own Scriptures; the gospel has fulfilled and superseded the Law of Moses and the expectations of the prophets. Those Jews who are truly believers in Jesus need to demonstrate their recognition that the Law and the rituals of their faith have thus been relativized as far as Gentile converts are concerned, and they cannot require new initiates to observe their demands. With both secular thinkers and Jews, Justin boldly appropriates his opponents' own territory, claiming that their ideals and hopes are realized in Christ.

Ultimately Justin's strategy did not convince, and his vigorous style of presenting his case in the context of philosophical disputation in particular did not save him from the judgment of political authorities who failed to see why his convictions needed to be expressed in such an exclusive fashion if they had so much in common with the positions of others. Nevertheless, though Justin's devotion to his philosophy brought him martyrdom in the end, his articulation of his faith as an intellectually coherent force was of great importance in his cultural environment.

Other Apologists

One of Justin's pupils in Rome was Tatian. Born in the period 125 to 130, he came from Mesopotamia, of Syrian parentage, and had been well educated in the Greek tradition. Converted to Christianity in Rome, he taught there for a time after Justin's death before returning to his native area. Tatian appears to have adopted there an extreme form of asceticism, which became known to its opponents as the "Encratite" heresy (from the Greek *enkrateia*, "continence") from its belief that baptized believers, as united directly to the Holy Spirit, should live as celibates and practice vegetarianism (see p. 314). We have two extant works by Tatian. One that we have noted already is his *Diatessaron*, or harmony of the four Gospels, which was widely used by Syriac churches in lieu of the individual canonical Gospels until the fifth century. The other is his *Oration to the Greeks*. This work, probably dating to the late 160s, is a lecture rather than an apology, but it is designed to set out Tatian's view of contemporary Graeco-Roman philosophy and religion.

Tatian had been converted after a pilgrimage that had taken him around several cities of the Roman Empire and brought him into close acquaintance with a range of religious and philosophical systems, including one of the mystery religions. All of these paths had failed to satisfy him. He presents Christianity as the only truth and seeks to establish its credibility both from its content and from its age. For him, there were no such people as "Christians before Christ"; the teachings of paganism were always in error. Tatian rails against the corruptions of the Roman Empire in law and politics, which in his eyes illustrate the bankruptcy of secular thinking. His vision was therefore much narrower than Justin's and his spirit much more polemical than his.

For all that, Tatian's diatribe against paganism is informed by a solid knowledge of its teachings, and his effort to convince others of his case is based on the assumption that human beings are rational beings who can be persuaded by a strong, logical argument. While his own personality reflects the struggles of an individual who found himself drawn more and more toward wholesale repudiation of the world, his cultural style as we have it in his *Oration* continues to deploy intellectual argumentation to present the gospel as a form of philosophy—despised and rejected by the world of Rome and Athens, but in reality the truth of God.

The more liberal style of Justin resurfaced in the work of Athenagoras, a Christian philosopher from Athens. We know almost nothing about his life, but around 177 he presented Marcus Aurelius and Commodus with an impressive work entitled *Plea for the Christians*. The address of a philosopher to rulers who were themselves philosophers, it sought to refute popular charges against the Christians and to argue that Christian belief was in harmony with the best of Greek philosophy. Athenagoras dismisses allegations that Christians are atheists and that they participate in "Thyestean feasts" and practice Oedipodean intercourse—that is, cannibalism and incest.[30] He argues that reason demonstrates that there is one God, the creator of all things, who is transcendent, eternal, and incomprehensible. But Christians are also able to assert these things in the light of the Scriptures, where the witness of the prophets testifies to the character of God as triune. The gods of pagan religion, with their physical properties and sexual dalliances, are ridiculous; Christians are right to refuse to sacrifice to them, because the true God has no need of human offerings.

At the same time, Athenagoras does not simply dismiss pagan veneration of the gods as idolatry; the gods are frankly said to be human creations, fabricated out of reverence for mortals who had first achieved or discovered something.[31] Athenagoras writes respectfully of the emperors, and his tone with regard to the structures of his political world is markedly different from Tatian's, but the emperor is to be honored, not worshiped. Athenagoras's concern is to commend the Christian faith as rational and attractive for those who are already of the mind that crude polytheism is problematic and to persuade them that the best answers to their questions are to be found in biblical revelation. Athenagoras is also credited with a work defending resurrection, which seeks to show that God is well capable, as creator of the body, of raising it to life and transforming it beyond death, so that human beings may realize their God-given destiny of living a perfect, embodied existence in the presence of God forever.

Some similar emphases to those of Athenagoras—albeit couched in a tone closer to Tatian's—are found in Theophilus, who was bishop of Antioch from 169. Theophilus wrote much, but of his writings only one work survives, a defense of Christianity in three books addressed to a friend named Autolycus, written around the year 180. It presents a rather disorganized argument against paganism, written to a Gentile by a converted Gentile but displaying many similarities to Hellenistic Jewish thought. Theophilus contrasts the true God with the gods of Graeco-Roman religion. God is made visible not in the form of idols but in creation and providence. The universe originates with God, not as a result of the imposition of order on preexisting matter, but as created out of nothing. The disclosure of God and of the moral standards enjoined in the Scriptures is not a recent human invention but a reality that predates the thinking of the Greek writers, philosophers, and poets. Christians think, speak, and act as they do because they have a love for truth, and their position is commended to Autolycus in the belief that all who similarly love truth ought to recognize the potency of the Christian case.

In addition to these works by Justin, Tatian, Athenagoras, and Theophilus, we know of a few other apologetic writers. We possess, via Eusebius of Caesarea, a few fragments of an apology addressed to Marcus Aurelius by Melito, bishop of Sardis, about 170. Melito appears to have seen the Roman world as specially prepared for the gospel in the providence of God, and he holds out the promise that the spread of Christianity brings blessing and prosperity to the empire. These views would be popularized considerably in the fourth century, especially by Eusebius, but it may be that Melito was the first to enunciate them. We also know the names of other apologists whose writings are lost, such as Aristo of Pella, Miltiades, and Apollinarius of Hierapolis, the last of whom was another petitioner of Marcus Aurelius.

The efforts of such figures confirmed to some pagan onlookers that Christianity was not just a superstition but a wholesale philosophy of life, implicitly comparable to the other schools of thought that could be found in the second-century world. This was how the Christians were seen by the great pagan physician and writer Galen, a native of Pergamum who traveled extensively around the Mediterranean world, studied in Alexandria, and lived for a time in Rome in the early years of Marcus Aurelius's reign. Galen disagreed with the Christians, seeing them, along with the Jews, as naive and dogmatic and in their arguments overly reliant on appeals to faith. Their God seemed to him capricious, and their doctrine of creation at odds with Greek cosmology. Nevertheless, Galen was impressed by the quality of individual Christian lifestyles, and he was prepared to treat the Christian way as a system of thought and behavior akin in principle to other philosophical traditions.

Galen's curiosity about the Christians helped to pave the way for other, more sustained engagement with the Christian faith on the part of pagan intellectuals. Our most valuable window into the nature of the relationship between secular and Christian thought in this period comes not from the apologists or those who, like Galen, observed aspects of Christian practice but did not have very extensive knowledge of Christian doctrine. The best picture is to be found among the sharpest and best informed critics of Christianity. It is from them that we learn of the kinds of intellectual criticisms that Christian thinkers took most seriously.

Celsus

The most famous of these intellectual critics was a Platonist philosopher named Celsus, who produced in the late 170s a work entitled *The True Discourse*, which mounted a sustained attack on Christianity. We cannot be entirely sure what prompted Celsus to write his work, but most scholars believe he was moved to respond to the Apologies of Justin Martyr. The majority of our text of *The True Discourse*—perhaps 70 percent in all—survives as quotations in *Against Celsus*, a Christian rejoinder produced by Origen more than a generation later, probably in the later 240s. We can only assume that these quotations are basically reliable, but it is of course impossible to be sure; certainly Origen elected to ignore parts of Celsus's work in which he had no interest but which may have been of importance to the weight of Celsus's overall argument. We know nothing of Celsus himself except what this text reveals, but it seems likely from his own evidence that he came from Syria.

Celsus's treatise is of major importance for three reasons. First, it is the oldest surviving attack on Christianity by a pagan intellectual for which we possess any substantial detail. Second, it is clear from what we have that Celsus was remarkably well informed about Christian beliefs. His polemic was formidable because it did not amount to a mere rehearsal of popular prejudices (though Celsus has plenty of harsh things to say about the character of contemporary believers) but was based on an impressive degree of acquaintance with Christian ideas and practices. He was the first opponent of Christianity to give serious attention to the figure of Jesus, and he recognized that it was not enough just to mock Christians for their attitudes and values; the credibility of their faith rested upon the logic of their claims about the one they called Savior and Lord. While Celsus's knowledge of the Scriptures did not cover much of what would be regarded as canonical, he knew at least the Gospels, especially Matthew's, and he was able to point out apparent discrepancies between them. He also knew Genesis and was able to cite works such as the *Epistle of Barnabas* and the *Book of Enoch*.

Celsus had a broad knowledge of Christian theology, and he was well aware of the differences that existed between Christian groups in his time. He had firsthand knowledge of Eastern Christian prophesying and charismatic phenomena such as speaking in tongues. He knew very well just how diverse were the opinions of those who called themselves followers of Jesus—there were Gnostic sects, movements pioneered by female apostles, Marcionites, and many other heretics besides—more, in fact, than Origen himself had heard of when he came to respond to Celsus's case. Celsus sought to show that the disunity and fragmentation of the Christian movement was testimony to its essential incoherence and falsehood in intellectual and moral terms. Christians only *looked like* a unified force because of their common hostility to their social world and their common fear of persecution.

The third reason why Celsus's work is of significance is that it established a precedent for later anti-Christian polemic on several issues, such as the nature of Scripture and the relationship between secular reasoning and Christian doctrine. Even if later writers did not use Celsus as a formal model, there is every probability that the nature of his attack on Christianity would have been known to at least some of them in broad terms. Celsus was long dead when Origen sought to refute his arguments; the fact that Origen still felt the need to counter his allegations may well suggest that they continued to attract some reasonably widespread interest among Christianity's foes. Many scholars believe it likely that Origen was in fact not the first Christian to respond to Celsus in print; at a time when the missionary expansion of the church had gathered some pace and Christianity was attracting a wider range of converts, the kind of opposition represented by Celsus offered a serious challenge indeed.

Celsus launched a multilayered attack on the Christians. As a Platonist, he found many of the core doctrines of Christian faith incredible. To his mind, an unchanging God who was not susceptible to suffering simply could not have become human, suffered, and died. Jesus was in fact a wonder-worker, whose miracles were performed by evil powers for evil ends. The moral character of his life was dubious rather than exemplary, and he died the ignominious death of a common criminal. The stories of his physical resurrection were myths, and Christians were in reality guilty of worshiping a dead man. The deity of Christ could not be proved by appeals to the prophecies of the Jewish Scriptures, for these were contradictory and unreliable and could just as easily be applied to someone other than Jesus—contemporary Christian prophets continued to deceive gullible people with their fantastic stories. Christian hope for the resurrection of the body and the consummation of all things was fallacious, for salvation must consist in the release of the soul from the contaminations of the physical world, and time could not be viewed in linear terms as a process that climaxes in an ultimate fate for creation of heaven or hell.

Celsus contended that Christianity could not appeal to Platonism to offer serious support for its ideas; it was in truth a medley of Jewish ideas mixed up with crude distortions of Greek concepts, tenable only for unintelligent and uncultured people. Greek sages had not borrowed from the Scriptures; Christians had stolen some of their notions from the Greeks and twisted them into caricatures of their original forms. Christianity was younger than and inferior to the splendors of Greek culture. The Christians' opposition to the imperial cult and the ancestral religious traditions of the Roman world showed their seditious tendencies, and it was therefore legitimate that the followers of Jesus should be executed and their movement should be driven from the earth. They were worse than the Jews, who, for all their idiosyncrasies, at least followed the customs of their fathers by observing their Law, celebrating their festivals, and upholding their religious and ceremonial practices. The Christians claimed to be an offshoot of Judaism, yet they had abandoned the substance of that inheritance, and their claims were in turn not recognized by the Jews themselves.

In Celsus's social and political criticisms of Christianity, we come close to one of the main motivating factors in his polemic: a concern that the Christians were a practical danger to the Roman world. As a sophisticated thinker, Celsus had his own doubts about the theology of polytheism at a theoretical level, but, like many intellectuals in antiquity, he opted for a social conservatism. The maintenance of good order depended upon the preservation of age-old religious customs, and in the absence of compelling reasons for adopting some alternative way of regulating human life, responsible people had a duty to uphold religious conventions and play their part in the preservation of cultural decency. The Christians, however, refused to do this, resisting their obligations to support the emperor, serve in the army, or hold public office, all of which duties were underpinned by religious symbolism. By challenging the traditional gods of the Roman order, the Christians were threatening the fabric of society.

Viewed as a whole, Celsus's attack on the teaching and behavior of Christians may be seen as an implicit acknowledgment of the cultural significance that Christianity had come to assume by his time. Its teaching was seen as something *worth* opposing both for its intellectual quality and for its practical implications. While it would clearly be an overstatement to suggest that in attacking Christianity Celsus was in any way giving in to it, it is certainly true that in framing his critique as he did, Celsus found himself having to chart a defense of paganism as an alternative to the Christian way of salvation. Although he offered a much more careful and even dispassionate critique than some of his ideological successors in the third or fourth centuries, the terms in which he conducted his engagement with Christian beliefs signaled a shift in the debate between paganism and Christianity.

Celsus's dispute with the Christians was a quarrel about the nature of religion in general. Was religion a matter of the beliefs and practices of a particular nation or group, or was it capable of transcending ethnic and social boundaries? If the latter, which was preferable—an inclusive polytheism supported by local traditions or a particularistic monotheism that contended that it alone possessed ultimate revelation? Celsus believed

Christianity to be dangerous because of what he saw as its sectarian tendencies and its spiritual privatizing of religion as something that assumed priority over political allegiances. But in trying to establish the grounds upon which people ought to believe that pagan philosophy and polytheism offered a better way, he was obliged to explain why this path was better as a way of life for all. In the process, he was implicitly accepting that the Christian gospel represented a wide-scale threat to the Roman way of organizing religion. Henceforth, there would be a conflict between two essentially different ways of understanding religious activity.

The Consequences of Critique

The effects of the intellectual critique of Christianity by secular thinkers in the second century were by no means entirely negative. The presence of such weighty opposition lent impetus to serious Christian thinking, and led to the emergence of a less occasional and more systematic style of Christian theologizing in response to the challenges raised. In handling the attacks of pagan polemic and the misrepresentations of Christian ideas, church leaders were obliged to explore the logic and the implications of their theological claims on a larger canvas than ever before.

As the faith was consolidated and the internal structures of its authority became more defined, theology moved from being primarily apologetic or practical to become a more ambitious and wide-ranging project, designed not only to meet ad hoc objections and distortions but to portray the gospel as a complete and compelling system of thought. The apologists' emphasis on categories such as the *Logos* and the oneness and goodness of God continued to influence the results. In other respects, however, Christians were also starting to evolve new and still more elaborate ways of configuring their doctrines as a conceptual scheme. In the West as well as the East, the results would be considerable.

8

CHRISTIAN THOUGHT IN THE WEST

▼

Gaul

Christianity seems to have first reached Gaul in the early second century, carried by believers from Asia Minor. As we saw in the previous chapter, the churches in the Rhone valley suffered persecution in 177 when Pothinus, the elderly first bishop of Lyons, and a group of other local believers were martyred for their faith. It is clear that by this time the Christians were well established at least in that region of Gaul, and a core among them was probably made up of Asians. It was in Lyons, the most important city in Roman Gaul, that Pothinus's successor, Irenaeus, another Asian, emerged as the first great systematic theologian of the Christian church.

Irenaeus

Irenaeus (ca. 140–200) was born into the church of Smyrna and was influenced by Polycarp. After moving at some point to Gaul, probably via Rome, he settled in Lyons and became a presbyter of the church. On his

225

return from a visit to Rome in 177 in the aftermath of the local persecution, he was elected bishop in succession to Pothinus. In his thought as in his life, Irenaeus belonged to both the East and the West, and one of the reasons his theology was of such importance was that he was able to operate within a western European context as someone who had a sound knowledge of Greek Christian thinking and was able to continue to write in Greek. As bishop, he proved an energetic pastor and teacher, devoting much of his efforts to the combating of Gnosticism, which in the form of a Valentinian sect (see pp. 165–68) was a serious force in the area around Lyons. Irenaeus produced a number of written works, but apart from some fragments, only two of these survive intact, neither of them in its original form. His influence, however, was far greater than the scale of his literary legacy might lead us to suppose.

The first of Irenaeus's extant writings is a work written in the early 180s, in five books, entitled *On the Detection and Refutation of "Knowledge" Falsely So-Called*, more commonly known as *Against All Heresies* (or simply *Against Heresies*), the title given it in an early Latin translation. The second is a short manual of instruction entitled *The Demonstration of the Apostolic Preaching*, dating to the early 190s, which was discovered in an Armenian translation in 1904.[1] The *Demonstration* was written to provide teaching for one of Irenaeus's friends. Its main objective is to demonstrate that the Christian faith is a fulfillment of the Jewish Scriptures, and there is accordingly much use of the *proof from prophecy* with regard to Christ.

It is on *Against Heresies*, however, that Irenaeus's status as a creative theologian chiefly depends. The work is a mine of information on the history of Gnostic sects in the second century, the subject of its first book, and even in the light of the modern discoveries of Gnostic texts at Nag Hammadi it remains a key source for our knowledge of Gnostic ideas. Irenaeus took care to familiarize himself with the essential principles upon which his opponents based their arguments, and he succeeded in presenting their views with an impressive degree of evenhandedness. His argument is disorganized in terms of structure, but it adduces a series of rebuttals of Gnostic teaching, based on reason (book 2), doctrine (book 3), and the sayings of Jesus, especially his parables (book 4). The final book (5) looks at other teaching of Jesus and Paul and offers a defense of the resurrection of the flesh, in opposition to Gnostic denials of this doctrine.

In so far as it is possible to isolate two essential themes in Irenaeus's theology, they are: first, his stress on the essential relationship between creation and redemption, and second, his emphasis on the incarnation.

Irenaeus insists that there is one God who creates and saves. There can be no question of creation being the work of a lesser deity, or of the material world being intrinsically corrupt. God always has with him his Word and his Spirit, pictured by Irenaeus as God's "two hands," by which he acts to create, sustain, and redeem. God's purpose for human beings, created in his image and likeness, is that they might enjoy fellowship with him and even participate in the divine nature.

Irenaeus sees human beings as composed of three elements—body, soul, and spirit—with the soul representing the image of God. In the fall, the divine likeness was lost, but the divine image remains (Irenaeus's distinction between "image" and "likeness" in Genesis 1:26–27 is dubious in exegetical terms). God permits evil in order to instruct creation by discipline and experience; history is a process by which God educates humanity toward maturity and the recovery of the divine likeness. The various covenants described in the Hebrew Scriptures (with Noah, Abraham, and Moses) were means by which God progressively revealed his will to men and women as they were ready to receive it. The incarnation was the climax of this process, for it was the entrance into human form of God himself, who constitutively effected for humans what they were incapable of doing for themselves—namely, bringing their humanity back into its proper relationship with God.

For Irenaeus, it is vital that the divine Word assumed full human flesh and suffered and died as a human being in order that he might represent humanity to God. Irenaeus draws particular attention to Paul's image of Christ as the "second man" and the "last Adam" (1 Cor. 15:45–49; see Rom. 5:12–21). The work of Christ is to *recapitulate* the original creation.[2] Such recapitulation does not take place simply because of the incarnation as a material act; it also depends upon the whole course of Christ's life, death, resurrection, and ascension. By living a perfect human life and triumphing at every stage over the power of evil, Jesus avoided the errors of the first Adam, reversed their ultimate effects, and restored humanity to its original glory in fellowship with God. The final consequence of his participation in the human condition is that human beings come by grace to participate in the divine nature (2 Peter 1:4).

Salvation, in Irenaeus's perspective, is never just a spiritualized affair or a release from the limitations of a body of flesh. He sees the kingdom of God as very much a physical phenomenon, and he teaches the prospect of an earthly millennial reign of God as part of the eschatological vision for creation. His millenarianism, based on a fairly literal reading of the vision in Revelation 20:1–6 of a future thousand-year reign of God on earth, would in time render his writings less influential in the

East than they proved to be in the West, as Greek theology on the whole came to be less enamored of such a literal interpretation of Revelation's language.[3] Irenaeus's holistic conception of creation's ultimate destiny was nevertheless consonant with many of the key emphases of Greek Christian thought, and his understanding of human deification would in time become a hallmark of Eastern doctrine.

Irenaeus produced a remarkably developed theology, shaped at every turn by a rich synthesis of Scripture and tradition and by a trinitarian conception of God. His fundamental conviction was that heresies such as Gnosticism were best tackled not by random responses to individual challenges but by the exposition of the overall logic of the Christian faith as it had been handed down in an orthodox tradition of teaching. His key significance lay in the fact that he attempted for the first time to synthesize the teachings of the Scriptures as a unitary force against the fragmented and changing claims of heretical alternatives. For the sheer expansiveness of his vision, and for his serious efforts to coordinate the various strands of his belief within an internally consistent framework of ideas, Irenaeus ranks as one of the greatest of early Christian thinkers.

The Church of Rome

Although Irenaeus painted a picture of the true church as a catholic and universal entity, he also chose to mention the church of Rome in particular as a powerful instance of the apostolic succession. He was able to quote the list of venerable bishops of Rome going back to the martyrs Peter and Paul. His list is probably a hybrid of reliable information and some imaginative guesswork; his claim that the Roman Christian community was "founded and organized" by Peter and Paul is definitely an exaggeration, for as we saw earlier, there were Christians there before them. His concern, though, was to signal the unbroken continuity of apostolic authority vested in one episcopal lineage as an example of the orthodox tradition. He asserted that "every church, that is, the faithful everywhere, should be in agreement with [the translation is disputed] this church, on account of its pre-eminent authority."[4] In context, it is clear that Irenaeus did not intend the church of Rome to be seen as the ultimate arbiter of the teaching of other churches; his point is that this church, with its demonstrable heritage from the apostles, is an especially illustrious example of a church in which true doctrine will be encountered.

By implication, other apostolic foundations such as Corinth or Ephesus might represent the same quality. Similar claims had already been made for Corinth as well as Rome by Hegesippus, a converted Jew and writer against Gnosticism who traveled from Palestine to Rome in the mid-170s, associating with bishops and compiling evidence that "in every succession and in every city, what the Law and the prophets and the Lord preached is faithfully followed."[5] What mattered, in theory, was not the name of Rome as such; Rome simply happened to be the principal Western illustration of such ancestry and thus the obvious Western place to look for sound belief and practice.

All the same, by the time of Hegesippus or Irenaeus, Rome was in fact long established as the natural center of gravity in the Western church. The city's political and cultural status had made this likely all along, and the fall of Jerusalem in 70 had led to a drift of Christian personnel and a diversion of Christian energies more and more toward the West. All the empire's roads led to Rome, and a vast array of believers made their way there from all over the Roman world to work, to teach, to share their theological ideas, and to broaden their support (as Marcion and Valentinus both sought to do)—or, in cases such as that of Ignatius, to die for their faith. Considerable prestige attached to the fact that Rome was the place where both Paul and Peter had been martyred, and memorial shrines to both apostles were already established by the second half of the second century. The memory of others in Rome who had paid the ultimate price for their devotion was also strong.

The Roman church was already wealthy by this time, and it seems to have used its resources fairly generously to benefit Christians in other places. Eusebius cites a portion of a letter written around 170 by Bishop Dionysius of Corinth to Bishop Soter of Rome in which the Roman believers are praised for their long-standing generosity to "many churches in every city, relieving the poverty of the needy, and making provision for the brothers [doing forced labor] in the mines by the contributions you have sent from the beginning, and thus preserving the ancestral custom of the Romans, true Romans that you are."[6] Conversions were occurring among some members of prominent noble Roman families, especially among their women. The church of Rome could point not only to a splendid heritage but to signs of an assured cultural status, even in the midst of enduring popular opposition and criticism from pagan intellectuals.

Yet Roman Christianity in the late second century remained diverse in character. As a magnet for believers from East as well as West, Rome was a center in which many different practices and perspectives coalesced, for all the rhetoric of Christians like Irenaeus about its common pattern of life. The early impact of Montanism in Rome is one evidence of that; so, too, is the influence of teachers such as Marcion and Valentinus who, though they were finally branded as heretics, did succeed in attracting sizable numbers of followers in Rome. The Roman church was especially susceptible to such currents by dint of its size. More significantly, there is some evidence to suggest that a strong system of central episcopal control actually took some time to emerge in Rome, and although the bishops of Rome undoubtedly did become very powerful, there was a lengthy period in which the city's various communities of believers remained dominated by local presbyters. Although there were increasingly clear distinctions between these presbyters and the bishop, a thoroughgoing monarchical episcopate may not have been fully established in Rome until into the third century.[7] In this climate, it was not difficult for charismatic teachers who arrived from other places to gain significant groups of disciples in particular congregations.

In the later years of the second century and the first part of the third, the church of Rome witnessed a number of major controversies about matters of practice, doctrine, and discipline. It was only in dealing with these, and the issues they generated concerning relations with churches elsewhere, that Rome's claims to authority grew into the kinds of assumptions with which the church there would ever after become associated.

Dating Easter

The first of the formative controversies was the so-called "Quartodeciman" dispute concerning the date of a central Christian festival. From the first century onward, many Christians had celebrated an annual feast called *Pascha*, in memory of Jesus's death and resurrection. In Christian preaching, the name *Pascha* came to be variously interpreted. Some said it derived from the Greek verb *paschein*, "to suffer," and so referred to the suffering of Christ as the true "Paschal" or "Passover" Lamb (1 Cor. 5:7).[8] Others, particularly in Alexandria, claimed that it came from *pascha* (a Greek rendering of an Aramaic word), "passage," and thus alluded to the "passage" of Christ from death to life and its implications for the believer who participated in this journey through baptism and the Eucharist. This prototypical Easter observance was probably an all-night vigil that culminated in the celebration of the Eucharist.[9]

Churches in Asia Minor traditionally observed the feast on the same day as the Jewish Passover, namely, the fourteenth day of the Jewish

month of Nisan, regardless of which day of the week this date fell, hence
the name "Quartodeciman" ("fourteenth"). They maintained that their
practice derived from the example of the apostle John. In Rome, the
Pascha was not held annually until perhaps 160, but when it was kept,
it was celebrated on the *Sunday following* the Jewish Passover, that is,
the Sunday following the first full moon after the spring equinox. This
practice was also observed in a large number of other communities, both
in the West and in Egypt. The upshot was that once every seven years
some Christians were remembering Jesus's death on the same day that
others were celebrating his resurrection.

Eusebius tells us that Polycarp of Smyrna traveled to Rome in his
old age (in 154 or 155) to discuss with the Roman bishop, Anicetus,
a number of matters concerning the observance of Easter, including
the question of its date. At this stage, annual observance in Rome was
still not the norm, and Anicetus followed the principle assumed by his
predecessors, namely, that the Lord's resurrection was celebrated every
Sunday rather than just once a year. The meeting between Polycarp and
Anicetus produced no agreement, but they parted on good terms and
pledged to respect each other's positions.[10]

In Asia there seems to have been some determination to retain the
fourteenth-day practice. In an influential sermon *On the Pascha* dating
to around 170, Bishop Melito of Sardis offered a forthright exposition
of the sacrifice of Christ as the fulfillment of the deliverance typified
by the Hebrew Passover. His appeal, however, was not to the continuity between Christianity and Judaism but to the absolute superiority
of Christ over the sacrifices of Jewish religious practice. Perhaps in
reaction against charges that the Quartodeciman position represented
a Judaizing tendency, Melito issued a bitter attack on Judaism, blaming "ungrateful Israel" for its crime in failing to recognize the Messiah
and in orchestrating his crucifixion. The tone of his rhetoric marked a
notably low point in early Christian anti-Semitism.

As far as the ritual practice of Easter observance was concerned,
discrepancy perhaps mattered little when believers were far apart. The
Christian communities in Rome, however, contained a large constituency of Asians, and once a system of yearly celebration was adopted,
the issue became a practical problem at a local level. A generation after
Anicetus had agreed to disagree with his Asian brethren, one of his
successors aroused considerable opposition by attempting to impose
uniformity of practice not only in Rome but also upon the churches
in Asia. Victor, bishop of Rome from about 189 to 198 or 199 (and the
first Roman churchman to use Latin as his regular language), called

for a standardization of the Sunday *Pascha* observance in all churches and threatened to excommunicate any communities that refused to comply. It is likely that his determination was provoked by a desire to curtail the activities of some of Rome's Asian Christians, among whom was a presbyter named Blastus who was said to have associations with a range of beliefs that Victor would have regarded as undesirable, not least Montanism.

Victor was opposed by a senior Asian bishop, Polycrates of Ephesus, and also by Irenaeus who, while keeping to the Roman practice himself (despite his Asian origins), argued that Victor's injunction was an abuse of authority that would needlessly divide the churches. Irenaeus's counsel prevailed, and Victor apparently countermanded his excommunication order. In the long term, the position sponsored by Victor would win out, and the Council of Nicaea in 325 would stipulate that Easter should be celebrated everywhere as a Sunday festival. Quartodeciman believers nevertheless continued to exist in Rome for some time, and there were further protests against the Sunday *Pascha* by Eastern churchmen in the fourth century. Though condemned by various church councils, Quartodecimans were still to be found in many places in the East for several centuries.

The Quartodeciman position was almost certainly the more ancient practice, but it lost out to sheer force of custom, reinforced by the weight of Rome's authority. Victor may have failed to get his way in the first instance, and serious division had been avoided between the churches of Asia Minor and Rome, but his actions were an ominous sign of how readily Christian communities, separated by differing traditions but with equal claims to apostolic precedent, could risk undoing their bonds of unity. They also showed how seriously Rome regarded its right to impress its views on believers elsewhere and how determined a forceful bishop could be in asserting such a position.

The Monarchian Controversies

The extent to which Rome still continued to be something of a melting pot of doctrinal influences was further illustrated by a series of controversies that began under Victor's episcopate and continued, in a course that took various twists and turns, under his successors, Zephyrinus (198/199–217) and Callistus (217–222). The so-called "Monarchian" controversies related to two fundamental areas of Christian belief: the person of Christ and the nature of God. They assumed a particular importance because they raised questions that continued to overshadow the doctrinal debates of the later third and fourth centuries.

The background to Monarchianism lay in the existing discussions of Greek theology about the relationship between Jesus and God and in the logic of traditional arguments against Gnosticism. The *Logos* theology expounded by Justin Martyr and the other apologists sometimes spoke of the divine Word as "another God" beside God the Father. It was argued that the Son derived his being from the Father but was distinct from him, in the way that one torch may derive its flame from another while remaining a genuinely separate torch. This position, however, appeared to threaten the coherence of Christian reasoning against Gnosticism. The Gnostics taught that there were two cosmic principles—good and evil, spirit and matter. Orthodox Christians like Irenaeus had of course contended that this was quite wrong; there could be no first cause other than the one, good Creator God. In the late second and early third centuries, a number of Christians began to fear that the *Logos* language of Justin appeared to introduce another divinity alongside the Creator and so compromised the singleness or *monarchia* ("single principle of authority") of God's being. Did not the *Logos* theology imply a doctrine of "ditheism"—the possibility of two gods rather than one—and thus tilt toward the very Gnostic errors its advocates were so anxious to condemn?

The Monarchians, or those who argued most strongly that the singleness of God's being was paramount, proposed two main alternatives to the *Logos* approach. One was to say that Jesus as God's Son was not "another God" but a normal human being endowed with the divine Spirit to a unique degree. Some such views were propagated at Rome by a number of individuals from Asia Minor in the period 199 to 230. Modern scholarship has often labeled these people "dynamic Monarchians" because they seem to have believed that the divinity of Christ was a divine power (*dynamis*) that descended upon him at his baptism, and that he was *adopted* as God's Son rather than *being* God's Son by nature. One who proposed this idea was a leatherworker from Byzantium named Theodotus (190s); another was a banker also named Theodotus, who taught that Jesus was the last and greatest of the prophets, divinely anointed to be a great "high priest in the order of Melchizedek" (Heb. 6:20–7:28). A leader in these circles for a time was one Natalius, who eventually made his peace with Pope Zephyrinus by recanting his views. Others nevertheless continued to espouse similar theories in subsequent years; another who became notorious for this teaching was a man named Artemon (ca. 230).

The details surrounding all of these people are not altogether clear, but they all evidently contended that their doctrine was conventional, arguing that a view of Jesus as a Spirit-anointed man fit the Synoptic Gospels' portraits of him as one who grew and developed in every sense. Some vaguely comparable ideas had indeed existed in the past: the prophet Hermas, whose visions are recorded in the *Shepherd* of Hermas, appears to have seen the Son of God and the Holy Spirit as essentially the same, and, as we have seen, the Jewish-Christian Ebionites had similarly held that Jesus was adopted as God's Son at his baptism. The notion that Christ was divine by degree rather than by kind would also resurface some years later in the Syrian church, in the teaching of Paul of Samosata, bishop of Antioch from 260, whose views were condemned by a synod at Antioch in 268 (see pp. 268–69).

As Rome's bishops recognized, the problem with all such thinking was plain: the Scriptures spoke of Jesus as filled with the Spirit and as one who walked a fully human path, but they also spoke unambiguously of his divine origins. According to the Gospels, Jesus was an object of worship in the earliest days of his earthly life, and his baptism had to do with his saving mission for others, not with his adoption by God. The Son of God was not just a regular human being elevated to divine status as a reward for living a holy life; he was in the first instance divine in his being. Those who taught that his nature was that of a "mere man" (in Greek, *psilos anthropos*, hence, to their opponents, the "Psilanthropists") fatally compromised the fundamental difference between his ultimate origins and the status of those he came to save. The "dynamic Monarchian" or "adoptionist" case was a false avenue.

The other kind of Monarchian position suggested in lieu of the traditional *Logos* theology commanded wider support, and the issues that it raised generated some of the most important theological reflection in the early Western church. The suggestion in this case was that God's *monarchia* should be thought of as a simple, undifferentiated reality, so that the terms *Father* and *Son* referred merely to different aspects of the same one God. Thus, it was argued, when God was seen as Creator, he was usually known as "Father," and when he was seen as Redeemer, he was usually known as "Son"—but there was only one personal being in view at all times. In fact, when Jesus was born, suffered, and died, God the Father just as much as God the Son was born, suffered, and died. Under the influence of language used by Tertullian to denounce such notions, the position would become known in many circles as "Patripassianism," from the Latin *pater*, "Father," and *passio*, "suffering," on the grounds that to say God the Father and God the Son were identical was to imply that the Father as much as the Son suffered on the cross.

These ideas were again popularized in Rome by immigrants from Asia Minor. The primary force was a native of Smyrna named Noetus, who arrived in Rome around 200, having apparently already been criticized for his teaching by Asian clergy. His ideas were taken up by a number of people, among whom we have the names of two individuals, Polemon and Praxeas. Some scholars have expressed doubt as to whether Praxeas as such actually existed, because the name means "busybody" and may be a nickname devised for some other person by Tertullian, who devoted a treatise to countering such beliefs (pp. 244–46). It is quite possible, however, that Praxeas was indeed a historical character. Other Monarchians after Noetus were Epigonus and Cleomenes.

Hippolytus and Callistus

The views represented by Noetus and the others were challenged by Hippolytus, one of the presbyters of the Roman church and one of its most capable theologians. Hippolytus (ca. 170–236) may well have been of Eastern extraction himself, and like Irenaeus, whose theology exercised some influence upon him, he wrote in Greek, the last significant figure in the Western church to do so.

Hippolytus argued that there was indeed one God but that it was necessary to distinguish between the Father, the Son, and the Holy Spirit. The three were distinct *prosopa*, or "persons." Despite Hippolytus's intellectual abilities, his way of establishing the distinctions between these "persons" was not very successful. He claimed that the *Logos became* the Son in the incarnation, and thus the term *Son* should only be used of the incarnate Christ, not of the preexistent Lord; in effect, Jesus Christ was only a creature to whom divinity had been assigned for the duration of his saving ministry. The Holy Spirit was in practice not all that significant, either. As was the case in much of the theology of the second and early third centuries (the same point can be made of the apologists), most of the attention in Hippolytus's reflection on the nature of God was focused on the Father-Son relationship.

Hippolytus was himself opposed by one of the deacons of the church in Rome named Callistus. Callistus was apparently a former slave who, according to Hippolytus, had been convicted of financial embezzlement and had served a sentence in the mines of Sardinia. Hippolytus was no doubt keen to blacken his opponent, and we cannot be entirely sure of the reliability of his allegations, but it does seem that Callistus had a checkered past. However, he was restored to the church by Zephyrinus and put in charge of a Christian cemetery beside the Appian Way on the south side of Rome (a recently developed property, it was the site of the increasing Christian practice of burying the dead in long underground tunnels or galleries, from which the name "catacombs" derived (from *ad catacombas* or "at the hollows").[11] Neither Zephyrinus nor Callistus was much of a theologian, and they both adopted language that appeared at one minute anti-Monarchian and at the next not too far removed from that of Noetus. Callistus quarreled with Hippolytus's theology, accusing him of ditheism for making what he alleged was too rigid a differentiation between the divinity of the Father and the divinity of the Son.

In 217, Callistus succeeded Zephyrinus as bishop of Rome, and Hippolytus refused to countenance his legitimacy. Hippolytus and his supporters operated as a dissident group among the Roman house-churches. Hippolytus was probably not a challenger for Callistus's position as bishop (or, as he has been conventionally described, an "antipope"), but his stance certainly amounted to a strong *de facto* refusal of Callistus's validity in office. Hippolytus's opposition to Callistus seemed to be confirmed by the latter's pronouncements on ecclesiasti-

Scene from a Roman catacomb. Illustration from FreeStockPhotos.com. Used by permission.

cal discipline. Callistus was prepared to grant pardon and reconciliation for believers who had committed even flagrant sins after baptism, provided they were penitent. He was also willing to allow clergy who had been twice married to continue in office, and he flouted Roman legal convention by recognizing marriages made between aristocratic women and men who were slaves or freedmen (these were normally allowed only on payment of considerable financial penalties). The church, he believed, was a mixed body, a combination of wheat and tares, which only God had the prerogative finally to disentangle; in its earthly expression, it necessarily remained a society with unworthy as well as holy members.

Callistus was a shrewd administrator and ecclesiastical strategist, and in relaxing some of the usual rules of the church's morality his actions enlarged its boundaries and increased the sphere of his own authority, for he was willing to admit into the fellowship of the official church those whom conventional disciplinary standards would previously have excluded. Callistus was probably content to accept baptized confessors from a wide variety of backgrounds by submitting them to a fairly simple rite of penitence, and his permissive stance on the background of Christian officials may well have been designed to accommodate the admission of leaders from other groups into the ranks of the mainstream church.

Sabellius: Modalist Monarchianism

While Callistus was bishop, a teacher named Sabellius, who seems to have originated in Libya, asserted a more sophisticated form of Monarchianism than that of Noetus and his followers. His theology, and ideas resembling it, would become known ever after as "Sabellianism." Modern treatments tend to label it "modalism," for according to Sabellius's logic, Father, Son, and Holy Spirit are simply different *modes* of being adopted by the one God at different times and for different purposes. God may be now Father, now Son, and now Holy Spirit, but God is never *simultaneously* all three. God may be deemed to act as Father in creation, as Son in redemption, and as Spirit in prophecy and sanctification, but God is not in essence all three at once. God should be thought of as the "Son-Fathering one," who projects the Son and the Spirit at the appropriate times in order to accomplish his purposes.

Callistus appears to have vacillated in his assessment of Sabellius's ideas before finally excommunicating him, and Hippolytus blamed him for allowing such errors to be spread. Callistus probably attempted to adopt something of a middle ground between Sabellius and Hippolytus, but his own rather confused formulations proved incapable of resolving the issues that Monarchianism had raised. He allowed for a distinction between the Father and the Son but also regarded the Son as equivalent to the flesh of Jesus and the Father as the divinity that inhabited this physical form.

After Callistus's death in 222 (he probably died in an outbreak of mob violence against the Christians), Hippolytus wrote a lengthy and blistering attack on false teaching entitled *Philosophoumena* or *The Refutation of All Heresies*.[12] In the eight books that survive out of the original ten, he upbraids a range of false teaching, especially the views of Gnostic sects, arguing that each one of his targets is an offshoot of pagan philosophy. In his own time, the corruptions of Callistus are said to be the worst excesses of all. Hippolytus's relationships in Rome remained strained under Callistus's successor, Urban (222–230), but he was finally reconciled with Bishop Pontian (230–235). In 235, following the accession of Maximin to the imperial throne, Hippolytus and Pontian together became victims of a renewed policy of political oppression; they were arrested and deported to Sardinia, where they both died.

North Africa

Monarchian views of God's nature continued to be held throughout the third century. Hippolytus's opposition to both modalism and laxity of moral discipline found strong parallels, but in a different register and with nuances all their own, in another vital center of the Western church—North Africa. At how early a date Christianity had spread to Roman North Africa—the coastal region comprising the approximate areas of modern-day Tunisia, Algeria, and Morocco—is unknown. Our first reference to believers there is to the martyrdom of the Scillitans in 180 (see p. 209). The territory was heavily shaped by European influences culturally and economically, and when Christians in Rome and other Western centers were still working with Greek texts, the believers in Carthage were already using a Latin Bible and holding their worship services in Latin.

It was in North Africa that the most robust formulations of a distinctively Western theology were first produced in the work of the gifted teacher Tertullian. They evolved in ways that were both consonant with and distinct from the patterns advanced by the church in Rome.

Tertullian: The First Latin Theologian

Tertullian (ca. 160–225) was the first Christian writer of any importance to express himself in Latin. He did write in Greek as well as in Latin, but none of his Greek works survive, and his great achievement was that he comprehensively laid the foundations for the transference of a hitherto overwhelmingly Greek-language theology into Latin. Educated in Carthage in the second half of the second century, he was raised in an environment in which cultural assets mattered. Carthage had evolved over the course of the first century into a splendid city of perhaps 90,000 people and the administrative capital of a very large territory. Though a Roman city,[13] it had a proud sense of its identity as a place where a high degree of Romanization did not automatically entail looking to Rome for all the answers. The distinctiveness of a North African heritage continued to be cherished, sometimes in conscious resistance to perceived encroachments from overbearing Italian influences.[14] The intelligentsia of Carthage knew that they had fine traditions of their own and that their city was a major place in its own right.

We know very little about the details of Tertullian's life or about the circumstances of his conversion to Christianity, though it has long been speculated that he was powerfully impressed by the witness of Christian moral behavior and perhaps especially by the courage of believers who suffered for their faith. There is no clear evidence to support the traditional view that he was a lawyer (despite his outstanding gifts as an orator, and despite the number of legal-sounding terms that can be found in his vocabulary), nor can we be sure that he was ever ordained as a presbyter, though this does seem likely. We do know that he was married and that his wife was a Christian, though at what stage she was converted we cannot say. He is said to have lived to a very old age, and despite his esteem for martyrdom, we may assume that he died a natural death.

Tertullian's Christian writing, produced in roughly the period 190–220, is pervaded by a very sharp contrast between secular paganism and Christianity, and a great deal of his work is concerned with exhorting followers of Christ to live up to the true standards of their faith. Around 208 he became a convert to the New Prophecy or Montanism, but although he advocated its teaching for the rest of his days, it is unlikely that he ever abandoned or was removed from the catholic church. In the later period of his writing, he fired some very severe criticisms at the shortcomings of catholic Christian morality and its representations among church leaders, and it is clear that he and his fellow Montanists found themselves increasingly marginalized within the church. Contrary to what has often been suggested, however, there is little reason to believe that they ever came to constitute a separate sect.

We possess more than thirty of Tertullian's treatises, a number of which are of importance as the first treatments of their themes in the history of theology, such as his exposition of the Lord's Prayer in his tract *On Prayer*. He wrote works of apology, works against heresy, and works on various moral and disciplinary subjects. Most of his apologetic texts were produced in his first phase of writing, in the later 190s. The brief work entitled *To the Nations* follows the pattern of existing Greek apologetics, arguing that conventional charges against the Christians (such as allegations of cannibalism and incest) were unjust and based on ignorance and that pagan deities were simply a projection of idealized human beings. *To the Nations* was probably a draft for a much more famous work, the *Apology*, which is often regarded as Tertullian's literary masterpiece.

Formally addressed to imperial governors and magistrates, especially those in Carthage, but really intended as much as anything for Christian readers, the *Apology* presents a fascinating depiction of Christian experience and a sophisticated effort to demonstrate the absurdity of pagan religion in comparison with Christianity. Tertullian's brilliant prose exposes the shoddy logic, cultural pretensions, and political injustices of polytheism and upholds the integrity and reasonableness of Christian beliefs and practices. His style, studded with many memorable aphorisms, offers far more than mere defense; drawing on a vast array of rhetorical gambits and literary figures of speech, he goes out of his way to embarrass his opponents and bolster the confidence of his believing readers with a virtuoso celebration of the superiority of Christianity.

Rebutting the misconceptions of Christian behavior as immoral, Tertullian taunts paganism for its own follies and crudities, arguing that persecution of Christians represents a violation of the conventional Roman commitment to freedom of religion. The cruel torturing of Christians is futile, he argues, if it is intended to stamp out the faith, because far from reducing the numbers of the faithful, it entices others who are attracted by the boldness and comradeship with which the sufferers face their punishments: "'See how they love one another!' they say—for they themselves hate one another. 'See how ready they are to die for one another!'—for they are more ready to kill one another."[15] Thus, to the persecutors, Tertullian extends this defiant challenge: "The more you mow us down, the more we multiply. The blood of the Christians is seed."[16]

As Tertullian sees it, hostility is, nevertheless, the believer's inevitable lot in this world, and he counsels withdrawal from political affairs, resistance to military service, and a firm avoidance of the contaminating effects of secular entertainment. For all that, Tertullian was not an anti-intellectual figure, determined only to lambaste secular culture and retreat into a ghettoized world in which knowledge is based ultimately on faith. He is famed for asking the series of rhetorical questions, "What has Athens to do with Jerusalem? What has the Academy to do with the church? What have heretics to do with Christians?"[17] The context for these questions is not, however, an argument against Christian knowledge of philosophy or literary culture as such, but an argument against systems of thought (chiefly doctrinal heresies) that are based upon something other than divine revelation. Heresy seeks to determine truth by human inquiry, and thus its intellectual roots are those of pagan philosophy; Christianity is a God-given wisdom received by faith, and it must not be corrupted by dialectical processes of reasoning based upon ordinary human confidence.

Tertullian was no obscurantist. His ways of reasoning and his conceptual approaches to theological issues were in fact shot through with philosophical influences (especially from Stoicism) and even with appeals to the natural witness of the human constitution to the truth of God. In his work *On the Testimony of the Soul*, he argues that the soul of the uneducated, ordinary person yields instinctive awareness of the reality of God's existence and character—even unthinking interjections such as the cry "Good God!" or the idiom "God bless you" betray an unconscious apprehension of divine truth. In another short piece, *On the Pallium*, he seems to suggest that the pallium, or cloak traditionally worn by the teacher of philosophy, may be symbolically donned by the Christian, who emerges at the end of the work as the devotee of "a better philosophy."[18] If there is renunciation of the world, there is equally, it appears, a kind of appropriation of its legacy; the believer is in some sense also a philosopher—only a true one. The *Apology* reveals an extensive knowledge of classical literary authorities, and its author's erudition as a scholar. Tertullian may have set pagan wisdom and Christian revelation in antithesis, but he was in no sense an unlettered philistine who saw secular culture as an influence only to be disowned.

In his antiheretical writings, Tertullian tackled a wide range of errors. *On the Prescription(s) of Heretics* sets out the guidelines against which heresy is to be assessed. The word *prescription(s)* (it is likely that the original form in the title was plural rather than singular, as traditionally assumed) implies not so much a technical legal process—the obtaining of an *injunction* against the heretics, as it were—as a logical refutation of heretical ideas or the adducing of intellectual objections to them. Heretics are presented as incapable of understanding the Scriptures, and since they refuse to submit to the rule of faith preserved in the Christian church, they forfeit the right to appeal to Scripture to justify their opinions. A work entitled *Antidote to the Scorpion's Sting* (in Latin, *Scorpiace*) depicts heresy as a scorpion, whose lethal bite could be dealt with only by applying the teaching of the Scriptures.

Tertullian countered Gnostic and Marcionite teaching in particular, affirming the goodness of creation, the reality of Christ's physical incarnation, and the resurrection of the flesh. Gnostic practices formed the background to his treatise entitled *On Baptism*, the first analysis of its subject in the Christian tradition. Tertullian wrote it in order to counter the baptismal rite practiced by a woman of a Gnostic sect. Important in many respects for its evidence of contemporary liturgy in North Africa, it is significant for its opposition to the baptism of infants. It offers the earliest clear evidence that this practice was taking place, and, in the same breath, the earliest indication of controversy about it—scholars continue to speculate as to whether it was the practice that was innovative or Tertullian's objection to it (see further pp. 278–79). Tertullian argues that since children may fall into sin when they grow up, they may thereby forfeit the salvation that was supposedly theirs by virtue of their baptism as babies. The seriousness of what baptism entails means that it ought to be undertaken only by mature people who go through a process of purification in preparation. The relationship of baptism and renunciation of sin is further explored in a separate work entitled *On Penitence*.

It is from one of Tertullian's antiheretical texts, *On the Flesh of Christ*, that we have inherited another of his most famous statements: "It is believable because it is foolish," usually mistranslated as, "I believe because it is absurd."[19] As with the question, "What has Athens to do with Jerusalem?" these words have frequently been misunderstood and taken to epitomize a supposed antirationalism on Tertullian's part. In fact, their context makes clear that they should not be read this way at all; Tertullian reasons that the crucifixion, death, and resurrection of Jesus are, as Paul himself characterized them, "foolishness" (1 Cor. 1:18–25). By alluding to Paul's argument, Tertullian uses the authority most revered by his Marcionite opponents to argue for the very thing that these critics denied—the reality of Jesus's physical sufferings and resurrection.

In the longest of all his extant works, the five-book treatise *Against Marcion*, Tertullian presents a full-scale argument against Marcionite dualism and its attendant sharp division between the Hebrew and the Christian Scriptures. Marcionite teaching posed a very considerable challenge in Tertullian's context, and his extensive and impassioned effort to demolish its logic (drawing directly upon Marcion's *Antitheses*) indicates how seriously he took it as a threat. In another substantial work, *On the Soul*, he seeks to refute Gnostic errors on the origin and nature of the soul. In the process, he repudiates a variety of philosophical psychologies, including the Platonist idea of the preexistence of the soul and the Pythagorean notion of the transmigration of the soul from one physical form to another. He advocates a "traducian" theory (from the Latin *tradux*, "shoot" or "sprout") that while the body is created at conception, the soul is inherited from the parents—a view that differed from the perspective held by a majority of early Christians that both body and soul are brought into existence directly at conception.

Tertullian's turn to Montanism did not signal a great shift in his theological outlook; indeed, his most important rebuttals of heresy belong precisely within his Montanist period. In reality, the moral and disciplinary stance that he adopted as a devotee of the New Prophecy was only a more thoroughgoing development of a rigorist tradition to which he had been attached since his initial conversion to Christ. North African spirituality in the third century became renowned for its resistance to compromise with the world, and the willingness of Carthage's Christians to submit to martyrdom testifies to an existing vision of faithful discipleship as an all-demanding commitment. Tertullian's predisposition was austere from the start. What Montanism afforded him was simply an inflation of existing ideals and an escalation of their practical corollaries. The demands of fidelity could be construed as the stringent obligations incumbent upon "the spiritual," and the power to realize such aspirations could be attributed directly to the enabling of the Paraclete, whose discipline brooked no compromise with the satanic agencies that lurked in lesser standards.

In his treatise entitled *On Patience*, composed around 200, Tertullian contrasts the Christian virtue of patience, exemplified supremely by Jesus himself, with pagan notions of detachment from one's circumstances. One of the essential qualities of spiritual patience, he argues, is that it is forward-looking rather than a matter of mere indifference. In this connection, it is permissible to flee from persecution with a view to survival, and patience is the ability to endure the inconveniences that flight entails. In the Montanist work, *On Flight in Persecution*, however, this allowance of flight is reversed: true believers must not run away from their oppressors but stay and face death bravely, strengthened by the presence of the Paraclete.

Similar emphasis on the cost of discipleship is to be found in Tertullian's pronouncements on issues of marriage and sexuality. In the first book of his pre-Montanist tract *To My Wife*, he had exhorted his wife not to remarry if he should die before her, and in a second book, written after some interval, he had counseled her that if she did take another husband, he must at all costs be a Christian. In his strongly Montanist work, *On Monogamy*, however, remarriage is declared to be utterly wrong because it is a betrayal of the believer's devotion to Christ and tantamount to bigamy. With the coming of the Spirit and the dawning of the last days, there could be no concessions, not even those granted by the apostles themselves. In a treatise entitled *On Modesty* (or perhaps *On Chastity/Purity*—the Latin *pudicitia* covers a range of meanings) he extols virginity as the sexual ideal and exhorts Christian married couples to abstain from sexual relations. In various other writings, he condemns idolatry, popular shows, and contemporary fashions in women's dress (including cosmetics and jewelry). Tertullian's ethical pronouncements were frequently narrow-minded and based upon dubious readings of biblical texts, and his tone was certainly calculated to infuriate many of his contemporaries.

Around 213, Tertullian issued a trenchant work, *Against Praxeas*, which has justly become one of his most-read texts. It is a sustained refutation of the logic of Monarchianism. He presents Praxeas as an enemy of prophecy as well as a proponent of Patripassian ideas: "Praxeas did a twofold service for the devil at Rome," he argues. "He drove away prophecy and introduced heresy; he put to flight the Paraclete and crucified the Father."[20] Tertullian contends that it is essential to discern *both* unity *and* plurality in God's actions. Like Irenaeus, he insists that creation and redemption are the work of one God, but he is equally insistent that this God carries out his will in the world in a threefold manner, acting simultaneously as the Father, the Son, and the Holy Spirit.

These distinctions are not simply impermanent appearances adopted by God at different stages for different purposes, but they are three ways in which God operates at once in the "economy" or "dispensation" of salvation history.[21] They are, as Tertullian puts it, "capable of being counted" as three, yet there is only ever one God. The Montanist Tertullian naturally gives a significant place to the Holy Spirit and does not concentrate on only the Father and the Son, as some earlier writers had tended to do. He adduces a wealth of biblical texts (drawing particularly upon John's Gospel) to establish that genuine distinctions do not entail fragmentation or a plurality of gods. Sometimes his exegesis is weak, but his main thrust is abundantly clear: threeness and oneness are not, in God, mutually exclusive.

How, though, is this combination of threeness and oneness to be characterized? Tertullian's answer proved highly seminal for subsequent reflection. There is, he submits, one divine *substantia*, "substance," subsisting in three *personae*, "persons," and the nature of God is best described by the word *Trinitas*, "Trinity." *Trinitas* was used by Tertullian for the first time; it translated a Greek word with the same sense, *trias*, "threeness," used already of God by the apologist Athenagoras. Tertullian may not have completely originated the use of *substantia* and *persona* as theological terms, but in treating them as he did, he furnished trinitarian doctrine with a technical vocabulary that would be used ever after by the majority of Western Christians.

It is not absolutely certain what the linguistic context for Tertullian's usage of these terms was. In the case of one of the words, at least the overtones were from secular philosophy. In Stoic thought, *substantia* referred to a kind of light, fine, invisible matter. So when Tertullian says that the three subsist as one "substance," he means that God is a single Spirit, and this Spirit is invisible and intangible but not entirely immaterial. For Tertullian, *substantia* is the Latin equivalent for the word generally used to describe God's essence in Greek: *ousia*, or "being."[22] This is not something that exists independently of the three but that which they have in common, or their shared foundational unity. It is what makes God one.

The Latin word *persona* translates the Greek *prosopon*, which Hippolytus used to describe the Father and the Son. We do not know if Tertullian followed Hippolytus or whether the influence was the other way around. Either way, the Latin term, like its Greek counterpart, had a history in the world of the theater. In the ancient theater, actors wore masks to allow their audiences to understand which character they were playing. A *persona* was originally a mask through which the actor spoke—*per-sonare* literally means "to sound through." From this the word developed the general sense of a *role* played by an individual. It is possible that Tertullian intends his readers to think of God as one divine actor playing three *roles* in a cosmic drama. It is vital to his logic, however, that God does not just adopt these distinctive roles at different points in the process, but *wears* them, as it were, all the time. The three "persons" in God are not autonomous selves in the popular modern sense of *persons* but three principles of operative individuality, always present in God's character.

The most serious difficulty with Monarchianism, according to Tertullian, was that it could not account for the cross, resurrection, and continuing presence of Jesus. If the Son was one and the same as the Father in the sense that either one was effectively all there was to God, how was the death of the Son not divine suicide? Faith's testimony was clear: the Son handed himself over to the Father in dying; the Father raised the Son from the dead; and the risen Jesus is both exalted at the right hand of God and present with his followers in the power of the Spirit. Unless God is simultaneously Father *and* Son *and* Spirit, it is impossible to make sense of the scriptural and experiential witness to the diversity within God's character. Only a trinitarian conception of God's nature could specify these things appropriately; the Monarchian position had no resources to do so.

Tertullian did not stop Monarchianism in its tracks, but he greatly influenced the subsequent course of trinitarian theology. His argument in the end fell short of an adequate account of the relationship between divine oneness and threeness, for in practice he subordinated the persons of the Son and the Spirit to the person of the Father, and he concentrated so much upon the *economy,* or the sphere of God's threefold operations in the world, that he never quite explained how the threeness that is witnessed in time and space relates to the essential, eternal being of God independently of creation. For its time, however, Tertullian's theology was a rather sophisticated attempt to explore the coherence of Christian claims about the relationship between Jesus and God.

The Legacy of Tertullian

Tertullian's influence in the West was considerable, both in his pioneering use of Latin and with respect to his ideas. Though unmentioned in the extant works of any of his contemporaries, he was undoubtedly read by many. Jerome, writing in the late fourth century, claims that Tertullian was studied daily by Cyprian, bishop of Carthage, in the 250s[23] and in North Africa Tertullian's views on spirituality and the purity of the church certainly affected conceptions of the Christian calling for generations. His uncompromising expressions of ethical seriousness also hinted strongly at the differences of thinking about the church and its salvation that existed between Rome and Carthage. In North Africa, the boundaries between church and world were sharper than they were in Rome, and martyrdom for the faith was increasingly seen not so much as a tragic possibility but as a spiritual aspiration.

The Montanism that colored Tertullian's specific delineations of ecclesiastical discipline would in time be crushed in both Carthage and Rome, but Tertullian's passion and originality ensured that the particularities of a North African vision, Montanist or otherwise, were given a prominence in the West that was not to go away. Although Roman Christianity would have its own purists and separatists, Latin theology was born in a milieu quite distinct from that of Rome, and the issues that Tertullian raised would in the course of the third century lead to significant tensions between Rome and Carthage. It is no surprise that Tertullian was never formally canonized by the church of Rome.

Minucius Felix

Tertullian's *Apology* in particular strongly influenced *Octavius*, an important work by a Roman writer, Minucius Felix. Composed some time in the first half of the third century, perhaps in the later 230s, *Octavius* is a stylish apology for Christianity. It purports to narrate a dialogue between two Christians, Minucius Felix and Octavius Januarius, with a pagan friend, Quintus Caecilius Natalis, on a walk from Rome to Ostia, the port of Rome, where most of the conversation takes place. Minucius Felix is said by the early fourth-century writer Lactantius to have been a leading advocate in Rome,[24] and his companions appear as men of similar social status.

Although the setting for the work is Roman, the background lies in North Africa; Minucius refers to the conversion to Christianity of prominent citizens in Cirta, the capital of Numidia. Cirta was also the hometown of Fronto, Marcus Aurelius's mentor, who had launched a scathing intellectual attack on the Christians more than a generation before, and it is likely that Minucius wishes to respond to Fronto's well-known criticisms; he certainly expresses a knowledge of some of Fronto's points. It is possible that he exploits a Christian-pagan debate that had actually taken place in a town such as Cirta.

Minucius's text is modeled on classical dialogue forms, and it draws heavily on Cicero, Seneca, and other Greek and Latin authors. There is no reference to Christ by name, and not a single quotation from the Scriptures, indicating that the intended readership was educated pagans rather than Christians. The argument is urbane and carefully constructed, and it ends with Caecilius conceding defeat and expressing a desire to become a Christian. Caecilius's defense of traditional Roman religion is shown to be untenable, his criticisms of Christian morality misconceived. It is the providence of the one transcendent God, not the supposed protection of the so-called gods of polytheism, that has governed Rome's history. This God is a reality to all rational creatures, and the claim that he has become human and acted to save men and women is entirely consonant with what intelligent people (like the Stoics) already affirm about the reality of divine immanence. The claims of pagan religions are riddled with absurdities, and the temples of the old gods and goddesses are filled with treasures brutally plundered from undeserving victims. Far from Christians being guilty of barbaric practices, they live upright, moderate, and peaceful lives, trusting in the prospect of a reward with God.

A great deal of Minucius's argument is derived from Tertullian, but his tone is much more restrained than that of the *Apology*. Pagan religion is vigorously criticized, but the criticisms are presented as reasoned objection rather than aggressive ridicule. There is none of Tertullian's militancy; pagans are to be won over by a tactful, carefully measured use of logic. Minucius is less interested than Tertullian in bolstering Christian assurance with grand claims about the success of the gospel or the glories of Christians' fortitude in the face of suffering. He writes in a Roman context in which Christianity has grown and made some important inroads among the privileged classes, and his attitudes to secular culture are not nearly as confrontational.

The work testifies, nevertheless, to the lingering influence of Tertullian's thought upon those who would respond to anti-Christian polemic and set out the facts about Christian belief. For all Minucius's diplomacy, the Christian case in *Octavius* is advanced with intellectual confidence and a firm conviction as to its cultural relevance. The dialogue does not mildly suggest that Christianity deserves to be tolerated; it assumes that the truth of the gospel should be acknowledged for what it is. The methods may differ considerably, but for Minucius, as for Tertullian, it is persuasion and conversion as much as self-justification that is in view. Western Christianity's most articulate spokesmen saw no reason to hide their light under a bushel, whatever the challenges of their social world.

9

ALEXANDRIAN CHRISTIANITY AND ITS LEGACY

▼

The Church in Alexandria

According to a tradition as old as the second century, the church in Egypt was founded by the evangelist John Mark, the cousin of Barnabas, sometime companion of Paul, and disciple of Peter. Mark was said to have been the first bishop of Alexandria and to have been martyred there in the year 68. We cannot tell if this tradition is reliable or whether it simply reflects a bid on the part of second-century Christians in the city, faced with challenges to their convictions, to associate their church with the authority of an apostolic emissary.[1] It is in many respects surprising that Paul himself did not seek to take the gospel to Alexandria, given the city's very large community of Hellenized Jews and the significant opportunities it would have afforded for spreading the faith into a different sector of the Mediterranean world. Perhaps he dreamed of doing so; we cannot know. Whatever the case, Alexandria was almost certainly the home of some of the Egyptian Jews who are said to have been present in Jerusalem at Pentecost (Acts 2:10), and the story of Jesus must have traveled there early, whoever its first bearers were.

By the second century, Alexandria ranked alongside Antioch and Rome as one of the most important sees of the church. Though, as we shall see in due course, there was much more to Egyptian Christianity in cultural and spiritual terms than simply the church in Alexandria, it was there that the Christian faith developed some of its most enduring conceptual forms. The city's status in political terms was no surprise. Founded by Alexander the Great in the fourth century B.C. and established as the capital of Egypt by Ptolemy I Soter (304–283/282 B.C.), Alexandria was the second city of the Roman world. A vital gateway for trade throughout the southern and eastern Mediterranean, it was also a dynamic cultural melting pot, sustaining the largest single community of Jews outside Palestine and a rich mixture of Semitic, Hellenistic, and African traditions. Renowned for its superb library and its traditions of scholarship, the ethos of both intellectual and religious life in Alexandria had always been eclectic and open to assimilating new ideas.

Alexandrian Christianity was strongly influenced by Gnosticism. The greatest of the Gnostic teachers, Basilides and Valentinus, had connections with the city, and their ideas owed much to the philosophical and spiritual character of that context. It is no surprise that the dominant forms of a Christian message in Egypt's capital over the period 130 to 180 reflected a fundamentally intellectual conception of faith as, in its highest form, a special *knowledge*. The kind of knowledge offered by a Gnosticized Christianity was assuredly different from most of the versions of wisdom prized by the philosophical sages, and it told a bleaker story about the nature of the physical universe. Its basic tenets would nevertheless have been easily understood by those who saw the pursuit of truth as the most pressing obligation for the human spirit. Alexandria had always been full of people on a quest for knowledge and full of teachers claiming to be able to impart it.

Pantaenus

Around 180, the most prominent Christian teacher in Alexandria was Pantaenus. A Sicilian by background and a convert from Stoicism, he is said to have been an energetic spokesman for the Christian gospel who traveled widely as a missionary in the East, perhaps penetrating as far as India. Unlike many of his contemporaries in Alexandria, Pantaenus was not a Gnostic, proffering a false form of knowledge, but he was a messenger of a faith that was intellectually respectable. He was head of what is said by Eusebius to have been a "school for believers," that is, a Christian school modeled on the principles of traditional Greek institutions such as Plato's Academy in Athens.[2] We cannot be sure whether such a school existed in a formal sense, but it is likely that Pantaenus was not a presbyter, operating within the normal structures of ecclesiastical leadership, but rather an independent instructor who took pupils on application, somewhat as Justin did in Rome.

The church in Alexandria seems to have absorbed early on the traditional Greek practice of professional scholars operating their own schools of learning with their own particular emphases and methods, and the pattern of Christian organization allowed independent teachers to hold authority alongside the institutional ministry of the regular clergy. Their teaching would have included not only issues of Christian doctrine but instruction in grammar, rhetoric, and matters of practical behavior. Pantaenus was evidently a particularly well-regarded example of such a teacher, and his activity did much to impress Alexandria's educated elite. He presented a version of Christianity that was neither obviously esoteric nor culturally inward-looking.

Clement of Alexandria

The most famous of Pantaenus's students was Clement. He was born around 150, perhaps in Athens. Like Justin before him, he had spent his youth on a quest for wisdom, and he had come to Christian faith via philosophical study. After professing belief in Christ, he had traveled widely around the Greek-speaking Mediterranean and sat at the feet of many distinguished Christian teachers. In one of his writings, he refers to some of the scholars he had heard. Tactfully, he does not name his mentors, but he writes: "One was in Greece—the Ionian; the next in Magna Graecia [southern Italy] . . . ; others were in the East, and in this region one was an Assyrian and the other a Palestinian, a Hebrew by descent. The last of all (in power he was the first) I met and in him I found my rest, when I had caught him hidden away in Egypt." This "Sicilian bee, gathering the spoil of the flowers of the prophetic and apostolic meadow,"[3] was almost certainly Pantaenus.

Clement was already a convert to Christianity. What Pantaenus offered him was an intellectually satisfying understanding of his faith, which stimulated him to devote the rest of his life to the task of exploring the Christian message and communicating it to others. Clement became a

teacher himself and subsequently succeeded Pantaenus as head of his
school. Like his mentor, he probably remained distinct from the regular
clergy. Though one tradition claims he was ordained as a presbyter not
long before his death, it is quite likely that he remained a lay instructor.
Strikingly, his writings reveal almost nothing about the organizational
life of the Christian community in Alexandria. He appears to have
left the city during the persecutions of 202 to 203 and to have gone to
Jerusalem, where he died some time around 215.

Clement wrote a considerable amount. Though some of his writings
have been lost, we have three substantial works and two shorter texts still
extant. The first of his major works is entitled *Protreptikos,* or "Exhortation." It is an apologetic text designed to persuade its readers of the truth
of Christianity and the errors of pagan religion. Clement's second book
is entitled *Paidagogos,* or "Tutor." Intended as a sequel to *Protreptikos,*
it addresses the person who has made the transition from paganism to
Christian faith and offers further practical instruction in the way of Christ.
A *paidagogos* in Greek was not a schoolteacher as such (the usual term for
that person was *didaskalos*), but a slave who trained his pupil in morals
and social etiquette before delivering him to the teacher who would give
him more scholarly teaching. In Clement's perspective, Christ, as the
divine Word, is the true tutor, who leads people into the real depths for
which all other learning is but preparatory. Clement presents a range of
Christian counsel on practical matters, including eating, drinking, social
activity, and entertainment. Much of what he has to say offers a fascinating
glimpse into the social world of Alexandrian Christianity in his time.

One might have expected Clement's third study to be entitled *Didaskalos,* or "Teacher," and to be an exposition of more advanced areas
of Christian doctrine. This was Clement's intention, but such a work
was never written. Instead, he produced a text entitled *Stromateis* (or
sometimes *Stromata*). The Greek means either "Patchwork coverlets"
(*Stromateis*) or "Bedding" (*Stromata*); the treatise is commonly known
in English as "Miscellanies." Such collage works were common in late
antiquity, and the genre was often adopted by writers who wished to offer
a diverse range of information and advice without having to maintain
a single theme consistently throughout. Clement seems to have deliberately chosen the form because it enabled him to discuss theological
and ethical matters in a suggestive rather than a prescriptive style. In
his view, the intrinsic mysteriousness of the deep things of God meant
that they were best dealt with in a series of allusive musings as opposed
to a bold, sequential argument. Quite simply, it was easier to produce
miscellaneous thoughts than advanced teaching.

Stromateis deals with the relationship of philosophy to Christianity as well as with a broad variety of doctrinal and ethical issues such as faith and repentance, martyrdom, sexual self-restraint, and asceticism. The text is incomplete as we have it, and it is possible that in later parts lost sections went on to discuss spiritual matters in greater depth. In addition to these three great works, Clement wrote a rhetorical exposition of the gospel story of the rich young ruler (Mark 10:17–31; cf. Matt. 19:16–30; Luke 18:18–30) traditionally called by its Latin title, *Quis Dives Salvetur?* ("Who is the rich man who will be saved?"), and a set of notes on the teachings of a Valentinian Gnostic, entitled *Excerpts from Theodotus*. A collection of some biblical exegetical studies is lost, but we know from other evidence that it set out a number of allegorical readings of scriptural texts.

Communicating the Faith

Clement's writings suggest that he saw his role as a Christian teacher in three ways. First, he was called to expound the Christian gospel for thinking people steeped in Greek culture. In certain respects, he can be regarded as a Christian version of the great Jewish intellectual Philo (from whom he learned much), attempting to present his faith as the highest form of the wisdom for which all honest philosophers had sought. As Clement saw it, if God is the good Creator, then God is the giver of every good thing, including the desire for knowledge. The seeds of truth are planted by God in all rational creatures, and philosophy is able to teach people much about the nature of God's truth. As the Law was for the Hebrews (Gal. 3:24–25), so philosophy is for the Greeks: a tutor to bring them to Christ.[4]

Like other apologists before him, Clement draws attention to some of the similarities between philosophical ideas and the teaching of Scripture. Though he can make the familiar claim that Plato and other thinkers plagiarized from Moses and the prophets without acknowledging their debts, he is also conscious of the need to make the simple style of the Scriptures palatable for people used to the more sophisticated conceptual methods of philosophical reflection. He resorts to allegorical exegesis to gloss over potentially awkward passages in the Jewish Scriptures and to argue that when these texts are read correctly, they point to Christ. The Savior of whom they speak is one whose teaching can be rendered into the moral categories of Stoic and Neopythagorean wisdom. Clement's theology is assuredly self-confident in that it sees Christianity as the climax and goal of everything to which secular philosophy had been moving, and it contains plenty of polemic against the crudities of polytheism. But it is never anti-intellectual or cheaply dismissive of classical culture as such.

In the second place, Clement believed he had a duty to defend the true Christian faith from perversions of it. His fire in this area is above all directed against the Gnostics, whose teaching was such a dominant reality in his immediate context in Alexandria. He deploys philosophy as well as the Scriptures to refute the logic of his opponents. Philosophy is presented as an enemy rather than a supporter of the Gnostics' views. The Gnostics purport to be interested in a higher knowledge, but in reality they show no signs of possessing it. The *gnosis* of which they speak is an illusion; the "true *gnosis*" is to be found in the knowledge of the God whose Word became genuinely incarnate in Jesus Christ. The "true gnostic" understands that the material world is not inherently corrupt but is the work of a good and benevolent Creator. Such a person appreciates that he is made in the image of this God and designed for fellowship with him.

The Christian life begins with faith, which is a basic apprehension of the elementary truths about God, but this faith is expressed in a rational manner in the daily discipleship of walking with God. On this journey, ethical endeavor is motivated not by fear of punishment or hope of reward but by a love of the knowledge of God for its own sake. Its ultimate end is to ascend to the vision of God beyond this present life and to become one with God in a mystical, spiritual union—an ideal that owes much to Platonist thought. The attainment of this final purpose is not, however, immediate upon death; it is reached only by a further process of purification and discipline. Clement is not much concerned with physical resurrection or the restoration of all things; his eschatological focus is on spiritual participation in the being of God. In this last respect, he perhaps unwittingly concedes too much to his Gnostic antagonists, but in much of his other argumentation, he succeeds in using Gnostic logic against itself to contend that real knowledge of God is grounded upon the revelation of God's character that has taken place in the incarnation, crucifixion, and resurrection of the divine Word.

Clement is sharply critical of the Gnostics because they are sectarians and because their ideas are in conflict with the apostolic faith. At the same time, he is very uncomfortable with the position of Christians who believe in a simple "orthodox" tradition that can supposedly be detached from wider currents of intellectual thought. Such people imagine that philosophy must be shunned as a danger to their faith, whereas the "true gnostic" recognizes that philosophy can in fact be used *against* error rather than in its furtherance. Clement's conception of the apostolic tradition is defined in more fluid terms than that of Irenaeus, whose work he knew and respected. Clement is much less interested in bishops as transmitters of the Christian faith. He himself had received it from a variety of mentors, not from "official" apostolic successors, and he sees himself as passing it on in a similar fashion, simply as a faithful teacher of the gospel rather than as one who claims a particular pedigree of ecclesiastical authority. The apostolic faith is essentially the faith that treats the Scriptures seriously and interprets them as pointing always to Christ. Where the Gnostics and other heretics such as Marcion go wrong is that they fail to honor the integrity of the Scriptures' unity and to discern the power of their witness to an incarnate Savior.

The third area of Clement's teaching lay in instructing Christians in ethics. He opposes the extreme asceticism of some of the Gnostics, arguing that God's material creation is primordially good, not evil; at the same time, he advocates a prudent and restrained enjoyment of its benefits. He firmly rejects the allegation that sexual relations are necessarily at odds with a spiritual existence and denies that marriage should be regarded only as a second best to the ideal of celibacy. Some believers may be called to a life of total denial, but not all. Luxury and indulgence are nevertheless vigorously discouraged. It is clear that Clement wrote for a constituency of affluent and privileged Christians in Alexandria, and he encourages them to practice moderation and frugality. They are not all necessarily to give away their wealth (despite the apparent injunction to the rich young ruler), but they are to shun ostentation and excess and to recognize their obligations to live as missionaries to their worldly neighbors in moral as well as intellectual terms. Clement's ethics owe a great deal to Stoic ideals of moderation, prudence, and detachment from passion. He also shares with both Stoic and Platonist thought a vision of the moral life as dynamic and progressive, and he recognizes that the community of the faithful includes people at various stages of spiritual development, according to their capacities and privileges. These ideas are combined with biblical images of the knowledge of God as an on-going journey of discovery, both in this world and in a life to come.

Clement epitomizes the style of Alexandrian Christianity—urbane, eclectic, and practical, concerned to impress the sophisticates of a cultural center with the truth of the Christian gospel without confining Christian beliefs and practices to an esoteric system suitable only for an elite. Many of Clement's apologetic gambits are not very original;

he follows in a well-trodden path of Christian rebuttals of paganism, and his arguments about the philosophers' debts to the Scriptures are familiar from Justin Martyr and other second-century presenters of the faith. At the same time, the tone that pervades his work is very different from that of his contemporary, Tertullian. Secular philosophy is not to be railed against as inimical to the truth and as the seedbed of heresy; it is to be deliberately accommodated as an important preparation for the gospel.

Clement's explorations of the relationship between faith and knowledge were among the first of their kind in the history of Christian thought, and his recognition of the need to present a version of spiritual knowledge that would simultaneously differentiate the Christian gospel from Gnosticism and communicate its intellectual coherence to those outside the church was critically important in its context. If, in the end, Clement's depictions of spirituality are rather too deeply marked by Platonist and Stoic assumptions to be easily assimilable today, that is not to say that his work did not represent a vital force in the communication of the Christian message in his particular world.

Origen

Clement's work in Alexandria was continued and taken further by Origen, who surpassed his predecessor in intellectual gifts and far outstripped him in literary output and influence. Though in his lifetime and—much more so—afterward he was notoriously controversial, in his writings Origen stands out as the greatest of all biblical scholars and theologians in the third century and one of the most remarkable figures in the history of the early church.

Born in Alexandria around 185, Origen came from a Christian background, though from a family that had perhaps converted not very long beforehand. His father, Leonidas, was martyred in the persecution of believers in the city in 202 or 203. According to Eusebius (a great admirer of Origen), the teenage Origen only narrowly escaped martyrdom himself when his mother hid his clothes to prevent him from venturing outside his house.[5] His upbringing was devout, with daily exposure to and memorization of the Scriptures, as well as an ambitious program of instruction in classical literature. On the death of his father, Origen was housed and supported by a wealthy Christian woman (whose Gnostic sympathies would later embarrass him), and he is said to have attended the lectures of a noted Platonist teacher, Ammonius Saccas. Eusebius (drawing on Origen's own letters and on stories told by his supporters a century later) claims that the young man was remarkable for his spiritual zeal as well as his intellectual abilities; he also reports the story that Origen chose to castrate himself in order to facilitate his teaching ministry among women, taking a literal approach to Jesus's reference to those who make themselves eunuchs for the sake of the kingdom of heaven (Matt. 19:12).[6] In his late teens, Origen became a teacher and was recognized by the church of Alexandria as the worthy successor to Clement, who had fled the city.

Origen built up a considerable reputation as a teacher, scholar, and ascetic, and in the ensuing years, he traveled widely to Rome, Palestine, Greece, and elsewhere both to visit other Christians and, at various times, to escape political tensions in Alexandria. His actions while he was away on one of these trips, around 215, got him into trouble with his bishop back in Alexandria, Demetrius, who seems to have become jealous of the prominent role Origen had developed as an itinerant consultant on theological questions and disciplinary troubleshooter. (Origen in turn appears to have despised his bishop's petty pride in his own power and his comfortable status as the head of a wealthy Christian community.) Demetrius objected to the fact that in Caesarea Origen had preached as a nonordained teacher in the presence of bishops. The bishops in question had no problem with this, but Demetrius reprimanded him for his presumption.

On his next visit to Palestine, Origen was ordained a presbyter by the local bishops, and for this (and some other reports of what he had recently been teaching when he was in Athens) Demetrius engineered his official condemnation by a synod in Alexandria. Although Demetrius died not long afterward, his successor upheld Origen's excommunication, and in the end, Origen moved permanently to Caesarea, where he taught for the rest of his days, supported by a rich friend and patron named Ambrose,[7] who paid for a team of stenographers to take down his wisdom. During the outbreak of political persecution under the emperor Decius around 251, Origen was arrested and tortured for his faith, and he died at Tyre about three years later, perhaps of the wounds he had suffered at that time.

The Biblical Scholar

Origen's literary output was enormous. It spanned studies on the text of Scripture, biblical commentaries, interpretation, antipagan polemic, heresy, dogmatics, spirituality, prayer, and mission. He produced in all approximately eight hundred works. Of these, the vast majority are lost, and many survive not in their original Greek but in Latin translation. What we do have, however, amounts to a substantial intellectual legacy, and it testifies amply to the versatility of Origen's mind and the depth of his cultivation not only in Greek literature and philosophy but also in the Hebraic context of Christianity's origins. Very unusually for the early centuries of the church, Origen was proficient in Hebrew as well as in Greek, and this ability set him apart as easily the most accomplished biblical scholar of his age.

Origen's masterpiece was the *Hexapla*, a compilation of six versions (the title means "sixfold" in Greek) of the Jewish Scriptures set out in parallel columns. In the first column was the Hebrew text in conventional usage among Jews of the day. This was followed by a transliteration of this text into Greek letters for the benefit of most readers. After this came the four main Greek translations in existence at this time: one by the Jewish proselyte scholar (and one-time Christian convert) Aquila (ca. late 130s),[8] another by the Jewish Christian Symmachus (ca. 180–200),[9] then the Septuagintal text, followed by a Jewish translation by Theodotion (ca. 150–200).[10] On some parts of Scripture, there were more than six versions; on the Psalms, one of the extra columns apparently drew on the text of a scroll that Origen had discovered hidden in a pot near Jericho.[11]

Most of the *Hexapla* is now lost, but the few pages that remain provide an enduring source of study for modern scholars. Debate persists about the original design of the columns, and many scholars now believe there never was an original Hebrew text in the first column, only a transliterated Greek version of it. Whatever the case, the sheer task of compiling and correcting such a work was huge and called upon all the energies of Origen's scribal assistants. It is likely that the only complete edition of the *Hexapla* was the original one; everyone else in a position to consult the work at all probably had access to just a portion of it.

The main aim of Origen in producing the *Hexapla* was to highlight the text of the Septuagint as the central one, in accordance with its essential place in all Greek-speaking churches. In his exchanges with Jews, he had run into a number of difficulties over the interpretation of scriptural passages on account of the fact that many Greek synagogues preferred to use one of the versions of Aquila, Symmachus, or Theodotion (Aquila's was the most favored) rather than the Septuagint. He believed that the Jews were prone to alter their texts of Scripture where it suited them, not least in order to tone down the force of messianic statements. It was vital to show that the Christians were using a true and reliable rendering.

Although Origen was keen to demonstrate the authority of a single text as the basis for preaching and teaching, he valued the variant readings offered by the other translations as providing stimulus for theological reflection. He did not seek to establish the veracity of the Septuagint in the usual manner of a textual scholar, by collating an array of manuscripts and building a critical text. Rather, he simply assumed that the Septuagintal text was automatically the best, and the others were there in order to shed light upon it. He carefully marked all clauses in the Septuagint that were not to be found in the Hebrew. In most cases this was to indicate that there were doubts as to their reliability, but not always; where there was support from other Greek versions, Origen believed the absence of a Hebrew original did not necessarily mean that the text was suspect. In the case of whole books or parts of books to be found in the Septuagint but not in the Hebrew (the literature that would later be deemed deuterocanonical or apocryphal), he assumed that the Septuagint was correct and the material was canonical—even if this meant that those passages could not be the basis of argument in dialogue with Jews or with some Christians.

Origen produced commentaries and homilies on almost every biblical book and a large number of *scholia*, or exegetical notes, on texts ranging from Exodus to the Gospel according to John. Sadly, a large proportion of all of these is lost, and some exist only in incomplete or fragmentary form. Many were deliberately suppressed or left uncopied owing to a fierce controversy concerning Origen's teaching that would flare up in the fourth century (see further p. 266). Others, conversely, were preserved by those who sought to defend him against his critics, though sometimes his would-be advocates sought to improve upon their hero by purging him of some of his more awkward statements. Among the most important of the commentaries and homilies to survive, albeit in incomplete form or in abridged Latin translations, are ones on Genesis, Psalms, Song of Songs, Matthew, John, and Romans.

On First Principles

The heart of Origen's approach to Scripture can be found in his treatise *On First Principles*. Its title in Greek is *Peri archon*, but only fragments of the original are extant (in a fourth-century anthology of Origen's works known as the *Philocalia*), and the work is often cited under the Latin name, *De principiis*, as we owe the survival of the rest of the text to a controversial, revisionist translation by a scholarly Western monk,

Rufinus of Aquileia (ca. 345–411). The treatise is highly significant for a number of reasons, but its primary importance is that it amounts in some sense to the first manual of systematic Christian theology. As we have seen, Irenaeus was a systematic theologian before Origen, but Origen went farther than Irenaeus in his endeavor to set out a coherent account of essential Christian truth-claims in a single literary study.

The context of *On First Principles* is anti-Gnostic, and Origen senses that the best way to refute Gnostic claims is not by adducing answers to individual points of belief but by elaborating a "connected body of doctrine" that will afford a panorama of Christian orthodoxy.[12] The content is influenced by Platonist philosophy, but the style is centered on scriptural exegesis. Origen seeks to expound the apostolic tradition in accordance with a fairly classical understanding of the rule of faith, using Scripture to ground his doctrinal claims. Like other writers, he refutes the Marcionite and Gnostic differentiation of the Jewish and the Christian Scriptures; these sacred writings are to be read as a unity, and the linchpin of their unity is the person of Christ. The entire text of Scripture comes from the Holy Spirit, and the interpretation of it is at the deepest level a spiritual affair, which only those with spiritual discernment will be able to accomplish. Origen's biblical interpretation was careful and sophisticated. He took great pains over the language of his text, endeavoring to identify its historical and geographical references and analyzing its semantic and rhetorical structures. All of the Bible's details matter to him.

At the same time, while Origen appreciates that a biblical passage may be taken at face value, in its literal or historical sense, he insists that this is only one level of its meaning, and an incidental or superficial one at that. At a deeper level, Scripture has a *spiritual* sense. For Origen, this is apprehended not just by a discerning of "types" of Christ in the Jewish Scriptures but by a process of reading the whole biblical narrative as conveying spiritual truth. The most common means of achieving this is by the use of allegory. So, for example, the Song of Songs is to be read as a depiction of the love affair between Christ and the church and also a picture of the relationship between the soul of the individual believer and God. Noah's ark speaks of the church, outside of which there can be no salvation. Joshua's conquest of Canaan can be seen as an image of the vanquishing of sin by Christ on the cross.

Allegorical exegesis was common in antiquity in the interpretation of classical authors such as Homer,[13] and it had already been widely applied to scriptural texts in the Alexandrian tradition by both Jewish and Christian writers, especially Philo and Clement, whose concern to find deeper meanings in sacred literature was fueled in part by Platonist assumptions that invisible, heavenly truth was necessarily represented in veiled or shadowy form in ordinary human language. What Origen did was to extend the range of allegory's possibilities, allowing in some cases for not just two sorts of meaning in the text but three, embracing not only the literal and the spiritual but also a moral dimension.

Just as the human being is made up of body, soul, and spirit, Origen reasons, so the biblical language has a literal sense (its "flesh"), a moral sense (its "soul"), and a spiritual sense (its "spirit"). Occasionally he envisions a fourth sense as well, an "anagogical" or prophetic meaning expressive of divine promises about the future, but for the most part he follows a twofold or threefold scheme. His methods would be criticized by many for detaching the import of Scripture from its obvious historical setting and opening the door for entirely subjective interpretations of biblical literature, but they would also be profoundly influential for a very large number of interpreters in later periods, in the fourth and fifth centuries and especially in the Middle Ages.

On First Principles covers, in four books, the doctrines of God, creation, anthropology, and eschatology or "the last things." Although Origen's concern is to follow the rule of faith, he also states at the start of the work that he intends to explore a variety of issues on which unambiguous answers are not given in Scripture, but on which it is legitimate to speculate in the light of the reason that God has given to human beings. The combination of a spiritual approach to Scripture and an enthusiasm for rational or speculative reflection lends his work a unique flavor. God is presented as utterly transcendent, absolutely one, of pure mind, immaterial, and beyond description. God can only be conceived through another, namely his Word or Son. The Son is eternally generated by the Father. The divinity of the Son is derivative, and in that sense the Son is subordinate to the Father, who is "God-in-himself"; but God never existed without the Son, and never *became* the Father. The Holy Spirit is less than the Son but greater than any created being. Together, the Father, the Son, and the Holy Spirit constitute three distinct but essentially unified *hypostaseis*, or "substantive beings," all eternally together.

According to Origen, prior to the existence of the physical world, God was not without his creation. A realm of rational or spiritual beings was created, dependent upon God but free to turn away from him. For no reason that we can explain, except perhaps that they became sated with adoration of God, these beings at length chose to rebel, and their inexplicable choice became the cause of the material world. Among the spiritual creatures, some sinned more heinously than others; demons were guilty of a more serious rebellion than angels, and some spirits transgressed more than angels but less than demons. For these last spirits, the physical world and human bodies were the consequence. The material world is not to be seen as a terrible accident, however, but as part of God's good purpose; it is a temporary order brought into being in order to educate and reorientate human beings back toward their maker.

In Origen's anthropology, each person's spirit preexists and has its own particular history in eternity. The lot of the individual in this life is determined by the degree of sin committed in this previous spiritual state; people are rewarded or punished in varying measure according to their actions prior to their bodily existence. Redemption consists in the soul's deliverance from the fetters of physicality and its ascent toward union with God. Although his enemies accused him of it, Origen does not suggest that spirits or souls can transmigrate from one body to another. Nevertheless, he sees earthly life as only one stage in the long process by which the soul is restored to its true destiny; the process takes time because God respects the freedom of what is created. In the end, there will be a "restoration" (Origen's word is *apokatastasis*, after Acts 3:21) of all things, and this may well mean that demons and even Satan himself, a fallen angel, will be restored to fellowship with God. The love of God is ultimately capable of conquering all.

Although Origen sees the fall as a universal reality, he argues that one spirit chose not to rebel against God. This created soul, he maintains, was united with the divine *Logos* in the incarnation. The union was so close that the soul was permeated by the divinity of the *Logos*, just as an iron bar, placed in a fire, takes on the properties of the fire.[14] The *Logos* remained unchanged in being yet genuinely united to the humanity of the fleshly Jesus, who developed, suffered, and died. As one with the created mind of Jesus, the *Logos* exercised direct and complete controlling power over his flesh, yet the *Logos* was not compromised in his divine inviolability.

Nor did the *Logos* supplant the human soul of Jesus. In a work only discovered in the twentieth century, the *Dialogue with Heracleides*, Origen makes it clear that it is vital for human salvation that Jesus should have possessed what in modern terms we might call "a full human psychology." In fact, Origen lays considerable emphasis on the fact that Jesus seemed to the average observer to be nothing more than an ordinary man; so great is the power of sin to limit human capacities that the incarnation necessarily involved the veiling of God's presence in the medium of creaturely flesh.

Not everyone can recognize the divinity that is present in the life of Jesus, Origen argues; the apprehension of spiritual truth always calls for faith and maturity. The initial attraction of Jesus may lie in his exemplary qualities as a human being, and spiritual progress consists in moving beyond this to higher and higher levels of appreciation of his divine perfection. All of this progress is enabled by the work of the Holy Spirit, who makes possible all development in faith, holiness, and communion with God. But the Spirit always respects and works with the capacities and inclinations of the individual's freedom. Within the confines of present earthly existence, all discernment is limited, and even after death the soul is not yet capable of sustaining the full splendor of divine reality. Origen posits a doctrine of purgatorial fire, consequent upon death, by which the soul is purified of its remaining corruptions and made fit for the presence of God.

Faith and Philosophy

Origen's theology presents a fertile synthesis of biblical ideas with a heavily philosophical inheritance. He issues many harsh criticisms of Plato, but he was undoubtedly affected by Platonist influences in a variety of areas, such as his doctrine of the preexistence of souls, his conception of the *Logos* as an intermediary or "secondary God," his view of evil as an absence of goodness, and his vision of the eschatological ascent of the soul away from the limitations of the physical world. In the details of several such themes, Origen made it very clear that he thought Plato's philosophy was in error, but he could hardly shake off its legacy. His style of arguing also owed much to Stoic logic. Many of his arguments were immediately controversial, not least his notion of ultimate universal salvation. He equally rendered some decidedly speculative accounts of aspects of cosmology: he regarded the stars, for example, as living entities, possessed of spirits of their own and capable of exercising influence over the natural order, not by dint of an astrological determinism but because of their intrinsic freedom as rational beings, able both to respond to and to reject the law of God.

The depth of Origen's immersion in Greek culture was perhaps both his greatest strength and his most serious weakness. Positively, he was unusually well equipped to take his Christian message to an educated constituency of Greek intellectuals. He could use categories such as *Logos* or the ascent of the soul to hint at some conceptual resemblances between the gospel and the ideas of secular thought, while at the same time chiding pagan opponents for their distortions of Christianity and the weaknesses of their own logic. In his massive work *Against Celsus*, he is able to argue as one kind of Platonist to another, insisting that the pagan critic Celsus (see pp. 220–24) had not only entertained erroneous views of such matters as Christian ritual practices or the relationship of Judaism and Christianity but also of the implications of freedom and change within a Platonist metaphysic. In his biblical commentaries and sermons, Origen shows unprecedented versatility in setting forth the spiritual profundity of scriptural texts as sources of meditation and moral instruction.

More negatively, however, Origen's debts to Greek philosophy meant that his particular formulations of the rule of faith went beyond the obvious logical parameters of Scripture in a number of respects, rendering his theology not only controversial but also very obviously a product of its time and place. Whatever may be appropriated from Origen by Christians in the twenty-first century, it is unlikely to be his belief in such phenomena as the preexistence of souls or the life of the stars.

Spirituality and Faithfulness

The spirituality of Origen's practical writings was nevertheless a landmark in early Christianity. *On Prayer*, written at Caesarea and dedicated to his patron Ambrose, is the first systematic treatment of its subject by a Christian author. Prayer is presented as a graced response to God, and its daily practice lies at the heart of the Christian life. Against those who maintain that prayer makes no difference if God is all-powerful anyway, Origen argues that prayer is the state of mind in which reason begins to think clearly about the possibility of knowing impossibilities. He depicts prayer as primarily contemplative, though also as something that is followed up in action. Of the four main types of prayer—adoration, petition, entreaty, and thanksgiving—adoration is first and foremost. At times when the believer does not know how to word his or her prayers, the Holy Spirit presents them to God on his or her behalf, rendering the person's deep yearnings articulate in God's hearing (Rom. 8:26–27).

Origen demanded the highest of moral standards from those who served the church, and he had some very sharp things to say about the conduct of clergy who in his opinion held loosely to the imperatives of self-denial and practical austerity. Much of what held good for clergy also applied to believers in general. In another work addressed to Ambrose,

Exhortation to Martyrdom, produced in the 230s, when persecution was a genuine possibility for some of his readers, Origen warns against the dangers of compromise with the world. It is not enough to remain inwardly true while outwardly one conforms to demands to sacrifice to the emperor or engage in idolatry; the faithful believer must be prepared to welcome suffering and death as the gateway to the presence of God. As an expression of the heart of one who would in the end face martyrdom himself, the work is all the more poignant. Origen never would be less than controversial, but his teaching and example as a scholar, ascetic, and mystic were crowned by his preparedness to pay the ultimate sacrifice for his faith.

Origen's Influence: Admirers and Opponents

One of Origen's pupils in Caesarea was a young man of aristocratic background named Gregory. Born into a prominent family in Pontus in Asia Minor around 212, Gregory had studied law in Berytus (Beirut) before he arrived in Caesarea. There he was converted to Christianity under Origen's influence and received instruction from him. Around 240 Gregory returned to Pontus as a missionary, becoming bishop of Neocaesarea in Cappadocia, where he enjoyed outstanding success in propagating his faith. He became particularly renowned for his ability to perform miracles such as exorcisms, and he acquired the designation Gregory *Thaumatourgos*, or Gregory "the Wonder-Worker."

Although he was nothing like the speculative thinker that Origen was, Gregory was an able and charismatic leader, and he sought to be a faithful devotee of his mentor's teaching, even if he did not always manage to express it in a very nuanced fashion. Partly through his influence, Origen's spirituality and exegesis would continue to affect Cappadocian theology for a long time to come, reaching its intellectual high point in the teaching of the great Cappadocian theologians of the late fourth century: Basil of Caesarea, his brother Gregory of Nyssa, and their friend Gregory of Nazianzus, to whom we shall come in the next volume in this series.

Origen also exercised strong influence in Palestine. Pamphilus (ca. 240–309), a presbyter of Caesarea and a teacher himself, transcribed a great proportion of Origen's writings (most of the ones used by Jerome in the late fourth century). He also wrote a defense of Origen against his critics, in collaboration with his pupil, the future church historian Eusebius; fragments of it survive in Latin translation.

In the same period, however, Origen was also vigorously attacked by a number of writers. One was Methodius, a scholarly bishop with links to Olympus in Lycia in southwestern Asia Minor (d. around 311), who challenged Origen's teaching with regard to the preexistence of souls and spiritual resurrection and asserted a more obviously biblical account of the Christian hope as encompassing physical resurrection and the continuation of earthly personal identity.[15] Over fifty years later, another still more forthright critic was Epiphanius, bishop of Salamis in Cyprus (ca. 315–403), who was a particularly zealous opponent of heresy. He wrote a work entitled *Panarion*, or *A Medicine Chest for the Cure of All Heresies*, in which he attacked a great range of doctrinal errors from both the past and the present. His efforts were driven by the presence in his own see of a significant group of Marcionites.

Although Epiphanius could not deny the lingering power of Origen's scriptural commentaries, he was passionately critical of his concept of spiritual resurrection, opposed to core aspects of his teaching on the Trinity, and dismissive of his practice of theological speculation more generally, which he regarded as a transgression of the clear bounds set by biblical authority. It was through Epiphanius's influence in particular that opposition to Origen spread to Palestine, where it sowed bitter divisions between some of the ablest minds in Christian scholarship in the late fourth century.

In the second half of the third century, though, Origen's sway in the East was considerable. Even where people disagreed strongly with his ideas, or where they were not intending to address the question of his orthodoxy as such, the ways in which Origen had expressed things tended to condition the style of their discussions. Origen's language with reference to God proved particularly significant in this respect. In opposition to all forms of Monarchianism, Origen had taught that God the Son was genuinely distinct from God the Father and that he did not originate as a creature or have his status conferred upon him honorifically but was eternally generated by the Father. At the same time, Origen's way of describing the divine character had suggested that the Son was in some sense subordinate to the Father. The Son was not part of the created order, Origen maintained, but he was the mediator between the one who is uniquely "God-in-himself"—the Father—and the world of creaturely reality.

Such views were also propounded by Dionysius, bishop of Alexandria from 247 or 248 to 264, who had been taught by Origen. Dionysius was a remarkable figure in a number of ways, and he represented his faith bravely in a time of serious persecution, suffering personal exile under the emperor Valerian.[16] He was not an unqualified Origenist, but the resemblances between his thinking and Origen's were marked. While in exile in Libya in the late 250s, Dionysius got involved in a dispute among some local believers about the appropriate way to envisage the relationship between God the Father and God the Son. He strongly asserted the distinction between the divine *hypostaseis*, or "persons," and went so far as to say that the Father and the Son were as different as a boat and a boatman; they were not "consubstantial" (*homoousios*). This way of putting things was abruptly criticized by his namesake, Dionysius, bishop of Rome (259/260–268), who denounced "those who divide the *monarchia* of God into three powers and separated *hypostaseis*." Dionysius of Alexandria replied that he did not deny the essential closeness in the relationship between the Father and the Son; they could be described as resembling a root and a plant or a source and a river; but there was nevertheless a distinction between them.

The dispute between Dionysius of Alexandria and Dionysius of Rome appears at first sight to be a hairsplitting debate over verbal niceties. In reality, it was considerably more serious than that. To the church of Rome, the kind of language used of God in the Greek East, especially where it was affected by Origen's authority, appeared dangerously akin to *tritheism,* or the notion that there were three gods rather than one. It seemed to posit a serious division in the fundamental unity of God's being. When the phrase "three *hypostaseis*" was translated into Latin, it came out as "three *substantiae*" (the Latin *substantia* was the literal equivalent of the Greek *hypostasis*), and this was plainly at odds with the phraseology that had been popularized in the West by Tertullian—that there were not three *substantiae* in God but *one*, subsisting in three *personae*.

The problem, of course, was that in construing the Greek so literally, Western translators failed to appreciate the precision of what Greek theology was actually saying. The Eastern position was not intending to suggest that there could be "three substances" or "three Godnesses" in God; it was simply using a different word for "persons." What Latin theology called *personae*, Greek called *hypostaseis*. The semantic confusion between the two sides would nevertheless become a serious issue in the fourth century. If the Westerners suspected the East of tritheism, Greek thinkers believed that in Rome the danger was precisely the opposite—a defense of modalism. So strong was the West's affirmation of the *monarchia* that the distinctions between the Father, the Son, and the Holy Spirit seemed to be collapsed altogether.

Paul of Samosata

The indirect implications of Origen's teaching not only were high-lighted in the sharpening tensions between East and West but could also be seen in debates within Eastern theology itself. In 261, a new bishop was appointed in Antioch, a native of Syria named Paul of Samosata. Paul is presented in a distinctly hostile fashion by Eusebius, who hints that his appointment was attributable to his associations with Queen Zenobia, who had recently established a rebel kingdom in Palmyra, a prosperous region that had been part of the Roman Empire since the first century.[17] Paul was no friend of Origen's theology, and his teaching implied that he did not approve of either the *Logos* doctrine or the principle of three distinct *hypostaseis* within God.

As far as Paul of Samosata was concerned, it seems, Jesus, though conceived of a virgin, was fundamentally a human being, one "from below," who happened in God's purposes to be specially and completely anointed by the Holy Spirit. It made no sense to profess a preexistent divine Son; Jesus was essentially a uniquely inspired man, inhabited by the same Spirit who had energized the prophets of old. Paul alleg-edly claimed that God and the *Logos* were simply *homoousios*, "of one substance," without differentiation.

For propounding such views, Paul was accused of heresy by a num-ber of other Eastern bishops in a series of meetings, and at a synod in Antioch in 268, he was condemned and officially deposed from his see. His ideas seemed unmistakably reminiscent of the sort of crude adoptionism sponsored by some believers more than a century earlier. Confident of the support of his political superiors in Palmyra and backed by a loyal following of local Christians, Paul did not give in easily, and he refused to hand over his church. He was only removed some four years later, in 272, when the emperor Aurelian overthrew the Palmyran kingdom and elected to assign its bishop's church to those "to whom the bishops of the religion in Italy and Rome should communicate in writing"[18]—the first recorded instance of an internal church dispute being determined by political authority.

Some of Paul's opponents were undoubtedly Origenists—they included individuals such as Gregory *Thaumatourgos*—and there was clearly a degree of political gamesmanship and ecclesiastical rivalry in operation in the context of his trial and its aftermath. It is not apparent, however, that the controversy was primarily about the degree to which Paul's teaching differed from Origen's as such. It was the nature of Paul's propositions about Jesus and the basis of his divinity that was the real issue. Paul's accusers insisted, on solid biblical and logical grounds, that Jesus had to be different not only in degree but also in nature from other human beings; he was not simply more inspired or more filled with the divine Spirit but was in himself divine by nature. The question was not whether Paul's doctrine was pro- or anti-Origen but what it implied about an understanding of Christian orthodoxy.

So keen were Paul's antagonists to assert the distinction between Jesus and other beings that they seem to have favored a formulation that was, if anything, a betrayal of Origen. They spoke of the *Logos* as functioning substantially within the flesh of Jesus as a soul animating a body. Taken literally, this formula compromised one of the most vital points in Origen's Christology (teaching about Christ)—the contention that Jesus possessed a created human soul. Efforts to avoid adoptionist or "degree" Christologies would run similar risks ever after, especially in the course of disputes between theologians representative of Alexandria and Antioch in the fourth and fifth centuries. How might Christians speak of the divine origins of Jesus without impugning the integrity of his humanity?

Origen had endeavored to hold together both the reality of Jesus's human nature and the doctrine of eternal Sonship, but his *Logos* theology, besides being tied to a Platonist metaphysic, also implied a subordination within God in which the Father was God in some essential sense in a way that the Son (or the Spirit) was not. Was it possible to assert *both* preexistent divine Sonship *and* equality across the distinctions in God, while also doing justice to the humanity of the incarnate one? Whether individual theologians wished to follow Origen or condemn him, and whether membership of one camp or another in that debate was deemed a criterion of orthodoxy, the issues that Origen's acute and imaginative thinking had raised could hardly go away. Thanks to his influence, the eclectic wisdom of the Alexandrian tradition would profoundly affect the course of Christian doctrinal discussion for generations to come.

10

WORSHIP AND PRACTICE

▼

Christian activity in the second and third centuries cannot be confined only to the intellectual and organizational work undertaken by the obvious leaders of the churches, or by a small number of gifted scholars and teachers such as those we have looked at in the preceding chapters. In all of the contexts we have considered, the ordinary, everyday life of the faith went on at its own level, and practical questions of belief, behavior, and spirituality were faced as much at the grassroots as in the thought of the individuals whose names have become famous. For the overwhelming majority of believers, vitality of spiritual experience was measured not with reference to works of literature produced by intellectuals but by the rhythms of the life of thanksgiving, prayer, instruction, and fellowship in which they shared each week with their brothers and sisters in Christ.

The process by which church structures had become more rigid and systems of doctrine had been differentiated had rendered the authority of the past uniquely important, and there was an enduring conviction that practices had to be anchored in existing patterns. Christians at all levels drew comfort and strength from the belief that what they were doing and saying when they worshiped was consistent with the faith of those who had gone before them, and that they shared in a spiritual communion that transcended their present—often trying—circumstances. There was a strong sense that the body of Christ embraced not only the living, or all those who currently confessed the name of Christ in truth, but also their ancestors in the faith, those who had died "in the Lord." The piety of earlier generations was, in a mysterious but vital fashion, part of the corporate experience of the community in the present day.

Evolving Approaches to Initiation

In apostolic times, baptism had generally followed quite quickly upon profession of faith, though it had always been necessary to ensure that those who sought to be baptized understood the basics of the faith and pledged to abide by its moral standards. As the number of converts from pagan backgrounds had increased, the obligation to extend this elementary instruction had increased along with it. The realities of persecution or opposition had also led Christians to be wary about admitting people too easily; those who sought to join could, after all, be false in their profession—infiltrators bent on spying upon the believers on behalf of hostile authorities or disrupting the life of the community for malicious reasons of their own. The conviction of believers that they were a special people, the chosen ones of God, had equally heightened the sense that although the gospel was for all, the advantages of full participation in its benefits were not to be dispensed lightly. All except some of the Gnostic sects restricted participation in the eucharistic meal to the baptized, but it was increasingly seen as important to ensure that the process of initiation itself was not administered lightly. If baptism was a once-for-all event, it was not to be undertaken with anything less than proper solemnity.

As we saw already in the *Didache* (p. 180), it had become standard by the late first or early second century to require converts to pass through a period as catechumens, or "those under instruction" (Greek *catechumenoi*), prior to admission to the full privileges of membership in the church. This phase of catechesis or teaching was undertaken by spiritual leaders, primarily bishops, and its combination of intellectual and ritual elements proved a powerful tool in the spread of the faith. To become a catechumen was to leave behind the status of a general inquirer or hearer and register a formal interest in joining the community, but it was not yet to be regarded as a full member. Those enrolled as catechumens were treated as believers, and they were accordingly part of the *synaxis* or assembly of the church for worship, but they were not as yet among "the faithful," "the chosen ones," or those with complete rights of belonging. They were not yet greeted with the holy kiss of peace, and they were dismissed from the worship service prior to the Eucharist.

The period of instruction for the catechumens might vary considerably, from an interval of a few days or weeks to as long as two to three years, depending on context. In many of the larger urban churches, catechumens received daily instruction; in other places the teaching took place only on Sundays. It became common for baptism to be administered at special times, and often just once in the year, except during periods of persecution, when normal patterns were disrupted and it was considered acceptable to baptize at any time. Easter was the most favored time because of its associations with the symbolism of sharing in the death and resurrection of Christ, and in Rome and North Africa in particular this was the preferred season for initiation. Pentecost was also quite popular in other places, as the climax of a post-Easter season celebrating the reality of the resurrection.

The instruction given to catechumens tended to begin with elementary moral teaching followed by some basic clarification about the nature of Christian confession. All of the teaching was intended to be based upon the Bible. Those under instruction would listen to the reading and exposition of Scripture in the regular church meetings and were expected to absorb and become gradually capable of recollecting scriptural material for themselves. Although the nature of the anticipated theological confession involved some specific aspects, overall the level of doctrinal knowledge required remained fairly limited; much of the substantive teaching was about practical matters of Christian behavior. The learner was left in no doubt about practices that were unacceptable and about occupations and recreational activities that were deemed to be at odds with God's Law.

Besides injunctions against crimes such as killing, theft, and all kinds of sexual immorality, catechumens were particularly warned about the evils of idolatry, which meant they could not participate in any public occasions in which the pagan gods were invoked, including sporting events, entertainment shows, and theatrical performances. Forbidden trades or professions included acting, working as a gladiator or a charioteer, being employed as a sculptor or an artist of religious idols, and engaging in roles that involved the taking of human life, such as holding office as a magistrate.[1] Catechumens were called upon to prove themselves different from the world around them; they had to display complete integrity and reliability in their daily lives, extend practical care to the needy, and avoid all kinds of compromising situations.

Candidates were examined individually to ascertain their progress, and in some contexts they were formally charged more than once during their preparation to renounce evil and live in consecration to the standards of Christ's way. In the later stages of their training, it was not unusual for ritual exorcisms to take place. Sometimes this was seen as ridding the catechumen of evil spirits, though more often it was a symbolic petition for the subsequent restraint of the powers of evil in the person's life. Such rituals were conducted by bishops, presbyters, or other senior leaders, but from around the middle of the third century onward, many churches came to have junior officials known as *exorcists* who carried out these functions.[2] It was normal for baptism to be preceded additionally by serious fasting and often by a sustained vigil of prayer. The particular obligations and tests applied to catechumens varied from context to context, but there was always a scrutiny of character, a consideration of the person's grasp of a core confession, and an emphasis upon the solemnity of the initiation to follow.

It had already become very common from the later first century, if not before, to baptize by pouring water over the candidate's head, but complete or partial immersion was certainly also practiced, both outdoors in rivers and lakes and indoors in household fonts. The *Didache* considers immersion in cold, running water to be the normal mode, but allows for pouring (and warm water) if circumstances so dictate.[3] Similar flexibility is shown in other second- and third-century writers. Approaches to the baptismal rite varied, but we have one particularly interesting account in the document known as the *Apostolic Tradition*, which contains a detailed description of what are claimed to be traditional rites and practices in the church, and much fascinating information on the consecration of leaders, sacred rituals, and various aspects of Christian ethics.

The *Apostolic Tradition* had a much stronger influence in Eastern churches than it did in the West, and its details survive not in the original Greek but in a range of translations and derivative texts. The document represents a complex mixture of traditions, and the history of its text has evoked a vast amount of scholarly attention, but in essence at least it can probably be dated to the early third century. Many scholars have believed that it is to be partly or wholly connected with the authorship of Hippolytus of Rome, and this remains a consensus assumption, but it is one that has recently been subject to criticism. Some recent analysts contend that the associations with Hippolytus are not secure, and indeed that the Hippolytus under whose name a number of important works of biblical commentary and theology have been preserved was not in fact Hippolytus of Rome but another author who operated in an Asian church context (cf. pp. 235–38). If this is true, the *Apostolic Tradition* would need to be located in the East, not the West.

The jury is probably still out on these claims. Certainly the traditions reflected in the church order cannot precisely be assumed to reflect standard practice in Rome in the early third century, or even the practice of a particular group at Rome, such as those who may have been led by Hippolytus. There is also no doubt that the impact of the text was much greater in the East than it was in Rome. Whatever the source of the work, however, its claims to represent traditional rites deserve to be taken seriously. Whether Western or Eastern in origin, its evidence, at least in part, may allow us to glimpse liturgical practices that go back into the later second century.

The *Apostolic Tradition* refers to a three-year period of catechesis as traditional.[4] This claim may or may not be authentic to the original work, but a process of due instruction was certainly regarded as normal. Candidates were anointed with consecrated oil to symbolize their exorcism and renunciation of evil. In order to be baptized, they undressed, and women untied their hair and removed any gold jewelry they were wearing. These actions were seen as representing dissociation from everything worldly; it was apparently thought that the devil might lurk in clothes or hair. Having descended naked into a baptismal font, their profession was tested by the bishop, who asked them a series of questions:

Do you believe in God the Father Almighty?

Do you believe in Jesus Christ, the Son of God, who was born of the Holy Spirit and the Virgin Mary, who was crucified under Pontius Pilate, and died, and rose again the third day from the dead, and ascended into heaven, and sat down at the right hand of the Father, and will come to judge the living and the dead?

Do you believe in the Holy Spirit, in the holy church, and the resurrection of the flesh?[5]

After each question, the candidate replied, "I believe," and was immersed in the font: the water was thus applied three times, not just once. After this, further anointing with oil took place, first by a presbyter and then by the bishop; in the latter case, the bishop placed a hand on the believer's head and *sealed* him or her by making the sign of the cross on the forehead. The process of chrismation (Greek, *chrisma*, "anointing") derived from Hebrew rituals for the consecration of priests and kings and was evidently seen as a vital element of the reception of the candidate into the community of faith, symbolic of the honor bestowed in becoming fully part of the "holy priesthood" of all believers in Christ (see 1 Peter 2:5, 9; Rev. 1:6; 5:10; 20:6). Once the baptismal process was complete, the newly recognized member would be admitted into the fellowship and allowed to participate for the first time in the Eucharist.

The evidence of the *Apostolic Tradition* is valuable for many reasons, not the least of which is its witness to the kind of confession the catechumen was required to make. Applicants for baptism, in this tradition at any rate, were not expected merely to acknowledge belief in one God or in Jesus but to give assent to some specific details on the status of Jesus as the Son of God the Father Almighty and on the manner of the Savior's coming into the world and his departure from it. Other elements deemed essential were belief in the Holy Spirit, in the church, and in the resurrection of the body. Nothing specific is affirmed of each of these, but their inclusion in the basic confessional requirements is significant. The doctrinal understanding expected of the initiate may have been limited, but it included some particular points that were obviously believed to lie at the heart of the Christian faith. The threefold structure of assent reflects the triune nature of the God into whose name the candidate was baptized (Matt. 28:19): the believer expressly acknowledged God the Father, God the Son, and God the Holy Spirit. Public entry into the family of God was not only through a simple declaration of faith in Jesus but by acknowledgment of God the holy Trinity.

In the context of baptism, the testing of such belief naturally took an interrogatory form; questions were asked and a simple response, "I believe," was given. In later times, the threefold pattern would also be used in what scholars call "declaratory" (as opposed to "interrogatory") creeds, in which more detail would be included on the essentials of Christian belief and recited rather than simply affirmed. The baptismal confession recorded in the *Apostolic Tradition* would in fact closely influence the evolution of the later creed that came to be known as the "Apostles' Creed," the most influential of all Western baptismal creeds, which is why the language quoted above from the *Apostolic Tradition* may sound quite familiar. Scholars call the confession recorded in the *Apostolic Tradition* the "Old Roman Creed" to distinguish it from its later descendant.[6]

Another prominent witness from the early third century suggests the existence of fairly similar baptismal practice elsewhere. In North Africa, Tertullian speaks of baptism as preceded by prayer, fasting, all-night vigils, confession of sin, exorcism, threefold immersion into each of the three persons of the Trinity in response to questions about the faith, anointing, the sign of the cross, and the laying-on of hands by the bishop prior to welcome to the eucharistic table. Tertullian describes an invocation of the Holy Spirit over the waters of baptism, and he sees the postbaptismal chrismation as directly evocative of the Holy Spirit's anointing of Jesus at his baptism in the Jordan. He attests that while a bishop normally conducted the baptism, it was possible for the process to be conducted by presbyters or deacons, and even on occasion by other believers; women, however, were excluded from this privilege.[7]

In a work known to us under the Latin name of the *Didascalia Apostolorum (The Teaching of the Apostles)*, we have important, if somewhat disjointed, information about order, worship, and administration in the Syrian church of the third century, recorded by an author who was probably a convert from Judaism. The *Didascalia* draws upon the *Didache* and various other sources, and in its complete form, it survives only in an early Syriac translation; the original Greek text has had to be reconstructed from extant fragments of a Latin version and from a fourth-century work known as the *Apostolic Constitutions*, which revises and incorporates some of its material. The witness of the *Didascalia* is only one piece of evidence, and caution is necessary in inferring conclusions about the Syrian tradition more generally from what it says. Nevertheless, a number of its claims square with other testimonies regarding early Syrian liturgy, and from the overall picture that we can assemble, there are some interesting features to notice.

In this Syrian context, candidates for baptism first expressed repentance and faith before being admitted to further instruction, but the nature of the instruction that followed is not entirely clear. When it came to the initiation rite, it appears to have been seen as particularly important that applicants were subjected to prebaptismal anointing with oil, which was regarded as a sign of their full identification with Christ, who was also anointed by the Holy Spirit at his baptism to enable him to fulfill his priestly and kingly roles. Such anointing might take place on the whole body and on the head. According to the *Didascalia*, in the case of women candidates the anointing of the body was preferably to be done by a female deacon (see pp. 304–5), but the actual baptism was to be performed by a man, either a bishop or another member of the clergy.[8]

Other sources from farther to the east, from the Syriac-speaking churches, also speak of the chrismation of both body and head, and similarly refer to the link between believers' baptism and the baptism of Jesus. It is likely that practices varied, and it is even possible that in some circles the anointing rather than the water baptism was seen as the central action. Scholars debate what such patterns imply about the evolution of baptismal liturgy in this Eastern context and why it may be that in Syria in particular the symbol of chrismation took place before the water rite. Whatever is said on these questions, it is clear that anointing was viewed in this tradition as an especially significant aspect of the initiation process.

Baptizing the Young

Both Tertullian (*On Baptism*) and the *Apostolic Tradition* attest that baptism was applied not only to adults but also to young children and babies.[9] In the liturgical procedure, children were apparently baptized first, then men, then women. In the *Apostolic Tradition*, it is said that "the little ones" who could not speak for themselves were spoken for by their parents or by some other family member. As we remarked in chapter 8, Tertullian's voice is the earliest incontestable witness to infant baptism, but it is notable that he also disapproves of the practice, arguing that it is better for people to be mature and to pass through a process of preparation before they are baptized. It seems clear from what both Tertullian and the *Apostolic Tradition* say that the baptism of infants was not an innovation in their times or over the past generation, and at least some third-century believers considered it to be an apostolic custom. It is, nevertheless, virtually impossible to determine just how far back the practice can be traced, since all of the earlier evidence, both in the New Testament itself and in other authors, is subject to many differences of interpretation.

It is possible that from quite early on babies born to parents converted to Christianity had been baptized, whereas babies born to already Christian parents had not. It is equally conceivable that from early times there had been a practice of baptizing quite young children but *not* babies and that the baptism of babies had developed first as an emergency measure that had then come to apply to younger and younger infants. As we noted in passing in chapter 4, in the case of the earliest Christian period, we simply do not have sufficient information on which to settle these matters with confidence, and it is almost certainly wrong to generalize with regard to the churches as a whole. Practices may well have varied, and it is possible that different principles applied to children in cases of household conversions from those that pertained to children born into already Christian homes.

Such matters still deeply divide Christians today, and disputes about the appropriate understanding of New Testament texts relating to baptism are unlikely to disappear. Whatever is to be said on the various sides of these debates, the reality is that neither an argument in favor of baptizing babies today nor an argument against the practice can be established conclusively on the grounds of historical evidence about the earliest customs of the churches. It is clear that in the late second and early third centuries infants were being baptized in at least a number of contexts and that a system of adults acting as sponsors was already in operation in these places. It is equally incontrovertible that this practice increased greatly over subsequent generations and received express theological justification from a number of Christian leaders.

At the same time, the practice of baptizing very small children or babies was undoubtedly opposed by some from the start, and the process of catechesis implies that regular baptismal instruction at least was aimed at those who were old enough to speak for themselves. There would always be many children of Christian parents who were not baptized in infancy, and even when individuals professed faith in their youth, it was by no means uncommon for them to defer their baptism until they were much older.

Eucharistic Practice

Baptism continued to symbolize enlightenment, cleansing, and adoption into God's family. The believer was henceforth said to be "sealed" with the Holy Spirit (Eph. 4:30; see also 2 Cor. 1:22; Eph. 1:13–14) and by virtue of this unrepeatable rite imprinted with a special character by God. To bear this spiritual seal was to be simultaneously assured of divine grace, summoned to holiness of life in conformity to Christ, and made the recipient of God's promises for eternal life. From around the middle of the second century onward, the newly baptized in some churches were given milk and honey along with the elements of their first Eucharist as tokens of their entry into the Promised Land of God's goodness (see Exod. 33:3).

In the later first century, the ritual of remembering Jesus had become separated from the common meal in which the first Christians had shared; the Eucharist was generally held on a Sunday morning, and the *agape* or love feast took place in the evening. By the middle of the second century, the *agape* was held only occasionally, and by the third century, if it survived at all, it was only as a kind of charity supper for the needy rather than a fellowship meal for regular worshipers.[10] It is not entirely clear why the *agape* tradition declined. The likeliest cause was the persistence of abuses such as those that Paul had condemned in Corinth (2 Peter 2:13; Jude 12), though it is also possible that there were problems in some places with the secular authorities, who clamped down on evening gatherings of all societies or clubs in the belief that they were a potential source of political trouble. To the average magistrate, Christian meetings would have fallen into the same category as other voluntary associations—and to some they seemed all the more dangerous because of the rumors of what went on in their midst.

As the connections between the Eucharist and the *agape* became more tenuous and the commemoration of Jesus was regarded as the focal point of Sunday worship, the ritual sequence of the thanksgiving began to alter somewhat. In early times, when the Eucharist was part of a common meal, the usual pattern appears to have reflected the shape of the Last Supper, which was itself embedded in customs surrounding Jewish formal meals. Bread was blessed, broken, and distributed to all present; then came the fellowship meal; and the blessing and sharing of the cup followed at the end. Though this was not always the approach, as we saw (see p. 121), it was probably the most frequent. Once the Eucharist and the *agape* became distinct events, however, the two main rituals of the thanksgiving were no longer separated by the fellowship meal, and they seem to have been located directly in a context of reading, exposition, and prayer.

The evidence in Justin Martyr's *First Apology* indicates such a pattern in one mid-second-century context:

> And on the day called Sunday an assembly is held in one place of all who live in cities or in the country, and the records of the apostles or the writings of the prophets are read for as long as time allows. Then, when the reader has finished, the president admonishes and exhorts [us] in a discourse to imitate these good things. Then we all stand up together and offer up prayers; and . . . when we have finished praying, bread and wine and water are brought, and the president likewise offers up prayers and thanksgivings to the best of his ability, and the people give their assent, saying "Amen"; and the elements over which thanks have been given are distributed, and everyone partakes; and they are sent through the deacons to those who are not present.[11]

Naturally we cannot assume that Justin's description would have held good for any and every Christian gathering; the *agape* did continue to feature at least intermittently in some churches well after his time. Nevertheless, Justin's words give a valuable picture of what was to him a standard form of liturgy, and they indicate the way in which the thanksgiving had developed in at least one tradition by this period. The eucharistic actions of eating and drinking came together, and they flowed out of an apparently more formal worship sequence. Interestingly, there is no reference to singing as a core element of the communion liturgy. This may possibly imply that sung praise had been particularly associated with the *agape* rather than with the Eucharist as such, though it is unwise to generalize on the basis of Justin's silence on the matter.

Some scholars have argued that the positioning of the Eucharist in a framework of reading, exhortation, and prayer represents a deliberate second-century fusion of the Christian communion rite with the kind of liturgy traditionally observed in a Jewish synagogue service. The combination of the thanksgiving with scriptural reflection and petition was not, however, an innovation; it was simply a formalization of existing practice. Christians had always focused on God's Word and prayed together when they gathered. All that had happened was that, with the sidelining of the fellowship meal, the remembrance of Jesus had assumed an even more obvious place at the heart of the worship. It is also notable that, despite the decline in the *agape*, the aspects of belonging and togetherness remain strongly emphasized in Justin's characterization; even those who could not be present at the assembly were taken portions of the communion elements and were thus embraced within the fellowship of the thanksgiving.

In Justin's account, the prayer said at the Eucharist is extemporaneous, and this is likely to have been the general rule. From other second- and third-century witnesses, we can possibly glimpse something of the broad pattern such improvised prayers may have taken. In accordance with Jewish traditions of giving thanks at meals, eucharistic prayers seem often to have consisted of at least two aspects: remembrance (Greek, *anamnesis*) and invocation (Greek, *epiclesis*). Remembrance meant recollecting the saving acts of God in the history of Jesus and perhaps reciting the words of Jesus at the Last Supper as an institutional narrative for the meal. Invocation meant appealing for the Holy Spirit to come upon the worshipers and to accept their thanksgiving. One particularly striking example of such a pattern is to be found in the *Apostolic Tradition*, which pictures the worship leader engaging in an opening dialogue with the congregation and then offering a formal prayer over the elements that clearly combines the two aspects of remembrance and invocation:

The Lord be with you.
    And with your spirit.
Lift up your hearts.
    We lift them to the Lord.
Let us give thanks to the Lord.
    It is fitting and right.
We give you thanks, O God, through your beloved Son Jesus Christ, whom in these last times you sent to us as Saviour and Redeemer and Messenger [literally "Angel"] of your will; who is your inseparable Word, through whom you made all things, and whom by your good pleasure you sent from heaven to a Virgin's womb, who was conceived and made flesh and manifested as your Son, born of the Holy Spirit and the Virgin;

Who, fulfilling your will and procuring for you a holy people, stretched out his hands when he suffered, that he might free from suffering those who have believed in you;

Who, when he was betrayed to a voluntary suffering to destroy death and break the devil's chains, to tread down hell and lead the righteous to the light, to fix hell's limit and to manifest the resurrection, took bread and gave thanks to you and said: "Take, eat, this is my body which is broken for you." Likewise also the cup, saying: "This is my blood which is shed for you. When you do this, do it in remembrance of me."

Remembering, therefore, his death and resurrection, we offer to you this bread and cup, giving you thanks that you have counted us worthy to stand before you and to minister to you as priests.

And we beseech you to send your Holy Spirit upon the offering of your holy church. Gather them together and grant that all who partake of the holy things may be filled with the Holy Spirit for the confirmation of their faith in the truth, that we may praise and glorify you through your Son Jesus Christ, through whom be glory and honour to you, Father and Son with the Holy Spirit, in your holy church, both now and for ever. Amen.[12]

There was, however, no standard form of such prayers in the second or third centuries, and just as the worship leader in Justin's picture prayed as his ability allowed, the *Apostolic Tradition* and other texts likewise granted freedom of expression according to the fluency of the person leading the worship. Some standard forms of wording did exist, and in the *Apostolic Tradition*, the leader is permitted to use these if he wishes, but they were by no means mandatory or universal in style. Only later on did eucharistic liturgies develop specific sequences, in which a prayer of *anamnesis* lay at the center and other elements, such as an institutional narrative, were structured around that. Even then, fixed forms were intended to facilitate formation in sound teaching and to assist with meaningful participation, not to reduce the liturgy to a series of mechanical steps. Practices still varied considerably, and several distinctive emphases can be found in Syrian, Egyptian, and Western forms. Many of the eucharistic rites consisted of several short prayers rather than a single, overarching prayer of thanksgiving, and Western liturgy was often briefer than Eastern.

One feature that did at length become widespread was the sense that the celebration of the Eucharist was a *sacrifice* or *offering* made by the assembled believers. Such ideas can be seen in the prayer recorded in the *Apostolic Tradition*, and they were already present in some measure in the first-century church. They derived from ancient Jewish convictions about the importance of rendering a spiritual offering of praise and devotion to God rather than a merely outward fulfillment of religious ritual. The terminology of the Eucharist from the start implied such associations, and the meal could be visualized as a "pure" or bloodless sacrifice of worship over against the literal blood-sacrifices of both Hebrew and Graeco-Roman religious practice.[13] This picture was held alongside the continuing belief that the eating and drinking were an actual participation in the body and blood of Christ and that the Eucharist was "holy food" for the nourishing of the faithful.

As we noticed in chapter 4, some early Christian ritual meals consisted of a variety of foodstuffs, and practices such as mixing water with wine or substituting water or milk for wine at the Eucharist continued in certain quarters for generations. Bread-and-water Eucharists were particularly common in Eastern Christianity, especially in Syria and Asia, and in these contexts, there was often much less enthusiasm for the idea of the Eucharist as a sacrifice. Sacrifice was seen as synonymous with false religion, and wine was shunned as an item associated with pagan ritual practice (meat was also avoided in the general diet for similar reasons). Many of those who held such views, however, either had or were alleged to have connections with traditions that were controversial on doctrinal or moral grounds, such as certain Gnostic sects and other radical ascetic movements. Resistance to sacrificial associations for the Eucharist did not entirely disappear, and there were later ascetic believers who also adopted bread-and-water rituals, but bread and wine were the most common eucharistic elements in the churches at large, and from around the middle of the third century they were generally standard. Some Eastern ascetics partook only of the bread in the Eucharist, and the same was often true of the sick; on the whole, however, it was not considered appropriate to receive only the bread or the cup; to use a later phrase, communion was normally "in both kinds."

Worshipers increasingly came to regard their "sacrifice" as in various ways evocative of Christ's offering of himself on their behalf. Jesus had given himself up in the belief that he was obeying God's will, and the believers saw themselves as following his priestly pattern when they celebrated the Eucharist. They were not repeating Christ's saving action every time they took communion, for that was both impossible and unnecessary; but they were recollecting and symbolizing anew his perfect work. The bread and wine were sacred symbols, figures, or "antitypes" of the body and blood of Jesus, and great solemnity and reverence were to attend their reception. Christian teachers insisted that the elements were never to be received in a casual manner, and extreme care had to be taken to ensure that no part of the sacred food and drink was dropped or spilled.

If it had been habitual among some of the very earliest followers of Jesus to remember their Lord several times in the week or even daily (Acts 2:46), in the second and third centuries it was also common to hold Eucharists in more contexts than that of Sunday worship. Depending on social circumstances and political freedom, communion was often celebrated in such places as cemeteries, prisons, and at the tombs of martyrs or other revered saints, and in many Christian communities in the third century there was a daily thanksgiving. Daily communion was especially common in the West; Eastern Christians, on the whole, tended to stay with the tradition of celebration only on Sundays or at special holy seasons. In the North African churches, believers seem regularly to have taken some of the consecrated bread home with them so as to be able to take communion in private. This practice probably originated during times of persecution, but it persisted in a number of both Western and Eastern contexts in later centuries.

Fasting, Prayer, and Praise

The practice of communal worship was bound up with other enduring routines, especially fasting and prayer. Wednesdays and Fridays came to be widely observed as Christian fast days, over against the Jewish fast days of Mondays and Thursdays (as the *Didache* directs).[14] Believers would typically abstain from food until the ninth hour of the day, or 3:00 p.m., at which time there would be a service of Bible reading and prayer prior to the taking of any food. The choice of the ninth hour may have been because this was the time at which Jesus had died (Matt. 27:46–50; Mark 15:34–37; Luke 23:44–46). In some later churches, there was also a celebration of the Eucharist at this hour. It was not considered appropriate to fast on Sundays, which were a time not only for remembering the death of Jesus but for rejoicing in his resurrection and anticipating the future arrival of the kingdom of God with power. Fast days came to be known in some quarters as "stations," evocative of the "watch" of dutiful soldiers.

Prayer naturally continued to be seen as an essential daily commitment. In the third century, the usual three times for prayer were widely correlated with the standard divisions of the working day in the Roman Empire, so that prayer typically took place at the third, sixth, and ninth hours of the day, or at approximately 9:00 a.m., 12:00 noon, and 3:00 p.m. It was common to have prayer at other times as well, such as on rising, at the lighting of the evening lamp, at bedtime, and at midnight. The extent to which individual Christians observed some of these hours must have varied considerably, depending on circumstances and on individuals' spiritual enthusiasm. The most ardent believers, such as ascetics, kept vigil most frequently; many others must have been unavoidably occupied with work during the daytime hours. Nevertheless, it was seen as obligatory for all Christians to pray at least in the morning and in the evening, and wherever possible at other times as well, such as at the taking of food. A threefold (9:00 a.m., 12:00 noon, 3:00 p.m.) or fivefold (these three plus morning and evening) sequence was probably very common in both the East and the West by the third century.

The observance of a daily "office," as it came to be known, generally involved not only prayer but Bible reading and singing as well, especially at the hours when people were at home or with their families. The Psalms in particular were much used, and attention was given to their many references to worship and petition as taking place at particular seasons of the day and night. Divided into sections and understood messianically, the Psalms, both read and sung, were powerful symbols of a daily offering of praise to God. We have very limited information on other hymnody in the second and third centuries, but there is no doubt that hymns expressly identifying Christ were in use. This is clear from Pliny's description of the Christians in Bithynia around 112: one of their practices was to "chant verses . . . in honour of Christ as if to a god."[15] In the third century, it was held that hymns addressing Christ as divine had been written and sung by believers from the earliest days of the faith.[16]

Examples of such worship from a later context can be seen in a collection of forty-two hymns known as the *Odes of Solomon*, which probably originated in the Eastern Syrian church in the late second century. Only discovered in their complete form in the early twentieth century, these hymns circulated in both Syriac and Greek. Their tone is both celebratory and mystical, and they include a considerable amount of material reminiscent of Gnostic sentiment,[17] but they were probably produced in orthodox circles. They contain some striking evocations of Christ as the Word and Wisdom of God incarnate, and in keeping with ideas discernible elsewhere in Syrian tradition, they picture the Holy Spirit as a feminine divine personification. The nineteenth *Ode*, exalting the virginal conception of Jesus, opens like this:

> A cup of milk was offered to me,
> and I drank it in the sweetness of the Lord's kindness.
> The Son is the cup,
> and the Father is he who was milked;
> and the Holy Spirit is she who milked him;
> Because his breasts were full,
> and it was undesirable that his milk should be released without
>   purpose.
> The Holy Spirit opened her bosom,
> and mixed the milk of the two breasts of the Father. . . .
> The womb of the Virgin took [it],
> and she received conception and gave birth.

Somewhat less striking language is to be found in a few fragmentary glimpses of other early hymns. There is a hymn of praise to Christ at the end of Clement of Alexandria's *Paidagogos*, which contains some impressive evocation of classical Greek verse, but this was probably not designed for use in church worship. There is also a much-discussed portion of a third-century trinitarian chant discovered on a scrap of papyrus from Oxyrhynchus in Egypt, which seems to include a rudimentary system of musical notation:

> While we hymn Father, Son, and Holy Spirit,
> Let all creation sing Amen, Amen.
> Praise, power to the sole giver of all good things. Amen. Amen.

A more extensive Greek hymn is the *Phos hilaron* ("Gladdening Light"), preserved in the later fourth century, by which time it was already said to be of ancient status. It is probably second-century in origin. Still sung in the liturgy of the Eastern church at the lighting of the evening lamp, it gives thanks for the cheerful light of nature given by God each new day, for the light of the lamp in the darkness of the night, and for the illumination brought by the light of Christ. The words of this hymn have been translated by notable English hymn-writers such as John Keble and Robert Bridges, and versions of it still appear in Western hymnbooks.[18]

All told, the literary evidence for the hymns sung by believers in the second and third centuries remains fairly slender, but there is no reason to doubt that Christians continued to find poetry and song to be an important media of worship, and sung praise played an enduring part in their routines. The Christians were known to their pagan critics as those who expressed themselves in song, and even if their activity was frowned upon—Celsus, for example, considered the believers' chants a dangerous thing, deadening the senses and jeopardizing the use of reason—its emotional power was acknowledged all the same.

Christian Assembly

It was considered vital that believers assembled for worship each Sunday morning, except in the most unusual of circumstances. In Justin Martyr's description of Sunday worship, it is significant that the gathering included all local Christians and that bread and wine from the thanksgiving meal were taken to those who could not be present. In some churches, it was considered inappropriate to hold more than one Eucharist in a town on the same Sunday on the grounds that the communion meal symbolized the unity of believers; several different Eucharists implied not oneness but fragmentation. In larger cities, where there had from early times been multiple congregations, this pattern was clearly not practicable, but efforts were made to emphasize local links as much as possible.

Throughout the second century, private houses continued to be the main meeting places, and the great majority of buildings used for worship were not identifiably Christian. The lack of special public buildings underscored the sense that the church was primarily a spiritual community; its members were a pilgrim people with no fixed abode in this world, worshiping a God who could not be confined to particular physical spaces. In general, believers still met in whatever local home had the most room to accommodate them. Gradually, however, some houses began to be formally adapted to serve as places of worship. By the early third century, in some places at least, we see the beginnings of what has come to be known, after Eusebius and other sources, as a "house of the church."[19] There is good evidence that Christians did have particular places of worship in a number of parts of the empire by this time, and in most cases these were probably some form of "houses of the church."

Our evidence for what such a building may typically have looked like is very limited; clearly it did not amount to an official church edifice of the kind that would appear in the fourth century. Nevertheless, we do have some indications as to its possible character. In 1931, when archaeologists were excavating the Roman fortress at Dura-Europos, a garrison town on the Euphrates in northwestern Syria destroyed by the Persians in 256, they discovered a fairly large house, constructed in the early 230s and renovated a few years later for use in Christian worship. On the outside, the building retained the appearance of a domestic residence; inside, a number of modifications had been made to facilitate liturgical practice. One of the public rooms had been enlarged, and a dais had been installed at its eastern end. In another room, originally an ordinary chamber, much more extensive conversions had taken place. This space had been turned into a baptistery, the earliest surviving example of its kind, with a font about a meter deep set in the floor at the western end of the room, covered with a decorated canopy. The walls of the room had been elaborately adorned with frescoes of biblical scenes, including depictions of Adam and Eve, David and Goliath, the Samaritan woman at the well, Jesus walking on the waters (clearly intended to symbolize the imagery of baptism), and Christ as the Good Shepherd (John 10:1–21; cf. Heb. 13:20; 1 Peter 2:25; 5:4).[20]

Baptistery from Christian house at Dura-Europos, Syria. Illustration from Dura-Europos Collection, Yale University Art Gallery, New Haven, CT. Used by permission.

We cannot assume that the Dura-Europos house was typical of all "houses of the church," and we need to be cautious about extrapolating general patterns from this one celebrated example. Many places of worship were doubtless different in form. Some, however, were probably similar to this Syrian case; it is unlikely that the changes made to a house in a rather remote town on Rome's Eastern frontier would have lacked all precedent or parallel elsewhere. Archaeological work in cities such as Rome, Carthage, and Antioch has revealed a transition in other contexts toward what have been called "halls of the church," where houses used for worship were greatly enlarged, given such features as raised pulpits for preaching or platforms to accommodate clergy as distinct from laity, and turned into essentially rectangular assembly halls. There was a gradual evolution toward more formal structures.

There is evidence from many cities and towns that civil officialdom began to recognize certain places of assembly as Christian property. Through all of these developments, Christians remained vulnerable to intermittent political pressure, and at various times in the third century, such places of worship were confiscated or destroyed by the authorities in a bid to stifle organized Christian activity. The case of the controversial bishop Paul of Samosata (pp. 268–69) showed that Christians might also quarrel among themselves over the possession of church property and appeal to secular powers to adjudicate. Such an appeal in itself may have been, as yet, unusual, but the incident stems from a period in which the authorities increasingly had to take account of the presence of "Christian" buildings. Whether their places of assembly were to be recognized, seized, or destroyed, the Christians were too numerous to be ignored.

Charity

Caring for the vulnerable continued to be regarded as a very important Christian responsibility. Money was routinely collected at church services and given to needy Christians locally or farther afield. In a society in which the contrast between rich and poor was enormous and obvious signs of privation were to be seen on every street corner, believers were also encouraged to give to the poor, the hungry, and the sick, and preachers regularly reminded their hearers of their responsibilities toward the outcasts and untouchables of their world. As the churches grew in organizational terms, they often developed schemes for the regular distribution of funds, and those in larger cities took on important roles as dispensers of charity in their neighborhoods. They also came to act as banks with which vulnerable individuals could lodge precious assets for safekeeping; the due maintenance of such deposits was seen as an important moral duty for church officials.

On the whole, Christian social thought remained fairly conservative, and there were few realistic opportunities to effect economic change on any significant scale. Teachers such as Clement of Alexandria were content to assure their more prosperous disciples that wealth was not necessarily an evil; riches were not to be abandoned wholesale but used for appropriate ends. Such arguments did little to disturb conventional economic patterns, and sometimes the impetus to share material privileges seemed to be blunted by an essentially spiritualizing interpretation of biblical teaching on the relative status of riches and poverty. Nevertheless, almsgiving was treated seriously, and believers were exhorted to pay due attention to their obligations. Those who hoarded their resources or feigned indifference to the plight of the weak were warned of dire spiritual consequences, while those who did disburse their assets were promised special divine favor.

Sacred Time

As we saw, many Christians from the first century onward observed an annual feast called *Pascha* in memory of Jesus's death and resurrection (p. 230), and in the second century, significant disputes arose concerning both the meaning of the term *Pascha* and the basis upon which the date of this festival was to be calculated. For the Quartodecimans, the *Pascha* did not necessarily fall on a Sunday; for others it did. These disputes endured into the fourth century and beyond, but by the late second century, a fairly large majority of Christians had come to agree that the annual remembrance of the death and resurrection of Jesus ought always to be a Sunday festival. Easter day was preceded by a period of fasting, and in many quarters, it was also followed by an all-night vigil, culminating in a celebration of the Eucharist. In Rome and in North Africa in particular, the last phase of the Paschal vigil became the context for the final initiation of catechumens, who were baptized at dawn and then admitted to the sacred meal.

In quite a number of churches, the fast on the Saturday prior to Easter came to be joined to the regular Friday fast, which was observed all year, to create a continuous, two-day period of preparation for the festival. In Egypt and Syria, the Paschal fast was even longer, lasting six days, from the preceding Monday to the end of the Saturday vigil, though it was generally recognized that fasting on the Friday and the Saturday was of primary importance, in recognition of the particular days on which Jesus was crucified, died, and lay buried. Such an acknowledgment reflects a move toward marking the three days of Friday, Saturday, and Sunday as the particularly sacred days of a larger Easter season. The routine of fasting prior to Easter tied in with the process of preparing catechumens for baptism, and it was probably in the third century that the custom first arose of observing a still more sustained period of preparation over the weeks leading up to Easter, in imitation of the forty-day fast kept by Jesus after his baptism (Matt. 4:1–11; Mark 1:12–13; Luke 4:1–13), which was calculated in Egypt to have fallen on 6 January. It was only in the early fourth century, however, that a season of Lent would become widely observed, and even then the precise length of the season still varied a good deal.

If 6 January was regarded by Egyptian believers as the feast of the baptism of Jesus, in other Eastern contexts, it had a different connotation. The third-century church of Jerusalem considered 6 January to be the date of the nativity and the visit of the Magi (Matt. 2:1–12), and a connection with the birth of Jesus was in fact standard in most of the churches of the Greek East.[21] Both traditions seem to have spoken of the date as the occasion of the *epiphaneia* or "manifestation" of the Christ, and by the fourth century, the feast of Epiphany would be one of the major festivals of the church. A connection with the baptism of Jesus would remain dominant in much of the East and an element in some traditions in the West. But in other Western contexts, different associations would prevail; the festival would be linked in particular with the visit of the Magi and with other incidents recorded in the Gospels, such as the first miracle of Jesus described in John's Gospel, the turning of water into wine at a wedding at Cana in Galilee (John 2:1–11), or with the transfiguration (Matt. 17:1–13; Mark 9:2–13; Luke 9:28–36).[22]

If Easter was preceded by some kind of period of preparation, it was followed by a fixed season of rejoicing. The Jewish Feast of Pentecost fell on the fiftieth day after the Passover and did not involve any special treatment of the intervening period, but Christians came to consider the entire fifty days as a time of celebration. Every day during this season was treated like a Sunday; fasting was forbidden, and there was no kneeling for prayer. As far as we can tell, little emphasis was placed as yet on the fact that the gift of the Holy Spirit was bestowed upon the first believers on the fiftieth day itself (Acts 2:1), though this connection would be stressed from the fourth century.

In addition to the emergence or consolidation of these major festivals of the church, local believers marked the anniversaries of the deaths of esteemed martyrs. These dates were regarded not so much as commemorations of deaths, but as birthdays, or the days on which the believers in question emerged victorious from their earthly trials and entered into a new life with their risen Lord in heaven. In the first instance, the celebration of such days was very much a local affair, tied to the existence of a martyr's tomb or remains within a community, but the commemoration of saints gradually became a more extensive convention, and days marking some of the more famous saints began to be observed in regions far beyond their own.

Theologians such as Origen saw the martyrs as especially eminent members of the "cloud of witnesses" (Heb. 12:1) who surround believers during their earthly existence. Assured of a special place of honor in the presence of God (Rev. 6:9–11; 7:9–17), they are capable of interceding for their brothers and sisters in the world who seek to imitate their faith and follow their example. Special times for acknowledging the devotion of these saints and appealing for their spiritual assistance were increasingly common.

Christian Art

The Christians of the first two centuries tended to regard visual art for religious purposes with great suspicion. They had two main reasons for this. In the first place, the Ten Commandments contained a strict prohibition on the manufacture and use of graven images (Exod. 20:4–6; Deut. 5:8–10), and this rule was considered binding by Christians as much as by Jews. The invisible God was not to be rendered visible according to the speculative craftsmanship of the human imagination but revered as a mysterious spiritual being. In addition, by deliberately *not* using religious and imperial images, cult-statues, and idols, Christians emphasized the distance between themselves and the pagan world. The images of the world were believed to be demonically inspired, and apologists such as Justin Martyr, Clement of Alexandria, and Tertullian adduced powerful arguments against pagan idolatry as foolish, corrupt, and blasphemous. Drawing on polemic used by the Hebrew prophets (e.g., Isa. 44:9–20; 45:20; Jer. 10:3–5; cf. Pss. 115:2–8; 135:15–18) and the denunciations of the first Christians (Acts 14:15; 17:29; Rom. 1:21–23; see also p. 382 n. 11), they inveighed against the superstition and absurdity of equating the characteristics of divinity with human products made from wood, metal, and stone.

Believers did, however, routinely depict symbolic aspects of their faith on a variety of everyday objects, including jewelry and household items such as tableware, drinking vessels, and lamps. Artistic decoration of such items was normal in antiquity, but in the Graeco-Roman world, it was common for the ornamentation to be mythological, obscene, or immodest in style. Christian leaders were naturally keen to discourage the use of objects that displayed scenes of sexual activity or heavy drinking, but they understood the possible value of physical items serving as reminders of spiritual truths. It was also possible to turn the less objectionable varieties of conventional symbolism to Christian usage, and in the second century, quite a number of "innocent" secular images were gradually adapted to a Christian context.

The clearest example was the symbol of the Good Shepherd. Depictions of a shepherd carrying his sheep were common in the pagan world, both in the context of funerary art (in which the god Hermes was regularly portrayed as a guide to the underworld) and as a personification of humanitarian concern or philanthropy. Christians were able to transfer the concept to the biblical notion of Christ as the heavenly pastor of the faithful. Another conventional pagan type was a female praying figure (*orans*) with outstretched hands, who was classically associated with a personification of the virtue of piety; in Christian circles, little or no visual adaptation was necessary to apply the image to a new setting.

In a world in which the faith continued to lack any official status, it was advantageous for the associations of Christian art to be ambiguous rather than specific. Signet rings, which were used constantly in ancient society to seal letters and guarantee their authenticity, often bore symbols that could convey Christian implications, such as doves, fish, ships, and anchors, but which could also readily be explained some other way. The dove might be seen as an emblem of the Holy Spirit; the fish (the commonest of early Christian images) might represent an acrostic of the Greek words for "Jesus Christ, Son of God, Savior," *IXTHUS*, which also was the Greek word for "fish"; the ship might suggest the ark of faith on the stormy sea of life; and the anchor might serve as a reminder of the "hope as an anchor for the soul" (Heb. 6:19)—but in each case the same iconography could be used by pagans with different meanings. Other ambiguous motifs included depictions of peacocks, lambs, vines or bunches of grapes, harvest scenes, and similar images drawn from the world of nature. Only from around the later second century did Christian associations begin to become bolder, and the symbols started to be identified more commonly with explicitly biblical themes. Even then, creative reinterpretation of pagan images continued for many generations.

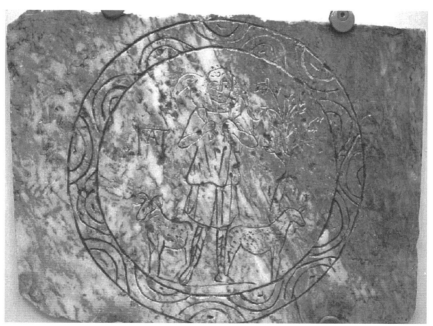

Depiction of Christ as the Good Shepherd, a favorite theme in early Christian art. Illustration from FreeStockPhotos.com

Aside from remarkable instances such as the frescoes found in the Dura-Europos house, most of our evidence for distinctively Christian art in the third century comes from funeral contexts. A good deal of it derives from Rome, though this is as much as anything an accident of history, the cultural significance of which should not be overstated; archaeology has also uncovered important material elsewhere in Italy, in Asia Minor, in North Africa, and in Gaul. The most striking Christian art, nonetheless, has been found in the underground burial sites, the catacombs, just outside Rome, especially the catacombs of Callistus, Domitilla, and Priscilla.

There was an established Roman tradition of adorning the walls and ceilings of burial chambers, and the frescoes from the catacombs continued to display many traditional images and motifs such as urns, garlands, birds, funeral banquets, and so on, as well as the ambivalent symbols of the praying figure and the shepherd. But there were also paintings with expressly biblical, and especially Old Testament, scenes, reflecting contemporary Christian concerns to read the Hebrew Scriptures as pointing figuratively to Christ and his salvation. Noah in the ark, Abraham about to sacrifice Isaac, Moses striking the rock, Jonah and the great fish, and Daniel in the lions' den were all common pictures. Where scenes from the Gospels were presented, they were usually of Jesus's miracles, such as the raising of Lazarus from the dead, though Jesus's baptism by John was also favored. The paintings were generally crudely executed and lacking in detail, but it must be remembered that they existed in poorly lit and cramped spaces. They were expressions of private Christian devotion intended to console grieving relatives and friends on visits to the graves of loved ones, not elaborate images designed for wider scrutiny.

Stone sarcophagi or coffins from the late third century have been found that are decorated on all external surfaces except the reverse with relief sculptures showing Christian scenes. Most of these caskets were carved out of white marble and were far too expensive for all but the wealthy to afford. The degree of detail in the scenes greatly exceeded that on frescoes, and there was often a range of biblical stories and conventional images on a single relief. The most splendid example is the so-called "Jonah sarcophagus," dating from around 270, now in the collection of the Vatican Museums. Its principal adornment is the story of Jonah, but there are also depictions of Noah's ark, Moses, and Jesus and Lazarus as well as some traditional Roman symbols intermingled with the biblical scenes.

There is good reason to believe that although Christians continued to deplore the evils of idolatry, they were prepared to differentiate between images as objects of worship and visual art as an expression of faith and a sign of belonging within the family of God. While there were some dangers in displaying Christian symbols too openly, there was an increasing willingness to revamp classical forms and to portray expressly biblical images in a variety of everyday contexts. In a society in which so many were illiterate, visual art had a teaching purpose, aiding devotion for many who could not read the Scriptures for themselves.

Scene from the third-century "Jonah sarcophagus," in the Museo Pio Cristiano, Vatican. Illustration from FreeStockPhotos.com. Used by permission.

In the representations of favorite scenes and images from the Hebrew Scriptures and the Gospels, ordinary believers were reminded of their communal identity with the people of faith in every age, and the artistic forms reflected the ways in which sacred texts were appropriated in Christian interpretation and worship. The art to be found on everyday objects also spoke to outsiders, providing non-Christians, too, with expressions of the Christians' beliefs and hopes concerning life and death and symbolizing their confidence that the world could not ultimately prevail against the message of their risen Lord.

11

MINISTRY AND MORALS

▼

Developments in Ministry

In the early second century, the ministry of the churches was still fairly fluid. While there was an increasing formalization of leadership roles, there was no uniform development. As we saw, the letters of Ignatius to the churches in western Asia Minor picture the bishop as a chief minister, flanked by a group of presbyters and assisted by deacons, but it is also clear that such a threefold ministry of bishops, presbyters, and deacons did not exist everywhere. Ignatius himself seems to have been the only bishop in Syrian Antioch, though there must have been several congregations besides his own in the vicinity, and in his letter to the Romans, he makes no mention of a named overseer, implying that the church of Rome was still governed by a board of elders. In the case of the other communities to which he wrote, Ignatius's concern that the bishop should be recognized as the focal point of order and unity testifies to the continuing diversity of practice in the communities he was addressing. As far as he was concerned, the emergence of a monarchical episcopate was a remedy for the dangers of anarchy in the churches.

Whatever some believers thought of them, charismatic prophets and teachers continued to operate in many churches. If, however, bishops could function as the arbiters of sound doctrine and good order, as Ignatius suggested, it was no surprise that ministry by bishops and their close assistants came to be especially promoted as the churches struggled to deal with their differences and as patterns of uniformity were grounded in appeals to apostolic tradition. Ignatius himself had not directly identified bishops as the successors of the apostles, but from around the middle of the second century it became increasingly common to trace the presence of monarchical bishops back to apostolic foundations. If the churches were keeping faith with their inheritance, they were doing so, it was argued, not least because they were led by those whose ministry stood in a lineage of apostolic authority.

Such logic is explicit in the writings of Irenaeus, who, as we saw, associates the maintenance of sound teaching with the influence of leaders who belonged to the apostolic tradition. Similar assumptions came to be widespread in the churches. Though formally regarded as the first among a body of equal presbyters, the bishop carried overall responsibility for teaching, for discipline, for communicating with other churches, and for ensuring the fidelity of the local community to wider patterns of belief and practice. The bishop was charged with protecting and promoting unity, both internally, among an individual church's own members, and externally, with believers in different places and in other times.

Presbyters are believed to have shared many of the functions of bishops, and they acted as advisers and supporters of bishops in the areas of discipline, procedure, and pastoral care. As the churches expanded, presbyters also assumed increasingly significant roles as delegated representatives of episcopal authority. They typically spearheaded evangelistic outreach in the name of the bishop, and they would lead worship and provide pastoral care for satellite congregations of the episcopal church. In the absence of a bishop, they could administer formal forgiveness to a penitent and preside at the Eucharist, something deacons expressly could not do. In some churches, particularly in larger centers with multiple congregations and especially diverse social constituents, the practical power exercised by presbyters was often considerable, and central episcopal control was not always easily secured, as may well have been the case in Rome itself as late as the third century.

The name *priest* was widely applied to bishops from the late second century, and from about the middle of the third century presbyters in general shared this designation. (Sometimes the bishop was known as the "high priest" to differentiate him from the other presbyters, who were simply "priests.") The sacerdotal dimension of the presbyteral role was greatly developed in the third century, and it became common to associate the sacred calling of Christian priests with the solemn charges given to the ancient Levitical priesthood.

Deacons' duties continued to include practical tasks such as the administration of charity and the distribution of alms. They also involved a number of liturgical functions: deacons typically read from the Scriptures, led certain prayers, uplifted offerings, distributed the consecrated elements at the Eucharist, and gave the signal for catechumens and those under discipline to leave the service prior to the eucharistic prayer. More powerful bishops had deacons as their secretaries, and a number of these officials came to be privileged confidants of their superiors, with a high degree of practical influence and a good chance of being favored for subsequent preferment. Though deacons might appear to have had rather menial responsibilities compared with presbyters, their closeness to the financial and procedural affairs of their churches brought some of them a greater degree of power than was evident on the surface.

Ordained Ministries

The evolution of all these ministries increased the distinction between those who occupied leadership roles and the believers in general, who made up the *laity* or the people of God (Greek, *laos*, "people"). In the New Testament context, the "people of God" included all Christians, who were all deemed to be a "holy priesthood" together (1 Peter 2:5, 9–10); now there was a stronger differentiation between leaders and other members of the church.

Leaders naturally remained part of the whole people of God, but it was increasingly suggested that those who were called to minister were in some sense different from other believers, and spiritual status of a special kind belonged to this group. The responsibilities of ministers were believed to be foreshadowed in the Law of Moses and sanctioned by the example of Jesus, who expressly commissioned particular individuals to go out and preach and teach in his name. In later Christian thinking, it would be said that a person with such a vocation had God as his "lot" (Greek, *kleros*, "lot," "portion," or "inheritance"; cf. Deut. 18:2), and to be a member of this constituency was to be *klerikos*, the root of our word *clergy*.

In principle, the choice of a candidate for ministry lay with the whole community; in practice, the opinions of bishops, and to some extent those of presbyters, were often highly influential, especially in cases in which the will of the people was divided. Bishops had primary charge of the process of consecrating others for leadership. Such consecration continued to be focused in an act of laying-on of hands and committing the person to God's service, inspired by the conviction that the spiritual gift was bestowed through this ritual (1 Tim. 4:14; 2 Tim. 1:6). The action was not to be undertaken lightly (1 Tim. 5:22), but only after a due process of approbation (1 Tim. 3:1–12; Titus 1:6–9). Presbyters might take part in the ceremony of consecration, but if the bishop's authority stemmed from the apostles, it was in the bishop's touch that spiritual power and catholic continuity were to be preeminently symbolized.

The earliest prescriptions for ordination are to be found in the first part of the *Apostolic Tradition*, which differentiates between officials whom the church appoints and those such as consecrated virgins or "confessors" (individuals who suffered for their faith but escaped martyrdom), who owe their position to a direct call from God. According to the *Apostolic Tradition*, when a bishop was being ordained, it was normal for other bishops from the local area to attend, and they alone would lay hands upon the candidate.[1] The standard time for ordination was during Sunday worship, and newly ordained presbyters would typically share in the celebrating of the sacred meal. It is clear, however, that there were exceptions to all of these practices, especially in situations of crisis or persecution, and many variations in ritual occurred in both the West and the East. In Egypt in particular, where the threefold ministry developed a good deal later than elsewhere, episcopal consecrations regularly took place without the presence of visiting bishops until well into the third century.

There is little evidence prior to the late second century as to how ministers in general were maintained. The example of the apostolic period included both a system in which leaders often partially or entirely supported themselves, and at the same time, the principle that workers were worthy of their hire (1 Cor. 9:1–18; 1 Tim. 5:17–18). Giving to prophets, teachers, and other leaders continued to be seen as an important duty in the subsequent generations, grounded in biblical principles about devoting the firstfruits of labor to those who serve in such ways and showing hospitality to visitors who minister "in the name of the Lord." Nevertheless, many teachers continued to work in other capacities and were expected to do so. The first clear indications of clergy being paid for their services as a matter of routine seem to lie in Montanist circles. Elsewhere, many continued to engage in other paid employment either on a full-time or a part-time basis, and it was presumably only in the larger, urban churches that it was first possible for bishops and other workers to be entirely supported out of the resources of the local believers. Where wealth increased, bishops and presbyters were doubtless the first to receive support, and it would not have been unusual for senior clergy to be paid while more junior officials continued to earn some or all of their living through other work.

The more the sense of spiritual eminence attaching to ordination grew, the more it seemed natural to seek to relieve those who occupied the major positions of ministry from the mundane demands of daily life. Ordained leaders had to continue to prove their suitability in office, and those who failed badly or fell into gross sin were believed to have betrayed their calling. In extreme cases, they were removed from office because they were no longer worthy of their position. Major problems would ensue when large numbers of clergy at once proved unfaithful in the face of persecution. In addition to the primary orders of bishops, presbyters, and deacons, the third century witnessed the evolution, in the larger churches at least, of other more junior offices, such as those of subdeacons, acolytes (primarily assistants of presbyters and deacons at the Eucharist), exorcists, readers, and doorkeepers. These positions were not as yet systematized, however, in any formal order that was applicable in different contexts elsewhere.

In major sees—Rome, Alexandria, Antioch, Ephesus, or Carthage—bishops came to be regarded as superiors over the other bishops in their provinces and as overseers of large territories of believers, stretching far beyond their immediate neighborhoods. Rome claimed authority over the whole of Italy, Sardinia, and Sicily; Alexandria over Egypt and Libya; Antioch over Syria and Cilicia; Ephesus over western Asia Minor and Phrygia; and Carthage over Roman North Africa. Rome also aspired to overall responsibility for Gaul; Carthage did the same with Spain. Rome in particular was increasingly prominent in the West as a whole, leading to tensions both with North Africa and farther afield. Some of these territorial claims would in time be recognized by official legislation, but the challenges they presented to ecclesiastical unity would only intensify as the generations went on.

Women's Roles

Compared with the situation in some of the house-churches of the first generation or so, women came to occupy a more restricted place in ministry in the second and third centuries. We have few further glimpses of female household leaders or patrons; presbyters and bishops were overwhelmingly male, and appeal was often made to passages such as 1 Corinthians 14:33–35 or 1 Timothy 2:11–15 to validate this state of affairs. In church orders such as the *Didascalia*, it is said to be for men, not women, to baptize and to teach,[2] and similar emphases are found in authors such as Tertullian.[3] In a number of the writings of church leaders, there is sharp polemic against women usurping male roles.

The teaching of the Pastoral Epistles (1 Tim. 2:8–15; 3:1–13; 5:1–16; 2 Tim. 3:1–9; Titus 2:1–15) or the "household codes" of Ephesians (5:22–6:9) and Colossians (3:18–4:1) was cited in support of arguments that women were to be submissive to male authority, not only within the structures of marriage and society as a whole but also within the family life of the church. Male leaders made much of the dangers of women devoting themselves to activities and interests that dishonored the gospel or detracted from the position of men. Women were to practice the art of being inconspicuous and not do anything to draw attention to themselves, least of all anything that might elicit sexual attraction. Tertullian's denunciations of female preoccupations with dress, cosmetics, and jewelry typify such a mind-set, and similar reasoning can be found in other writers. In many cases, the arguments were linked to appeals for sexual abstinence and the prizing of virginity, reflective of a growing tide of asceticism (see further below, pp. 311–16). Women who were deemed to overstep their place in the organization of the church's life could be portrayed as dangerous temptresses, disrupting the natural order of things and luring men away from the truth with their seductive feminine wiles.

The associations of false teaching and female sexual temptation were already clear in the condemnation of the prophetess Jezebel, who misled the faithful in the church of Thyatira in Revelation 2:20–25. They were also prominent in the characterization of some Gnostic cults: Simon Magus's sect operated with the aid of a former prostitute (p. 167), and Apelles, a Gnostic teacher in Rome and former disciple of Marcion, is said to have come under the spell of a female visionary named Philumene and collected her prophetic oracles.[4] Even though there was in fact little evidence that women were routinely much more liberated in some of the fringe sects than they were in the mainstream churches, as a result of such associations those circles that gave a significant place to women were often viewed with suspicion. A particularly obvious charge was the allegation of links with Montanism, for the New Prophecy openly gave women a higher degree of recognition in ministry than was often available elsewhere, and the churches in Phrygia in particular may have been more amenable to female leadership than was the case anywhere else. There is no doubt that the place Montanism afforded to women as prophetesses and leaders was problematic to many Christian men, for whom such a situation was further evidence of the movement's error.

For all the restrictions, women were not altogether excluded from positions of ministry. There are indications that at least some women continued to exercise certain prophesying, teaching, and pastoral roles in this period, and a number administered baptism. There were well-educated, articulate women who played significant parts in instructing others, both formally and informally. Women undoubtedly feature a great deal less than men in the narratives of the sources upon which we have traditionally relied for our understanding of the period, and in general they did not hold anything like the same degree of prominence within the obvious structures of leadership, but this does not mean they were of no importance in the churches. The evidence for women's positions is not confined to literary texts; archaeology has yielded other clues, especially gravestone inscriptions, which mention a variety of ministry functions performed by women long after the first century. Both the dating and the interpretation of some of this material are controversial, and its overall import can be exaggerated, but there are reasonable grounds for supposing that women did have important responsibilities in many churches.

A critical reading of the literary sources themselves also reveals a slightly more nuanced picture than may at first appear. In the apocryphal *Acts of Paul and Thecla*, Thecla is a young woman who is converted by the apostle Paul in Iconium and persuaded to renounce marriage. Miraculously delivered from death, she devotes herself to working in the service of Paul's gospel, and though she becomes separated from Paul, she goes on to engage in significant missionary work of her own, baptizing and teaching. Thecla is probably a fictional character, fashioned after the conventions of a heroine of a Greek romantic novel, but her depiction in the story may well reflect a concern on the part of a late-second-century author to portray a liberated woman, exercising independence and fulfilling an important role as a Christian leader. Though controversial with many—Tertullian deplored the appeal to her example by women who sought to administer baptism,[5] and others also regarded her reported activity as dangerously aberrant—Thecla became a much-admired exemplar in later generations in both the East and the West, and her cult was especially popular in Asia Minor and Egypt. It is likely that there were more than a few women who aspired to operate in ways akin to those of this literary type, and Thecla may conceivably represent a stylized amalgam of the claims of actual female evangelists who appealed to the authority of Paul in defense of their ministries.[6]

Other female role-models of a nonfictional variety[7] appear strikingly in the narratives of Christian martyrs. Women such as Blandina (p. 208) and Perpetua and Felicitas (pp. 210–11) demonstrate the idealization of the godly woman as a steadfast witness to Christ even in the face of death. Some scholars have suggested that since so many recorded martyrs were female, the Roman authorities may have regarded some of the women in question as individuals with a degree of standing in the Christian movement. This argument is difficult to prove, but there is no doubt that the characterizations of female heroism in the accounts of Christian martyrdom reveal a number of women as shining exemplars of the ultimate in spiritual devotion, whose courage must have appeared to their persecutors to be the equal of any man's.

Female Deacons

A diaconal role of some kind was probably held by women from early times, and although 1 Timothy 3:11 was often read as a reference to deacons' "wives" rather than to "women who are deacons" (the more logical rendering of the verse), women continued to function in such a capacity in several churches, especially in the East.[8] The word *deaconess* itself does not appear prior to the fourth century. Pliny's letter to Trajan concerning the Christians in Bithynia refers to two female servants who had been interrogated and tortured, whom Pliny says the Christians called *ministrae*, "female ministers."[9] It is not entirely clear what the import of this term is here; it may well mean that the women were simply "slaves" in the ordinary sense of the word rather than "ministers" in a church context. It is possible, however, that these women were some sort of recognized servants of the church.

In the *Didascalia*, certainly, female deacons are seen as an official group. In this Eastern context at least, they had charge of female candidates for baptism and took responsibility for anointing them and giving them further instruction after they had been initiated (though the baptism itself had to be conducted by a man). Female deacons were regarded as ministers to women more generally and as those who performed a vital role in the church by drawing alongside other females to a degree that was not appropriate for men. They looked after the sick, the convalescent, and the needy of their own sex, and engaged in a range of practical good works.[10]

The functions of such women overlapped in some measure with those traditionally performed by older widows. At the time of the Pastoral

Epistles, there was already a list of widows who were eligible for financial support from the church (1 Tim. 5:3–16). To qualify for admission, women had to be over sixty years old, of good character, and well-known for their practical Christian behavior, "such as bringing up children, showing hospitality, washing the feet of the saints, helping those in trouble and devoting [themselves] to all kinds of good deeds" (1 Tim. 5:10). Younger widows, who sometimes had a tendency to pursue less worthy ends, were encouraged to remarry, and women who were capable of being supported by children, grandchildren, or other family members were also not to be included on the list of widows, so that the church would not be burdened with unnecessary responsibilities.

The ministry of older widows continued to be of significance in the churches, but there were efforts to restrict their activities as well. In the *Didascalia*, where the age threshold for official widows is taken to be fifty rather than sixty, such women are not permitted to minister to anyone without the authority of a bishop or a deacon, and they are not to offer benefactions to others on their own account. They are not to teach in any official sense, and they do not share in the female deacons' role of anointing candidates for baptism. Their primary duties are prayer, fasting, and tasks such as visiting the sick.[11] It is in fact possible that the official recognition of the roles of female deacons was designed to define the limits of the influence of widows in the churches; by creating a class of women who were openly acknowledged to be accountable to episcopal control, it was possible for female ministries to be regulated within particular boundaries.

Admission to a particular female ministry was not seen as ordination to a liturgical role comparable to that of a bishop or a presbyter, or even to that of a male deacon. Women who took up such a responsibility were appointed with episcopal blessing, but they were not ordained in the full sense of the word. The injunctions placed upon women in ministry were also often stricter than those for men. There were seldom as yet any age stipulations for male officials, nor were male clergy in general expected to remain celibate, as widows clearly were. Women were sometimes also subjected to greater testing prior to being appointed to special status: the *Apostolic Tradition*, for example, enjoins that widows who have been recently widowed, even if they are of mature years, are not necessarily to be trusted; in order to be suitable for ministry, a woman needs to have lost her husband a long time previously.[12] This concern for candidates to be mature and of a settled temperament and proven faithfulness hints at the kind of role such female servants of the church were expected to play. They were to be helpers whose tasks were of an essentially practical nature.

Despite attempts to present such female duties as less significant than the responsibilities carried out by ordained men, it seems clear that in some cases women deacons did play a significant part in church services, and it was certainly not unusual for them to be involved in the instruction of other women. Some of these roles were controversial with some men, and later church assemblies made various attempts to curtail them through legislation, but they were not stifled altogether. The very persistence of efforts to restrict the activities of women testifies to the endurance of quite prominent female ministries in many places.

Assessing the Evidence

All told, the evidence for the participation of women in leadership roles in the churches beyond the first century is much less extensive than it is for the activities of men, and there is no doubt that in the majority of Christian contexts there was a demarcation between functions available to males and those that were possible for females. The tasks women were allowed to carry out were often practical or menial in nature, or heavily concentrated upon mission toward and care for their own sex. In some circles, women were active as teachers, prophetesses, and ministers, but in the majority of churches there were no female bishops or presbyters, and where women performed diaconal functions, their responsibilities were seen in the main as a good deal less significant than those of men. If they were distinguished from the laity in general, they were still subordinate to male clergy.

Scholars continue to debate the reasons for the shift in the position of women within the churches in the second century. Some contend that from quite early on there was a degree of tension concerning the place of women in the Jesus movement and maintain that in the later New Testament period we already see the beginnings of a triumph of the repressive over the liberating, a process that was sealed beyond doubt in the second century. Some men, it is said, had always been uncomfortable with the degree of opportunity afforded to women to participate openly in Christian leadership, and in the end, this male perspective prevailed so that women were systematically marginalized in ministry and kept within the traditional constraints of an essentially patriarchal social system.

On a more general slant, it is often argued that the diminishing of women's public roles was a close corollary of the increasing institutionalization of Christianity. As the churches grew and became more formally organized, so the freedoms originally afforded by the household setting were gradually curtailed; women were more and more subjected to the authority of a predominantly male leadership, and their tasks and opportunities were defined with reference to men's perceptions of what was "naturally" appropriate rather than by the standards of equality established in Christ. As the churches expanded, so they slipped ever more deeply into the patterns of their surrounding society—a world in which the position of women was severely controlled by the conventions of male power.

The evaluation of these arguments is a complex business, involving some difficult sociological and historical analysis, and a detailed engagement with all of the evidence is not possible here. It is worth stating, however, that some of the arguments for a deep fissure concerning the status of women in the earliest churches lack credible support. It is also possible to exaggerate the impression that misogyny was to be encountered at every turn in the communities of the second century and beyond. While there certainly was a good deal of rhetoric about the status of women from which most modern Christians might rightly recoil, it is unreasonable to suppose that women in the churches were in practice completely dominated by men or to imagine that they did not exercise a range of significant ministries as sponsors, missionaries, and exemplars of the gospel. It is undoubtedly a great pity that we do not hear more about these activities and that the majority of the women remain obscure or nameless, but from what we do know, it is evident that women's roles were much more important than might at first be supposed.

In the end, Christianity did become less egalitarian in the generations after the apostles, but in the midst of this development lay a striking phenomenon: in terms of society as a whole, the Christian churches contained disproportionate numbers of women. A significant proportion of primary converts to Christianity had probably always been women (a fact that chauvinistic pagan critics were eager to point out as evidence of the gospel's absurdity), and there is good reason to believe that the moral ideals held by the Christian movement contributed to further increases in the number of women within the churches. In Graeco-Roman society, the main method of population control was the exposure of infants, and girls were much more likely to be exposed than boys. Though controversial with some, such infanticide was widely defended by ancient thinkers, and it was upheld in law; but Christians, like Jews, regarded it as abhorrent. Christians and Jews were equally firmly opposed to abortion, which was also very widespread in ancient society, and which, aside from its consequences for birth statistics, was extremely dangerous to women, resulting in many deaths. The probable consequence of these beliefs was that in comparison with pagan society, where males greatly outnumbered females, the ranks of Christians and Jews contained a high proportion of women.

This fact in itself may of course only make the restriction of women's roles in the churches seem all the more unreasonable, but it is clear that women were not put off from becoming Christians by the ways in which the communities of believers were organized. In truth, though the opportunities accessible to women in the churches had become narrower overall, Christianity still offered women a number of freedoms that were not generally available to females in society as a whole. In Christian morality, men as well as women were expected to remain virgins until they married, and sexual infidelity on the part of a husband was considered to be just as bad as it was on the part of a wife. Men had obligations pressed upon them to be faithful to their spouses and to cherish their wives and treat them with proper respect. These principles represented a radical contrast with the double standards of pagan sexual ethics, which prized chastity among women but allowed extensive freedom to men.

Women in the churches almost certainly had more say than their pagan counterparts about whom they married, and they could expect a higher degree of security in their marriages, thanks to the strong condemnation of adultery and the equally strong discouraging of divorce. If they were widowed, especially after being married for some years, they were not necessarily expected to remarry, unlike most women at that time, but were if anything encouraged to remain single and devote themselves to Christian service instead.

Women who became Christians while married to unconverted men had from earlier times been encouraged not to leave their marriages, if possible, but to remain as a witness to their husbands (1 Cor. 7:12–16; 1 Peter 3:1–2). There is plenty of evidence that women were frequently the major catalysts for the spread of the faith within their households and that, especially among the upper classes of society, it was often through the influence of women in particular that the gospel made inroads. In this respect, the ministry of women cannot be confined to only the public activities of church life.

At one level, the formal place of women within the parameters of a patriarchal social system may in the end not have altered much, despite the signs of promise in the earliest communities and the potential that lay at the heart of the Christian message for a more radical degree of social change. At another level, however, through their work as missionaries within their households and families, devoted women were of incalculable importance to the development of the churches.

Discipline and Penance

As the warnings concerning moral failure and apostasy in the New Testament writings showed, there had from early times been a strong emphasis on the importance of baptized believers living changed lives. To fall into sin was to betray the universal Christian obligation to pursue holiness, and as the teaching of Jesus himself had made clear, sin was not necessarily an open or obvious affair but an evil that lurked in human motives, thoughts, and desires (Matt. 5:21–30; 7:1–6). There were different degrees of sin, and some offenses were graver than others (1 John 5:16–17), but to offend in one point was to be guilty of transgressing the whole law of God (James 2:8–11). Willful apostasy was a dreadful thing (Heb. 6:4–6; 10:26–31; 2 Peter 2:20–22).

Although there were powerful imperatives to pursue perfection (Matt. 5:48; 19:21) and hints that a measure of such maturity was in some sense possible (Eph. 3:14–19; Phil. 3:15–16; Heb. 6:1; James 1:4), it was recognized that believers were still inherently frail, fallible creatures who would inevitably fail and require daily forgiveness. Sinful behavior was held to be a structural absurdity for the person "born of God" (see 1 John 3:4–10), but those who claimed that they were altogether without sin deceived themselves (1 John 1:8–10). First-century practice had involved the public condemnation of unrepentant offenders (1 Cor. 5:1–5, 12–13; 1 Tim. 5:20) and the extending of forgiveness to those who expressed genuine confession and contrition (2 Cor. 2:5–11). The truly penitent were to be assured of pardon, restoration, and acceptance; those who persisted in sin were to be censured, placed under discipline, or excluded from communion for their own good. And as a last resort, the unrepentant were to be banished from the assembly of believers and treated as outsiders or heathens. It was believed that Jesus had entrusted the power of both judgment and forgiveness to the church (Matt. 18:15–18), and that by virtue of the gift of his Holy Spirit, his apostles had been granted the authority to pardon or retain sins (John 20:21–23; cf. Matt. 16:18–19). Reconciliation with God and reconciliation with the church were seen as closely related conditions.

In the early second century, the author of the influential *Shepherd* of Hermas impressed upon his readers that sins committed after baptism were capable of being remitted at least once through a process of penance. There were evidently many Christians who held that baptism rendered the believer enduringly spotless and that there was no further place for repentance or remission thereafter. Although firmly ruling out liberal assumptions that there could be multiple absolutions for persistent sins of the same kind, the *Shepherd* is concerned to stress that there could be at least one further opportunity for forgiveness of an offense subsequent to baptism. To such arguments, Tertullian in his Montanist days would sharply object, and others too were resistant to the popularity of the *Shepherd* on similar grounds, regarding its widespread reading in Christian circles as dangerous for morals. But its case was, in fact, for a middle way between an entirely rigorist and a wholly lax interpretation of discipline.

By the later second and early third centuries, there were fairly established patterns of penitential discipline. Believers who fell into sin typically went through a public process of abasement and censure before the church. Either voluntarily or under threat of excommunication, they were formally counted as penitents and automatically excluded from the Eucharist. Those under discipline continued to attend the first part of the worship service but were dismissed along with catechumens prior to the communion ritual.[13] They submitted to a public rebuke in the presence of the congregation and engaged in a full and contrite confession of their sin, an act commonly known under its Greek name of *exomologesis*.

The repentance was often carried out in sackcloth or rags, and due signs of emotional humiliation were expected. A verdict was pronounced by the bishop, specifying what was required of the offender. The nature of the sentence varied according to the sin, but it almost always involved a course of fasting and prayer, and often some almsgiving as well. The congregation was asked to pray for the transgressor's forgiveness and seek mercy on his or her behalf. Once the offender had fulfilled his or her period of discipline, the penitent sought reconciliation and was formally restored to fellowship and participation in the full rites of the church. As Easter became increasingly important as a baptismal season, it also became common in many churches for penitents to apply for restoration at this time.

Not surprisingly, there were involved debates about how particular sins were to be classified. Many bishops were prepared to grant absolution for sins such as fornication, adultery, or idolatry, and some were willing to forgive even murder. Others considered some of these offenses far too serious to be dealt with by the church at all; in such cases, exclusion from full communion had to be permanent rather than temporary, and the sinner could only be prayed for and commended to the mercy of God. Distinctions began to be pressed concerning sins that led "to death" (1 John 5:16–17) and those that did not, and there were different assessments of what specific lapses meant for the professing Christian. In most circles, there was a sense that penance could not be viewed simply as a sentence of judgment but also as a reformative or therapeutic process, intended to heal and restore rather than to punish in anything other than symbolic terms; but there were inevitably wide discrepancies about what such healing required. There were doubtless abuses of power by some leaders and spurious displays of contrition by some offenders.

In the most rigorist circles, those who apostatized from the faith were considered to be beyond the pale. As we shall see in the next chapter, sharp disputes broke out in the West in the third century over how to deal with believers—including church leaders themselves—who yielded to political pressures and betrayed their pledge to remain faithful to Christ no matter what the consequences.

Christians as Ascetics

The ancient Mediterranean world had a long history of asceticism. Greek culture bequeathed the word *askesis* (meaning "exercise" or "training"), and its moral philosophers produced various recipes for the restraint of bodily appetites and mental emotions and for detachment from material things. The itinerant teachers of Cynicism propounded a message of indifference to physical possessions and the pursuit of wisdom through poverty and simplicity, and Pythagorean, Platonist, and Stoic prescriptions for the good life all proposed their own particular patterns for transcending physical desires. Judaism also possessed notable traditions of individual and communal self-denial in consecration to God, and in early Christian times the Essenes and other ascetics of the desert such as the scholars of Qumran or the contemplative Therapeutae of Egypt combined their attachment to the Law of Moses with a philosophy of withdrawal from the world.

According to the Gospel accounts, Jesus had summoned people to deny themselves and take up their cross and follow him (Mark 8:34), even at the cost of shunning family ties (Matt. 10:34–37) and losing their lives for his sake (Matt. 10:38–39; John 12:25; cf. Mark 10:29–31). He had spoken of the dangers confronting the wealthy (Luke 5:20–26;

cf. Matt. 19:23–24; Mark 10:23),[14] called upon the affluent to sacrifice their possessions for the poor (Matt. 19:21; Mark 10:21), and sent out his messengers with neither equipment nor wallet (Matt. 10:9–10; Luke 9:3; 10:4). He had urged his disciples to practice not only watchfulness, prayer (e.g., Matt. 24:36–51; 25:1–13; 26:41), and fasting (Matt. 6:16–18; Mark 2:18–22), but more radical forms of self-denial as well. He had spoken of those who "renounced marriage because of the kingdom of heaven" (Matt. 19:12), and taught that the privileged ones who attained to the resurrection and the age to come would "neither marry nor be given in marriage" but become "like the angels" (Luke 20:34–36).

In early Christian circles, leaders such as James the brother of Jesus had been renowned for their devotion to the disciplines of prayer and fasting. The primitive community in Jerusalem is said by Luke to have practiced common ownership of property (Acts 2:44–45; 4:32–36). Paul had attacked the teaching of those who considered it wrong to eat certain foods, but he had also spoken frankly of the need to "put to death the misdeeds of the body" (Rom. 8:13) and confessed his own determination to discipline his body like an athlete in training (1 Cor. 9:24–27). His personal preference was not to marry but to remain single, in the expectation that the coming of Christ was imminent and that it was better not to become encumbered with worldly attachments. In Paul's eyes, the prospect of Jesus's return in glory also implied that men who had wives were to live as those who did not (1 Cor. 7:1–40).

It is clear that there were tensions about the implications of such self-denial. While Paul referred to the value of the single state, he also acknowledged that marriage in the Lord was good (1 Cor. 7:39) and conceded that if Christian husbands and wives chose to hold back from sexual relations, they ought to do so only for limited periods, in order to devote themselves to prayer (1 Cor. 7:1–7). A majority of believers did continue to marry and raise children. At the same time, some married Christians also chose to abstain from sex, believing they were thereby demonstrating a mastery of the flesh. In certain circles, marriage was repudiated altogether (1 Tim. 4:3); *enkrateia*, "continence" or "self-control," was prized as an ideal and the body was regarded as a site of pollution, defilement (Rev. 14:4), and distraction from the spiritual life.

To pagan observers, the mores of the average Christian believer, particularly in sexual matters, seemed strict enough already. Marital fidelity was prized, adultery and fornication were sharply condemned, and, as we have noted, standards of conformity were just as applicable to men as to women. Homosexual practice, which was widely accepted in the ancient world, was also condemned (Rom. 1:26–27; 1 Cor. 6:9–11; 1 Tim. 1:10). If believers had money, they were regularly reminded of their obligation to extend charity to the needy and not to hoard their wealth for selfish ends. Although aspects of Christian teaching on a number of these subjects reflected assumptions about nature, possessions, and the status of the body that could be paralleled in pagan thinking, there is no doubt that, in comparison with the standards of Graeco-Roman society at large, Christian behavior had quite particular parameters.

For some Christians, however, ordinary norms were not enough; even if these conventions were already rigorous by worldly measures, it was necessary to go further still in order to demonstrate wholehearted consecration to the heavenly calling of God in Christ Jesus (Phil. 3:14). As Paul's ethical counsel had repeatedly suggested, nothing was as powerful an incentive to renunciation of the world as the conviction that the time was short. But even as the years had gone on and the parousia had been delayed, the desire to rise above the preoccupations and desires of ordinary life did not fade. As the faith encountered opposition and believers suffered for their confession of Christ, the reality of persecution added its own weight to the argument that the life of the body was inherently precarious and not to be valued. Individuals in many Christian circles felt themselves drawn to a dismissal of normal relationships, the surrender of property, and the adoption of a simple, uncluttered life, dedicated to prayer, meditation, and charitable activities.

Such devotion sometimes won admiration from pagan onlookers, who were occasionally impressed by the degree to which the followers of Jesus were prepared to deny themselves in the interests of their faith. However, as the mistaken views that Paul had countered in Colossae and elsewhere showed, it was quite possible for professing Christians to use ascetic principles as a basis for spiritual pride and to behave in ways that denigrated the goodness of God's creation. Such dangers were particularly obvious in the teachings of some of the Gnostics, who took the ideal of spiritual discipline to be the hallmark of a privileged elite and whose notions of the superiority of spirit over matter were directly at odds with wider biblical principles and the implications of Christian hopes concerning physical resurrection. The need to differentiate between appropriate and inappropriate applications of ascetic ideas became one of the important issues in second-century polemic against Gnosticism. It was also present in the opposition to the beliefs of the Marcionites, whose interpretation of some of the teachings of Jesus in Luke's Gospel led them to eschew marriage and observe a modest dietary regime.

Both the Marcionites and the Gnostics based much of their thinking on the idea that the world of physical reality was intrinsically flawed or malign. Others, however, argued for self-denial on different grounds, believing that the material world was not necessarily wrong in itself but that certain forms of attachment to it presented a hindrance to personal devotion. In Eastern Syrian Christianity, where the origins of Christianity were significantly Jewish, many believers inherited a strong orientation toward some of the kinds of ascetic ideals sponsored by Jewish traditions (though there were also some Greek influences). *Enkrateia* was especially valued in this region, and prominent among the advocates of such continence was the late-second-century writer Tatian (see pp. 217–18). Tatian and his followers maintained that abstinence from sexual activity was vital to life in the Spirit, and there were additional obligations to abstain from meat and from the drinking of wine, which were closely associated with the fallen material world. Similar ideas were held by other Syrian Christians, who connected themselves with the name of the apostle Thomas. In these circles, it was held that all candidates for baptism were committed to a life of celibacy.

While such views came to be widely dismissed elsewhere as heretical, and although their probable effect in practice was that many people simply elected to put off baptism rather than pay its required price for most of their lives, they were nevertheless widespread in parts of the East, especially beyond the frontiers of the Roman world. Many of their devotees, both male and female, were among the most active of Christian missionaries in the rural territories of the east and the north. In the apocryphal *Acts of Thomas*, written in Syriac around 220, continence is associated with the attainment of immortality, and sexual activity is regarded as the focal point for all the forces of evil that assail human existence. Thomas, idealized as a militant challenger of the moral standards of a corrupt world, is described as successfully urging a newly married couple to desist from sexual congress and devote themselves to the cultivation of spiritual virtues. Parallel notions are to be found in works such as the Greek *Acts of Paul and Thecla*, in which virginity is commended as the truly spiritual state and the heroine steadfastly resists marriage and keeps her flesh pure.

Extreme versions of asceticism were often alleged against movements that were controversial for other reasons, and in some cases there is little doubt that the charges were exaggerated. The ambitions of groups such as Montanism presented inevitable challenges to conventional structures of authority, and they were problematic both for their criticisms of mainstream behavior and their claims to represent more desirable patterns of spirituality. Self-denial and control of the body's desires were often directly linked with particular evidences of spiritual power and prophetic authority. The cultivation of a style that purported to achieve not only moral but also spiritual superiority over the attainments of regular believers directly confronted bishops and priests with the possible shortcomings of their own behavior.

For all the conceivable ambiguities and the potential for abuse, the aspiration to otherworldliness was deeply rooted. Much philosophical and spiritual impetus was given to ascetic ideals in the theology of the Egyptian tradition, especially in the late second and third centuries, and above all in the writings of Origen. As we saw in chapter 9, Origen's thought was governed by a sense of the spiritual life as an all-demanding pursuit of the knowledge of God, which in turn called for an unqualified commitment to self-discipline, prayer, and the holiness without which no one would see the Lord (Heb. 12:14). As a young man, Origen had reportedly taken Matthew 19:12 literally, determinedly scarring his body for the sake of his Christian calling. In his later teaching, he made much of the image of the holy martyr, whose fidelity to his vocation leads him to demonstrate the ultimate kind of renunciation of the world. In the end, Origen came to pay such a price for his own steadfastness. His preaching and writing contributed to a tradition of idealized spirituality that combined scriptural images with elements drawn from the philosophies of the Greek world—from Platonism, the vision of the sage as one who ascends above the distractions of the world en route to the goal of union with God, and from Stoicism the notion of the truly wise man as the one who is unafflicted by passions and desires for things that are transient and incidental to inner happiness.

The details of the prescription for a higher-tier existence varied, but by the third century, there were many who held that there were two types of believers: those who lived an ordinary Christian life in sincere commitment to the teaching of Jesus and the traditions of their community, and those who were pledged to a still nobler path, destined for spiritual perfection. The ultimate in the attainment of this perfection was physical martyrdom, but other forms of self-sacrifice were tokens of a living pursuit of transcendence: poverty, chastity, and, above all, the preservation of virginity. Those who obeyed such a calling, it was supposed, would merit a more abundant heavenly reward. The poor and the celibate were frequently attributed with special intercessory powers, and their prayers were said to be of outstanding worth in God's sight. Only through severance from conventional social patterns could such status be achieved. Sometimes it seemed as if people who were content to belong in the ordinary category of believer were hardly to be thought of as genuine followers of Christ at all, and a life lived in the mundane context of family relations and paid employment was scarcely to be deemed Christian. Only those who were prepared to sacrifice all were worthy to be considered true servants of the kingdom of God. The old dangers of pride and hierarchical behavior never would die.

The distinctions in spiritual status somewhat mirrored the gaps that already existed between laity and leaders, but they were also much more fluid; it was certainly not necessary to be ordained in order to aspire to a higher spiritual life. As a number of scholars have suggested, this presented opportunities to believers who might otherwise not have attained to any particular status in the churches—in particular women, who, though they had fewer openings to be leaders in an official sense, had significant opportunities to express their piety and their independence from a world administered by men by devoting themselves to asceticism.

In its own ways, ascetic Christianity yielded a certain reconfiguring of gender stereotypes. In Christian moralizing, idealized men were now increasingly depicted in what, by classical standards, were subtly *feminized* terms, as those who cherished the sanctity of their virginity and kept themselves undefiled for God. Idealized women appeared, in their celebrated emancipation from worldly concerns, somewhat akin to men, for conventionally it was for the most part only men who could have exercised such social and intellectual independence. In the complex synthesis of influences that pervaded Christian asceticism, long-standing assumptions were transposed, and the images of the sons and daughters of God confronted the world's ideas of strength and weakness.

12

FAITH AND POLITICS

The First Half of the Third Century

The first part of the third century witnessed varying fortunes in the political status of the Christians in the Roman Empire. The stability and prosperity that had characterized the Roman world in the later years of the second century were followed by a period of relative decline. There were serious military troubles on the frontiers, especially to the north and east, with barbarian incursions on the Rhine and the Danube and the beginnings of problems with a revived Persian Empire. There were also mounting economic and social difficulties, with monetary devaluation, agrarian unrest, and urban decline; plagues and famines were also rife. From the 230s onward, the pressure would be more or less constant, as emperor followed emperor in rapid succession and major military and political upheavals brought one of the worse periods of crisis in the history of the Roman imperial system.

Even before the 230s there were signs that trouble was brewing, and there were intermittent outbreaks of hostility toward Christians in various places. The persecutions under Septimius Severus in the earliest years of the century were continued by his son, Marcus Aurelius Antoninus, better

317

known as Caracalla (211–217). As was often the case, the repression was particularly severe in North Africa, where the proconsul Scapula ordered Christians to be exposed to wild beasts and burned alive for their faith. In what was perhaps his final tract, *To Scapula*, Tertullian endeavored to persuade this governor that Christians were no threat to the empire. The effort to stamp them out would result in failure, he warned, for the people of God thrive on persecution; more ominously, it would also incur divine retribution. Pagan critics might fear that it was Christianity that threatened *their* world by disrupting the favor of the gods; to the zealous Christian spokesman, it was those who oppressed the true faith who risked bringing dreadful punishment upon their order by their shedding of innocent blood. In an age of political uncertainty, the prescriptions for stability could cut both ways.

Under the emperors Elagabalus (218–222) and Alexander Severus (222–235), Christians were allowed to exist in freedom. Popular hostility remained widespread, and there were a number of localized incidents of oppression, but there was little in the way of organized trouble from the center. There continued to be Christians in quite prominent positions in the imperial household, and others exercised important influences elsewhere. A learned and well-traveled Christian writer from the East, Sextus Julius Africanus, was admired by Alexander Severus for his impressive and wide-ranging scholarship and played a prominent role in the planning of a grand new library for the Pantheon in Rome.[1] Alexander was even persuaded to build a private shrine that contained images of Abraham and Christ alongside pagan religious representations. It was reported that Alexander's mother, Julia Mamaea, invited Origen to speak with her and tell her more about Christianity. It is unlikely that Alexander himself was anything other than curious or open-minded concerning the faith, but his position certainly made life much easier for the churches than it had been a couple of decades or so earlier.

Alexander Severus's policy was, however, directly reversed by his successor, the Thracian soldier Maximin (235–238). Maximin blamed the political failures of Alexander's regime specifically on the fact that he had allowed the Christians to prosper, both in the provinces and at his court. The imperial household was purged, and a number of prominent Christians were sent into exile, including both Pontian, bishop of Rome, and Hippolytus. In Cappadocia, there was vigorous persecution under the governor Serenianus, who burned down places of worship and caused believers to flee to other provinces. Perhaps for many Christians the threat of persecution was even greater than the likelihood of physical assault, for it was in these years that Origen, in Caesarea, wrote his *Exhortation to Martyrdom*, encouraging his readers not to flinch in the face of trial but to welcome death if need be. Perhaps not many of them were called to face death, but Origen's work expressed something of the mood of the times.

Maximin was nevertheless removed from power in 238, and under his successors, first the boy-emperor Gordian III (238–244) and then Philip the Arab (244–249), the Christians were once more tolerated. In fact, the condition of Christianity in the 240s not only improved again but advanced markedly, with significant expansion of the church's numbers, especially in the East. There were even rumors that Philip himself was a Christian. Such notions were not well-founded, despite their lingering attractions for fourth-century writers; nevertheless, there were good reasons why the Christian faith might have looked attractive to more people in these years of escalating socioeconomic and political turmoil.

There was a decline in the prestige of local urban cults and a weakening in enthusiasm for traditional religions. Christian spokesmen were offering a message that was increasingly confident in intellectual terms, and they were showing evidences of success sociologically. Figures such as Origen proclaimed a faith that appealed to educated intellectuals, and they were prepared to tackle head-on the objections that had been adduced so damagingly by pagan opponents such as Celsus. The feats of missionary bishops such as Gregory *Thaumatourgos* showed that Christian spokesmen could impress a pagan populace with their spiritual energies, and their would-be critics could hardly gainsay the fact that they championed a faith for which ordinary people were prepared, if necessary, to die.

Secular Challenges: Neoplatonism

Even so, it would be quite mistaken to suppose that Christianity in the 240s was *popular* in cultural terms or to think that there was a complete disillusionment with conventional religions. For one thing, the latter could still put on a good show. In April 247, Philip led the cultic celebration of one thousand years of Rome's history; a millennium of prosperity under the supposed protection of the traditional gods was acknowledged with three days and nights of expensive revelry, and coins were issued proclaiming the happiness of the age. Such diversions were, in reality, window-dressing, for the political peace was in serious danger of crumbling under the weight of invasions from the Goths, economic extortion by corrupt officials, and social oppression in the provinces from heavy-handed bureaucrats and mutinous soldiers. Nevertheless, the display showed that pagan religion was still very much at the heart of political image-making, and its symbolism still made the largest impact on popular emotions.

Secular philosophy was also fully capable of mounting powerful challenges to Christian belief. Plotinus (ca. 205–270), an Egyptian-born scholar who had studied in Alexandria under one of Origen's teachers, the elusive Ammonius Saccas, before moving to Rome to set up his own school in the mid-240s, propounded a dynamic interpretation of Platonism. His ideas, known to us from the fifty-four treatises posthumously collected and arranged in a series of six groups of nine (hence their name, *Enneads*, from the Greek for "groups of nine") by his eminent pupil Porphyry (ca. 232–303), offered a complex mixture of rationalism and contemplative mysticism that drew on a variety of philosophical influences besides Plato.

Plotinus regarded the ultimate reality at the top of the hierarchy of being as the One or the Good, the first principle that transcended all thought and speech. Emanating from the One was Mind, or the divine world of the Forms or Ideas. Then came Soul, the intermediary between the intelligible and the material realms. Matter was the furthest removed from the One, and its only goodness came from the form that was imposed upon it by Soul. Evil was an absence of goodness, and thus an absence of being. Human souls were derived from the One and could aspire to unity with it via a process of purification and contemplation, by which they ascended beyond the deficiencies and flux of the world of the temporal to the pure simultaneousness of the eternal. Recognition of one's spiritual kinship with the One was the beginning of the soul's return to its true origin and its proper destiny.

Plotinus was aware of Christian ideas, and he directed polemic against Gnostic views concerning spirit and matter. He was equally opposed to conceptions of the material world as created and redeemed by the direct action of God, for as he saw it, matter had to be the lowest form of being and the farthest from the One. What he offered instead was a sophisticated Neoplatonist synthesis of speculative metaphysics and ascetic ethics.[2] Variously capable of being read as a peculiar form of monotheism or a certain kind of pantheism, his system appealed to many intellectuals and attracted a significant following not only in Rome but much farther afield. Neoplatonism came to serve as one of the major alternatives to Christian belief for those who rejected the conventions of traditional Graeco-Roman religion. In time, it would also exercise a potent influence on Christian thinkers themselves. Its doctrine of three *hypostaseis*, the One, Mind, and Soul, seemed beguilingly comparable to the Christian notions of a trinitarian God, and its emphasis on self-denial and contemplation would find its way into various forms of Christian mysticism.

In reality, however, Neoplatonism was a long way from informed Christian logic on almost everything, despite its considerable importance in the shaping of many subsequent expressions of Christian theology. Its triad may have had three *hypostaseis*, but their status was nothing like that of the three divine persons of the Christian God. The Christian doctrines of the goodness of creation and of redemption by divine incarnation were ruled out on the grounds that matter was evil. The ascent of the soul toward the One took place via a natural process of reason and abstraction from the world of the senses, and there was no conception of salvation as holistic, embracing every aspect of human existence, and achieved not by natural effort but by divine grace.

The distance between the champions of a Neoplatonist philosophy and Christianity was graphically illustrated in the work of Plotinus's disciple Porphyry. Porphyry, a native of Tyre who had studied in various centers of learning before becoming a student of Plotinus in Rome, was a man of great learning and a prolific writer. Skeptical about all forms of popular religion, he was bitterly antagonistic toward the Christians, with whom he may have had some contact as a young man. As well as works such as *Philosophy from Oracles*, which contained a number of "oracles" against Christianity from various traditional religions,[3] he wrote a fifteen-book treatise *Against the Christians*, which developed a powerful, systematic assault on the Christian Scriptures and their teaching. Attacked by many later churchmen, Porphyry's onslaught was still considered to be worth refuting by prominent Christian thinkers as late as the fifth century, and it was ordered to be burned by imperial edict in 448. Our access to its argument today is only through the scattered fragments preserved in the writings of its numerous opponents.

Besides the high-flown attacks on Christianity among an educated elite, there also remained pervasive popular resentment of Christians. One instance was evidenced in Alexandria in 248. Incited by a pagan priest, a number of believers were set upon by a mob. Some were subjected to a popular lynching; others were dragged into the temples and forced to offer sacrifices; and the property of Christians was looted and destroyed in a popular rampage. The pretext was that they had refused to participate in the imperial celebrations, but the real reasons, as ever, were more arbitrary. As they had always been, the Christians were scapegoats for a general assortment of contemporary economic and social woes and the victims of petty grievances in a social context that was anything but happy beneath the surface.

Decius

Hearing of the events in Alexandria from his base in Caesarea, Origen saw them as presaging a period of more widespread persecution. He was right. Philip, having failed to deal personally with the problem of the Goths on the Danube frontier, appointed the best military commander at his disposal, Decius, the urban prefect of Rome, to oversee the process. Decius rewarded his master's confidence swiftly and so captured the loyalty of his troops that they declared him emperor in Philip's stead. After a period of attempted negotiation, Decius and Philip fought it out in battle; Philip was defeated and committed suicide, and in October 249, Decius was officially installed as his successor.

Decius declared himself a restorer of Rome's traditional values—a new Trajan, dedicated to the renaissance of the ideals of the one who had been hailed as "the best of emperors." On 3 January 250 he solemnly performed the annual sacrifice to Jupiter and the Roman gods in the Capitoline temple in Rome and accompanied the ritual with an edict that similar sacrifices should be offered throughout the empire. Decius's injunction was not directly targeted at the Christians, but they were inevitably likely victims; if they did not obey the command to sacrifice, they would be regarded as political subversives, guilty not only of disobedience to the law but of offending the gods and jeopardizing the concord of the empire. The penalty for such behavior was death.

The advent of Decius thus launched the first systematic and empire-wide attack on the Christians since the beginnings of the church. In chronological terms, the assault did not last long. Decius was killed in battle against the Goths (against whom he had rashly launched a further campaign) in June 251, and his religious policy was discontinued. In respect of its impact upon the churches, however, the effects of the persecution were considerable, both in the immediate and the long term.

One of the first Christians to suffer, within a matter of days of Decius's edict, was Fabian, the energetic leader of the church of Rome for the past decade and a half; his see was left vacant until March of 251. Another early victim was Babylas, bishop of Antioch, whose fame as a martyr came to be much celebrated in both East and West in later centuries. To ensure compliance with the emperor's orders, the authorities decreed that every person throughout the empire had to obtain a special certificate or *libellus* proving that the statutory sacrifice had been performed in the presence of designated officials. Archaeologists have uncovered a number of these documents from the sands of Egypt, and it is clear from the wording of them that they were deliberately designed to identify those who would not obey Decius's mandate. A commission was established in each city, and every individual had to obtain its signature, certifying that the sacrifice had duly taken place, accompanied by a cultic libation and eating of the sacrificial meat.

All over the empire, there was a rush to comply. In Carthage, the crowds queued up in such numbers at the temples to collect their piece of paper that the system could scarcely cope. Christian resistance, for the most part, was weak. In Smyrna, the bishop, Euctemon, led his congregation in person to the temple, and the situation was probably much the same in many places. There was widespread Christian acquiescence, especially among those who risked the confiscation of property. Some believers managed to flee and go into hiding, such as the bishops Cyprian of Carthage and Dionysius of Alexandria (the latter after he had been rescued from imprisonment), who administered their flocks from exile by secret correspondence.

Others managed to bribe less hostile commissioners to give them certificates stating that they had sacrificed when they had not. This practice was frowned on by Christian leaders, but in the aftermath of the troubles those who had resorted to this expedient were considered to have compromised less than their brothers and sisters who had given in and obeyed the law. A few bravely held out and paid the ultimate price, such as a presbyter in Smyrna named Pionius and a small group of his followers, who refused to copy their bishop and yield to the authorities despite appeals not to throw their lives away. Overall, however, the number of deaths was low; confronted with the choice of obeying Christ or the emperor, a large majority of believers, including a great many of their leaders, took the easy way out.

Compromise and Its Implications

Decius's persecution may have been short-lived, but it had forced a vast number of Christians to concede officially the supremacy of Caesar over their Lord. The requirement to sacrifice to the gods was not followed up with any sustained attempt to wipe out Christianity as such. As long as the stated rituals were performed, it was still possible to be Christian. But what kind of Christian? The effects of Decius's measures were felt not so much in the statistics of the churches' membership as in their theology, their self-image, and their discipline.

Thousands of believers had "lapsed" and compromised their convictions, but most of them still considered themselves followers of Jesus. No doubt many suffered from a bad conscience, but they assumed that they were capable of being restored and of making amends once the political climate improved. Established patterns of penitential discipline taught that even serious sin committed after baptism could be forgiven, provided that the guilty showed signs of genuine contrition and submitted to a process of supervised good behavior, under exclusion from the Eucharist. In the West, especially in North Africa and in Rome, the legitimately consecrated bishop was seen as the uniquely qualified person to grant such restoration, the one in whose hands lay the keys of the kingdom. However, many Christians in these areas and elsewhere were unwilling to apply to their bishops for remission, feeling that it was inappropriate to do so. Why seek forgiveness from a leader who had himself run away when times were hard? How could reconciliation be granted by clergy who had also personally buckled under pressure?

There was a good deal of disorganization. Some bishops treated the lapsed more leniently than others. Christians who faced severe demands from one bishop often sought an easier route to restoration, and certain other clergy elected to forgive penitents on no authority other than their own. In the absence of an obvious caste of respected leaders, laypeople also came to exercise considerable influence. Those who had suffered imprisonment, torture, and privation for resisting the authorities (and some of them were still in prison when Decius fell) were considered to be "confessors"—people who had held tenaciously to their beliefs under severe pressure. The status of such confessors had developed over earlier periods of persecution, when individuals who had suffered but survived had come to acquire aspects of the same spiritual eminence that attached to the martyrs themselves. In the wake of the persecution at Lyons in 177, those who had been imprisoned were deemed to have earned the right to forgive the sins of believers who had lapsed; in Rome it had been accepted that confessors were in a position to be admitted to the ranks of deacons or presbyters without formal ordination.

Cyprian of Carthage

In Carthage, the fugitive bishop Cyprian found on his return in 251 that his church was dominated by confessors. He had suffered a serious loss of public esteem in his absence, and Christians who had formerly been incarcerated had usurped his authority. The confessors, held by many to be specially anointed by the Holy Spirit, were taking it upon themselves to sign certificates authorizing the clergy to restore transgressors to communion. Cyprian was simply expected to endorse their decisions. Leniency was to be the order of the day.

Cyprian had not been a Christian for very many years himself. Born in Carthage around 200 to a respectable and affluent pagan family, he had had a successful career as a teacher of rhetoric. According to his own account of his spiritual journey, he had nevertheless grown disillusioned with the vanity and selfishness of his society and had finally found peace in the gospel of Christ. He was baptized about 246. In a culture of rigorist spirituality, he seems to have proved himself to be a particularly zealous Christian, dedicating himself so wholeheartedly to a life of celibacy, poverty, and Bible study that he was deemed a worthy candidate for the bishopric of his city only two years later. On his accession to that office, he is said to have sold his property to provide alms for the poor (though his friends bought back some of it for him).

Cyprian was a dedicated and efficient leader of his church, extending notable help to victims of plague in North Africa in 252–253,[4] raising money to ransom prisoners taken by barbarians (thus combining charity with missionary expansion, in a fashion that would be much used by later bishops), and coordinating the bureaucracy of his clerical order with aplomb. Like many bishops, he was an extensive letter-writer, and his extant correspondence constitutes a vital body of evidence on both church and society in his time. Some of his letters amount to virtual treatises on topics of theological importance such as the nature of the Eucharist. Cyprian was greatly impressed by the work of Tertullian and inherited from him a very strong sense of the moral obligations incumbent upon the church. These ideas were fleshed out in a number of ethical and spiritual treatises, on subjects such as the benefit of patience, work, and almsgiving, virginity, and the teaching of the Lord's Prayer.

Unlike the later Tertullian, however, Cyprian had not considered it his duty to avoid flight from martyrdom at all costs. In exile he had labored to encourage his harassed flock and bolster the confidence of those of his clergy who had remained, expressing his horror at the extent of the current apostasy from the faith and portraying it as a divine judgment on the church for its worldliness and lack of spiritual fiber. Though he had escaped himself, he was firmly opposed to easy restoration for those who had lapsed in his absence, and he counseled that there should be no formal overtures of forgiveness until outward conditions had returned to normal and he and his fellow bishops were able to resume their proper positions.

Nevertheless, Cyprian did not—and in the circumstances could not—take a totally strict line on the reconciliation of backsliders. His hero Tertullian, after initially believing in the possibility of restoration after grave sin, had gone on to reject it, moved by the stringency of a Montanist ethic. Cyprian's sympathies for Tertullian's rigorism were deeply felt, but he did not share the later Tertullian's Montanist assumptions, and although he took an extremely serious view on the heinousness of apostasy, he could not in the end endorse the idea that those who had betrayed their Lord by sacrificing to the gods were beyond all hope of forgiveness. In a work entitled *On the Lapsed,* he makes no bones about the dreadfulness of lapsing and warns his readers of the terrible dangers of incurring God's judgment. At the end of the treatise, though, having impressed upon them the magnitude of such sins, he extends the assurance that God is gracious and will pardon, as long as there are true signs of repentance and altered conduct.

As far as the practicalities of restoration to communion were concerned, Cyprian conceded that confessors could make recommendations, but only bishops had the authority to arrive at final decisions, for they were God's specially commissioned representatives. This policy was validated at a council of bishops held in Carthage later in 251, once the political situation had stabilized somewhat. It was agreed that penitents should be examined individually and have their offenses classified on a case-by-case basis, with the bishop in each instance having determinative power. No one should be irrevocably barred from the possibility of penance, nor should there be a straightforward lowering of hurdles. Those who had obtained certificates without actually sacrificing were to be restored to the church after varying periods of discipline; those who had sacrificed could be readmitted only on their deathbeds; and clergy who had lapsed were not to be allowed to reenter their orders.

These decisions were unsatisfactory in the eyes of a number of Christians in Carthage, and they broke away from Cyprian and set up their own congregation. They were led initially by a deacon but subsequently elected their own bishop, Fortunatus, as a rival to Cyprian. Cyprian was deeply disturbed at the actions of these dissidents. In a treatise entitled *On the Unity of the Catholic Church*, he spelled out in forceful terms his conviction that schism is a violation of the essential nature of the church. The "unity" of the church, he argued, really referred to its "uniqueness." The one catholic church found throughout the world is the exclusive home of truth, and divisions in it are the work of Satan. The church may have many members and exist in many different circumstances, but it is one body.

The focus of this unity, according to Cyprian, is to be found in the church's bishops; it is their presence that guarantees the cohesion of the diverse members of the body. Those who refuse to recognize the authority of duly appointed bishops are not only insubordinates or shabby witnesses who damage the public image of the Christian gospel: they are people who cast their own salvation into jeopardy. In distancing themselves from the authority of properly constituted leadership, they cut themselves off from the one catholic community and thus call into serious question the authenticity of their own faith. To forsake the catholic bishop is to forsake the catholic church.

Cyprian's argument is striking in two respects: first, for the weight he attaches to episcopal authority, and second, for his contention that the catholic church is the exclusive home of salvation. In his perspective, the integrity of the church is sustained by the unity of its bishops worldwide. Whatever the roles of other spiritually gifted individuals such as confessors might be, they cannot usurp the place of those who are officially appointed to episcopal rank. The power of bishops does not rest upon a principle of literal apostolic succession, but catholic bishops are nevertheless those whose teaching and functions are in demonstrable continuity with the doctrine and practice of the apostles. The origins of the church's unity lie with Jesus's appointment of a single apostle, Peter, as the one who held the keys of the kingdom. The other apostles were of the same status as Peter, and remained worthy of equal honor, but Jesus bequeathed the privilege of the keys to Peter first.

The manuscript tradition of *On the Unity of the Catholic Church* contains two versions of Cyprian's argument in this area.[5] One version deploys the uniqueness of Peter to illustrate the oneness of the church: Jesus elected to appoint the individual man Peter first to show that the church can only be one. The other version speaks of Peter's primacy as the first holder of the keys: Peter is chosen first, and it is specifically upon him as the "rock" that the church is built (Matt. 16:18). The second version is akin to later arguments in favor of the primacy of the see of Rome. Scholars have long debated the coexistence of the two strategies in the Cyprianic text. It is possible that Cyprian first used the argument from primacy, but without direct allusion to Rome, and then later altered it himself to the more guarded argument on unity in order to distance himself from claims that the see of Rome was uniquely privileged. Cyprian regarded all bishops as theoretically equal, and in the later 250s he would have a sharp disagreement with his Roman counterpart, in which it was plain that he did not recognize any special jurisdictional authority in the Roman see. Perhaps he added the unity argument in the context of that dispute. An alternative explanation is that the point about primacy does intentionally allude to Rome but is a later interpolation into Cyprian's text. The first account is perhaps more likely, however. Whatever the origin of the reasoning, Cyprian's idealization of the episcopate as the ground of the church's unity is clear.

The other remarkable aspect of Cyprian's case is his claim that "outside the church there is no salvation." This claim would become famous in later tradition,[6] but it is basic to Cyprian's reasoning. His original contention, in context, is not so much that the church is the sole mediator of grace as this might later be understood but that the catholic church is, in all its diversity, the universal home of all who truly follow Jesus. "You cannot have God for your Father," Cyprian argues, "if you do not have the church for your mother."[7]

Rome: Novatian

The context for Cyprian's teaching was not just his local situation in Carthage. In Rome, too, there were serious divisions surrounding the treatment of the lapsed. In the late teens and early twenties of the third century, the issue of restoration after lapses had already been highly contentious between Callistus and Hippolytus. As we might expect, it resurfaced with a vengeance in the wake of the Decian persecution following the martyrdom of Fabian on 20 January 250, during which a large number of Roman Christians had apostatized.

With most of the remaining church's activity forced underground, it was not possible to elect a successor to Fabian, and affairs were overseen by a presbyter named Novatian, who was highly regarded for his learning and his intellectual abilities. He was the author of an impressive Latin treatise, *On the Trinity*, the most ambitious treatment of its kind in Western theology to date. While much indebted to Tertullian, it advanced beyond previous Western accounts in emphasizing the eternity of God the Son.[8] Doctrinally orthodox, Novatian was an acute thinker and an elegant stylist, and he was well liked by many.

Novatian also took a rigorous attitude toward the lapsed. In his eyes, believers guilty of such serious sins as murder, adultery, and apostasy could not be granted remission; all that the church could do was appeal for mercy for them at God's final judgment. Primarily because of his hard-line stance on discipline, he was rejected as a candidate for bishop when the opportunity at last arose to appoint a new one in the spring of 251; there were simply too many lapsed Christians in Rome for whom his policy, if implemented, would have signaled the end of their belonging to the organized church. Cornelius, a more liberal presbyter who took the view that the lapsed could be restored after due penance, was elected instead. Novatian and his supporters, who included a sizable contingent of confessors, refused to recognize Cornelius, and they formed a separate community with Novatian as the "real" bishop. Both parties appealed to church leaders throughout the empire for support.

Novatian won some significant backing in a number of quarters, in southern Italy, Gaul, North Africa, and Asia Minor. Cyprian, however, wavered. Though inclined to support Novatian's high moral stance, he finally conceded that Cornelius was a faithful and virtuous leader and that, having been ordained first, he deserved to be acknowledged as the official bishop. Novatian, for all his abilities, was guilty of "schism," or "tearing apart" the unity of the catholic church.[9] In his letters to Cornelius, Cyprian made clear his belief that it was he, not Novatian, whom he regarded as his worthily appointed episcopal brother.

The political interlude that enabled the appointment of Cornelius in Rome did not last long. There was a further outbreak of persecution under Decius's successor Gallus (252–253) in which Cornelius was arrested and sent into exile outside Rome, where he died soon afterward. Cornelius's replacement, Lucius, lasted only a few months. By this time, Novatian's supporters in Rome had started to dwindle somewhat, as they saw that his status was not being widely acknowledged by other churches, and many of them were readmitted to the main community. Novatian nevertheless managed to hold on to his congregation, and he developed a significant teaching ministry. He wrote a number of further treatises on moral and spiritual themes, all with debts to Tertullian and with some similar Stoic influences (only a few of these works survive). He may have died as a martyr in the serious persecutions under the emperor Valerian in 258.

Despite the ultimate failure of Novatian's attempt to reform the church in Rome, his separatist sympathizers both there and farther afield endured for a long time. Typically styling themselves as *Cathari*, "pure ones," and regarding all other believers as compromised by their churches' lax attitudes to sin, the "Novatianists" continued in various parts of Europe, in Constantinople (where they had a particularly strong presence), and elsewhere in Asia into the fifth century. The sect was still significant enough to be mentioned in Alexandria in the early seventh century.

Rome: Stephen

Cyprian may have sided with the winning party in Rome in the case of the Novatianist controversy, but his good relationships with Rome became severely strained during the episcopate of Lucius's successor, Stephen, who was consecrated in May 254. Cyprian had accepted that regular believers who had compromised their faith might be restored, but what about the case of clergy? Not long after Stephen's consecration, a clash occurred over the question of how to treat erring leaders.

Cyprian took it upon himself to advise Stephen that two Spanish bishops who had procured *libelli* to say that they had sacrificed must not be allowed to challenge the status of those who had subsequently been appointed in their stead. As far as Cyprian was concerned, the buying of certificates of compliance, though a lesser offense than actual sacrificing, was, in the case of leaders, a bar to restoration to office; the guilty could return only as penitent laymen. Stephen, on the other hand, judged that those who had originally been properly consecrated deserved to be restored if they were truly contrite. Cyprian and Stephen agreed that the authority of the church was vested in its bishops, but they differed as to what the implications of this authority were in practice. Could bishops directly remit the sins of delinquent clergy, or was a more protracted process of penitence required?

The fundamental issue on which the two leaders disagreed, though, was not discipline as such but baptism. Cyprian believed baptism was not valid unless it was administered by an official of the catholic community, for only such a person was qualified by the gifting of the Spirit to perform the rite. This meant that baptisms carried out by schismatics were by definition invalid; those who administered them were severed from the one Spirit-anointed body of Christ and were thus incapable of communicating the gifts of the Spirit to the candidates. For Stephen, however, the status of the minister was irrelevant; what mattered was the faith of the convert and the basic regularity of the process—it must be done in water and into the triune name.

Cyprian's position was firmly grounded in the tradition of the North African church, which he consciously sought to follow. There it was simply assumed that individuals who had been baptized by anyone other than catholic clergy had not genuinely been baptized at all and so were subject to the usual process of preparation and initiation required of all converts. Because the earlier rite was formally invalid, this process was not a *rebaptism* but a first *real* baptism. Baptisms performed by Novatianists were no better than those carried out by heretics, despite the fact that the Novatianists baptized into the triune name.

Cyprian had strong support for his argument not only in North Africa but elsewhere. In Cappadocia, Firmilian, bishop of Caesarea, had followed a similar practice with converts from Montanism and had been supported in it by his Asian colleagues. In Stephen's view, however, all that was necessary when people came into the catholic community out of a schismatic or heretical context was that hands should be laid upon them, and the Spirit would be conveyed to them through that process. It had been the usual practice in Rome over many years for penitents to be received not by baptism but by the laying-on of hands. If Cyprian and his allies followed one established convention, Stephen could appeal to another.

The rift was serious. Stephen denounced Cyprian in very severe terms as a "false Christ," refused to grant an audience to a delegation of North African churchmen, and threatened to excommunicate those in North Africa and Asia Minor who followed Cyprian's teaching. Cyprian, for his part, convened a gathering of North African clergy in September 256 at which he consolidated support for his position and dismissed the legitimacy of Stephen's attempt to impose his will on other churches. Cyprian maintained that no bishop was in principle higher than any other, and no good argument could be adduced in favor of the spiritual primacy of the see of Rome. (It was perhaps at this stage that his original language in *On the Unity of the Catholic Church* was altered.) Confronted with a deep division between Rome and other churches, Cyprian's foundational doctrine of the unanimity of bishops was in jeopardy; his way of defending it was to argue that all bishops were equal, and each was responsible to God alone.

Further Persecution and a Working Solution

The outcome of the crisis was affected by events in the political arena. In the summer of 257, the emperor Valerian (253–260) initiated a new wave of persecutions. His edicts were specifically aimed at the church and its leaders. Christians not only had to acknowledge the Roman gods but were also forbidden to assemble for worship or visit Christian cemeteries. In the following year, Valerian ordered the arrest and punishment of bishops, presbyters, and deacons; prominent laypeople were to have their property confiscated and lose their status; aristocratic women were to be exiled; and civil servants who professed Christianity were to be reduced to slavery.

Valerian's measures, like Decius's, were generated by political and fiscal realities; once again the Christians were convenient targets in a situation of serious military pressure and economic malaise, especially since the larger churches such as Rome and Carthage appeared to be escaping the financial strictures affecting society at large and to be doing rather well in terms of resources. After tolerating Christianity in the initial years of his reign, Valerian determined to dismantle the organizational power of the Christians by focusing his attacks particularly on their leaders, their assets, and their channels of social respectability.

Stephen was arrested and put to death on 2 August 257. In Carthage, Cyprian was also detained and summoned before the proconsul, Galerius Maximus. Condemned as a prominent ringleader in a system opposed to the religion of Rome, he refused to recant and died bravely on 14 September 258. Meanwhile, Stephen's successor, Sixtus II, had accepted overtures from Dionysius, bishop of Alexandria (himself a victim of the persecution and sent into exile) in an attempt to mediate between Rome and Carthage. It was agreed that baptism by schismatics and heretics was invalid, but it was also acknowledged that in some circumstances those who had been baptized this way could be admitted to the church after penance and the laying-on of hands. In other words, Rome and Carthage would agree to disagree. The tensions would remain for generations to come, but at least schism had been avoided, even if the compromise had been achieved amid the brutal circumstances of persecution. Sixtus himself did not have long to live; he was seized along with a group of his deacons and executed on 6 August 258.

The Impact of the Troubles

The persecutions of Valerian were halted by his successor, Gallienus, in 260 to 261, and a number of Christian churches and cemeteries were restored in response to episcopal appeals. The troubles of the 250s had cost more than a few lives, not least among some of the church's esteemed leaders. But, for all the tragedy of individual cases, the persecution did not have a negative impact on the long-term strength of the Christian cause or the statistics of its position in Roman society.

For the most part, the remainder of the century was relatively calm for Christians in political terms. There was a brief threat of trouble under the emperor Aurelian in 274 to 275 when it was decreed that the Sun god was to be worshiped as "Lord of the Roman Empire," and it seemed that believers would be an obvious target for refusing to obey.[10] But the threat passed; Eusebius says that Aurelian changed his mind concerning the oppression of Christians.[11] In any case, Aurelian met his end in a military coup in April of 275. In many parts of the empire—North Africa, Egypt, Asia Minor, and Syria—the churches grew relatively undisturbed except for scattered incidents of local trouble. Christians were able to hold responsible civil offices, and in some instances their superiors turned a blind eye when they avoided their official responsibilities to promote the imperial cult or ensure that due sacrifices were made to the traditional gods.

Viewed in the larger scale of church history, the main significance of the political challenges of the mid-third century was not as much the physical effects of the repressions as such, grim though they were, as the varying positions that emerged among Christians in the midst of the trials with regard to the nature of episcopal authority, schism, baptism, and penance. The issues that had surfaced so powerfully in the debates between Rome and North Africa would continue to shape crucial areas of theological discussion and affect the structural unity of the Western church for a very long time to come. Eventually Rome would manage to induce the North Africans to abandon the austerity of Cyprian's sacramental position, but even in the fifth century, it remained necessary for the great Augustine of Hippo to suggest that his theology of a necessarily mixed church was not a betrayal of the African tradition.

The oppressions of Decius and Valerian did not succeed in crushing the churches, but they forced Christians, especially in the West, to think more systematically than ever before about the *nature* of the body of Christ and about the kind of relationship that existed between baptism and holiness. In the wake of the unavoidable realization that Christians could fail, dismally and in large numbers, to stand up for their Lord when the going got seriously tough, the church was forced to evolve a more elaborate practical system for dealing with those who lapsed. And in the light of the reality that the church's leaders could talk about catholicity and shared traditions of doctrine but still bitterly disagree about pressing practical matters of procedure, there was an obvious obligation to explore further the question of how believers were to deal with their differences.

The disputes were most acute in the West, but they were not confined there. As the differences of opinion between Rome and Alexandria over language for God (see pp. 266–67) and over baptism showed, they also reflected conflicts of perspective between the West and the East. The debates of the third century exposed the significant tensions that could exist between those who alike professed orthodoxy, especially when some bishops, not least some of those in Rome, saw it as their prerogative to determine practices elsewhere.

If the delicacy of relationships and the challenge to define the boundaries of discipline and purity had been highlighted by political pressures, there was far more self-examination yet to come for the churches. The end of the third century was to see a still more savage effort on the part of the secular powers to strike at the Christian movement.

Diocletian and "The Great Persecution"

Diocletian became Roman emperor in November 284. A few weeks later, he elected to share his responsibilities with a colleague, Maximian. Maximian would govern the Western provinces while Diocletian took charge of the East. In 293, each ruler appointed a deputy to serve as "Caesar" to his "Augustus." In the West, Maximian chose Constantius; in the East, Diocletian appointed Galerius. The diffusion of power among this "tetrarchy," or "rule of four," was designed to promote stability and forestall the possibility of military coups by ensuring that the empire's chief military commanders already held political authority. The empire was not formally carved up into four parts, but each of the rulers concentrated his attentions upon a particular region, while maintaining a commitment to the unity of the imperial order and the primary legitimacy of Diocletian.

After two generations of socioeconomic and military turmoil, Diocletian's regime initiated a concerted effort to deal with the empire's structural problems. There was significant reorganization of the army and provincial administration as well as a range of measures to inject life into the imperial economy, including a readjustment of prices and an overhaul of the taxation system. Along with these policies was a concern to revitalize cultural, moral, and religious life as well. In the cities of the empire, public buildings that had fallen into disrepair were resurrected, and serious attention was given to the promotion of

Roman coin (c. A.D. 290) showing the emperor Diocletian. Illustration from Otago Museum, Dunedin, New Zealand. Used by permission.

traditional cults, especially the cult of the emperor.

For well over the first decade of Diocletian's reign, Christians were able to function much as they had done over the preceding generation, and their presence in some senior administrative positions and within the imperial household itself continued to be tolerated. Lactantius (ca. 250–325), later a major Christian apologist, served as a teacher of Latin literature and rhetoric at Diocletian's court in Nicomedia in Asia Minor, and he was converted to Christianity at some stage during these years. Gradually, however, the Christians started to become a target of serious political hostility. The loyalty of the imperial army was a major concern, and there were increasing difficulties with Christians who either refused to perform the customary rites symbolizing obedience or indeed held out against military service altogether. A number of believers were expelled from the army in the East, and elsewhere there were isolated cases of martyrdom among soldiers.

At a sacrifice in Antioch in 298 attended by Diocletian and Galerius, the augurs found themselves unable to read the normal signs in the livers of the sacrificial animals after some Christians present were observed to have made the sign of the cross, and in the winter of 302 to 303, the oracle of Apollo at Miletus informed the emperor that the Christians were to blame for false prophecies being given. There was an intensification of anti-Christian propaganda with the dissemination of the works of Porphyry and other critics. At the same time, Lactantius's former teacher, Arnobius, an African from Sicca in Numidia, and formerly a firm enemy of Christianity, became convinced of the truth of the religion he had set out to attack and ended up writing a defense of the faith against some of the charges adduced by Porphyry and his kind.[12]

Diocletian concluded that Christianity was once again disrupting the stability of the state, and steps needed to be taken to deal with its representatives. Various advisers encouraged him in these judgments, among them, perhaps, Galerius and the Neoplatonist governor of Bithynia, Sossianus Hierocles, who in subsequent years proved a fierce opponent of Christianity. In late February 303 the first in a series of edicts was issued against the Christians, and an intense attack was launched on their rights and their property.

In the first instance, Diocletian appears to have sought to avoid blood-shed; unlike in Valerian's persecution, there was no threat of a death penalty as such. The oppression was nevertheless severe and wide-ranging in its effects. Places of worship were destroyed; the first target was the Christian edifice opposite the imperial palace in Nicomedia. Property was confiscated from places of worship, Scriptures were handed over to the authorities for burning, and clergy were removed from their offices and rounded up for torture. Believers with significant social status were stripped of the privileges attaching to birth or accomplishments in public service. They were also effectively prevented from pursuing justice through the courts, for participation in legal cases required a formal offering of incense prior to the presentation of a petition. At the imperial court, Christian officials were removed from office. Things were made worse by the outbreak of fires on separate occasions at the emperor's palace; Christians were held accountable and subjected to brutal fates, including death by burning.

A few months later, the pressure escalated still further. A second edict, published in the summer of 303 and seemingly directed primarily at the eastern empire, demanded that bishops and other clerics be arrested. It was already becoming clear that persecution inevitably involved blood-shed, and in a number of areas of the East, ordinary Christians were starting to pay the ultimate price for their faith when they resisted the seizure of church property. The main cost, though, at this stage was borne by clergy. As in previous repressions, however, the authorities found that they could scarcely implement the practical requirements of the legislation. There simply was not enough prison space to ac-commodate the numbers of church officials under detention, and the emperor was obliged to order that clergy be freed after being forced to sacrifice to the gods.

In 304, Diocletian fell ill and became unable to carry out his impe-rial duties. Galerius, whose hostility to Christianity seems to have been sharp from the beginning, issued a further edict that now commanded that "all citizens in every country in each city offer sacrifices publicly and libations to the idols."[13] The primary focus of the edict was again the East, but the law also seems to have been applied, albeit with less fanatical rigor, in the West. The issue now was not just about the public status and civil rights of Christian leaders or organized Christianity but about the position of all who professed faith. To refuse to sacrifice to the gods was, once again, an offense punishable by death. As in such circumstances in previous years, quite large numbers of Christians capitulated. At the same time, a great many also refused to comply and held out to the last. Some deliberately sought martyrdom or placed themselves in inevitable mortal danger by resisting the authorities. Those who survived the dreadful tortures inflicted by their captors were often maimed and scarred for the rest of their days.

The range and intensity of the sufferings visited on Christians during what became known as "the Great Persecution" varied considerably. The trial was most severe and long-lasting in the East, where Galerius pursued the Christians with passionate determination. In Palestine, Syria, and Egypt, a number of executions took place, though more were deported or imprisoned than martyred. In North Africa, as we might expect, there was a stronger measure of Christian defiance, and appeals were made to the traditions of resistance a century and more earlier. In the small settlement of Abitina (in modern Tunisia), the entire Christian community of forty-seven believers continued to meet even after their bishop had apostatized, before finally being arrested and taken to Carthage for trial and execution. In the Western provinces generally, though, there was much less systematic oppression; under Maximian, the most obvious impact of the authorities' actions was to be seen in confiscated property.

There was a measure of relief for Christians in both parts of the empire following the joint abdication of Diocletian and Maximian on 1 May 305. Constantius became Augustus in the West, and Galerius in the East. Nominally, Constantius was the senior of the two. But Galerius remained in a powerful position, so that the two new Caesars, Severus in the West and Maximin Daia in the East, were both associates of his. Constantius did not renew the persecution with any significant vigor in the West, though places of Christian worship were destroyed in Gaul, Spain, and possibly Britain. Much ecclesiastical reorganization and reorientation was necessary, as can be glimpsed from the detailed injunctions set out by a council of Spanish bishops held at Elvira near Granada some time around this period,[14] which stressed the importance of proper moral behavior among both clergy and laity, the evils of worldliness, and the necessity of regular attendance at worship. Among Elvira's eighty-one canons were severe penalties for apostasy and other sins as well as a stipulation that married bishops, presbyters, and deacons practice sexual abstinence and not have children. The climate was undoubtedly one in which moral reformation and the sharpening of Christian order and discipline were seen as very important. Nevertheless, as far as most Western believers were concerned, the worst of the horrors of persecution were over.

In the East, there was also an easing of the pressure, but in this case, it turned out to be only a brief respite. Before long, Galerius had redoubled his efforts to crush the Christians. With Diocletian out of the way in his retirement palace at Spalato (Split) on the coast of Dalmatia, his successors pursued a forceful agenda. In 306, a further edict was promulgated by Maximin, which again required all to sacrifice, regardless of age or sex, and stipulated that the names of those who did so were to be checked against official lists in each city. Dreadful punishments were visited upon any who refused to comply, though increasingly imprisonment or forced labor was imposed rather than execution. At the same time, Maximin promoted the reorganization of the pagan priesthood and encouraged propaganda attacks on Christian beliefs and practices.

The Rise of Constantine

Meanwhile, however, other momentous political developments were afoot in the West. In July 306, Constantius died at York, and the Roman legions stationed there declared his son Constantine to be the new Augustus of the West. Constantine's election in this way represented an usurpation of the right of Severus, Constantius's Caesar, to succeed as Augustus and produced a very delicate political situation. After a series of dexterous maneuvers, Constantine managed by 310 to get himself acknowledged as the undisputed ruler of the Gallic provinces and Spain. Events had conspired to assist him. Maxentius, son of Maximian, had seized control of Italy and Africa and had repulsed moves by Severus and Galerius to make him relinquish them. In 307, Severus had been captured and forced to commit suicide. He had been succeeded (much to the chagrin of Maximin) by Licinius, another of Galerius's close confidants, but Licinius had proved too slow in regaining Italy, and he had left the way clear for Constantine to upstage him. By 310, Constantine was poised for an invasion of Italy.

In the spring of 311, Galerius fell ill. While dying and in considerable pain, probably from cancer, he issued an edict[15] stating that his desire in treating the Christians as he had was simply to induce them to return to the religion of their ancestors. Now, in his extreme condition, he granted the churches an amnesty and permitted freedom of assembly, with the request that they pray for his health and for the security of the Roman state. In his weakened state, possibly he did have second thoughts about the policy he had pursued over the past decade. More likely he recognized that his strategy had failed to produce the religious conformity that he desired.

Whatever the case, neither his orders nor his appeal for prayer changed anything. Galerius died only a week after his edict, unaided by anyone's supplications. Maximin quickly gained control of the eastern provinces, and fierce persecution continued in many areas, promoted by popular hatred of Christians and hostility from local political leaders. Cities were induced to seek the expulsion of "atheists" from their boundaries. The brutality was worst in Egypt, where the punishments by decapitation and fire wreaked a terrible toll and left very dark scars on the memory of the Coptic church ever after. Casualties included the bishop of Alexandria and many other clergy and laypeople, who were variously put to death by beheading, burning, and other ghastly means. However, Maximin's aggression was increasingly opposed by both Licinius and Constantine, both of whom favored a policy of acceptance of the Christians. Licinius managed to seize the Balkan provinces, while in 312 Constantine, having defeated the Franks in the north, marched south into Italy to challenge Maxentius, whose presence was an obstacle to his obvious ambition to be sole emperor.

The Battle of the Milvian Bridge

After some fierce fighting in the north of the country, Constantine headed toward Rome. On 28 October 312, he faced Maxentius in battle at a spot five miles to the north of Rome, close to the crossing over the Tiber known as the Milvian Bridge (which still survives). Maxentius might well have elected to remain secure behind the walls of Rome and settle in for a siege; instead, he foolishly chose to march out of the city and face his challenger in the field, with the Tiber at his back. Despite having inferior numbers, Constantine triumphed, and as the defeated forces retreated, thousands were drowned in the river. Among them was Maxentius himself. Constantine's victory was purported to be the result of divine blessing—and the blessing not of the pagan deities but of the Christian God. Later reports claimed that Constantine had experienced a powerful vision of Christ prior to the battle and that his soldiers had fought under the sign of Christ and his cross (see further pp. 343–46). On the day after the battle, the conqueror entered Rome in triumph and was proclaimed Augustus; the West was his.

The Milvian Bridge, near Rome, scene of Constantine's victory over Maxentius in A.D. 312. Illustration from N. Lenski. Used by permission.

Constantine issued orders that the persecution of Christians should cease in all areas. The measure was aimed primarily at Maximin in the East, for Maxentius had of late exercised a broadly tolerant approach in the West, which had brought a marked change in North Africa especially. At Maximin's court, the report of Constantine's victory was hardly good news. Maximin had endeavored to assist Maxentius by invading Licinius's territories and heading west in a bid to thwart Licinius's capacity to abet Constantine's strategy. Now Maxentius was no more, and there was pressure to desist from oppressing the Christians. He started to distance himself from some of the consequences of the persecution in the East, and in late 312, he issued an edict of tolerance, granting the right of Christians to persist in their beliefs. No mention was made of a restoration of the right to build places of worship, but Christians were supposed to be free once again to hold their views if they insisted on doing so. Paganism was to be encouraged by example, not forced upon people by coercion. Maximin's word was not trusted, however, for his record was appalling, and many Eastern Christians continued to live in fear.

A few months later, in February 313, Constantine and Licinius met in Milan. An alliance was cemented between them by the marriage of Licinius to Constantine's half sister Constantia, and together the two rulers agreed on a policy of religious liberty in their joint territories. Two months after their meeting, Licinius defeated Maximin at Adrianople and took full control of the East. In June 313, he issued a circular to his provincial governors in Constantine's and his names that claimed to present the detail of the decisions reached in Milan. It asserted that the persecutions of Christians were officially to cease, that lands and properties belonging both to individual believers and to the churches as corporate entities were to be restored, and that there was to be freedom for all to worship according to their conscience. There was a resolution "to grant both to the Christians and to all people full authority to follow whatever religion each person has desired; whereby whatsoever divinity dwells in heaven may be appeased and made propitious towards us and towards all who have been placed under our authority."[16]

Maximin retreated through Asia Minor to Tarsus and took his own life. The last vestiges of harassment of believers in the East died away. After all the suffering of the past eleven years, the persecution that Diocletian had launched was finally over.

The "Edict of Milan"

The agreement of Constantine and Licinius came to be known as the "Edict of Milan" and ranks among the most famous of all political watersheds in the history of the Christian church. In fact, a formal edict as such was never issued in Milan; we have no evidence of any text issued prior to the statement promulgated some months later by Licinius in the East. It is clear, however, that the two leaders had concurred in their strategy, and Licinius's orders to his officials bore their joint authority.

Constantine had adopted a policy of tolerance toward the Christians over several years, partly because he saw an opportunity to make personal political capital out of appearing more generous than the imperial colleagues whose status he was set on challenging. From the beginnings of his rise to power in 306, he had extended liberty to the Christians in his dominions, and when he embarked on his campaign against Maxentius, he had been happy to make use of believers in various capacities; one of his senior advisers was Ossius of Cordoba, a bishop in exile from Spain. Following his defeat of Maxentius, Constantine had immediately ordered the cessation of persecution everywhere. As far as he was concerned, the agreement in Milan was consonant with the attitude he had adopted over some time. For Licinius, too, a lenient treatment of the Christians had been a way of differentiating his political claims from those of Maximin.

For Constantine, though, the so-called Edict of Milan had a history in more than just politics. It was in reality the judgment of an emperor who had already begun to sponsor Christianity at a different level, and in a fashion that none of his imperial predecessors had ever come close to doing.

LOOKING FORWARD,
LOOKING BACK

A Christian Emperor?

The origins of Constantine's identification with Christianity are difficult if not impossible to pin down. The stories we have inherited have been conditioned entirely by his Christian apologists, who celebrate his turn to Christ as a triumph of grace and the providential dawning of a new age of divine favor for the Roman Empire. His victory at the Milvian Bridge is typically attributed to his commitment to the Christian God, of whose reality he is said to have already become convinced. Lactantius says that before his encounter with Maxentius, Constantine had directed his troops to paint the sign of the cross on their shields as a talisman.[1] The cross was depicted in the form of a Chi-Rho monogram, a symbol that had come to be widely used as a badge of Christian identity, based upon the first two Greek letters (*chi* and *rho*) of the name *Christos*, "Christ." The emblem would also later appear on Constantine's coins.

According to Eusebius, writing in elaborate praise of Constantine after

Example of Chi-Rho symbol.
Illustration from FreeStockPhotos.com.
Used by permission.

Part of statue of Constantine, in Rome. Illustration from author.

his death, Constantine told him toward the end of his life that after having prayed to "the Supreme God" for assistance in battle,[2] one day while out marching with his troops, he suddenly saw a cross of light written in the noonday sky, and with it the words, "In this sign conquer." The image was visible not only to him but also to his soldiers. The following night, it is claimed, Christ appeared to him in a dream and commanded him to make a copy of the sign to use as his emblem in war. Constantine duly commissioned his craftsmen, who produced a standard consisting of a tall pole and a crossbar adorned with the Chi-Rho motif. It was under this sign of Christ and his cross that Constantine's holy army conquered.[3]

Constantine's open identification with the Christian cause seems clear-cut from around or before the time of his defeat of Maxentius, and writers such as Eusebius consider Constantine to be the leader of a holy war, driven by a mission to establish a model regime based upon Christian principles. Constantine steadily extended his power in the decade after Milan, and by the end of 324, he was sole ruler of the Roman world. Over all these years, both before and after he became sole emperor, he bestowed vast privileges upon the Christians. No longer was Christianity to be a fringe or clandestine movement but rather an entity with express legal rights and social advantages. Legislation was passed granting recognition to the church as a public body and affording its clergy extensive rights and benefits, including exemption from taxation and municipal obligations. The churches received enormous financial largesse and were allowed to inherit legacies from rich individuals. Places of worship destroyed in the persecutions were rebuilt, and huge amounts were spent on the construction of elaborate new churches not only in Rome but much farther afield, in Palestine, Asia Minor, and elsewhere.

In the 320s, Constantine conceived plans for a grand new capital in the East to be built on the ancient site of Byzantium on the Bosphorus and known as "Constantinople." The idea was said to have been granted by divine revelation: Constantinople was supposedly to be a Christian metropolis, undefiled by pagan cults and associations, the center of a new Christian empire. A genuinely splendid city was dedicated with great pomp in 330, though all but one of Constantinople's church buildings were completed after Constantine's death. A new senatorial elite, enticed to the East by various promises of status and wealth, was summoned to worship the "God of Victory" each Sunday and required to listen to the emperor's counsel on religious and moral matters. The dream seemed to reflect Constantine's ambitions for a transformed world.

Nevertheless, there were from the start many ambiguities about Constantine's adoption of Christianity. The military sign mentioned by Lactantius was perhaps an adaptation of an existing Roman cavalry standard. At any rate, the emblem came to be known as the *Labarum*, which may imply that its shape was capable of being associated with the *labrys* or double-axe—a traditional symbol of the cult of Zeus. Other evidence also suggests that Constantine experienced a vision in a similar context but claimed that what he saw was a manifestation of the Sun-god rather than Christ's cross. Certainly his profession of Christian faith did not stop him showing considerable support for aspects of pagan religion. He retained the pagan title of *Pontifex Maximus* and did little if anything to curtail the imperial cult. Although it appears that he came to deplore animal sacrifices in civic contexts (and to favor the appointment of Christian officials who would not perform them), there is no evidence that he discontinued them.

The coins Constantine issued in his early years as emperor included images of *Sol Invictus*, "the Unconquered Sun" (as well as symbols of various other pagan gods), and the still extant triumphal arch later erected in Rome to celebrate his victory over Maxentius also depicts *Sol Invictus* as Constantine's protector, referring simply to "the divinity," unspecified. When in 321 he declared the first day of the week a public holiday (or at least a day when nonessential labor was discouraged and public institutions such as the law-courts could be open only for the charitable purpose of freeing slaves), his stated reason was to respect "the venerable day of the Sun."

If there is any truth in the story of Constantine's vision of the cross in the sky, it is conceivable that he somehow associated the deity who had traditionally served as his personal guardian, the Sun-god, with the identity of the God of the Christians. It was not difficult to align such conventional images with the scriptural idea of Christ as "the sun of righteousness" (Mal. 4:2). Christian preachers had often connected the notion of Christ as the light of salvation with the nature of the sun as the source of human light, and there had long been popular rumors in some quarters that Christians were involved in a version of sun-worship because they met together on Sundays. A mosaic from a late-third- or early-fourth-century tomb found under St. Peter's in Rome expressly depicts Christ as Apollo the Sun-god in his chariot, and Constantine utilized an image of Apollo in a public statue of himself in Constantinople.

Constantine did not receive Christian baptism until his last days, though he had spent many years closely involved in doctrinal and disciplinary affairs of great significance for the future of the Christian cause in both the East and the West. His theological acumen had not been very high, and his attitudes toward the champions of conflicting ideas had changed according to circumstances and advice. By the time of his death in 337, the churches had undergone massive changes in their social, economic, and political fortunes, but he had by no means turned the Roman Empire into a Christian realm, nor had his identification with the faith brought straightforward or uniform advantages for those who professed the name of Jesus.

Persecution and political interference were certainly far from over; indeed, in a number of ways the kinds of political pressure to which the churches were exposed had only broadened and become more complex. Recognition and privilege also meant susceptibility to imperial manipulation, and disputes about doctrine and spirituality were now fought out on a much more conspicuous field where the stakes for winners and losers were higher than ever before. As was already well and truly evident by the early 320s, Constantine's world was a place where differences between believers could be taken to new dimensions. A great age of high-profile theological debate had begun in which orthodoxy could be directly associated with imperial policy and heresy could be seen as an expression of dissent that went beyond the concerns of ecclesiastical discipline.

The exact nature of Constantine's personal faith is in the end enigmatic, and the implications of his actions for the long-term development of the church are likely always to be interpreted in widely differing ways. Some see the age of Constantine as a providential turning point in which the Christian community was blessed with preferential treatment and opportunities that ensured an unprecedented expansion of the gospel. Others consider the process of change that evolved in the early fourth century to be one of the worst disasters ever to befall the Christian faith—a catastrophe that corrupted the church's moral integrity, diluted its spiritual distinctiveness, and rendered its doctrine and practice liable to political influences and cultural fads in ways that would never be undone.

Looking Back

The arguments adduced on both sides of this debate are complex, and a proper evaluation of the evidence would carry us beyond the boundaries of this book. We shall take up these issues in a little greater depth in the subsequent volume in this series. Rather than looking forward and attempting to assess the prospects for Christianity in the wake of Constantine's conversion, it is instructive at this juncture to look back at the journey we have taken in the story so far.

Whatever is to be said about the changes brought about under Constantine, there is no doubt that the followers of Jesus had come a very long way from the assumptions and hopes of the group of believers who had gathered in Jerusalem in the year 30. No one at that time could possibly have supposed that the convictions and dreams of this small band of Jews in an unfashionable part of the Roman Empire would one day have had such an impact upon the world. The story that the crucified Jesus had been raised to life, that he had been vindicated by God and been "made . . . both Lord and Christ" (Acts 2:36), and that God had acted definitively in him for the salvation not only of Jews but of Gentiles as well, had traveled far beyond its original setting in Palestine and far beyond the constituencies to whom Jesus himself had first announced the coming of the kingdom of God.

The message concerning the Jewish Jesus had long outlasted the circumstances of the Palestinian Judaism of Jesus's own time, not least the religious order based around the temple in Jerusalem. It had also made astonishing inroads into the imperial system at its height, the very system that had sentenced Jesus to death and sought to stifle the activities of his most ardent followers. It had won over not just the poor, the humble, and the desperate, but intellectuals, officials, and those at the highest levels of political authority. Devotees of widely differing religious and philosophical assumptions had been persuaded of the truth that Jesus was Lord, and people of all kinds of ethnic and social backgrounds had been prepared to give their lives for this conviction, refusing to subordinate the honor of their Savior to the prerogatives of any earthly potentate.

It is, without doubt, a remarkable story of expansion, transformation, and social change. At the same time, it would be a great mistake to suppose that it had all been easy or to think that the emergent churches had been on a smooth course of onward and upward progress at every stage. The growth of Christianity had been affected by many kinds of struggles and difficulties, and even the high points on the journey had invariably been complicated by ambiguities and the evidences of human failing. The faith had advanced at enormous cost, through blood, toil, sweat, and tears, and the developments that had ensued in the process had sometimes been negative as well as positive. Sometimes those who claimed to speak in Jesus's name had behaved very badly toward one another and toward others. Sometimes the liberating power of the gospel had been tragically eclipsed by agendas of human power, greed, and selfishness. Sometimes sociocultural conventions rather than the logic of holiness and self-denial had dominated believers' attitudes. At other times, the spiritual and otherworldly aspects of the faith had been stressed to the detriment of its physical and temporal dimensions.

The differentiation of the Jesus movement from its roots in Judaism had been a lengthy and painful business, in which equally sincere believers in Jesus differed sharply about the status of the Mosaic Law, about the terms of inclusion for Gentile converts, and about the function of the Jewish Scriptures among the community of the new covenant. There had been enduring arguments among the apostles, their co-workers, and other Christian teachers about what it meant to live a Christian life and about the entailments of showing that one belonged to the people of God. These debates had affected all kinds of areas, from the ways in which Christians narrated the ministry and sufferings of Jesus in the writing of their gospels to the manner in which they came to look upon those who persisted in their attachment to Judaism. The issues had also been sharpened by escalating degrees of antagonism toward Christian believers within Judaism.

In the rhetoric that had surrounded the eventual partings of the ways between the two faiths, it had been all too easy for Christians to forget just how Jewish Jesus himself was and how essentially Jewish "the Way" had remained to an earlier generation—including Paul himself, the most passionate pioneer of mission to the Gentiles. It had been too easy for these Gentiles to forget that they were only "grafted" into the Jewish stock (Rom. 11:11–24) and that it was "Israel," for all its sin and blindness, that had remained the vital focus of God's covenant purposes. Although there had been a deep concern among most Christians to identify the work of Jesus as the fulfillment of Jewish expectations, there had also been mounting difficulty in relating to those of Jewish faith who insisted otherwise. Various positions had been adopted, and the issues had been much affected by political events in Palestine, but undoubtedly there had been a hardening of attitudes toward Jews who persisted in their traditional loyalties. As the perspectives of the first Jewish Christians had been steadily eclipsed, the seeds had been sown for some of the most tragic consequences of later Christian hostility to Judaism.

In the second century, Christian reflection had been much preoccupied with the question of authority and with the specification of a
line of belief and practice that was in continuity with the teaching of
the apostles. This too, as we saw, was not straightforward, for there
was much diversity and there were many challenges to the principle of
a unified tradition, especially from the ideas of those who came to be
known by the generic labels of Gnostics, Marcionites, and Montanists.
The delineation of the parameters of a catholic faith had been a complex and heavily politicized process, and there would always be those
who dissented from the orthodoxy and the patterns of ministry that
emerged, those for whom the claims to consensus and legitimacy were
too narrow, too exclusive, and too authoritarian. Nevertheless, in the
recognition of a fundamental, apostolic tradition, in the exploration of
the status and scope of a body of Christian Scripture over against—yet
in vital continuity with—the Scriptures of Judaism, and in the elaboration of a more formal system of church authority structured around a
particular lineage of official leaders, the believing communities of the
second century had shaped the boundaries of mainstream Christian
thinking and action for the future.

As the churches had grown, Christian convictions had been severely
tested by many different kinds of opposition, ranging from everyday popular
scorn, through the reasoned attacks of pagan intellectuals, to intermittent
outbreaks of organized persecution from the civil authorities. All of these
pressures had been serious, and in their different ways they had challenged
the followers of Jesus about the coherence and integrity of their claims
and about whether they were prepared if necessary to suffer for their faith.
Up to the second half of the third century, the call to face torture or death
was not as common as many Christians today imagine it to have been, but
the sufferings inflicted upon some believers in the occasional bursts of
political repression that did take place were nonetheless appalling.

In their own ways, these troubles had strengthened the Christian witness,
for although there had been many defections from the Christian communities, the courage and resolve of the strongest believers had inspired others
to keep going, and led outsiders to inquire further about the nature of this
faith that seemed to enable people if not to prosper then at least to die
well. The intellectual assaults for their part had stimulated some sophisticated thinking among the most educated believers on the relationship
of Christian ideas and values to the teachings of secular philosophy and
other religious systems. Some of the most seminal works of early Christian
theology from authors such as Justin, Irenaeus, Clement of Alexandria,
Tertullian, and Origen had been produced in climates in which there was

a conscious need for intellectual apologetics or for a reasoned exploration of the inner logic of the gospel. The approaches had varied quite widely, but the underlying motivations had not been so different.

External pressures, however, had not always yielded positive results. The persecutions of the middle years of the third century had generated considerable problems of organization and discipline for the churches, especially in North Africa, in Rome, and in the East. While the statistical impact of the trials on the churches' membership had been relatively limited, their theological and spiritual significance had been great. Christians had had to face up to dealing with a widespread failure of nerve and the implications of large-scale capitulation to the demands of the world. The highly charged debates about the purity of the church and its sacraments, the nature of schism, and the authority of Christian leaders had produced some theological argumentation of enduring importance, but they had also thrown into relief divisions that would not go away. The differences between rigorists and pragmatists and the rivalries between opposing factions in major churches would continue to fester in ugly and intensifying ways long after the original causes of the tensions had passed into history.

The Great Persecution had been the most sustained attack ever launched upon Christians by the Roman authorities, though its effects had been much nastier in the East than in the West. It too would provoke further long-term problems, but if there were any illusions that the repressions might crush the Christian communities once and for all, such ideas proved to be just that—illusions. The ending of the persecution had coincided with the rise of Constantine, the legalization of Christianity, and all the profound changes that we have noted in the churches' social conditions.

At one level, things continued as before. The emergence of an imperial regime that directly favored Christianity did not alter the fundamental character of the gospel or revolutionize the demands of genuine discipleship of Jesus. At another level, however, from the early fourth century onward the air that Christians breathed would never be entirely the same again. In order to understand the extent to which this was so, it is necessary to explore this momentous period in more detail. We must try to assess why things happened as they did and consider their implications for the long-term unfolding of the Christian faith. But that is a subject for another book.

TIME LINE
OF EARLY CHRISTIANITY

The dating of many events, personalities, and texts is highly controversial, especially in the first and early second centuries. The following time-chart assumes approximations in several instances; specialist discussions of chronological questions can be found in some of the literature cited in the Suggestions for Further Reading.

Date	Major Developments
ca. 30	Crucifixion and resurrection of Jesus
30s	Peter, James, John as main leaders in Jerusalem
mid-30s	Martyrdom of Stephen Conversion of Paul
early 40s	Martyrdom of James son of Zebedee Itinerant ministry of the Twelve under way Mission by relatives of Jesus under way in Galilee James emerges as the primary leader in Jerusalem
mid-40s–mid-60s	Missionary work and Epistles of Paul
ca. 49	Council of Jerusalem
early 50s (?)	Epistle of James
60s–70s	Epistles of Hebrews, 1 Peter (?), Jude
62	Martyrdom of James brother of Jesus
64	Fire of Rome and persecution of Christians by Nero Martyrdom of Peter at Rome
ca. 65–68	Martyrdom of Paul at Rome
late 60s (?)	Pastoral Epistles
late 60s–early 80s	Synoptic Gospels

Date	Major Developments
66–73	Jewish war with Rome in Palestine
70	Fall of Jerusalem and destruction of temple
early 80s	Acts of the Apostles
late 80s (?)	Nazarenes cursed in Jewish synagogue prayers
ca. 90	Gospel according to John
early 90s	Emperor Domitian demands worship as a god Persecution of Christians Book of Revelation *1 Clement*
90s	2 Peter and Johannine Epistles
ca. late 90s–110	*Epistle of Barnabas* *Didache*
ca. 100–180	Growth of Gnosticism
ca. 110	Martyrdom of Ignatius of Antioch
ca. 112	Correspondence of Pliny and Trajan
132–135	Bar Kochva revolt in Palestine
ca. 140	*Apology* of Aristides
140s–150s	Marcion active (excommunicated in 144) *Shepherd* of Hermas (?)
150s	Disputes begin about dating of Easter
ca. 151	*First Apology* of Justin
155–156	Martyrdom of Polycarp
late 150s	Justin's *Dialogue with Trypho the Jew*
ca. 160	Tatian's *Diatessaron*
161–180	Persecutions under Marcus Aurelius
early 160s	*Second Apology* of Justin
165	Martyrdom of Justin
late 160s–170s	Growth of the New Prophecy/Montanism Apologetic works by Tatian and Melito
177	Athenagoras's *Plea for the Christians* Massacre of Christians at Lyons
ca. 178	Celsus's attack on Christianity in the *True Discourse*
180	Theophilus's *Apology* to Autolycus Death of Christians at Scillium near Carthage
180s–190s	Pantaenus active as Christian teacher in Alexandria Ministry and writings of Irenaeus of Lyons
ca. 190	Muratorian fragment
190–220	Tertullian's main period of writing in Carthage
190s–ca. 215	Teaching and writing of Clement of Alexandria
199–220s	Quartodeciman dispute and Monarchian controversies
202–203	Persecutions under Septimius Severus Martyrdom of Perpetua and Felicitas in Carthage

Date	Major Developments
ca. 208	Tertullian becomes a convert to Montanism
211–217	Persecutions under Caracalla
ca. 213–early 230s	Hippolytus active in Rome
ca. 215 (?)	*Apostolic Tradition*
ca. 215–early 250s	Teaching and writing of Origen in Alexandria and Caesarea
235–238	Persecutions under Maximin
late 230s	Minucius Felix's *Octavius*
240s–260s	Ministry of Gregory the Wonder-Worker in Cappadocia Influential work of Platonist scholar Plotinus
248	Cyprian becomes bishop of Carthage
249–251	First empire-wide persecutions under Decius Thousands of Christians lapse, complying with orders to sacrifice to the pagan gods
250s	Intensifying disputes between Rome and Carthage over the treatment of the lapsed Writings of Cyprian
251	Novatian and his followers separate from other Christians in Rome
ca. 254	Death of Origen
257–260	Persecutions under Valerian
258	Martyrdom of Cyprian
268	Paul of Samosata deposed as bishop of Antioch for allegedly teaching Monarchian views of Jesus
270s–280s	Intellectual attacks on Christianity by Plotinus's disciple Porphyry
284	Diocletian becomes emperor
293	The tetrarchy of Diocletian and Maximian, Galerius and Constantius formed
303–304	The Great Persecution Arnobius's *Against the Pagans*
304–313	Lactantius works on the *Divine Institutes*
305	Diocletian and Maximian abdicate
306–312	Easing of persecution in West under Constantine and Severus Further oppression in East under Galerius
311	Galerius issues edict of tolerance After Galerius's death, continued persecution under Maximin, especially in Egypt
312	Constantine defeats Maxentius at Milvian Bridge
313	"Edict of Milan" issued by Constantine and Licinius: universal tolerance
324	Constantine becomes sole emperor

SUGGESTIONS FOR FURTHER READING

There is a vast literature on almost everything to do with early Christianity, and numerous catalogs and indexes record a flood of annual additions to this bibliography. Material of many kinds influenced the writing of this book; the following suggestions are only a small selection of pointers for readers who would like to pursue particular topics in more depth. The list is restricted to literature available in English, though very extensive resources are to be found in other languages, especially in French, German, and Italian. The selection is also confined to book-length studies, though an enormous amount of journal articles exist on all topics, and vital discussions often take place in this context. The list reflects a wide range of historical and theological perspectives and is not necessarily representative of the interpretations offered in this book.

Sources

1. New Testament

Consult established major commentary series such as the *International Critical Commentary* (Edinburgh: T. & T. Clark), *Black's New Testament Commentary* (London: A. & C. Black), *New International Commentary on the New Testament* (Grand Rapids: Eerdmans), *Word Biblical Commentary* (Waco: Word Books), and *Baker Exegetical Commentary on the New Testament* (Grand Rapids: Baker), or the emerging *New Cambridge Bible Commentary* (Cambridge: Cambridge University Press). Early

Christian treatment of biblical texts can be studied in the valuable new series, Ancient Christian Commentary on Scripture (Downers Grove, IL: InterVarsity Press). Several other series focus on the application of New Testament texts to contemporary Christian life; a new project, the *Two Horizons Commentary* (Grand Rapids: Eerdmans), is endeavoring to consider the significance of biblical material for today in constructive dialogue with the disciplines of modern theology.

A great many surveys of New Testament literature and its context exist. By way of two recent examples:

Achtemeier, P. J., J. B. Green, and M. Meye Thompson. *Introducing the New Testament: Its Literature and Theology.* Grand Rapids and Cambridge, England: Eerdmans, 2001.

Burkett, D. *An Introduction to the New Testament and the Origins of Christianity.* Cambridge: Cambridge University Press, 2002.

At a more introductory level:

Exploring the New Testament. Vol. 1: *A Guide to the Gospels and Acts.* Edited by D. Wenham and S. Walton. Vol. 2: *A Guide to the Letters and Revelation.* Edited by I. H. Marshall, S. Travis, and I. Paul. Downers Grove, IL: InterVarsity Press, 2001–2002.

See also reference works below for dictionaries of New Testament material.

2. Other Texts

Dead Sea Scrolls

Barthélemy, J., J. T. Milik, et al., eds. *Discoveries in the Judaean Desert.* Oxford: Oxford University Press, 1955–.

Garcia Martínez, F. *The Dead Sea Scrolls Translated: The Qumran Texts in English.* 2nd ed. Translated by W. G. E. Watson. Leiden, Netherlands: E. J. Brill; Grand Rapids: Eerdmans, 1996.

Vermes, G., *The Complete Dead Sea Scrolls in English.* New York and London: Allen Lane/Penguin Press, 1997.

New Testament Apocrypha

Elliott, J. K., ed. *The Apocryphal New Testament.* Oxford: Oxford University Press, 1993.

Schneemelcher, W., ed. *New Testament Apocrypha*. 2 vols. Edited and translated by R. McL. Wilson. Louisville: Westminster/John Knox Press; Cambridge, England: James Clarke, 1991–1992.

Gnostic Scriptures

Bentley, L. *The Gnostic Scriptures: A New Translation with Annotations and Introductions*. Garden City, NY: Doubleday, 1987.

Robinson, J. M., ed. *The Nag Hammadi Library in English*. Rev. ed. San Francisco: Harper and Row, 1988.

3. Ancient Christian Authors

Various English-translation series exist for ancient Christian authors. Among the most important are:

Ancient Christian Writers. Edited by J. Quasten and J. C. Plumpe. Westminster, MD, and New York: Newman Press, 1946–.

Ante-Nicene Christian Library. Edited by A. Roberts and J. Donaldson. Edinburgh: T. & T. Clark, 1867–1872; New York: Christian Literature Co., 1897.

The Fathers of the Church. Washington, DC: Catholic University of America Press, 1946–.

Library of Christian Classics. Edited by J. Baillie, J. T. McNeill, and H. P. van Dusen. Philadelphia: Westminster; London: SCM, 1953–69.

The Library of Early Christianity. Washington, DC: Catholic University of America Press, 2002–.

Oxford Early Christian Texts. Edited by H. Chadwick. Oxford: Oxford University Press, 1970–.

The Oxford Library of the Fathers. Edited by M. Dods. Edinburgh: T. & T. Clark; New York: Eerdmans, 1838–1881.

A Select Library of Nicene and Post-Nicene Fathers of the Christian Church. Edited by P. Schaff and H. Wace. Reprint. Grand Rapids: Eerdmans, 1975.

The Apostolic Fathers

Holmes, M. W., ed. *The Apostolic Fathers: Greek Texts and English Translations* (Grand Rapids: Baker, 1999), updated edition of the translation by J. B. Lightfoot and J. R. Harmer.

Other Authors

Texts and English translations of such authors as Josephus, Philo, Pliny, Tacitus, Suetonius, Dio Cassius, and Eusebius can be found in the Loeb Classical Library series (Cambridge: Harvard University Press; London: Heinemann, 1912–).

4. Useful Anthologies

Bettenson, H., ed. *The Early Christian Fathers*. Oxford: Oxford University Press, 1969.

Jurgens, W., ed. *The Faith of the Early Fathers*. Collegeville, MN: Liturgical Press, 1998.

Stevenson, J., ed. *A New Eusebius: Documents Illustrating the History of the Church to AD 337*. Rev. ed. by W. H. C. Frend. London: SPCK, 1987.

Wiles, M., and M. Santer, eds. *Documents in Early Christian Thought*. Cambridge: Cambridge University Press, 1975.

Valuable collections of texts on a variety of doctrinal, social, and moral themes, accompanied by introductory essays, can be found in the following series:

Message of the Fathers of the Church. Wilmington, DE: Michael Glazier; Collegeville, MN: Liturgical Press, 1983–.

Very useful material can also be found in:

Ferguson, E., ed. *Early Christians Speak: Faith and Life in the First Three Centuries*. 2 vols. to date. Abilene, TX: Abilene Christian University Press, 1999–2002.

5. On the Role of Archaeological Resources

Frend, W. H. C. *The Archaeology of Early Christianity: A History*. London: Geoffrey Chapman; Minneapolis: Fortress Press, 1996.

Snyder, G. F. *Ante Pacem: Archaeological Evidence of Church Life before Constantine*. Macon, GA: Mercer University Press, 1985.

6. On Legal Texts

Coleman-Norton, P. R. *Roman State and Christian Church: A Collection of Legal Documents to AD 535.* 3 vols. London: SPCK, 1966.

Reference Works

Ackroyd, P. R., and C. F. Evans, eds. *The Cambridge History of the Bible.* Vol. 1: *From the Beginnings to Jerome.* Cambridge: Cambridge University Press, 1970.

Altaner, B. *Patrology.* 6th ed. translated by H. C. Graef. Freiburg, Germany: Herder; Edinburgh and London: Nelson, 1960.

Armstrong, A. H., ed. *The Cambridge History of Later Greek and Early Medieval Philosophy.* Cambridge: Cambridge University Press, 1967.

di Berardino, A., ed., with bibliographies by W. H. C. Frend. *Encyclopaedia of the Early Church.* 2 vols. Cambridge, England: James Clarke, 1992.

Chadwick, H., and G. R. Evans, eds. *Atlas of the Christian Church.* London: Guild Publishing, 1987.

Cross, F. L., ed. 3rd ed. revised by E. A. Livingstone. *The Oxford Dictionary of the Christian Church.* Oxford: Oxford University Press, 1997.

Evans, C. A., and S. E. Porter, eds. *Dictionary of New Testament Background.* Leicester, England, and Downers Grove, IL: InterVarsity Press, 2000.

Ferguson, E. *Backgrounds of Early Christianity.* 3rd ed. Grand Rapids: Eerdmans, 2003.

————, ed. *Encyclopaedia of Early Christianity.* Rev. ed., 2 vols. New York: Garland, 1997.

Green, J. B., S. McKnight, and I. H. Marshall, eds. *Dictionary of Jesus and the Gospels.* Leicester, England, and Downers Grove, IL: InterVarsity Press, 1992.

Hawthorne, G. F., R. P. Martin, and D. G. Reid, eds. *Dictionary of Paul and His Letters.* Leicester, England, and Downers Grove, IL: InterVarsity Press, 1993.

Hornblower, S., and A. Spawforth, eds. *The Oxford Classical Dictionary.* 3rd ed. Oxford: Oxford University Press, 1996.

Kelly, J. F., ed. *The Concise Dictionary of Early Christianity.* Collegeville, MN: Liturgical Press/Michael Glazier, 1992.

Kelly, J. N. D. *The Oxford Dictionary of Popes.* Oxford: Oxford University Press, 1986.

Martin, R. P., and P. H. Davids, eds. *Dictionary of the Later New Testament and Its Developments.* Leicester, England, and Downers Grove, IL: InterVarsity Press, 1997.

Quasten, J. *Patrology.* 3 vols. Utrecht, the Netherlands, and Antwerp, Belgium: Spectrum; Westminster, MD: Newman Press, 1962–64. Supplemented by 3 further vols. by A. di Berardino. 1978–2001.

van der Meer, F. N. S., and C. Mohrmann, eds. *The Atlas of the Early Christian World.* Translated by M. Hedlund and H. H. Rowley. London: Nelson, 1958.

Other Historical Guides

Introductory

Brox, N. *A History of the Early Church.* Translated by J. Bowden. London: SCM Press, 1994.

Chadwick, H. *The Early Church.* Harmondsworth, England: Penguin, 1967.

Frend, W. H. C. *The Early Church.* Reprint. London: SCM Press, 1982.

Grant, R. M. *Augustus to Constantine: The Thrust of the Christian Movement into the Roman World.* New York: Harper and Row, 1970.

Hazlett, I., ed. *Early Christianity: Origins and Evolution to A.D. 600.* London: SPCK, 1991.

Hinson, G. *The Early Church.* Nashville: Abingdon Press, 1996.

Lietzmann, H. *A History of the Early Church.* Parts 1–2, vol. 1. Translated by B. L. Woolf. Foreword and bibliography by W. H. C. Frend. Cambridge, England: James Clarke, 1993.

McKechnie, P. *The First Christian Centuries: Perspectives on the Early Church.* Downers Grove, IL: InterVarsity Press, 2001.

Markschies, C. *Between Two Worlds: Structures of Earliest Christianity.* Translated by J. Bowden. London: SCM Press, 1999.

Patzia, A. G. *The Emergence of the Church: Context, Growth, Leadership and Worship.* Downers Grove, IL: InterVarsity Press, 2001.

Rousseau, P. *The Early Christian Centuries.* London: Darton, Longman and Todd, 2002.

Trocmé, E. *The Childhood of Christianity.* Translated by J. Bowden. London: SCM Press, 1997.

More Advanced

Chadwick, H. *The Church in Ancient Society: From Galilee to Gregory the Great.* Oxford History of the Christian Church. Oxford: Oxford University Press, 2001.

Esler, P. F., ed. *The Early Christian World.* 2 vols. London and New York: Routledge, 2000.

Frend, W. H. C. *The Rise of Christianity.* London: Darton, Longman and Todd; Philadelphia: Fortress Press, 1984.

On Ideas, Doctrine, and Practice

Daley, B. E. *The Hope of the Early Church: A Handbook of Patristic Eschatology.* Cambridge: Cambridge University Press, 1991.

Daniélou, J. *A History of Early Christian Doctrine before the Council of Nicaea.* 3 vols. Translated by J. A. Baker and D. Smith. London: Darton, Longman and Todd; Philadelphia: Westminster, 1964–1977.

Evans, G. R., ed. *The First Christian Theologians: An Introduction to Theology in the Early Church.* Oxford and Malden, MA: Blackwell, 2004.

Grillmeier, A. *Christ in Christian Tradition.* Vol. 1: *From the Apostolic Age to Chalcedon (A.D. 451).* Rev. ed. translated by J. Bowden. London and Oxford: Mowbrays, 1975.

Hall, C. A. *Reading Scripture with the Church Fathers.* Downers Grove, IL: InterVarsity Press, 1998.

———, *Learning Theology with the Church Fathers.* Downers Grove, IL: InterVarsity Press, 2002.

Hall, S. G. *Doctrine and Practice in the Early Church.* London: SPCK, 1991.

Kelly, J. N. D. *Early Christian Creeds.* 3rd ed. London: Longman, 1972.

———. *Early Christian Doctrines.* 5th ed. London: A. & C. Black, 1977.

Pelikan, J. *The Christian Tradition: A History of the Development of Doctrine.* Vol. 1: *The Emergence of the Catholic Tradition (100–600).* Chicago and London: Chicago University Press, 1971.

Prestige, G. L. *God in Patristic Thought.* 2nd ed. London: SPCK, 1952.

Wilken, R. *The Spirit of Early Christian Thought: Seeking the Face of God.* New Haven and London: Yale University Press, 2003.

In the Beginning

Bockmuehl, M. *This Jesus: Martyr, Lord, Messiah*. Edinburgh: T. & T. Clark, 1994.

──────, ed. *The Cambridge Companion to Jesus*. Cambridge: Cambridge University Press, 2001.

Carroll, J. T., and J. B. Green, eds. *The Death of Jesus in Early Christianity*. Peabody, MA: Hendrickson, 1995.

Davis, S. T., D. Kendall, and G. O'Collins, eds. *The Resurrection: An Interdisciplinary Symposium on the Resurrection of Jesus*. Oxford: Oxford University Press, 1997.

Hengel, M. *The Cross of the Son of God*. Translated by J. Bowden. London: SCM Press, 1986.

Marshall, I. H. *The Origins of New Testament Christology*. Rev. ed. Leicester, England: Apollos, 1990.

O'Collins, G. *Christology: A Biblical, Historical, and Systematic Study of Jesus*. Oxford: Oxford University Press, 1995.

Sanders, E. P. *The Historical Figure of Jesus*. Harmondsworth, England: Allen Lane/Penguin, 1993.

Wright, N. T. *The New Testament and the People of God*. Minneapolis: Fortress Press, 1992.

──────. *Jesus and the Victory of God*. London: SPCK; Minneapolis: Augsburg Fortress Press, 1996.

──────. *The Resurrection of the Son of God*. Minneapolis: Augsburg Fortress Press, 2003.

Chapter 1

Expert treatments of a number of the themes touched upon in this chapter can be found in series such as the *Cambridge Ancient History* and the *Cambridge History of Judaism* (Cambridge: Cambridge University Press). Other helpful resources include:

Barclay, J. M. G. *Jews in the Mediterranean Diaspora: From Alexander to Trajan (323 BCE–117 CE)*. Edinburgh: T. & T. Clark, 1996.

Barnes, J. *Aristotle*. Oxford: Oxford University Press, 1982.

Boardman, J., J. Griffin, and O. Murray, eds. *The Roman World*. Oxford and New York: Oxford University Press, 1988.

Dillon, J. *The Middle Platonists: A Study in Platonism 80 BC–AD 220.* London: Duckworth, 1977.

Fitzmyer, J. A. *The Dead Sea Scrolls and Christian Origins.* Grand Rapids: Eerdmans, 2000.

Freyne, S. *Galilee from Alexander the Great to Hadrian, 323 BCE to 135 CE: A Study of Second Temple Judaism.* Edinburgh: T. & T. Clark, 1998.

Garnsey, P., and R. P. Saller. *The Roman Empire: Economy, Society and Culture.* London: Duckworth, 1987.

Goodman, M. *The Roman World, 44 BC–AD 180.* London and New York: Routledge, 1997.

Grant, R. M. *Gods and the One God: Christian Theology in the Graeco-Roman World.* London: SPCK, 1986.

Hare, R. M. *Plato.* Oxford: Oxford University Press, 1982.

Hayes, J., and S. Mandell. *The Jewish People in Classical Antiquity: From Alexander to Bar Kochba.* Louisville: Westminster/John Knox Press, 1998.

Inwood, B., ed. *The Cambridge Companion to the Stoics.* Cambridge: Cambridge University Press, 2003.

Jones, A. H. M. *The Later Roman Empire, 284–602: A Social, Economic, and Administrative Survey.* 3 vols. and maps. Oxford: Blackwell, 1964.

Keppie, L. J. F. *The Making of the Roman Army: From Republic to Empire.* London: Batsford, 1987.

Klauck, H.-J. *The Religious Context of Early Christianity: A Guide to Graeco-Roman Religions.* Translated by B. McNeill. Edinburgh: T. & T. Clark, 2000.

Lim, T., et al., eds. *The Dead Sea Scrolls in their Historical Contexts.* Edinburgh: T. & T. Clark, 2000.

Long, A. A. *Hellenistic Philosophy: Stoics, Epicureans, Sceptics.* 2nd ed. Berkeley and Los Angeles: University of California Press, 1986.

MacMullen, R. *Roman Social Relations, 50 BC–AD 284.* New Haven: Yale University Press, 1974.

Martin, L. H. *Hellenistic Religions: An Introduction.* New York: Oxford University Press, 1987.

Millar, F. G. B. *The Emperor in the Roman World (31 BC–AD 337).* London: Duckworth, 1977.

Novak, R. M. *Christianity and the Roman Empire: Background Texts.* Harrisburg, PA: Trinity Press International, 2001.

Rist, J. M. *Stoic Philosophy.* Cambridge: Cambridge University Press, 1969.

Saldarini, A. J. *Pharisees, Scribes and Sadducees in Palestinian Society: A Sociological Approach*. Rev. ed. Grand Rapids: Eerdmans, 2001.

Sanders, E. P. *Judaism: Practice and Belief 63 BCE–63 CE*. London: SCM Press, 1992.

Schürer, E. *The History of the Jewish People in the Age of Jesus Christ*. 4 vols. Rev. ed. translated by G. Vermes, F. Millar, and M. Black. Edinburgh: T. & T. Clark, 1973–1984.

Turcan, R. *The Cults of the Roman Empire*. Translated by A. Nevill. Oxford and Malden, MA: Blackwell, 1997.

Chapter 2

Much of the most useful work on this period is to be gleaned from commentaries on Paul's letters and on the Acts of the Apostles. The following are also valuable:

Barnett, P. *Jesus and the Rise of Early Christianity: A History of New Testament Times*. Downers Grove, IL: InterVarsity Press, 1999.

Culpepper, R. A. *John, the Son of Zebedee: The Life of a Legend*. Columbia, SC: University of South Carolina Press, 1994.

Esler, P. F. *Community and Gospel in Luke-Acts: The Social and Political Motivations of Lucan Theology*. Cambridge: Cambridge University Press, 1987.

Green, M. *Evangelism in the Early Church*. London: Hodder and Stoughton, 1970.

Hengel, M. *Between Jesus and Paul: Studies in the Earliest History of Christianity*. Translated by J. Bowden. London: SCM Press, 1983.

Hill, C. C. *Hellenists and Hebrews: Reappraising Division within the Earliest Church*. Minneapolis: Fortress Press, 1992.

Kee, H. C. *Christian Origins in Sociological Perspective*. London: SCM Press, 1980.

Perkins, P. *Peter: Apostle for the Whole Church*. Columbia, SC: University of South Carolina Press, 1994.

Theissen, G. *The First Followers of Jesus: A Sociological Analysis of the Earliest Christianity*. Translated by J. Bowden. London: SCM Press, 1978.

Winter, B. W., et al., eds. *The Book of Acts in Its First-Century Setting*. 5 vols. to date. Grand Rapids: Eerdmans; Carlisle, England: Paternoster Press, 1993.

Witherington III, B. *New Testament History: A Narrative Account.* Grand Rapids: Baker; Carlisle, England: Paternoster Press, 2001.

Wright, N. T. *The New Testament and the People of God.* Minneapolis: Fortress Press, 1992.

Zetterholm, M. *The Formation of Christianity in Antioch.* London and New York: Routledge, 2003.

Chapter 3

Much of the best literature consists of commentaries and specialist monographs on Paul's letters. The following works present a wide range of perspectives on the context and motivations of Paul the man and Paul the theologian:

Barclay, J. M. G. *Obeying the Truth: Paul's Ethics in Galatians.* Edinburgh: T. & T. Clark, 1988.

Barrett, C. K. *Paul: An Introduction to His Thought.* London: Geoffrey Chapman, 1994.

Boyarin, D. *A Radical Jew: Paul and the Politics of Identity.* Berkeley and Los Angeles: University of California Press, 1994.

Bruce, F. F. *Paul: Apostle of the Free Spirit.* Rev. ed. Exeter, England: Paternoster Press, 1980.

Dunn, J. D. G. *The Theology of Paul the Apostle.* Grand Rapids: Eerdmans, 1998.

———, ed. *The Cambridge Companion to St. Paul.* Cambridge: Cambridge University Press, 2003.

Fee, G. D. *God's Empowering Presence: The Holy Spirit in the Letters of Paul.* Peabody, MA: Hendrickson, 1994.

Gorman, M. J. *Paul's Narrative Spirituality of the Cross.* Grand Rapids: Eerdmans, 2001.

Hays, R. B. *Echoes of Scripture in the Letters of Paul.* New Haven and London: Yale University Press, 1989.

Horrell, D. *The Social Ethos of the Corinthian Correspondence: Interests and Ideology from 1 Corinthians to 1 Clement.* Edinburgh: T. & T. Clark, 1996.

Horsley, R. A., ed. *Paul and Empire: Religion and Power in Roman Imperial Society,* Harrisburg, PA: Trinity Press International, 1997.

Kim, S. *Paul and the New Perspective: Second Thoughts on the Origin of Paul's Gospel.* Grand Rapids: Eerdmans, 2002.

Meeks, W. *The First Urban Christians: The Social World of the Apostle Paul.* New Haven and London: Yale University Press, 1983.

Murphy-O'Connor, J. *Paul: A Critical Life.* Oxford: Oxford University Press, 1996.

Oakes, P., ed. *Rome in the Bible and the Early Church.* Carlisle, England: Paternoster Press; Grand Rapids: Baker, 2002.

Roetzel, C. J. *Paul: The Man and the Myth.* Columbia, SC: University of South Carolina Press, 1998.

Sanders, E. P. *Paul and Palestinian Judaism.* London: SCM Press, 1977.

———. *Paul.* Oxford: Oxford University Press, 1991.

Wenham, D. *Paul: Follower of Jesus or Founder of Christianity?* Grand Rapids: Eerdmans, 1995.

Witherington III, B. *The Paul Quest: The Renewed Search for the Jew of Tarsus.* Leicester, England, and Downers Grove, IL: InterVarsity Press, 1998.

Wright, N. T. *The Climax of the Covenant: Christ and the Law in Pauline Theology.* Edinburgh: T. & T. Clark, 1991.

———. *What St. Paul Really Said.* Oxford: Lion; Grand Rapids: Eerdmans, 1997.

Ziesler, J. A. *Pauline Christianity.* 2nd ed. Oxford: Oxford University Press, 1990.

Chapter 4

Aune, D. E. *Prophecy in Early Christianity and the Ancient Mediterranean World.* Grand Rapids: Eerdmans, 1983.

Barrett, C. K. *Church, Ministry and Sacraments in the New Testament.* Carlisle, England: Paternoster Press, 1985.

Bauckham, R. *God Crucified: Monotheism and Christology in the New Testament.* Carlisle, England: Paternoster Press, 1998.

Beasley-Murray, G. R. *Baptism in the New Testament.* London: Macmillan, 1962.

Bradshaw, P. *Early Christian Worship: A Basic Introduction to Ideas and Practice.* London: SPCK, 1996.

Campbell, R. A. *The Elders: Seniority within Earliest Christianity.* Edinburgh: T. & T. Clark, 1994.

Ferguson, E., ed. *Christianity and Society: The Social World of Early Christianity.* New York: Garland, 1999.

Finn, T. M. *From Death to Rebirth: Ritual and Conversion in Antiquity.* Mahwah, NJ: Paulist Press, 1997.

France, R. T. *Women in the Church's Ministry: A Test-Case for Biblical Hermeneutics.* Carlisle, England: Paternoster Press, 1995.

Grant, R. M. *Early Christianity and Society.* San Francisco: Harper and Row, 1977.

Hartman, L. *"Into the Name of the Lord Jesus": Baptism in the Early Church.* Edinburgh: T. & T. Clark, 1997.

Hays, R. B. *The Moral Vision of the New Testament: Community, Cross, New Creation: A Contemporary Introduction to New Testament Ethics.* San Francisco: Harper San Francisco, 1996.

Hellermann, J. H. *The Ancient Church as Family.* Minneapolis: Fortress Press, 2001.

Hurtado, L. W. *One God, One Lord: Early Christian Devotion and Ancient Jewish Monotheism.* 2nd ed. Edinburgh: T. & T. Clark, 1998.

————. *At the Origins of Christian Worship: The Context and Character of Earliest Christian Devotion.* Grand Rapids and Cambridge, England: Eerdmans, 2000.

————. *Lord Jesus Christ: Devotion to Jesus in Earliest Christianity.* Grand Rapids and Cambridge, England: Eerdmans, 2003.

Kodell, J. *The Eucharist in the New Testament.* Wilmington, DE: Michael Glazier, 1988.

Malherbe, A. *Social Aspects of Early Christianity.* Philadelphia: Fortress Press, 1983.

Malina, B. *The New Testament World: Insights from Cultural Anthropology.* Louisville: Westminster/John Knox Press, 1993.

Martin, R. P. *Worship in the Early Church.* Reprint. Grand Rapids: Eerdmans, 1964.

Matera, F. *New Testament Ethics: The Legacies of Jesus and Paul.* Louisville: Westminster/John Knox Press, 1996.

McDonald, J. I. H. *The Crucible of Christian Morality.* London and New York: Routledge, 1998.

Meeks, W. *The First Urban Christians: The Social World of the Apostle Paul.* New Haven and London: Yale University Press, 1983.

Minear, P. *Images of the Church in the New Testament.* Philadelphia: Westminster Press, 1960.

Nock, A. D. *Conversion: The Old and the New in Religion from Alexander to Augustine of Hippo.* Oxford: Oxford University Press, 1933.

Osiek, C., and D. Balch, eds. *Families in the New Testament World: Households and House Churches.* Louisville: Westminster/John Knox Press, 1997.

Patzia, A. G. *The Emergence of the Church: Context, Growth, Leadership and Worship.* Downers Grove, IL: InterVarsity Press, 2001.

Stark, R. *The Rise of Christianity: A Sociologist Reconsiders History.* Princeton, NJ: Princeton University Press, 1996.

Witherington III, B. *Women in the Earliest Churches.* Cambridge: Cambridge University Press, 1988.

Young, F. *The Theology of the Pastoral Letters.* Cambridge: Cambridge University Press, 1994.

Chapter 5

Barton, S. C. *The Spirituality of the Gospels.* London: SPCK, 1992.

Bauckham, R. J. *Jude and the Relatives of Jesus in the Early Church.* Edinburgh: T. & T. Clark, 1990.

———. *James: Wisdom of James, Disciple of Jesus the Sage.* London and New York: Routledge, 1999.

———, ed. *The Gospels for all Christians: Rethinking the Gospel Audiences.* Edinburgh: T. & T. Clark, 1998.

Blomberg, C. *Jesus and the Gospels: An Introduction and Survey.* Leicester, England: Apollos; Nashville: Broadman and Holman, 1997.

Burridge, R. A. *What Are the Gospels? A Comparison with Graeco-Roman Biography.* Cambridge: Cambridge University Press, 1992.

———. *Four Gospels, One Jesus? A Symbolic Reading.* London: SPCK, 1994.

Chilton, B., and J. Neusner, eds. *The Brother of Jesus: James the Just and His Mission.* Louisville: Westminster/John Knox Press, 2001.

Dunn, J. D. G. *The Partings of the Ways: Between Christianity and Judaism and Their Significance for the Character of Christianity.* London: SCM Press, 1991.

———. *Jesus Remembered: Christianity in the Making.* Vol. 1 to date of projected 3–vol. series. Grand Rapids: Eerdmans, 2003.

Hengel, M. *The Four Gospels and the One Gospel of Jesus Christ.* Translated by J. Bowden. London: SCM Press, 2000.

Horbury, W. *Jews and Christians in Contact and Controversy.* Edinburgh: T. & T. Clark, 1998.

Klijn, A. F. J., and G. J. Reinink, *Patristic Evidence for Jewish-Christian Sects*. Leiden, Netherlands: E. J. Brill, 1973.

Lieu, J. M. *Image and Reality: The Jews in the World of the Christians in the Second Century*. Edinburgh: T. & T. Clark, 1996.

———. *Neither Jew nor Greek? Constructing Early Christianity*. Edinburgh: T. & T. Clark, 2002.

Painter, J. *Just James: The Brother of Jesus in History and Tradition*. Minneapolis: Fortress Press, 1999.

Stanton, G. N. *The Gospels and Jesus*. Oxford: Oxford University Press, 1989.

Tugwell, S. *The Apostolic Fathers*. London: Geoffrey Chapman, 1989.

Wilson, S. *Related Strangers: Jews and Christians, 70–170 CE*. Minneapolis: Augsburg Fortress Press, 1996.

Chapter 6

Bauer, W. *Orthodoxy and Heresy in Earliest Christianity*. Translated by R. A. Kraft and G. Krodel. Philadelphia: Fortress Press, 1971.

Blackman, E. C. *Marcion and His Influence*. London: SPCK, 1948.

Bruce, F. F. *The Canon of Scripture*. Glasgow, Scotland: Chapter House, 1988.

Dunn, J. D. G. *Unity and Diversity in the New Testament: An Inquiry into the Character of Earliest Christianity*. London: SCM Press, 1977.

Evans, G. R. *A Brief History of Heresy*. Oxford and Malden, MA: Blackwell, 2003.

Frend, W. H. C. *Saints and Sinners in the Early Church*. London: Darton, Longman and Todd, 1985.

Hanson, R. P. C. *Tradition in the Early Church*. London: SCM Press, 1962.

Hoffmann, R. J. *Marcion on the Restitution of Christianity: An Essay on the Development of Radical Paulinist Theology in the Second Century*. Chico, CA: Scholars Press, 1984.

Hultgren, A. J. *The Rise of Normative Christianity*. Minneapolis: Fortress Press, 1997.

Kelly, J. N. D. *Early Christian Creeds*. 3rd ed. London: Longman, 1972.

Logan, A. H. B. *Gnostic Truth and Christian Heresy: A Study in the History of Gnosticism*. Edinburgh: T. & T. Clark, 1996.

Lüdemann, G. *Heretics: The Other Side of Early Christianity*. Translated by J. Bowden. Louisville: Westminster/John Knox Press, 1996.

Markschies, C. *Gnosis*. Translated by J. Bowden. Edinburgh: T. & T. Clark, 2003.

Metzger, B. M. *The Canon of the New Testament: Its Origin, Development and Significance*. New York: Oxford University Press, 1987.

Rudolph, K. *Gnosis: The Nature and History of Gnosticism*. Translated by R. Wilson. Edinburgh: T. & T. Clark, 1983.

Tabbernee, W. *Montanist Inscriptions and Testimonia: Epigraphic Sources Illustrating the History of Montanism*. Macon, GA: Mercer University Press, 1997.

Trevett, C. *Montanism: Gender, Authority and the New Prophecy*. Cambridge: Cambridge University Press, 1996.

Turner, H. E. W. *The Pattern of Christian Truth: A Study in the Relations between Orthodoxy and Heresy in the Early Church*. London: Mowbrays, 1954.

Williams, M. A. *Rethinking "Gnosticism."* Princeton, NJ: Princeton University Press, 1996.

Young, F. M. *The Making of the Creeds*. London: SCM Press, 1991.

Chapter 7

Barnard, L. W. *Justin Martyr: His Life and Thought*. Cambridge: Cambridge University Press, 1967.

Bauckham, R. J. *The Theology of the Book of Revelation*. Cambridge: Cambridge University Press, 1993.

Benko, S. *Pagan Rome and the Early Christians*. London: Batsford, 1984.

Bowersock, G. W. *Martyrdom and Rome*. Cambridge: Cambridge University Press, 1995.

Brown, P. R. L. *The Cult of the Saints: Its Rise and Function in Latin Christianity*. London: SCM Press, 1981.

Chadwick, H. *Early Christian Thought and the Classical Tradition: Studies in Justin, Clement, and Origen*. Oxford: Oxford University Press, 1966.

Edwards, M., M. Goodman, and S. Price, eds. *Apologetics in the Roman Empire*. Oxford: Oxford University Press, 1999.

Frend, W. H. C. *Martyrdom and Persecution in the Early Church*. Oxford: Blackwell, 1965.

Grant, R. M. *Greek Apologists of the Second Century*. London: SCM Press, 1988.

Hargis, J. W. *Against the Christians: The Rise of Early Anti-Christian Polemic.* New York: Peter Lang, 1999.

Hemer, C. J. *The Letters to the Seven Churches of Asia in their Local Setting.* Sheffield, England: Sheffield Academic Press, 1986.

Hoffmann. R. J., ed. *Celsus on the True Doctrine: A Discourse against the Christians.* New York: Oxford University Press, 1987.

Lane Fox, R. *Pagans and Christians.* Harmondsworth, England: Viking Press, 1986.

Osborn, E. F. *Justin Martyr.* Tübingen, Germany: J. C. B. Mohr [Paul Siebeck], 1973.

———. *The Emergence of Christian Theology.* Cambridge: Cambridge University Press, 1993.

Perkins, J. *The Suffering Self: Pain and Narrative Representation in the Early Christian Era.* London: Routledge, 1995.

Salisbury, J. E. *Perpetua's Passion: The Death and Memory of a Young Roman Woman.* New York: Routledge, 1997.

Skarsaune, O. *The Proof from Prophecy: A Study in Justin Martyr's Proof-Text Tradition: Text-Type, Provenance, Theological Profile.* Leiden, Netherlands: E. J. Brill, 1987.

Sordi, M. *The Christians and the Roman Empire.* Translated by A. Bedini. London and Bologna, Italy: Cappelli, 1983.

Thompson, L. L. *The Book of Revelation: Apocalypse and Empire.* Oxford: Oxford University Press, 1997.

Wagner, W. H. *After the Apostles: Christianity in the Second Century.* Minneapolis: Fortress Press, 1994.

Wilken, R. L. *The Christians as the Romans Saw Them.* New Haven and London: Yale University Press, 1984.

Winter, B. W. *Seek the Welfare of the City: Christians as Benefactors and Citizens.* Carlisle, England: Paternoster Press; Grand Rapids: Eerdmans, 1994.

Chapter 8

Barnes, T. D. *Tertullian, a Historical and Literary Study.* Rev. ed. Oxford: Oxford University Press, 1985.

Behr, J. *Asceticism and Anthropology in Irenaeus and Clement.* Oxford: Oxford University Press, 2000.

Bray, G. L. *Holiness and the Will of God: Perspectives on the Theology of Tertullian.* London: Marshall, Morgan and Scott, 1979.

Brent, A. *Hippolytus and the Roman Church in the Third Century: Communities in Tension before the Emergence of a Monarch-Bishop.* Leiden, Netherlands: E. J. Brill, 1995.

Clarke, G. W., ed. and trans. *The Octavius of Marcus Minucius Felix.* Ancient Christian Writers series. New York: Newman Press, 1974.

Grant, R. M. *Irenaeus of Lyons.* London and New York: Routledge, 1997.

Lampe, P. *The Christians of Rome in the First Two Centuries.* Translated by L. Holland and M. Steinhauser. London: Burns and Oates, 2000.

Lawson, J. *The Biblical Theology of Saint Irenaeus.* London: Epworth Press, 1948.

MacKenzie, I. M. *Irenaeus' Demonstration of the Apostolic Preaching: A Theological Commentary and Translation.* Aldershot, England: Ashgate, 2002.

Minns, D. *Irenaeus.* London: Geoffrey Chapman, 1994.

Osborn, E. F. *Tertullian: First Theologian of the West.* Cambridge: Cambridge University Press, 1997.

Rankin, D. *Tertullian and the Church.* Cambridge: Cambridge University Press, 1995.

Raven, S. *Rome in Africa.* 3rd ed. London and New York: Routledge, 1993.

Wingren, G. *Man and the Incarnation: A Study in the Biblical Theology of Irenaeus.* Translated by R. Mackenzie. Edinburgh and London: Oliver & Boyd, 1959.

Chapter 9

Behr, J. *Asceticism and Anthropology in Irenaeus and Clement.* Oxford: Oxford University Press, 2000.

Chadwick, H. *Early Christian Thought and the Classical Tradition: Studies in Justin, Clement, and Origen.* Oxford: Oxford University Press, 1966.

———, ed. and trans. *Origen: Contra Celsum.* Cambridge: Cambridge University Press, 1965.

Clark, E. A. *The Origenist Controversy: The Cultural Construction of an Early Christian Debate.* Princeton, NJ: Princeton University Press, 1992.

Crouzel, H. *Origen: The Life and Thought of the First Great Theologian.* Translated by A. S. Worrall. Edinburgh: T. & T. Clark, 1989.

Edwards, M. *Origen against Plato.* Aldershot, England: Ashgate, 2002.

Griggs, C. W. *Early Egyptian Christianity, from its Origins to 451 CE*. 3rd ed. Leiden, Netherlands: E. J. Brill, 1993.

Hanson, R. P. C. *Allegory and Event: A Study of the Sources and Significance of Origen's Interpretation of Scripture*. London: SCM Press, 1959.

Kamil, J. *Christianity in the Land of the Pharaohs: The Coptic Orthodox Church*. London and New York: Routledge, 2002.

Lilla, S. R. C. *Clement of Alexandria: A Study in Christian Platonism and Gnosticism*. Oxford: Oxford University Press, 1971.

Osborn, E. F. *The Philosophy of Clement of Alexandria*. Cambridge: Cambridge University Press, 1957.

Scott, A. B. *Origen and the Life of the Stars*. Oxford: Oxford University Press, 1991.

Simonetti, M. *Biblical Interpretation in the Early Church: An Historical Introduction to Patristic Exegesis*. Translated by J. A. Hughes. Edinburgh: T. & T. Clark, 1994.

Trigg, J. W. *Origen: The Bible and Philosophy in the Third-Century Church*. Atlanta: John Knox Press, 1983.

———. *Origen*. London and New York: Routledge, 1998.

Young, F. M. *Biblical Exegesis and the Formation of Christian Culture*. Cambridge: Cambridge University Press, 1997.

Chapter 10

Aland, K. *Did the Early Church Baptize Infants?* Translated and edited by G. R. Beasley-Murray. London: SCM Press, 1963.

Avila, C. *Ownership: Early Christian Teaching*. Maryknoll, NY: Orbis, 1983.

Bacchiocchi, S. *From Sabbath to Sunday: A Historical Investigation of the Rise of Sunday Observance in Early Christianity*. Rome: Pontifical Gregorian University Press, 1977.

Bradshaw, P. F. *Daily Prayer in the Early Church*. London: SPCK; New York: Oxford University Press, 1981.

———. *Early Christian Worship: A Basic Introduction to Ideas and Practice*. London: SPCK, 1996.

Cantalamessa, R. *Easter in the Early Church: An Anthology of Jewish and Early Christian Texts*. Translated by J. M. Quigley and J. T. Lienhard. Collegeville, MN: Liturgical Press, 1993.

Cerrato, J. A. *Hippolytus between East and West: The Commentaries and the Provenance of the Corpus*. Oxford: Oxford University Press, 2002.

Connolly, R. H. *Didascalia Apostolorum: The Syriac Version Translated and Accompanied by the Verona Latin Fragments.* Oxford: Oxford University Press, 1929.

Dix, G., ed. *The Treatise on the Apostolic Tradition of St Hippolytus of Rome.* Rev. ed. by H. Chadwick. London: SPCK, 1968.

Finney, P. C. *The Invisible God: The Early Christians on Art.* Oxford: Oxford University Press, 1994.

Hengel, M. *Property and Riches in the Early Church.* Translated by J. Bowden. London: SCM Press, 1973.

Jensen, R. M. *Understanding Early Christian Art.* London and New York: Routledge, 2000.

Jeremias, J. *Infant Baptism in the First Four Centuries.* Translated by D. Cairns. London: SCM Press, 1960.

Jungmann, J. A. *The Early Liturgy to the Time of Gregory the Great.* Translated by F. A. Brunner. Notre Dame, IN: University of Notre Dame Press, 1959.

Mathews, T. F. *The Clash of Gods: A Reinterpretation of Early Christian Art.* Princeton, NJ: Princeton University Press, 1993.

McGowan, A. B. *Ascetic Eucharists: Food and Drink in Early Christian Ritual Meals.* Oxford: Oxford University Press, 1999.

McKinnon, J. W. *Music in Early Christian Literature.* Cambridge: Cambridge University Press, 1987.

Milburn, R. L. *Early Christian Art and Architecture.* Berkeley and Los Angeles: University of California Press, 1988.

Quasten, J. *Music and Worship in Pagan and Christian Antiquity.* Translated by B. Ramsey. Washington, DC: Pastoral Press, 1983.

Westermeyer, P. *Te Deum: The Church and Music.* Minneapolis: Fortress Press, 1998.

White, L. M. *The Social Origins of Christian Architecture.* 2 vols. Valley Forge, PA: Trinity Press International, 1996–97.

Yarnold, E. J. *The Awe-Inspiring Rites of Initiation: The Origins of the R.C.I.A.* 2nd ed. Collegeville, MN: Liturgical Press, 1994.

Chapter 11

Brown, P. R. L. *The Body and Society: Men, Women and Sexual Renunciation in Early Christianity.* New York: Columbia University Press, 1988.

Clark, G. *Women in Late Antiquity: Pagan and Christian Lifestyles.* Oxford: Oxford University Press, 1993.

Davis, S. J. *The Cult of Saint Thecla: A Tradition of Women's Piety in Late Antiquity.* Oxford: Oxford University Press, 2001.

Eisen, U. E. *Women Officeholders in Early Christianity.* Translated by L. M. Mahoney. Collegeville, MN: Liturgical Press, 2000.

Jensen, A. *God's Self-Confident Daughters: Early Christianity and the Liberation of Women.* Louisville: Westminster/John Knox Press, 1996.

MacDonald, M. Y. *Early Christian Women and Pagan Opinion: The Power of the Hysterical Woman.* Cambridge: Cambridge University Press, 1996.

Meeks, W. *The Origins of Christian Morality: The First Two Centuries.* New Haven and London: Yale University Press, 1993.

Sawyer, D. F. *Women and Religion in the First Christian Centuries.* London and New York: Routledge, 1996.

Schüssler Fiorenza, E. *In Memory of Her: A Feminist Theological Reconstruction of Christian Origins.* New York: Crossroads, 1983.

Shaw, T. M. *The Burden of the Flesh: Fasting and Sexuality in Early Christianity.* Minneapolis: Fortress Press, 1998.

Telfer, W. *The Forgiveness of Sins: An Essay in the History of Christian Doctrine and Practice.* London: SCM Press, 1959.

Thurston, B. B. *The Widows: A Women's Ministry in the Early Church.* Philadelphia: Fortress Press, 1989.

von Campenhausen, H. *Ecclesiastical Authority and Spiritual Power in the Church of the First Three Centuries.* Translated by J. A. Baker. London: A. & C. Black, 1969.

Chapter 12

Burns, J. P. *Cyprian the Bishop.* London and New York: Routledge, 2001.

Clarke, G. W., ed. and trans. *The Letters of St Cyprian of Carthage.* 4 vols. Ancient Christian Writers series. New York: Newman Press, 1984–89.

DeSimone, R. J. *The Treatise of Novatian the Roman Presbyter on the Trinity.* Rome: Institutum Patristicum Augustinianum, 1970.

Evans, R. F. *One and Holy: The Church in Latin Patristic Thought.* London: SPCK, 1972.

Frend, W. H. C. *Martyrdom and Persecution in the Early Church.* Oxford: Blackwell, 1965.

Greenslade, S. L. *Schism in the Early Church.* 2nd ed. London: SCM Press, 1964.

Gregory, J. *The Neoplatonists.* 2nd ed. London and New York: Routledge, 1998.

Hinchliff, P. *Cyprian of Carthage and the Unity of the Christian Church.* London: Geoffrey Chapman, 1974.

Hoffmann, R. J. *Porphyry's* Against the Christians: *The Literary Remains.* Amherst, NY: Prometheus Books, 1994.

Lane Fox, R. *Pagans and Christians.* Harmondsworth, England: Viking Press, 1986.

Sage, M. M. *Cyprian.* Cambridge, MA: Philadelphia Patristic Foundation, 1975.

Simmons, M. B. *Arnobius of Sicca: Religious Conflict and Competition in the Age of Diocletian.* Oxford: Oxford University Press, 1995.

Walker, G. S. M. *The Churchmanship of St. Cyprian.* London: Lutterworth Press, 1968.

Wallis, R. T. *Neoplatonism.* 2nd ed. London: Duckworth, 1995.

Looking Forward, Looking Back

Barnes, T. D. *Constantine and Eusebius.* Cambridge, MA, and London: Harvard University Press, 1981.

Baynes, N. H. *Constantine the Great and the Christian Church.* 2nd ed. Oxford: Oxford University Press, 1972.

Cameron, A. *The Later Roman Empire,* A.D. *284–430.* London: Fontana; Cambridge: Harvard University Press, 1993.

Drake, H. A. *Constantine and the Bishops: The Politics of Intolerance.* Baltimore: Johns Hopkins University Press, 2000.

Jones, A. H. M. *Constantine and the Conversion of Europe.* London: Macmillan, 1962.

Kee, A. *Constantine versus Christ.* London: SCM Press, 1982.

Lieu, S. N. C., and D. Montserrat, eds. *Constantine: History, Historiography and Legend.* London and New York: Routledge, 1998.

MacMullen, R. *Christianizing the Roman Empire (AD 100–400).* New Haven and London: Yale University Press, 1984.

Pohlsander, H. A. *The Emperor Constantine.* London and New York: Routledge, 1996.

NOTES

Chapter 1: The World of Jesus's First Followers

1. Britain (though only part of it as it is today) became a Roman province in A.D. 43, a few years after the time of Jesus, though it had also been invaded by Rome in the first century B.C.

2. The title "Caesar Augustus" was applied to all emperors in the first century. From the early second century onward, "Caesar" was sometimes used of an heir to the throne or an assistant ruler, but "Augustus" always designated a reigning or senior emperor.

3. The Greek of popular usage was known as *koine*, "the common tongue," to differentiate it from the more formal classical Greek from which it was derived. Greek continued to be widely used in Christian circles in the West until the late second century, when it began to be replaced by Latin.

4. "Hellenistic" in this context refers broadly to the period from Alexander the Great (356–323 B.C.) to the conquest of Egypt, the last part of Alexander's kingdom, by the Romans under Octavian in 31 B.C. The world of Alexander and his successors was characterized by a widespread diffusion of Greek culture, not least in terms of religious and philosophical ideas.

5. The movement to which he gave rise also came to be known as the Peripatetic tradition, probably from the *peripatos* or covered courtyard attached to the Lyceum.

6. The deep rivalries between the Jews of Samaria and Judea dated from at least the fourth century B.C., and in the eyes of most Judean Jews, the Samaritans had been corrupted by their long-standing accommodations with the religious and moral culture of the Assyrians. Some Samaritans had opposed the rebuilding of Jerusalem after the Babylonian exile, and the Samaritans had built a temple of their own on Mt. Gerizim in the early fourth century B.C. This site was destroyed by the expansionist Hasmonean (Maccabean) ruler John Hyrcanus around 128 B.C., which had further fueled antipathies. The Samaritans accepted only the Law of Moses as their Scriptures, and they looked forward to the coming of a new Moses, a reformer who would restore true worship on Mt. Gerizim. In the time of Jesus, there was strong racial hatred between Jews and Samaritans—which makes some of the positive references to the Samaritans in the Gospels especially striking (see Luke 10:33; 17:16; John 4:1–42; cf. Matt. 10:5; Luke 9:52–53; John 8:48).

7. It also came to be cited in the form of the Roman numeral for seventy, LXX, after Latin renderings became available in the late second century A.D.

8. His work on the Jewish war was originally written in Aramaic, but this version is lost, and our text of the treatise is in Greek. Josephus's other writings were originally produced in Greek.

Chapter 2: Spreading the News

1. As we shall see, it is also only in this first phase of his travels that Paul's activities can really in any sense be depicted as a kind of missionary journey, for in later periods his work was concentrated much more upon extended stays in strategic urban centers.

2. In reality, the Christian movement remained a predominantly urban affair for a long time to come, partly on account of language barriers among those in the country.

3. Some scholars speculate that he may have been a distant kinsman of Paul's.

4. This dating depends upon the association of the letter with a context prior to the so-called apostolic council of Acts 15:6–29 (see pp. 73–75) and the locating of Paul's ministry in southern rather than northern Galatia.

Chapter 3: Paul: Missionary, Teacher, Martyr

1. The emperor Caligula had also issued orders to have a statue of himself set up in the temple in A.D. 39–40. The scheme had never materialized; the Roman governor of Syria had wisely resisted, and Caligula himself was assassinated in January 41, leaving his explosive plans unfulfilled.

2. Its harbor required regular dredging to deal with the problem of silt, and by the middle of the first century, the importance of Ephesus as a port city had begun to wane.

3. It certainly does not survive in its original form. Some scholars believe that part of it is to be found in 2 Corinthians 10–13, though the evidence for this is debatable.

4. A number of scholars posit an imprisonment setting in Ephesus for some of these letters, but the evidence for such a setting is, to my mind, not very compelling. The Pauline authorship of some or all of these letters is also disputed. See further pp. 93–96, 126–27.

5. For some particular examples of Paul's female companions in ministry, see p. 116.

Chapter 4: Being Christian

1. The gist of these estimates comes from some much-discussed figures by the sociologist Rodney Stark, in his work *The Rise of Christianity: A Sociologist Reconsiders History* (Princeton, NJ: Princeton University Press, 1996), 7.

2. The idea that the very poor were disproportionately represented in the Pauline churches continues to have its supporters, but it is opposed by much of the best scholarship on the social makeup of the communities with which Paul engaged.

3. Although in many ways—as critics of Paul's gospel have often pointed out—the advice is nonrevolutionary in social terms, urging obedience and duty rather than emancipation, it is also the case that Paul sees slaves, including miscreants such as Onesimus, as fellow believers as well as servants, who are to be treated accordingly by their Christian owners (Philem. 16; cf. Eph. 6:9; Col. 4:1).

4. We must bear in mind that the application of such weighted, modern terms to the structures of ancient societies requires considerable caution. There was also a great deal of variation and flux, or what sociologists call "status inconsistency," among these groups.

5. Arguments that the Erastus of Romans 16:23 is not to be identified with such a figure are unconvincing.

6. It must also be remembered that to be literate, and especially to be able to write, as many early Christians could, was to belong to an educated elite in ancient society.

7. The background lies in a famous story recorded by the Roman poet Ovid in *Metamorphoses* 8.626–725. In this story, the gods Zeus and Hermes are said to have visited the city incognito and not been received as hospitably as they deserved, with the result that Lystra missed out on various divine blessings. The citizens this time were evidently determined to ensure that they did not repeat the mistake.

8. Communication was probably impeded by language barriers; neither Paul nor Barnabas would have known the local Lycaonian language (Acts 14:11).

9. The term was used by Jews for the *assembly* of the covenant people as a whole (e.g., Deut. 23:3; Neh. 13:1; cf. Acts 7:38).

10. This form, rather than the masculine "Junias," is probably the original name of the person mentioned by Paul.

11. There is no evidence to suggest that married women took a more prominent role in ministry than unmarried women.

12. Similar sentiments can be found in classical and Jewish authors in antiquity, but Christian hostility was much stronger. Instruments such as pipes, flute, lyre, harp, cithara, and Eastern sambuca (a four-stringed triangular guitar) were repeatedly attacked as synonymous with settings from which Christians were supposed to distance themselves, especially the world of the theater, drunken wedding-banquets, and dinner-parties. The trumpets, cymbals, harps, and lyres mentioned by the psalmists were often interpreted allegorically. Musical imagery continued to be deployed widely, as it had been from early times (e.g., 1 Cor. 13:1; 14:7–8; cf. 1 Cor. 15:52; 1 Thess. 4:16; Rev., *passim*), but instruments were overwhelmingly seen as illustrative rather than literal media. Sacred dance (see 2 Sam. 6:12–16; Ps. 149:3) was also nonexistent as a worship form among most early Christians, and there would be much denunciation of dancing as another form of secular entertainment. Though there were some significant traditions of ritual dancing in later contexts, especially in the church in Ethiopia, on the whole, dancing was equated with worldly behavior or the activities of false sects.

13. The injunction to Corinthian women to "remain silent," "as in all the congregations of the saints" (1 Cor. 14:33–35) has been variously interpreted, but unless it is an interpolation of a non-Pauline comment into Paul's text (a theory favored by some scholars) it needs to be read in the light of an overall context in which women are clearly envisaged by Paul as praying, prophesying, and taking active, audible parts in worship. It is possible that Paul is in fact seeking to restrain certain women in Corinth from taking such a prominent role in the weighing of prophecy that good order (the primary concern in the context of these verses) is being violated; instead of disrupting worship by commenting on the content of prophetic messages, these women should "ask their own husbands at home" (v. 35).

14. First Tim. 3:11 also refers to the qualifications necessary for female deacons (though the language has often been translated otherwise, to refer instead to deacons' wives). On the later roles of such women, see further pp. 304–6.

Chapter 5: Israel Old and New

1. The most natural association is with James himself, and the letter can plausibly be dated to some time in the early to mid-50s (some would say even earlier), though a large number of scholars believe that the document postdates James and was written in his name by an author who sought to claim his authority.

2. Martin Luther in the sixteenth century, for whom the letter was "a right strawy epistle," is undoubtedly the most famous, but there were many who had similar misgivings in the early Christian period.

3. Such a position would come to be labeled in general "antinomian," literally "anti-law."

4. In later tradition, James was said to have been known as "James the Just" because of his devotion to Torah and to the practical expression of his faith.

5. Eusebius records the later tradition that the relatives of Jesus were known as the *Desposynoi*, "the Master's people," because of their witness to their kinsman (Eusebius, *Ecclesiastical History* 1.7.14).

6. The usefulness of such a strategy was already under some pressure by the mid-60s, however, and this in its own way had contributed to the instability of the period.

7. A few volunteers did go to Palestine from some quarters, and certain activists who escaped after the war and fomented anti-Roman behavior elsewhere were suppressed by force in Egypt and Cyrenaica, but in several cases this was with the cooperation of Jewish authorities.

8. A candidate from Paul's circle remains a strong possibility. Barnabas and Apollos have both been suggested; neither association can be proved.

9. Many scholars believe that the letter was not penned by Jude himself, though a reasonable case can be made that it was.

10. It claims to have been written from Rome (called here "Babylon," as in Revelation; see pp. 195–96 [and p. 382 n. 9]), with the assistance of Silas (1 Peter 5:12–13). If it is by Peter, as quite early tradition believed, it must obviously predate the destruction of the temple by several years. A large number of modern scholars dispute the plausibility of Petrine authorship on stylistic and other grounds. The evidence in either direction is not altogether conclusive.

11. This fact is implied in the headings given to each of the canonical Gospels in the second century: each one is said to be the Gospel *"according to"* the author, not the Gospel *"of"* the author. The writer is regarded as a witness to a single shared message, not the creator of a particular message of his own.

12. The interrelationship of the three documents is a much disputed affair among scholars. A large number of critics have posited the existence of a separate tradition (or set of traditions) labeled "Q" (for the German *Quelle*, "source") alongside Mark as a source for Matthew and Mark (especially on the sayings of Jesus), and various attempts have been made to identify the process by which this material evolved and its particular theological genealogy. Others dispute this hypothesis and propose a variety of other possibilities. Many of the classic arguments have tended to focus on the relationships in literary terms only and have somewhat neglected the degree to which all of the Gospels reflect oral traditions at base, which naturally overlapped and varied in a range of ways.

13. Albeit not of an order that cultural sophisticates of the Graeco-Roman world would naturally have considered especially impressive.

14. The twelfth of the *Eighteen Benedictions*.

15. This was presumably aimed at Jewish Christians in particular, but it possibly included all Christians in general.

16. This was in accordance with techniques that were widely used within first-century Judaism itself, especially in Alexandria, where *Barnabas* almost certainly originated. On Philo, see p. 46; compare Paul's allegorical treatment of the story of Hagar and Sarah in Galatians 4:21–31.

17. It is also conceivable that it had reached much farther west than Rome. Even if Paul himself did not reach the western Mediterranean (and, as we saw, he may have done so), there is every probability that over the ensuing decades other missionaries had carried the faith farther west from Rome.

18. The relationship between old and new Israel affects at some level (albeit with somewhat differing perspectives) a great deal of the literature that from the seventeenth

century onward has been known as the work of the Apostolic Fathers, including Barnabas, Clement, Hermas, Ignatius, and Polycarp, as well as some additional texts. We shall be considering several of these writings in the next two chapters.

19. Jerome, *Epistle* 112.13.

Chapter 6: A Catholic Church?

1. Thomas's bones are said to have been moved to Edessa in Syria in the late fourth century, and in the twelfth century they were taken to Italy.

2. On the tradition that the church in Alexandria was begun by the evangelist Mark, see p. 249.

3. In some versions of the legend, Addai is associated with the disciple Thaddaeus.

4. There are also warnings against receiving false teachers (e.g., 2 John 10–11).

5. W. Bauer, *Orthodoxy and Heresy in Earliest Christianity*, trans. R. A. Kraft and G. Krodel (Philadelphia: Fortress Press, 1971).

6. Albeit Rome did not and could not entirely succeed in fulfilling such an ambition.

7. The chronological sequencing of the Epistles and the relationship between their author or authors and the writer of John's Gospel are all the subject of significant scholarly dispute. There is not space to enter into the details of these arguments here.

8. Ignatius, *Letter to the Smyrnaeans* 1.1–2.

9. Ignatius, *Letter to the Trallians* 9.1–2.

10. The term *Docetists* seems to have been first used by Serapion, bishop of Antioch at the turn of the second and third centuries. Forms of docetism varied somewhat, but arguments against what amounted to docetic ideas of one kind or another were mounted by a wide range of Christian teachers throughout the second century. Ignatius is only one example.

11. Despite the sensationalist claims made by some modern writers, the Gnostic gospels are of only limited value for the history of Jesus himself. The earliest of them, the much-discussed *Gospel of Thomas*, the Greek of which dates to the third quarter of the second century, has been elevated by a few scholars to the putative status of a fifth canonical Gospel. But although it may perhaps preserve a few genuine words of Jesus not to be found in the canonical Gospels, much of its material is derived from Matthew and Luke, and its overall style, character, and theology are very different. At no stage in mainstream early Christian tradition was the *Gospel of Thomas* seriously treated as comparable to the canonical Gospels.

12. Basilides' teaching was similar in certain respects, but his influence was smaller, being largely confined to Egypt.

13. One of Christianity's more formidable opponents, the late-second-century writer Celsus (see pp. 221–24), called the consensus tradition "the church of the multitude" or "the Great Church" (Origen, *Against Celsus* 5.61), a name that exercised a lengthy influence.

14. Irenaeus, *Against Heresies*, 1.10.1.

15. Despite its conventional designation, it is not a "second letter" by Clement of Rome (see pp. 179–80), but an anonymous homily or word of exhortation.

16. *2 Clement* 2.4.

17. Irenaeus, *Against Heresies*, 3.11.8.

18. Some might argue that Tatian's attempt to reduce the fourfold plurality to a single version, and the similar attempts in many subsequent harmonies of the Gospels, however well-intentioned, were rather misguided in that they necessarily diminished the richness that we have in possessing four (though not forty-four) canonical Gospels as opposed to only one.

19. Muratorian Fragment, lines 77–80.

20. Cold, running water was symbolic of the "living" water of the new life in Christ.

21. *Didache* 15.1.

22. Though the tradition arose that Clement himself was in fact a monarchical bishop of the church of Rome, in a direct line from Peter (between Peter and Clement were Linus [see 2 Tim. 4:21] and Anacletus/Anencletus), it was almost certainly the case that Clement and his predecessors were simply the leading members on a collegial board, not sole bishops. While there were prominent Roman bishops in the second century, a strong monarchical episcopate may not have evolved there until the early third century.

23. The document was possibly (though not necessarily) assembled out of two separate pieces.

24. Not least in our own, when a good deal of "New Age" spirituality has clear resonances with some rather old Gnostic assumptions.

Chapter 7: External Pressures: Suffering for and Defending the Faith

1. Suetonius, *Claudius* 25.4.

2. Tacitus, *Annals* 15.44.

3. Ibid.

4. Ibid.

5. Nero's second wife, Poppaea, whom he had married after the murder of his first, Octavia, in 62, is said by Josephus to have been friendly toward Jews, and she was perhaps a "God-fearer" (Josephus, *Antiquities of the Jews* 20.195).

6. Dio Cassius, *History* 67.14.

7. The Christians of the imperial household would also be subjected to some fierce purges in the third century when the political tide was most strongly opposed to their faith.

8. The John who wrote Revelation was said by some from the second century onward to have been John the apostle, who, it was assumed, had been exiled temporarily to Patmos from his base at Ephesus. However, such an identification was also challenged rather widely in the early church, and it is rejected by a majority of scholars today. In style, Revelation is quite different from John's Gospel or the Johannine Epistles, and there are many other features that make a common authorship unlikely. The writers may well have come from a similar theological background (Revelation employs some designations for Christ that are to be found elsewhere only in John's Gospel, namely, "Word of God" and "Lamb of God"), but the strong probability is that the prophet John was a different figure from John the apostle.

9. Revelation is saturated with evocation of the Jewish Scriptures, not least prophecies against Babylon (cf. Rev. 18:1–19:8 with Isa. 13:1–14:23; 21:1–10; 47:1–15; Jer. 25:12–38; 50:1–51:64). There is also allusion to the oracles against the power of Tyre in Isaiah 23:1–18; Ezekiel 26:1–28:19. The name "Babylon" probably denotes Rome in 1 Peter 5:13.

10. Thus, while Revelation adopts the language and imagery of the first-century Roman world, its essential theological message has a great deal to say to Christians in every age about the nature of God and about what it means to anticipate the final triumph of his rule.

11. E.g., Acts 15:20, 29; 21:25; 1 Cor. 6:9–11; 10:1–14; 2 Cor. 6:16; Gal. 5:20–21; Eph. 5:5; 1 Thess. 1:9–10; 1 John 5:21; Rev. 2:14–16, 20–25; 21:8; 22:15. For evidence of the tensions that ensued within Christian circles when some believers adopted a freer attitude toward idols and their associations, see 1 Corinthians 8:1–11:1.

12. On Christian attitudes to religious symbolism more generally, see further pp. 292–96.

13. He is so named to distinguish him from his uncle, "Pliny the elder," who was also an important author.

14. Pliny, *Epistle* 10.96.

15. On the actual practices that presumably provoked such charges, see pp. 112–22.

16. Pliny, *Epistle* 10.96.

17. Ibid.

18. Ibid., *Epistle* 10.97.

19. Eusebius, *Ecclesiastical History* 4.9.1–3.

20. Ignatius, *Letter to the Romans* 5.2–3.

21. *Martyrdom of Polycarp* 9.3.

22. *Letter to Diognetus*, 5–6.

23. Eusebius (ca. 260–340), whose *Ecclesiastical History* is cited a number of times in this book, is an invaluable if complex source for the development of Christianity from apostolic times up to his own day. On Eusebius and his work, see further the second volume in this series.

24. Eusebius, *Ecclesiastical History* 5.1.55.

25. Ibid., 6.2.2–6.

26. By the later second century, the North African church already included a number of Christians of some wealth.

27. Tertullian, *Apology* 40.2.

28. The term *pagan* did not in fact become a generic label for non-Christians in the Latin-speaking churches until the fourth century. One of the meanings of *paganus* in secular Latin usage was "country-dweller," and it is possible that what Christians came to mean when they used it was that those who practiced other forms of religion were "rustics"—they were like people who lived in rural areas, which remained less affected by the gospel than the cities and towns. (An alternative explanation is that a *paganus* was a "civilian," or one who had not been enrolled in the army of Christ.) Although it is strictly anachronistic to use words such as *pagan* and *paganism* in a general sense prior to the fourth century, they remain serviceable as shorthand designations for most scholars (though some are troubled by their lingering pejorative overtones).

29. Eusebius, *Ecclesiastical History* 4.3.1–2.

30. Ibid., 5.1.14. In Greek legend, Thyestes had seduced his brother's wife and had subsequently been invited to a banquet at which his own sons were served up to him; Oedipus had unwittingly killed his father and married his mother.

31. This argument goes back to Euhemerus, a Sicilian philosopher of the late fourth century B.C.

Chapter 8: Christian Thought in the West

1. An Armenian text of *Against Heresies* also survives.

2. The term evokes Ephesians 1:10, which refers to God's ultimate purpose to sum up all things in Christ. Like a number of Irenaeus's key terms, it also had a background in classical rhetoric, in which it referred to the summarizing or recapitulating of a narrative.

3. There were, however, strong millennial views among many Gnostics and Montanists, and also in writers such as Justin Martyr.

4. Irenaeus, *Against Heresies* 3.3.1.

5. Eusebius, *Ecclesiastical History* 4.22.1–3.

6. Ibid., 4.23.10.

7. The term *pope* (Greek, *pap[p]as*, Latin, *papa*, "father") did not become confined to the bishop of Rome until the sixth century; previously, it was used in the West as an honorific designation for any bishop. In the East, it was usually reserved for the bishop of Alexandria, who may still be thus designated. The office of the papacy as exclusively Roman became formalized in medieval times, in the light of the powerful assertion of the

magisterial status of the Roman See over earlier centuries, especially the fourth. On the concept of a leader as a spiritual "father," see generally 1 Cor. 4:15; 2 Cor. 6:13; Phil. 2:22; 1 Thess. 2:11; 1 Tim. 1:2; 2 Tim. 2:1; Titus 1:4; Philem. 10; 1 Peter 5:13; 3 John 4.

8. The sacrifice of Jesus as "the Lamb of God" (John 1:29, 36) is also connected with the Passover offering in John's Gospel, where his death takes place on the day of preparation for the Passover, at the hour when the lambs are being slaughtered for the feast (John 19:14). When the soldiers refrain from breaking Jesus's legs, this is also said to be in fulfillment of scriptural injunction against breaking the bones of the Passover lamb (John 19:31–37; cf. Exod. 12:46; Num. 9:12).

9. The name "Easter" itself did not come into use until much later, in the context of the English church in the seventh century. It probably derives from the Saxon term for the spring festival in honor of the pagan goddess of the dawn, Eostre, and thus reflects a synthesis of religious influences in that setting.

10. Eusebius, *Ecclesiastical History* 5.24.14–17.

11. From an early date, burial of the dead was seen as an important work of Christian charity (especially toward poorer people), following Jewish traditions. It was later regarded as one of the "corporal works of mercy," alongside feeding the hungry, giving drink to the thirsty, clothing the naked, harboring the stranger, visiting the sick, and caring for the imprisoned (see Matt. 25:35–36). Prior to the early third century, there were few indications on gravestones that the deceased were Christian, though the increasing commemoration of martyrs' graves obviously left no doubts in these cases. The third century saw the acquisition of Christian cemeteries by larger churches such as Rome and Carthage, but relatively few burials were expressly marked as Christian until the fourth century. In the late fourth and fifth centuries, those known as *fossores* or *fossarii*, "diggers," who collected corpses, sold grave spaces, and oversaw the running of complexes such as the catacombs in Rome, were quite a powerful subclerical order within the church. The practice of cremation was strongly rejected as being at odds with Christian belief in the resurrection of the body, and its general demise in later Roman society was due to Christian influence.

12. The association of this work with Hippolytus of Rome is disputed by some scholars, and a great deal of uncertainty also surrounds the authorship of other works traditionally ascribed to him, including commentaries on Daniel and on the Song of Songs. Some recent scholarship argues strongly for an Eastern origin for some or all of these texts (see pp. 274–75). The attribution of *The Refutation of All Heresies* to Hippolytus of Rome nevertheless continues to have supporters.

13. Roman Carthage, established as a colony by Augustus, was a different city from the Carthage that the Romans had destroyed in 146 B.C. at the climax to the third in the bitter series of Punic wars. The former Carthaginian Empire at its height had been the primary obstacle in Rome's quest for supremacy in the western Mediterranean. Its demise brought about the origins of what became the Roman province of North Africa, which expanded considerably over time but was from the earliest a highly important source of grain, taxes, and other imports for the Romans.

14. In reverse, some Romans nursed ancient suspicions about *Punica fides*, or the alleged untrustworthiness of the Carthaginians.

15. Tertullian, *Apology* 39.7.

16. Ibid., 50.13.

17. Tertullian, *On the Prescription(s) of Heretics* 7.9.

18. Tertullian, *On the Pallium* 6.2.

19. Tertullian, *On the Flesh of Christ* 5.4.

20. Tertullian, *Against Praxeas* 1.5.

21. The Greek word *oikonomia* originally described "the way in which a household was run," and so "the administration of affairs" in political, commercial, or administrative terms. It was used by Irenaeus to describe the manner in which God ordered the affairs of history to bring about salvation, loosely evoking the appearance of the term in Ephesians 1:10 (cf. the somewhat different sense of a ministerial "commission" in 1 Cor. 9:17; Eph. 3:2, 9; Col. 1:25). The Latin equivalent was *dispensatio*, "dispensation."

22. However, the *literal* equivalent in Latin for *ousia* was in fact not *substantia* but *essentia*. In the course of the doctrinal debates of the third and fourth centuries, considerable confusion would be engendered by the rendering of such Greek theological terms with Latin words carrying different (and often blunter) nuances.

23. Jerome, *On Famous Men* 53.

24. Lactantius, *Divine Institutes* 5.1.21.

Chapter 9: Alexandrian Christianity and Its Legacy

1. The church in Egypt would also deeply cherish the tradition that it was to Egypt that the infant Jesus was taken by his parents in flight from King Herod (Matt. 2:13–15).

2. Eusebius, *Ecclesiastical History* 5.10.1–4.

3. Clement, *Stromateis* 1.1.11.1–3.

4. Galatians 3:24–25 describes the Law as a *paidagogos* "to lead us to Christ."

5. Eusebius, *Ecclesiastical History* 6.2.2–6.

6. Ibid., 6.8.1–2. However, in a later exposition of Matthew 19:11–12 (Origen, *Commentary on Matthew* 15.1), Origen criticizes those who take Jesus's words literally.

7. Not to be confused with the much more famous Ambrose who was bishop of Milan in the later fourth century.

8. Aquila is said by Epiphanius of Salamis to have been converted to Christianity during a stay in Jerusalem but excommunicated for his refusal to abandon his interest in astrology. He then became a Jewish proselyte and learned Hebrew under rabbinical instruction. His rendering of the Scriptures into Greek was extremely literal in style.

9. Little is known of Symmachus. Christian authors variously claim that he was an Ebionite or a Samaritan who became a Jewish proselyte. His translation was much more readable than Aquila's.

10. Like Symmachus, Theodotion remains obscure, though again there are varying contentions that he was a Jewish proselyte or an Ebionite. Epiphanius says he was a Marcionite, which is very improbable. His text has proved valuable to scholars working on books such as Jeremiah and Job, whereas Origen used it to fill in the gaps in the Septuagint's rendering.

11. Eusebius, *Ecclesiastical History* 6.16.3.

12. Origen, *On First Principles*, pref. 10.

13. Homer's *Iliad* and *Odyssey* were standard texts in ancient education, with an almost biblical status in the schooling of children.

14. This is an image that was much used in various connections in early Christian reflection upon the person of Christ.

15. Among Methodius's many writings (and the only one of them to survive in its entirety) is a remarkable dialogue entitled *Symposium*, or *On Chastity*, which offers a creative Christian rereading of Plato's *Symposium*, extolling the excellence of virginity as an expression of the desire of the soul for God and praising Christ as the Bridegroom of the church.

16. Dionysius became notable for his views on the origin of the book of Revelation, which he argued could not have been written by the same author as John's Gospel because of its language and style. His scholarly exposition of this argument was provoked by an

encounter with some Christians who held to a literal interpretation of the millennium. Dionysius insisted that Revelation 20:1–6, and indeed the Apocalypse as a whole, needed to be read allegorically, not literally.

17. Eusebius, *Ecclesiastical History* 7.30.1–17.

18. Ibid., 7.30.19.

Chapter 10: Worship and Practice

1. Generally speaking, soldiers were allowed to become catechumens, but individuals who were already catechumens were forbidden from joining the army.

2. Their other duties included laying hands upon *energumens*, or the mentally sick, who were also for the most part excluded from participation in the Eucharist. The Roman church of the mid-third century had more than forty exorcists.

3. *Didache* 7.1–3.

4. *Apostolic Tradition* 17.

5. Ibid., 21.

6. Obviously the argument that the *Apostolic Tradition* reflects an Eastern rather than a Western source impinges upon the validity of such terminology. The title of the "Apostles' Creed" for the more famous later Western statement of faith derives from the late fourth century, by which time there was a legend that each of the twelve apostles contributed one of its clauses under the inspiration of the Holy Spirit. The earliest evidence for that creed's present form is to be found in the early eighth century, though very similar formulas existed from the fifth, and its core affirmations have clear connections with the much older confession preserved in the *Apostolic Tradition*.

7. References to several of these details are to be found in Tertullian's work, *On Baptism*; others come from other texts by Tertullian.

8. *Didascalia Apostolorum* 3.12.

9. Tertullian, *On Baptism* 18; *Apostolic Tradition* 21.

10. It survived longer in the Ethiopian church than elsewhere.

11. Justin Martyr, *First Apology* 67.3–7.

12. *Apostolic Tradition* 4.

13. Malachi 1:11 was one biblical text that came to be cited in support of the idea of "pure" sacrifice (e.g., *Didache* 14.1–3).

14. *Didache* 8.1.

15. Pliny, *Epistle* 10.96.

16. Eusebius, *Ecclesiastical History* 5.28.5, citing an unknown third-century author.

17. The Gnostics made extensive use of hymns, though only parts of these survive, typically in the writings of orthodox opponents. Some other important examples of Syriac hymns are preserved in the apocryphal *Acts of Thomas*, a work produced around 220. Though this work is Gnostic in origin, the hymns it cites probably also belonged to other circles in eastern Syria.

18. Classic versions include Keble's "Hail! Gladdening Light" and Bridges's "O Gladsome Light, O Grace."

19. Eusebius, *Ecclesiastical History* 7.30.19.

20. Archaeologists also unearthed a Jewish synagogue close to the Dura-Europos house, which was also impressively adorned with scenes from the Hebrew Scriptures.

21. Other speculative dates for the nativity included 20 May, proposed by Clement of Alexandria. The later convention of 25 December was a Western choice, and although it is just possible that it had already been identified by some in the third century, the first hard evidence for its observance dates to the church of Rome in the 330s.

22. The transfiguration was later commemorated on a feast day of its own on 6 August.

Chapter 11: Ministry and Morals

1. *Apostolic Tradition* 2.
2. *Didascalia Apostolorum* 3.12 (baptism); 3.6 (teaching).
3. Tertullian, *On Baptism* 17.5; cf. *On the Prescription(s) of Heretics* 41.5.
4. Eusebius, *Ecclesiastical History* 5.13.2.
5. Tertullian, *On Baptism* 17.5. One might surmise that Tertullian's attitude could conceivably have changed following his turn to Montanism, though there is no obvious evidence of this fact.
6. Some scholars have argued that some of the apocryphal *Acts of Paul and Thecla* may have been written by women who chose chastity as a form of autonomy from the structures of patriarchal society and as a protest against the restrictions of a male-dominated church. The evidence for these claims is, however, hard to sustain.
7. Though nonfictional, their characterizations are strongly influenced by literary conventions.
8. There is reason to believe that female diaconal roles were much slower to develop in the Western churches than they were in the East.
9. Pliny, *Epistle* 10.96.
10. *Didascalia Apostolorum* 3.12–13.
11. Ibid., 3.1–11.
12. *Apostolic Tradition* 11.
13. In parts of Asia Minor, those under discipline for less serious offenses were apparently permitted to remain for the offering of the thanksgiving, but they were debarred from receiving the elements; as was the case with all offenders elsewhere, those who had committed graver sins had to leave before the communion rite commenced.
14. Luke's Gospel in particular emphasizes Jesus's exhortations to his disciples to minimize their attachments to the present age, and Luke's version of the Beatitudes of Matthew 5:3–12 (Luke 6:20–26) has Jesus blessing not "the poor in spirit" (Matt. 5:3) but simply those "who are poor" (Luke 6:20), while pronouncing woe on the rich, the well-fed, and the comfortable (Luke 6:24–26; cf. 1:53).

Chapter 12: Faith and Politics

1. Julius Africanus's writings included a history of the world, which calculated that the faith represented in the Jewish Scriptures was the oldest religion known to humankind, and a vast encyclopedia, dedicated to Alexander Severus, on natural history, medicine, warfare, magic, and many other topics. These works survive only in fragments.
2. To call it "Neoplatonism" is to use a modern description: Plotinus and his disciples thought of themselves simply as followers and interpreters of Plato.
3. The work, however, was intended to show overall that traditional religions supported belief in a single supreme being. Porphyry was prepared to acknowledge that Jesus was a great moral teacher, but he was very critical of Jesus's followers for allegedly misrepresenting his status by claiming that he was divine. Porphyry's later writings were more openly dismissive of Jesus.
4. More than a year after his return from exile.
5. Cyprian, *On the Unity of the Catholic Church* 4–5.
6. The best-known version derives from Cyprian, *Epistle* 73.21. *On the Unity of the Catholic Church* 6 suggests that, "There is [no] escape for one who is found to be outside the church."
7. Ibid. This is an influential claim also made by Cyprian in a number of other places.

8. The title of the study as we have it was perhaps added later, since Novatian manages to deal systematically with the character of God as Father, Son, and Holy Spirit without ever using the word *Trinity* as such.

9. "Schism" (cf. 1 Cor. 1:10; 11:18; and especially 12:25; also John 7:43; 9:16; 10:19) was from the second century onward distinguished from "heresy." To separate from the catholic community on doctrinal grounds was heresy; to leave on some other basis, and so to violate the bonds of love that bound true believers together, was schism.

10. Christian leaders, however, had also appealed to Aurelian when it suited them, such as in the request of the Eastern bishops to the emperor to remove the controversial Paul of Samosata from the bishop's house in Antioch in 272.

11. Eusebius, *Ecclesiastical History* 7.30.20.

12. Arnobius's treatise *Against the Pagans* is a diffuse and hastily written work in seven books. In content it is more of a counterattack on paganism than a vindication of Christianity, revealing a good deal more about pagan religions than about Christian teaching.

13. Eusebius, *The Martyrs of Palestine* 3.

14. The date is unclear. The council is traditionally dated ca. 306, but it may have been as late as 310.

15. The edict was issued not only in his own name but also in the names of Constantine, Licinius, and Maximin.

16. Lactantius, *On the Deaths of the Persecutors* 48.2; cf. Eusebius, *Ecclesiastical History* 10.5.2–17.

Looking Forward, Looking Back

1. Lactantius, *On the Deaths of the Persecutors* 44.5–6.

2. Elsewhere, Licinius is said to have done something similar prior to his decisive battle with Maximin, as the result of a vision. The title "Supreme God" was also used in pagan rituals.

3. Eusebius, *Life of Constantine* 1.28.

INDEX

Page numbers in italics refer to maps and illustrations.